DATE DUE

NATIONS OF THE MODERN WORLD

MOROCCO	Mark I. Cohen and Lorna Hahn
NIGERIA	Sir Rex Niven *Colonial Service, Nigeria, 1921–59; Member of Northern House of Assembly, 1947–59*
NEW ZEALAND	James W. Rowe *Director of New Zealand Institute of Economic Research, Inc.* Margaret A. Rowe *Tutor in English, Victoria University, Wellington*
PAKISTAN	Ian Stephens *Formerly Editor of* The Statesman *Calcutta and Delhi, 1942–51; Fellow of King's College, Cambridge, 1952–58*
SOUTH AFRICA	John Cope *Formerly Editor-in-Chief of* The Forum; *South African Correspondent of* The Guardian
SUDAN REPUBLIC	K. D. D. Henderson *Formerly of the Sudan Political Service; Governor of Darfur Province, 1949–53*
TURKEY	Goeffrey Lewis *Senior Lecturer in Islamic Studies, Oxford*
THE UNITED STATES OF AMERICA	H. C. Allen *Commonwealth Fund Professor of American History, University College, London*
WEST GERMANY	Michael Balfour *Reader in European History, University of East Anglia*
YUGOSLAVIA	Muriel Heppell and F. B. Singleton

WEST GERMANY

WEST GERMANY

By
MICHAEL BALFOUR

FREDERICK A. PRAEGER, *Publishers*
New York · Washington

BOOKS THAT MATTER

Published in the United States of America in 1968
by Frederick A. Praeger, Inc., Publishers
111 Fourth Avenue, New York, N.Y. 10003

© 1968 in London, England, by Michael Balfour

Library of Congress Catalog Card Number: 68-19844

Printed in Great Britain

Preface

THERE ARE many books about the history of Germany and almost
as many about West Germany today; there are considerably
fewer which try, as this one does, to interpret the second in the
light of the first. But to make such an attempt in three hundred
pages has repeatedly called for complex processes to be summed
up in a few lines and judgments passed on difficult problems in a
couple of sentences. I cannot expect that I have always achieved
the accuracy and balance which I have sought, nor can I expect
everyone to agree with my inclusions and omissions. Of the latter,
only some are inadvertent.

In the first four chapters, I have had in mind the technique of
the film cameraman, putting the subject into perspective by
'tracking in' from far away with the detail getting greater as the
objective gets closer. Some of the ground I had already covered in
The Kaiser and His Times and *Four-Power Control in Germany 1945–46*.
Where I could not think of a better way of expressing what I have
said already, I have not hesitated to repeat myself.

Having been rash enough to express views about politics,
economics, strategy, philosophy, theology and social affairs, I hope
I may be excused for not venturing on literary and aesthetic
criticism. But when my publishers asked me to provide illustrations,
I decided against reproducing yet once again such familiar faces
as Bismarck and Adenauer and have instead tried to give the book
an extra dimension by showing something of Germany's cultural
heritage. Some readers may find my selection curious: I can only
assure them that it has not been casual. I would like to call particular
attention to the detailed notes on some of the illustrations at the
end of the book.

I have interpreted my subject as permitting me to deal with
Germany as a whole down to partition. After that event, I have
only written about the German Democratic Republic (to which a
separate volume in this series is to be devoted) in so far as I thought
this necessary to an understanding of the Federal Republic.

I have tried to economise on words by providing a number of

statistics: I hope that the Appendix containing these will be treated as an integral part of the text. But I decided with regret that I was incompetent to embark on the considerable task of providing figures for the East which would be properly comparable with those for the West.

I have many debts—to my wife, for typing the whole text twice; to Dr Elizabeth Wiskemann, for her advice on the earlier chapters; to Mr Victor Earl and my daughter Corinna, for help with the statistics; to Hans Deichmann, for enabling the final revision to be made by an Italian peasant; to Professor Bernhardt of Frankfurt University for checking the Annexe on the Voting System; and to many other friends and colleagues who have provided information and advice.

An Englishman who writes critically about another country in these days may be thought to expose himself to the charge of living in a glass house. But if any reader feels disposed to bring such a charge, I would remind him of R. L. Stevenson's rejoinder when told that some of his remarks about Edinburgh had given 'proportionable pleasure' to a rival city. 'To the Glasgow people I would only say one word but that is of gold: *I have not yet written a book about Glasgow.*'

New Year's Day 1968   M.L.G.B.

Contents

Map

Germany, showing the Federal Republic, the D.D.R. and lands formerly German, now under Polish and Russian administration *facing page* 300

List of Illustrations

Acknowledgements

ACKNOWLEDGEMENT for kind permission to reproduce illustrations is made to the following bodies, to whom the copyright of the illustrations belongs:

Verlag Karl Alber, Freiburg i. Br.: 1
Städtisches Fremdenverkehrsamt, Bamberg: 2 (photograph by Foto-Limmer, Bamberg)
Rheinisches Bildarchiv, Cologne: 3a
Ullstein Bilderdienst, West Berlin: 3b, 10a, 10b
Musée d'Unterlinden à Colmar (Ht-Rhin): 5
Verwaltung de Staatlichen Schlösser und Gärten, West Berlin: 6 (photograph by Walter Steinkopf)
Städtisches Verkehrsamt, Landsberg a. Lech: 7
Stiftung Preussischer Kulturbesitz (Staatliches Museum, Dahlem, and Nationalgalerie, Charlottenburg, West Berlin): 8, 9b (photographs by Walter Steinkopf)
Kunsthalle, Bremen: 9a (photograph by Stickelmann, Bremen)
Paul Klee Stiftung, Berne, and Cosmopress, Geneva: 11
Professor Walter Gropius: 12
Rembrandt Verlag, West Berlin: 13
Peter Tunnard, London: 14 (from the collection of the Hon. Anthony Samuel)
Verkehrsamt Berlin: 15 (photograph by Harry Wagner)
The German Tourist Information Bureau, London: 16 (photograph by Karl Heider, Coblenz)

Part One

Chapter 1

From Tribe to National State: The First Reich

Origins

How the name German originated is a thing about which nobody seems sure. According to one theory it means 'a man who shouts', and so a warrior; according to another it means 'a neighbour'. The earliest peoples to be known by it lived in the first millennium B.C. in Denmark and South Scandinavia, from which, as population outgrew supplies, they made periodic excursions to warmer and wealthier climes. These tribes had various names, such as Teutons and Cimbrians. The term German may have been applied collectively to them all, which would suggest a common origin further back, and this would seem to be supported by the fact that they appear to have spoken dialects of a single tongue. Alternatively 'German' may have been the title of the tribe which came most frequently into collision with its Celtic neighbours further west and which by design or accident managed to give them the impression that it had the whole mass behind it.

During the second and first centuries B.C. these tribes shifted southwards and westwards, presumably in the face of fresh groups arriving from the north and east. They pushed the Celts, who had previously inhabited the area between the Elbe and Rhine, over the latter river and in some cases followed them across it. When about A.D. 98 the Roman historian Tacitus set out to shame his decadent fellow-countrymen by comparing them with the noble savages in 'Germania', he defined the area as lying between on the one hand Gaul and the Alps from which it was separated by the Rhine and the Danube, and on the other the Sarmatians and Dacians (on the plains of Russia) from whom it was divided by mountains and mutual terror! The two Roman provinces of High and Low Germany hardly came into this area at all. Their eastern boundary lay along the Rhine to the neighbourhood of Mainz and then cut across to the upper Danube. A move to press further

forward met with disaster in A.D. 9 when the Cherusci under a chief
whom the Romans called Arminius (a name which the patriotism
of later Germans has transliterated into Hermann) annihilated the
Roman general Varus and a couple of legions at the battle of the
Teutonic Wood, which many centuries later was located near
Detmold and later still near Hildesheim. The result was that much
of modern Germany and most of the peoples who were to settle
there never came under Roman law or absorbed Roman culture.
Some later writers have blamed upon this omission many of the
faults which they found in German behaviour; at the very least it
made the Germans different from their Latinised neighbours.

As the Roman Empire staggered to its collapse, its armed forces
grew incapable of keeping at a safe distance the tribes from whom
they were increasingly recruited; north-west and western Europe
saw successive inroads of the Germani or their fellows. Thus the
Franks (or free men) went to France, the Lombards to Italy, the
Visigoths to Spain. But as soon as one group moved off, another
emerged to replace it from the vast reservoir of the northern plains.
As a result present-day Germany came to be inhabited by
Bavarians, Swabians (or Alemanni), Thuringians, Franconians,
Frisians, Saxons, and Lorrainers, loose agglomerations with little
apparent cohesion or political connection. About the sixth century
an adjective derived from the root 'thoid' (or people) began to be
applied to the language of the tribes remaining between the Rhine
and the Elbe, who still had to be converted to Christianity (a
process in which the Englishman Boniface had a large hand two
centuries later). In old High German 'thoid' became 'diutisk'
which gradually developed into 'diutsch' and so into 'deutsch'—
the name used to describe themselves by the people whom this
book is about.

In the eighth century the seven tribes, in common with many
other folk, fell under the overlordship of the Emperor of the
Franks. Such cohesion as this involved was threatened when the
Frankish Empire broke up after Charlemagne's death in 814. But
the eastern part of it remained united under King Louis, who
although a Frank used the title 'Germanicus'. In 843 his domains
were given recognised form by the Treaty of Verdun which (in
view of the fact that Franks and 'diutisks' could no longer understand one another) had to be drafted in both languages. It was
this Treaty which is generally taken to mark the beginning of
what, looking backwards, we can see to have been German history.
Then in 911 the seven tribes, tired of being ruled by outsiders,
made Conrad of Franconia their King. Almost immediately we

find his realm being described in Latin as *regnum teutonicorum*—the Kingdom of the Teutons, while in the course of the next century *Teutonici* came into use to describe its inhabitants.

Up to this point, and indeed for another century, the history of Germany did not basically differ from that of areas further west. In all cases loose tribal groupings were being consolidated together under the domination of strong and ambitious kings. Indeed the process was so successful that the consciousness of common destiny which the rulers instilled into their subjects never became altogether effaced and thus proved a factor of decisive importance in later history. 'By 1075 Germany had far outstripped France and England . . . and was already on the path leading to more modern forms of government . . . Had his success proved durable, it is scarcely doubted that Henry IV (1056–1106) would have created a great German state coeval with Norman England and Philip Augustus.'[1]

This, however, was not to be. It was not simply that Germany lacked the clear-cut frontiers of France and Britain, though the resulting exposure to invasion was certainly a distracting factor. The main cause of the failure began by making a major contribution to the success. For in 942 Otto King of the Germans was elected King of the Romans and thus became the heir to the Emperors (though the title Roman Emperor did not come into use until later). This ensured him the powerful support of the Church, many of whose dignitaries in Germany and North Italy acted virtually as imperial officials. But in 1075 the great Pope Gregory VII (Hildebrand) decided to put an end to this practice and immediately clashed with Henry IV. The struggle which led to the Emperor standing barefoot in the snow at Canossa may have served the cause of liberty and true religion by preventing the Popes from degenerating into Imperial lackeys, but its effects upon Germany were disastrous. Instead of devoting themselves to consolidation of their hold on the country, successive Emperors were tempted or forced to try and assert themselves against the Papacy; the Church, instead of acting as their ally, only too frequently sought to undermine their authority.

One step to this end was the claim that succession to the Imperial throne did not go by hereditary right but that each new occupant had to be elected by his immediate vassals. The result was a series of disputed successions and debilitating bargains : the central authority grew weaker instead of stronger. In their search for allies, the rulers of the First Empire (*Reich*) were drawn into

---

[1] G. Barraclough, *Factors in Modern German History*, p. 17.

controversies all over Europe but particularly in Italy. From time to time a great man like Frederick Barbarossa (1152–90) rose above the difficulties, and thereby secured among his subjects a loyalty which, lingering long after his death, acted itself as a unifying factor. But henceforward the two major posts in Christendom were kept apart by mutual suspicion; attention was distracted from the task of ruling Germany by the fear of losing ground against Rome. The people who profited most from this situation were the princes who should have been subordinate. In the end it was one of these families, the Habsburgs, who in 1438 succeeded in appropriating the Imperial throne and, by dint of judicious marriages, keeping it as family property. In their hands the Empire regained for a time a good deal of its glory but lost the closeness of its connection with Germany. For it was in the basin of the middle Danube that Habsburg possessions and interests were concentrated (except when Charles V (1500–58) ruled Spain and Naples as well). Many of their subjects were not Germans at all, in many of the areas inhabited by Germans their authority was slight and many of the ends to which the Imperial resources were devoted were of dubious benefit to Germany.

The later history of Germany has been dominated by the fact that during the Middle Ages the process of political consolidation was not carried through. Britain and France may have had certain climatic and geographical advantages which Germany lacked. But the thing which gave Britain her outstanding advantage and made her the scene of that technological break-through known as the 'Industrial Revolution' derived from the achievements of the Normans, Plantagenets and early Tudors. The three main spurs underlying that Revolution are accumulation of capital (with means of transferring it from savers to effective spenders), technical invention (which presupposes the accumulation of knowledge and is particularly important in its application to communications), and growth of population. The vital precondition for all three developments is stable and effective government with all that this can bestow in the way of security, peace and a reliable undiscriminating legal system. The accidents or, if one prefers, the destiny of history placed Britain in a specially favourable position for establishing such government and its accompaniments. Their progressively accelerating development involved an early swelling in the numbers of merchants, well-to-do landed gentry, professional men and craftsmen. This in turn meant that the crucial conflict between a monarchy tending to absolutism and the various elements composing the 'middle classes' who had within them the seeds of the democratic state was in Britain fought at a relatively early stage and settled decisively in favour of the popular side. This shift of power intensified the awareness of common involvement which had been growing under a reasonably enlightened royal government since mediaeval days; the resulting cohesion (or, to use a simpler term, patriotism) considerably increased the international effectiveness of the state. True, the power of the King was in the seventeenth century replaced by that of an oligarchy. But the oligarchy was never a closed one, owed much of its resources to its connection with commerce and took care to see that commercial interests got free play. Moreover, the doctrines evolved to justify the Revolution continued to dominate orthodox thought, so that when the social transformations wrought by the Industrial Revolution began to gather way, there were within the ruling élite enough believers in the principle of liberty to provide a focus for the dissatisfied and to offer what proved to be a justified hope that the necessary adjustments could be made without having the social fabric again torn apart by the spiritual and material destruction of revolution.

In Germany, by contrast, the preconditions for these developments were lacking. At the end of the Middle Ages the land of the *Deutsch* was an idea rather than a political reality. A dawning awareness of this fact and a consequent sense of frustration may have been responsible for a wave of interest which arose in the fifteenth century about the distinctive features of German culture. Historical studies flourished as never before; several of the first books to be printed were concerned with the German past. This was the century which created the myth of Barbarossa sleeping in his cave, a common enough form of folk legend but significant in that it projected its adherents forward from an unsatisfactory present to the future greatness which would follow his reawakening. This was also the time that the words 'of the German nation' were added to the title 'Holy Roman Emperor'. The towns were growing in wealth and enterprise. Already the dominant economic force in Central Europe, they might soon have seized the political initiative. From the Low Countries a cultural flowering comparable to the Italian Renaissance spread at the end of the fifteenth century all the way up the Rhineland and into southern Germany; Grünewald, Hieronymus Bosch, Erasmus, Dürer and Cranach were all born between 1450 and 1480. Nine new universities were established between 1450 and 1517. For a moment Germany seemed to have a chance of catching up on her omissions. In fact, the full damage done by those omissions was just about to be revealed.

The Reformation and Religious Wars

The ferment of new thought awoke in Martin Luther (1487–1546) an intense religious experience which spread from theology to morals and thence to politics. The success of the Reformation owed not a little to a widespread dissatisfaction which projected on to the venal and decadent leaders of the Catholic Church responsibility for the weakness and misgovernment of which the Germans were becoming so conscious. It has been described[1] as 'Germany's belated revenge for the continuous thwarting of her destinies by the Papacy from the eleventh century onwards'. But a substitute had to be found for the Papal authority which was being rejected and this was almost inevitably the local secular power. In England, where this power had already been established on a national plane, the extra title of Head of the Church made the single central ruler even stronger. But in the lands of the Germans where effective power was split between many princes and each was free to choose his creed, this process of secularisation had a disintegrating effect, especially as the minority remaining true to the old faith included the Emperor.

The introduction of religious differences added a new dimension to the political rivalry already existing between the princedoms and in the absence of a dominating authority, there was no way of settling these differences except by arms. Luther revived and extended the Pauline and Augustinian doctrine that it was faith alone which could save souls from damnation. In the hands of his successors this tenet degenerated into an intense preoccupation with the details of the correct faith. A national disposition to abstract argument was fostered at the expense of humanist culture. As the hopes aroused by the early Reformation proved illusory, questions of abstruse theology such as the relations between the various persons of the Trinity came to be discussed with an intensity of passion reminiscent of the early Christian Church. The prayer of one theologian was that God might fill him with hatred of heretics. His colleague whose eyesight was ruined by writing too many controversial pamphlets is no bad symbol of the age. It was not an accident that in Germany the Wars of Religion lasted for thirty years, reduced the population by some thirty-five

[1] J. A. Hawgood, *Evolution of Germany*, p. 149.

per cent and at their end in 1648 left the country divided into 234 territorial units.

Emphasis on the direct responsibility of the individual to God might have been expected to foster a critical attitude towards the State. But Luther's belief in original sin led him to a pessimistic view of human institutions and a distrust of the masses, which was intensified when in 1525 the excitement of defiance to the existing order spread from the religious field to the secular and burst out in the Peasants' Revolt. By throwing his authority against the rebels, Luther may have lost a chance of making Protestantism a religion of the masses. But in the long run the support of the princes and organised authority was more important; without them the Reformation might have petered out as earlier movements had done. Yet by taking their side, he put control into their hands; they became the people who decided what kind of institutions should be created to maintain the new views. The Lutheran Church thus grew into a branch of the State, teaching that God had ordained princes to rule their peoples as fathers rule their families; the business of pastors was to save souls for a heavenly kingdom rather than to improve conditions in an earthly one. As all a ruler's subjects had to conform with his religious views, it was natural for his officials to collect from them along with other taxes the dues on which that Church depended. Those who disliked the religion of their ruler could usually find near at hand an alternative more to their taste much as inhabitants of Victorian cities 'sat under' one preacher after another until they found somebody congenial. (The 1565 Peace of Augsburg, which established this system, only covered the Roman Catholic and Lutheran religions; any others remained unprotected.) All of which goes to explain the virtual absence in Germany of the nonconformist dissenting tradition which has proved in Britain and America so potent a source of politics that were radical without being irreligious. Even in 1914 there were only 150,000 people in the whole of Germany claiming to belong to 'Free Churches'.

The endemic fighting made lives and property insecure, justice was hard to be had, the population fell instead of rising, saving, learning and invention languished. Awareness of common interest and the sense of being master of one's own fate, belief in ability to control one's own environment were all absent. The new trade routes, which brought so much stimulus to Western Europe, turned Germany into an economic backwater. The mouths of the Rhine, which might have provided an outlet to the Atlantic, passed at this very juncture under independent control. The middle classes lost ground instead of advancing. While Britain and France were entering on the most eventful period in their history and expanding in all directions Germany was at best stagnating.

Germany's Eastern Face

To say that Germany, being in the centre of Europe, has an eastern as well as a western frontier may seem a glimpse of the obvious but is all the same a truth of the first importance. For her history has been just as much affected by the lands to the one side as by those to the other, and as conditions in the two directions differed vastly, her people have had continually to reconcile dissimilar influences and problems. Germany taken as a whole belongs to Central rather than Western Europe.

When in the second century B.C. the Germanic tribes moved west and south, the gap left on the plains east of the Elbe was filled by Slavonic groups. These people, who in one or two cases even infiltrated west of the river, remained little affected in religion, society and farming methods by Mediterranean culture. As Central Germany developed, the Christian duty of converting the heathen on the east combined with a desire to get the land put to better use.

In Bohemia and Silesia the operation of conversion and colonisation went ahead fairly smoothly. In many parts of Eastern Europe, German-speaking settlers tended throughout the centuries to be welcome on account of their skills as traders and craftsmen; by the nineteenth century it was only a small exaggeration to say that one could travel by ox-cart from the Baltic to the Black Sea and stop each night in a German household. But further north the Prussians, a Slavonic people akin to the Latvians and Lithuanians, offered the fiercest resistance. A prominent part in subduing them was played by the Teutonic Knights, an order originally formed to free the Holy Land from the infidel which after the distraction of the Fourth Crusade decided to seek other areas for applying the techniques of the Church Militant. A first start in Transylvania proved abortive but in 1225 they moved on to north-east Germany and in fifty years of struggle succeeded in imposing on the Prussians not merely German habits but in some cases German names. In 1309 the headquarters of the Order was moved from Venice to Marienburg, south-east of Danzig. Nor was it only in Prussia that the original inhabitants became Germanised. In spite of a Slav counter-attack in the fifteenth century, a parallel assimilation was achieved widely in the conquered territories, though more among the owners of the lands than among the tillers of them, thus complicating the task of anyone so rash as to try and decide on strictly historical grounds to which state it is that they should now belong.

The process left a lasting mark on the men who conducted it. They came to regard as inferior beings all those—chiefly peasants —who kept any of their original characteristics, until the habitual attitude of the German to the Slav became one of disdain. On numerous occasions in coming centuries Germans and Russians were to cooperate. But this cooperation was never, in German eyes, quite between equals. Secondly they never felt quite secure against the possibility of a Slav counter-attack. In consequence great emphasis was laid on discipline, sacrifice, vigilance and valour.

At a relatively early stage the Emperor Conrad III had entrusted to a man called Albert the Bear (1100–70) the responsibility of turning part of Brandenburg into a strong point and as a result peasants from farther west were encouraged to settle in the swamps surrounding the village of Berlin. Three centuries later in 1415 a new ruler of Brandenburg became needed and the Emperor Sigismund gave the job to his friend Frederick Hohenzollern whose family, after originating on a Swabian hill-top, had for generations held an Imperial post in Nuremberg.

At the time of the Reformation a junior member of this family was Grand Master of the Teutonic Knights. He sought the advice of Luther and was told to renounce his vows, abolish the order, marry and found a dynasty. This comprehensive programme he executed in full. But early in the seventeenth century his line died out and the Lutheran Prussian Dukedom was as a result taken over by the Calvinist Elector of Brandenburg. And whereas the German peasants needed to colonise the Slav lands had had to be tempted by offers of exceptional privileges, a variety of forces had combined towards the end of the Middle Ages to turn them back into serfs bound to the land and dependent on the landlord for justice. The towns decayed in the religious wars, except for a few ports through which the surplus corn, grown by large-scale farming on the noble estates, was shipped to satisfy deficiencies farther west. Manufacturing was almost non-existent and from 1400 to 1650 the landowners, or 'Junkers', dominated the country.

Under Frederick William, who was known as 'the Great Elector' and reigned from 1640 to 1688, the Hohenzollerns began to get the upper hand: in 1701 his son Frederick ventured to take the title of 'King in Prussia'. The family held the view that a medium-sized state such as theirs could only prosper by exploiting the differences between its bigger neighbours. In view of Prussia's limited resources, the essential minimum of strength which this policy implied could be achieved only by the strictest care and control in the use of those resources. The situation was in many ways parallel to that of Soviet Russia in the 1930s and '40s and of other developing countries in Africa and Asia today. But the basic industry to which the fruits of economy were devoted was war, and since mercenaries were on the whole too expensive, Prussia anticipated revolutionary France by creating a national army. On this Frederick II (the Great, 1712-86) spent two-thirds of his revenue and in it one-sixth of the adult male population was required to serve; by his death it was practically as big as the French. Its officer corps was imbued with a high sense of duty— 'a moral compulsion which forced them, out of respect for themselves and their calling, to bear hardship, danger and death without flinching and without expectation of reward. This feeling of honour, the King believed, could only be found in the feudal nobility, not in other classes and certainly not in the bourgeoisie which was driven by material rather than moral considerations and was too rational in moments of disaster to regard sacrifice as either necessary or commendable.'[1]

A bargain was accordingly evolved by which the King was given the right—and the money—to maintain a standing army while the supply of officers became a monopoly of the nobility. The pay which the nobles thus obtained eked out the inadequate revenue of their estates which were, however, made inalienable. A further innovation was the development of a General Staff to plan and conduct campaigns.

To raise the money and the men, however, a civilian service was needed and it was to the bourgeoisie that the Kings originally turned for staffing this. In more than one respect it set the pattern for modern bureaucracies. As early as 1700 the principle of entrance by examination was established (although at the same time other posts were sold to the highest bidder!) and in 1723 it was laid down that applicants for senior grades must have had a university education. By the end of the eighteenth century, officials had acquired security of tenure against arbitrary dismissal. Stein was to say later that 'we are governed by paid, book-learned and disinterested property-less bureaucrats'. The officials, like the officers, were expected to serve the King rather than the public and to hold their tongues about work which so often had a military importance. Such servants proved their value in enabling the

[1] Gordon A. Craig, *The Politics of the Prussian Army*, p. 16.

monarchy to assert itself against the aristocracy and were sometimes rewarded by ennoblement. But once the struggle was over, nobles too were taken into service, particularly at the local level, and the mediaeval conception of society as divided into 'estates' was assimilated to the eighteenth-century concept of royal absolutism. The pillar of Prussian administration became the *Landrat* or district officer who tended to be at one and the same time a magnate nominated by his peers and a permanent official nominated by the King.

This absolutism was tempered in three ways. First the government was amongst the most up-to-date in Europe, inspired by the advanced ideas of the Enlightenment and tolerating almost any form of religious view. The King encouraged his subjects to reason for themselves, provided only that they obeyed his orders. Compulsory education was introduced in Prussia in 1717, 150 years ahead of England and France (though this did not prevent there being generals in the Prussian army who could not write their own names!). The *Allgemeines Preussisches Landrecht,* promulgated in 1794, provided a comprehensive, clear, uniform and impartial code of justice which was not superseded for over a century. Secondly, the King accepted the same standards as he imposed and regarded himself as the first servant of his people, even if he took his own decisions as to what their interests were. When the ruler was mediocre, the system was indifferent—but the Hohenzollerns managed to produce more above-average rulers than most dynasties. Finally, Prussia was successful, growing rapidly in size and international reputation. In 1739 it seized Silesia from the Habsburg Empire. In 1792 and 1793, it acquired large areas of Poland, even though it came off relatively badly in the final partition of 1795 which extinguished the existence of an independent Polish state. The human reluctance to jump off bandwaggons would by itself be enough to explain why the most autocratic state in Germany was also the only one to succeed in evoking among its subjects an effective loyalty as well as a sense of national identity. But in addition, as has been shown, most of the people who could have spread disaffection had been found a job in the State machine.

This was the austere and elevated climate in which was formulated the philosophy of Kant, the descendant of a Scottish immigrant and Germany's most profound thinker (1724–1804). Kant struggled to reconcile in the circumstances of eighteenth-century Prussia the two values of freedom and order, just as in the field of knowledge he sought to reconcile freedom with the universal law of cause and effect which man seems to find in nature. He held that the factor most distinguishing men from animal creation was their intuitive awareness of an inner moral law embodying the spirit of reason. Human conduct was to be judged, not by the nature and consequences of acts but by the motives of the actors. An act was moral in proportion as it was motivated by reason; the test of such motivation lay in whether the principle involved in the act could be universally applied. For unless such universal application were possible, the act itself could not be absolutely disinterested and this all truly moral acts were required to be. The 'categorical imperative' incumbent on men was always so to act that the action could be taken as the basis of a universal law. Sympathy and compassion were to be excluded as motives of moral action since they confused the application of reason. The starting point of Kant's thought may have been his hatred of tyranny. But in the effort to render external tyrants unnecessary, the individual was required to impose on himself an even more rigorous code than the King of Prussia imposed on his subjects. A man could be allowed to be free only if he was completely subject to an inner control.

In this way the tenets of the Prussian state were provided with an intellectual justification derived in part from the liberal tradition of Western Europe but capable of independent development.

Western Germany and the French Revolution

Germany as a whole took over a century to recover from the Thirty Years War. During the period French influence was persistent in politics and literature while artists, architects and musicians took their inspiration from Italy. It was the age of despotic rulers, supported by mercenary armies, a necessary episode in the rebuilding of the social fabric but hardly an inspiring one. The passion which had resulted from allowing religion to influence politics ebbed in proportion as respect for reason grew, and even those princes who still insisted on their subjects conforming to their own religion usually took more mundane considerations as a guide in making policy. But this solution increased the differences between the various parts of Germany. In the north and east the Protestants held their ground and though the Pietists here revived an emotional intensity of personal belief, this led to individual charity rather than to concerted social action, to withdrawal from the world rather than to attempts at improving it. According to Heine the choice was between mystics without imagination and dogmatists without intelligence. In the south and west Catholicism succeeded under Habsburg leadership in re-establishing its hold and these areas were in consequence brought within the orbit of the Mediterranean Counter-Reformation, having baroque as its distinctive art accompaniment.

With the major exception of Prussia, none of the German states had a sufficient record of success to inspire its subjects with any strong feelings of pride or loyalty. But on the other hand there was no widespread discontent. The nobility, old and new, played no intellectual role comparable to that of their fellows in France. The middle classes only grew slowly and were composed more of officials, lawyers, teachers, clergy and merchants than of manu-facturers. They it was who provided the protagonists of a slow cultural revival which at first was largely rationalist in character and regarded the enlightened individual as a citizen more of the world as a whole than of the principality in which he happened to live. Ruling should be left to those with special qualifications for the task. As Goethe put it, the common people were better at dealing blows than at deciding policy.

Gradually, however, signs of a national revival appeared, start-ing with an academic reassertion of the values of German learning and the German cultural heritage. The common language and the memory of a common history, the two great legacies of the mediaeval Reich to modern Germany, began to be recognised as the essential links uniting the inhabitants of the many and varied political fragments into which the area had been splintered. Look-ing round the outside world, those inhabitants of the area who had attained the level of self-consciousness needed for effective reflection could not help noticing that elsewhere links of language and culture had become the keystones of the most successful politi-cal societies yet evolved. In France and Britain (and to a lesser extent in Spain, Holland and Scandinavia), national feeling had grown spontaneously as a loyalty to a homogeneous social structure evolved under a settled central government and enjoying the highest level of prosperity yet known to man. From this observa-tion it was but a step for Germans to conclude that since they had a common language and history, they ought also to have a common government and that lack of such a government might be a major reason for their relative backwardness. German national spirit was thus much more of a self-conscious growth, based on a deliberate imitation of what had happened unintentionally else-where, and drawing its emotional **drive from** a sense of deprivation.

'The revival of Germany did not begin at the altar but in the lecture-hall.'[1] In France and Britain the facts preceded and formed the basis for theory; in Germany the theory was taken over ready-made by the intellectuals in the population and adopted as an ideal to which the facts must be altered to fit.

The execution of this process was notoriously accelerated by the French Revolution. This movement provided the world with an unprecedented demonstration of what could be achieved by a resolute and fanatical government able to fire its people with enthusiasm and so to mobilise the full resources of the nation. In face of the whirlwind, the cosmopolitan rationalism of Goethe's Weimar and the Spartan discipline of Frederick's Potsdam alike proved inadequate. The Germans were first inspired and then humiliated. One result was a wave of romantic dissatisfaction with rationalism which had its roots in Pietism and in the enthusiasm for folk-lore and primitive culture. Along with this went a wide-spread (though by no means universal) desire to emulate France in exploiting the national idea for political purposes and in securing, if necessary by political concessions, popular support for a war to liberate and even unify Germany. The Revolution must be fought with its own weapons. The problem, as the patriots saw it, was how to rouse the population to enthusiasm and evolve a determination which would triumph over all obstacles. The views of Clausewitz, formed at this time, take as their starting point the question 'how a community which has rested on a merely cultural basis could be turned into a community with a political will—a self-conscious national state capable of defending itself and keenly concerned about its freedom and external prestige'.[2]

It was as a step towards this end that in the years following their defeat by Napoleon at Jena (1806), the Prussian authorities put in hand an overhaul of their society—principally accomplished by non-Prussians in the King's service such as Stein, Hardenberg, Scharnhorst and Gneisenau. Outmoded economic restrictions were removed, the towns were given a certain amount of self-government and in the countryside the serfs were emancipated. The professional standing army, on whose size Napoleon had set a limit, was reorganised and supplemented by a popular short-service 'Home Guard' (*Landwehr*). The responsibilities of the General Staff were increased. The reformers sought to sacrifice all other values to the re-establishment of Prussia as a major European Power. The

---

[1] T. Heuss, *Friedrich Naumann*, p. 360.
[2] G. Ritter, *Staatskunst und Kriegshandwerk*, I, p. 71

resulting excitement carried the country into the coalition which overwhelmed Napoleon in 1813 and again two years later.

An atmosphere of this kind favoured the development of that emphasis on the individuality of peoples which distinguished German thought for the following 140 years. In 1807 Fichte began to give a political application to the academic interest in national characteristics. This occurred as a reaction against the universalism of the 'enlightenment', against the domination of France over Germany and against the Napoleonic attempt to unify Europe. Such a view came easily to Germans since the Roman theory of 'natural law' with its emphasis on universalism, the intellect and the individual had always had less influence on the east than on the west side of the Rhine. Each people was thought of as a separate entity with distinct characteristics and capacities; the differences were more significant than the similarities. Moreover, the State rather than the individual was the embodiment of the national identity and as such the repository of ultimate values.

With Kant, resistance to the State could still be justified if its own principles could be shown to lack universal application. Hegel (1770-1831), however, went a step further for, in an effort to find a compromise between liberal values and Prussia's authoritarian bureaucracy, he transferred the highest seat of reason from the individual to the community : the world was then faced with the paradox that only in obedience to the State could the individual be truly free. Moreover, there could be no higher authority than the individual State : the final arbiter in international affairs must therefore be force (though the road to this conclusion was often smoothed by a facile optimism which suggested that once the national will rather than a ruler's whim became everywhere sovereign, states would have the same view of world politics and so live in peace with one another).

It may be that, because in Western Europe government on the whole was well established over wide areas, political theorists tended to emphasise freedom and individual rights; in Central and Eastern Europe where the defects caused by division were easier to see, they gave priority to order and the rights of the State. Now the exaltation of individual rights at the expense of government authority clearly leads to selfishness and anarchy, while the opposite process leads to despotism and injustice. The idea of holding the two in balance is more easy to express than to execute. Equilibrium can be achieved verbally by saying that the highest freedom consists in obedience to law as the embodiment of reason and that social liberty is a consequence of, rather than a check on,

the power of the State. But in practice this formula tends to be
given one of two slants. Either existing law is attacked in the name
of freedom as a palpably inadequate embodiment of reason. Or
else obedience is demanded, in the name of reason, to law equated
with the current demands of the government, even where this
appears to be at the expense of the individual.

Germany in the nineteenth century was to exhibit examples of
both deviations. The main stream of thought continually slipped
into an uncritical assertion of the rightness of whatever happened
to be; the assailants of the *status quo,* handicapped by lack of
political experience, carried the demand for liberty to excessive
lengths.

We may today find it hard to understand how Hegel's philosophy
could ever have obtained such wide acceptance as an account
of reality. But not only did it provide an intellectual justification
for the kinds of policy which historical forces were rendering
attractive to many Germans. No other philosopher since Aquinas
had provided the world with a coherent system claiming to explain
not only logic, metaphysics and morals but politics, history, society
and aesthetics into the bargain. Moreover, developing an initiative
of Kant's (the 'Copernican Revolution') he argued that our ideas
about all these matters were affected as much by the man viewing
as by the thing viewed, so that subject and object were inextricably
linked. In this he showed the way to Marx and many other later
thinkers. The involved character of his language, instead of being
an obstacle to understanding, chimed in with national habits of
thought. Many decades of critical reflection were needed to see the
edifice in perspective and separate the grains of lasting truth from
the vast architecture in which they were embedded. In the interval,
the spurious elements had done as much as the valid ones to
influence the way men acted.

Hegel, though by birth a Swabian, was a professor at the
University of Berlin, founded in 1812 by William von Humboldt
as an integral part of the Prussian revival. In a country where
nationalism began as an intellectual exercise and all professors are
appointed and paid by the State, universities have an obvious
political role. Berlin in particular deserved its description as the
'1st Guards Brigade of Learning'. For this was the intellectual
power-house where not only Hegel but such historians as Ranke,
Droysen and Treitschke generated the distinctive view of the
world and of Prussia's place in it which Germany was to offer as
its gospel, a coherent and comprehensive alternative to the rational
individualism stemming from the Graeco-Roman tradition.

Yet paradoxically von Humboldt, so far from designing the university as a political weapon, made the freedom of the professor to teach and of the student to learn into one of the fundamental principles of his system. He was also the founder of the tradition that research, the advancement of learning, is not merely the primary function of a university but an ideal means of stimulating students to independent thought. In textual, historical and biblical criticism German scholarship was to dominate the nineteenth century and be a major factor in changing its view of the world. Yet such is the domination of environment over thought that when it came to the values which their own nation was accepting as guides, the function of German scholars turned only too often from criticism to inculcation.

There was a further consequence of the doctrine that all students, no matter what their future profession, were to be taught as though they were destined to be scholars. For precision and thoroughness thereby gained status in public life, perhaps at some cost to a sense of proportion. This trend was reinforced by the requirement that virtually all candidates for administrative posts should pass an examination in law, so as to ensure that they understood the principles of the system which they would be called on to apply.

The Failure of the Liberals

In 1803 Napoleon rationalised Germany, apart from Prussia, by expelling Austria and reducing the remaining units from three hundred to thirty; three years later he prevailed on the Habsburg Emperor to abolish the Holy Roman Empire. The statesmen who met in 1815 at the Congress of Vienna found it difficult to put the clock completely back and accordingly confirmed these changes with minor variations, linking the German states in a loose confederation. The rulers of Bavaria, Saxony and Württemberg, whom Napoleon had promoted to be Kings, were allowed to keep their title and Hanover (ruled until 1837 by the King of England) was given the same rank. At the last moment Prussia, as compensation for leaving some of her Polish acquisitions in Russian hands, was given considerable areas of the Rhineland and Westphalia which she did not welcome (since they meant that her territories were divided into two large blocks with no geographical connection) and in which she was not welcomed (since her dour methods contrasted unfavourably with twenty years of French rule). As a result of this and earlier transactions her predominantly Lutheran population of 6 million was increased to 10, of whom 5, including a million Poles, were Catholic. But the victory had been won by the government and the popular movement was allowed little share in its fruits. The poorer peasants, although technically freed from the land, became more dependent than ever on the Junker landlords. The limited self-government allowed to the towns was not extended to the country districts. The *Landwehr* continued but was looked at askance by the professional soldiers who were elevated into a closed caste with restricted admission and special privileges.

The problem for German nationalists prior to March 1848 was to find a rallying point. The obvious leader for a united Germany might seem to be the Austrian Emperor. But less than a third of his dominions was included in the German Confederation and of the twelve million people who were so included almost half were Slav. His predecessors had signally failed to rouse an adequate consolidating loyalty in the days when this might have been done spontaneously and nobody could rate high the chances of holding together a population still retaining cultural badges of membership in so many different national groups. Clearly, however, an identification of the Empire with Germany would be bound to alienate the Emperor's non-German subjects, and the interests of the Habsburg dynasty were for that reason only very partially German. Yet though unwilling to risk the loss of their non-German interests by taking a lead in unifying Germany, they realised that for Germany to become united would involve the splitting up of their domains. They were wedded to the existing order because any change must be to their disadvantage. Some of the other German princes, such as the Wittelsbachs in Bavaria, had managed to rouse a limited local loyalty. But neither it nor their lands spread wide enough to provide the basis for a national state, which must inevitably spell the end of their own independence. The most to be hoped for was that their ruling classes would be sufficiently conscious of their German attributes to offer only formal opposition to unity. This left the nationalists with a choice between throwing out the dynasties by a revolution or building the new state round Prussia.

From 1815 onwards two-fifths of those Germans who were not Habsburg subjects lived in Prussia so that a united nation which left them all out would have made nonsense. But the leaders of the national movement, basing themselves on English and French examples, took it for granted that a national state must have a liberal constitution and therefore associated unification with the establishment of responsible representative government. The demand for this also reflected the early stirrings in Germany of the Industrial Revolution and the pressure of groups whose economic situation was improving for a corresponding improvement in social status. The *Zollverein* or Free Trade Area set up between 1828 and 1835 under Prussian leadership (but excluding Austria) did something in the short term to relieve the pressure for unification (particularly by making trade easier between Prussia's various parts) but in the long term increased that pressure by hastening technological change. Significantly it was Prussia which in Silesia and the Ruhr valley possessed two of Europe's chief coalfields.

But though there were considerable liberal elements in Prussia, and particularly in the western provinces, the last parts of Germany to be affected by industrialisation were her core provinces east of the Elbe. Here an independent middle class was still small, the ruling class consisting of landowners and of officials of various kinds closely assimilated to them. Liberalism, so far from attracting the Junkers, was anathema to most of them and rather than pay the price of recasting their society in order to become leaders of Germany, they preferred, like the Irishman asked whether he would rather be a Christian or a gentleman, to remain as they were.[1]

Moreover, they were bound to have misgivings about a course which would estrange them from their natural allies, the Russian nobility, besides carrying a grave risk of collision with Austria, still the moral leader of the Germans, and with France whose position in Europe was bound to be impaired by the rise of a strong united Germany.

The biggest mistake of the Liberals in the years before 1848 was their failure to realise the importance of having organised force at their command. This was not simply due to lack of practical experience, though they certainly paid the price of their relative immunity from military service. Doctrinaire theories borrowed from England and elsewhere fostered the idea that any army beyond a national militia would menace individual liberties. Accordingly, they not only failed to organise a citizen force which could stand up to the royal armies (though this began to happen in Berlin during the 1848 rising) but they also disregarded the impossibility of defying Austria without the armed strength needed to make the

---

[1] The constitution of Pomerania (actually a province of Prussia) was alleged to consist of the single clause 'We will proceed as we have always proceeded'.

defiance successful. A self-appointed Assembly at Frankfurt (composed predominantly of self-employed intellectuals rather than merchants or manufacturers) drew up in 1848 a constitution for Germany but was powerless when Austria, Prussia and Hanover rejected it. Plumping for an arrangement which left Austria out (the 'small-Germany' solution) they offered the German crown to King Frederick William of Prussia; when he refused it, the gathering broke up. When the King tried to set up a union of his own, Austria threatened war and by the Agreement of Olmütz (1850) forced him to abandon the scheme.

Thereafter the Liberal cause might have foundered altogether if the economic tide had not been steadily strengthening the middle classes. The groups ranged against them were neither effete nor incompetent nor half-hearted. They believed that they had saved Germany from chaos by their firm stand in 1848–50 and saw no reason why they should not repeat the process whenever necessary. Moreover, the middle classes were beginning to doubt their ability to keep a revolution within bounds. For the struggle to break the political power of the landowners had been postponed in Germany to an epoch in which working-class consciousness was beginning to stir. Marx, born and educated in Germany, was doing his best to spread the idea that the proletariat should exploit the bourgeois revolution as a stepping-stone to their own dictatorship. Not for the last time those Germans who wished to put their fellow-countrymen in control of their own destiny shrank from the action needed to do so for fear that, once the impetus was created, it might hurtle beyond the goal. And indeed, if the Liberals had been strong enough to put up a fight, the result might well have been a civil war into which most of Europe would gradually have been drawn.

Yet a widespread desire for German unity persisted and was reinforced when Italy became united in 1859. The failure of 1848-50 deepened the sense of frustration which the years after 1815 had aroused, and produced a reaction against what were regarded as the unpractical policies responsible for failure. Many of those reaching manhood between 1850 and 1870 were not only obsessed with the problem of unification but convinced that policies of realism (*Realpolitik*) could alone be expected to overcome the obstacles. Realism involves a hard-headed assessment of values and a readiness to sacrifice subordinate ones to the top priorities. And whereas for a moment after 1806 it had been to liberalism that concessions were called for in the name of nationalism, now they were to be made to conservatism. The primacy which these men and women gave to the advancement of the national cause at the expense, if necessary, of freedom is one of the dominating facts of the next seventy years, since this was the generation which was to provide Germany's leaders between 1880 and 1914.

After 1848 all the indications pointed to Prussia as the focus of German unity and to lack of international influence as the price for remaining disunited. But the Prussian élite still feared that a united Germany would mean the ruin of all the things which they valued, while the other states of Germany were too proud of their own identities to accept a merger reducing them to the level of Prussian provinces. Moreover, an all-German government, to deserve the name, had to be responsible for the defence and foreign policy of its territories. Yet these two prerogatives and the control thereby ensured over the Kingdom's destinies were precisely what the Prussian leaders felt least inclined to surrender.

Although the Liberals probably had a majority among the Prussian voters and although a more liberal ministry was called to power in Prussia in 1858, the history of the next four years showed how deeply rooted was the opposition to concessions. The crucial clash came on the question of what form the army was to take and where control of it was to rest. Strategic developments had outmoded the *Landwehr* and made it an obstacle to the organisation of an efficient striking force. Accordingly, the War Minister Roon wanted to convert it into the regular army's reserve. As proposed, the reform involved the adaptation of the nation to militarism whereas the reforms of 1806-14 had sought to make the army a reflection of the nation. The Prussian Parliament (*Landtag*) tried to restore the balance, and when it was disregarded, sought to enforce its will by the power of the purse. The men round the King took the view that military arrangements were his personal concern as commander-in-chief and advised him to stand firm. This he readily did, dissolving Parliament. But, even though the constitution divided voters into three classes according to wealth and allowed 3 per cent, 12 per cent and 85 per cent of the total each to elect an equal number of Deputies, the opposition came back in greater strength. Still the royal group would not give way. The King's obstinacy seemed destined to make his name a stock example of the social havoc done by misplaced pertinacity.

From this predicament King William was not only saved but in the short space of eight years raised to the position of German Emperor. The man chiefly responsible for this transformation was, of course, a highly-strung genius with an inordinate appetite and a squeaky voice called Otto von Bismarck. Bismarck once compared the statesman to a wanderer in a forest who knows the direction of his route but not the point at which he will emerge from the woods. He himself showed an unsurpassed skill in keeping in sight during his wanderings as many alternative routes as possible and postponing to the latest practicable moment a choice between them. Indeed he often managed to travel by several at once and contrive for them to converge at the same point. He ended his memoirs by defining the task of the policy-maker as being 'to foresee as accurately as possible the way in which other people are going to react in given circumstances' and his genius displayed itself in so adapting his own immediate behaviour so as to make those reactions yield their maximum contribution to his ultimate objectives. Men and ideas alike he regarded more as tools than as ends in themselves and while this goes far to explain his success in solving the problems which faced him, it also helps to explain why he left for those who came after him other problems even more intractable still. He understood to perfection the dynastic system in which he had grown up, but the new order of society which emerged during his lifetime filled him with foreboding rather than sympathy.

Between 1862 and 1870 Bismarck succeeded in defying the Prussian Parliament for four years, finding from a State-owned railway the cost of the military expenditure which it refused to grant. But in addition he had the insight to recognise that German unity in one form or another was inevitable and that the question facing Prussia was not therefore 'whether' but 'how?' Bent on avoiding the acceptance of someone else's terms, he engineered by a series of improvisations what was in effect the conquest of Germany by Prussia. In the war of 1866, with the help of Moltke's strategic gifts and the remodelled Prussian army, he overcame Austrian and Hanoverian opposition to German unity under Prussian leadership, and in the war of 1870 overcame that of France. He further kept these two wars from starting a European conflagration. But in addition he led Prussia to a position in which she could no longer refuse to assume the leadership of Germany and in which neither the other princes nor the Liberals could refuse to accept Prussian predominance. The exclusion of the Germans of Austria from the united national state in any case increased the chances of that state being dominated by the Protestant north rather than the Catholic south, and this helped to allay Prussian fears. Finally in the 1866 constitution of the North German Confederation, adapted in 1871 to become that of the

German Empire, he evolved a compromise which gave all groups enough of what they wanted to be acceptable to most of them.

Yet it is hard to contemplate this epoch-making result without pondering on the turn of chance or fate which provided that, when the man of genius appeared, he did so on the conservative side. If the Liberals had possessed a Bismarck or a Lenin in 1848, how differently the world might have developed! But was the absence of such a man due merely to the accidents of heredity or did the history of Germany prior to 1862 make it impossible for realists to be Liberal?

Chapter 2

The Second Reich

Internal Affairs Under Bismarck

IN JANUARY 1871 the victorious King William of Prussia was proclaimed German Emperor (*Deutscher Kaiser*, not Emperor of Germany). He thus became merely the senior rather than the superior of the other German princes. 'The Emperor is not my Monarch,' said a Württemberg politician. 'He is only the commanding officer of my Federation.' There were indeed those who maintained, with considerable legal justification, that the princes were subordinated to the Empire rather than to the Emperor, and in particular to the Federal Council or *Bundesrat*. To this body, which deliberated in private, each of the twenty-five member governments sent a delegation proportionate to its importance. Though all the votes of each delegation counted, each voted as a block (on the logical but unfounded principle that no government can be of two minds). Of the fifty-eight members, seventeen came from Prussia (which after its victories comprised in area and population about five-eighths of the Federation and completely surrounded twelve of the smaller states), six from Bavaria and four each from Saxony and Württemberg. As no proposal to change the constitution could go forward if fourteen votes were cast against it, this effectively gave either Prussia or the South German states acting together a guarantee against reforms of which they disapproved. The agreement of the *Bundesrat* was required before legislation could be submitted to the Imperial Assembly (*Reichstag*)[1] and it was to be consulted on all important questions including declarations of war.

The intention would appear to have been for the *Bundesrat* to become a sort of Cabinet, the supreme executive organ of the Empire. If so, the aim remained unrealised, and the Council steadily lost influence : in 1914 it was not consulted until after war had been declared. Instead the power passed progressively into

[1] This was the name habitually used in the First Reich for the body described in English as the 'Imperial Diet' (of Worms, Ratisbon, etc.).

the hands of its Chairman the Imperial Chancellor who was almost always also Minister-President of Prussia and, as such, the head of the Prussian delegation. There was no Cabinet in the English sense of the word. The State-Secretaries for Foreign Affairs, the Interior, Finance, Justice, Posts and (later) the Navy were regarded as officials, responsible to the Chancellor. There was no Federal Secretary of War : the Prussian Minister of War acted as chairman of the *Bundesrat* committee on the Armed Forces and appeared in the *Reichstag* to speak on military matters. This was because the Prussian army remained directly responsible to its King while absorbing the troops of all the smaller German states including Hanover. The armies of Bavaria, Saxony and Württemberg retained varying degrees of independence, though the Emperor could transfer an officer from any of them to the Prussian army regardless of the victim's wishes. The Prussian Parliament remained unaltered, including the three-tier voting for the *Landtag*.[1] Prussian Ministers often doubled their job with that of the corresponding Federal State-Secretary, the Chancellor always being Prussia's Foreign Minister (since her foreign policy was confined to relations with the other states in the Empire).

To this complex and conservative structure, however, Bismarck added a *Reichstag* elected by universal (male) suffrage as the Frankfurt Assembly of 1848 had proposed. This was something which in 1871 few other states in Europe possessed, and its radicalism alarmed the Conservatives. In practice, however, the *Reichstag* went far to justify its description by a Socialist as 'the fig-leaf of absolutism'. Apart from the fact that throughout virtually the whole of its existence it provided a majority ready to vote for the existing régime, its powers had three flaws. It could not initiate legislation, it did not appoint the Chancellor and at an early date it was compelled drastically to curtail its powers over the financing of defence. Membership was by law incompatible with membership of the *Bundesrat* and therefore in practice with the holding of ministerial office (though Civil Servants could stand for election as Deputies and, if successful, be given leave of absence while they sat).[2]

The *Reichstag* reflected public opinion and could stop government proposals, including taxation, from becoming law. But it

[1] See above, p. 35.
[2] It went without saying that an official would belong to one of the parties supporting the government and preferably the Conservatives. On one occasion when a nobleman who was a National Liberal Deputy and an aide-de-camp to the Kaiser voted with the Progressives he was deprived of his right to wear uniform !

could not enforce its own wishes. The parties were left free to criticise but given no chance of putting alternative policies into action themselves. They therefore tended to degenerate into irresponsible pressure groups more prone to split up than to coalesce.

According to the constitution 'the Emperor appointed the Imperial officials', including the Chancellor. Their tenure of office therefore depended not on the confidence of a majority in the *Reichstag* but on the will—one might almost say the whim—of the Emperor. What the constitution failed to lay down with clarity was where the powers and duties of the Emperor ended and those of the Chancellor began. It is true that there was a clause requiring the Chancellor to countersign and take responsibility for all royal decrees and orders. But if a Chancellor ever showed reluctance to act in this way, all the Emperor had to do was to replace him with someone more compliant—there was to be no lack of candidates. In theory, of course, the *Reichstag* could have forced the Emperor's hand by refusing to vote for the measures of any Chancellor who did not follow the policies it favoured. But not only had the Prussian Parliament come off worst when it tried to do this in 1863. Most Deputies would have recoiled from the idea of forcing on the Emperor a Chancellor of their own choosing. To decide who should govern the country was not regarded as part of a politician's business. As a result the country came to be governed by a virtually uncontrolled bureaucracy.

This bureaucracy was older than the legislature and correspondingly disdainful of it. But bureaucrats have a different approach to problems than politicians and Germany subsequently suffered from having administrative rather than political judgement brought to bear on the formulation of policy. This weakness was aggravated during the 1880s by the gradual elimination of liberally-minded officials from the Prussian service (from which Reich officials were largely recruited) which meant that the people running the country were often at variance with public opinion.

Dependence on the Emperor was by no means the only problem facing the man who combined the offices of Imperial Chancellor and Prussian Minister-President. He had to work at the same time with two parliamentary bodies, the *Reichstag* and *Landtag*, each chosen on a very different basis. How could he hope to do this if their political complexions began seriously to diverge? Moreover, although the Chancellor was largely concerned with foreign policy (defined for obvious reasons in the constitution as a Federal matter) he had no legal right of control over the armed forces which reported direct to the Emperor. Bismarck, whose policy from 1863 to 1866 had alone enabled this situation to persist, defended it on the ground that, if the Chancellor were allowed control over the armed forces, it might be very hard to prevent the *Reichstag* from interfering in matters of vital national security. Yet if the Chancellor was denied the powers needed to keep military and political policies in tune, the only constitutional possibility of reconciling them rested with the Emperor. Bismarck was usually able to get William I to do as he wished. But in 1871 William was already seventy-four.

Such then was the form of the Federation into which by 1871 most people speaking German had been collected together (though there were many left outside in Switzerland, in Austria and in isolated groups throughout Eastern Europe). Bismarck had squared the constitutional circle though by a formula which did not allow for easy revision. But the inhabitants of the new Empire were still far from being an integrated community. Conservatives looked suspiciously at Liberals, aristocrats at bourgeoisie, industrialists at workers, soldiers at civilians, Protestants at Catholics, North at South, Christians at Jews. In the past, centrifugal forces had often proved too strong. Could they now be held in check? Could the political system be adapted to the consequences of the industrial and social growth which was just beginning to get under way?

A challenge arose immediately. The doctrine of Papal infallibility, promulgated by the Vatican Council just as the Franco-Prussian war was breaking out, was not only a slap in the face to liberal opinion, but precipitated disputes inside the Catholic Church which raised the whole question of its relation to the State. In the controversy which followed laws were passed giving the Imperial and Prussian governments powers over education and the appointment of bishops, establishing civil marriage and expelling the Jesuits and other non-German priests and nuns. Bismarck saw in the Catholics, who composed a third of the population and founded the Centre Party to represent their interests in the *Reichstag*, the allies of all those elements of whom he was most suspicious—the South Germans and Hanoverians who had opposed Prussian leadership and now wanted to limit the Federal government's powers, the Austrian conservatives who resented a German Empire from which they were excluded, the French right-wing who longed to avenge the 1870 defeat, and the Poles who threatened German security in the eastern provinces, not to mention the Danes, Hanoverians and Alsatians. The legislation was thus a logical continuation of the campaign for a unified

Germany; the idea of fighting clerical obscurantism was supported with enthusiasm by the Liberals who called the policy 'the cultural struggle' (*Kulturkampf*).

Bismarck, however, found that the course which his Ministers supported on grounds of principle raised almost as many political problems as he had expected it to solve. Persecution had its usual effect of strengthening the will to resist, while Protestants at court and among the Prussian Conservatives were so hostile to Liberalism that they made common cause with the Catholics. By the end of the 1870s the Chancellor had had enough. The accession of a new Pope, Leo XIII, gave him a chance to start negotiations which gradually moved to an amicable settlement in 1887. The State established its right to supervise education and have a say in the appointment of bishops. The Church went a long way to germanise its clergy. The Centre Party, afraid of the attack being renewed, took care to give no grounds for a charge of disloyalty. Bismarck had thus succeeded in neutralising a possible source of division.

One of his motives for relaxing the *Kulturkampf* was his view that the gravest threat to the State was in future likely to be social rather than religious. In 1875 the two working-class parties founded by Marx and Lassalle had sunk their differences to form the Socialist Workers' Party. In the 1877 elections the votes given to this rose by nearly 50 per cent (350,000 to 500,000). Continued progress at a similar rate would create serious difficulties. In 1878, taking advantage of two attempts on the Emperor's life, Bismarck introduced legislation to impede Socialist agitation. This enabled him to recover Conservative support but forfeited that of Progressive opinion. To carry it through, he counted on Catholic willingness to uphold social order. He did not confine himself to repression. In a series of laws between 1883 and 1889 he inaugurated, for the first time in history, an imaginative system of social insurance and labour arbitration designed to reconcile the workers to their conditions. They, however, were slow to appreciate benefits bestowed by a political system in which they had little say.

Events were to show that few people were in fact more orderly and law-abiding than the average German worker. But their leaders continued to talk for a long time in terms of revolution; Bebel had in 1871 pointed at the Paris Commune as a weak prelude to what would happen before long in Germany. The most intense venom was reserved for any revisionist who challenged the view that revolution was both necessary and bound to come. Indeed the attitude of the ruling classes made it hard to see how the workers could get what they wanted otherwise than by revolution and it was only after a sort of revolution that their demands were in the end met. The owners of property can hardly be blamed for taking the threat of revolt seriously. Germany's lack of any tradition of religious radicalism meant that socialism, as generally on the continent, was materialistic, opposed to religious belief as well as to private ownership of the means of production. In the eyes of all respectable citizens, this combination put the party beyond the pale. Nobody belonging to it could be regarded as a loyal citizen; its participation in the conduct of political affairs was unthinkable. Such an attitude, which has only faded very gradually, did much to induce among large sections of the German middle classes an attitude of passive acceptance of government.

The process of consolidating the rest of German society behind the government was taken a step further when increasing quantities of cheap overseas and Russian grain began to arrive on European markets, thanks to overseas investment, better communications, the introduction of iron steamships and the opening of the Suez Canal. This struck at the livelihood of the big landowners east of the Elbe who seemed likely to lose not only such foreign markets as Britain but also the home market in Germany. Heavy industry (as distinct from commerce) was equally anxious for protection while getting established. The constitution empowered the Imperial government to raise revenue only by indirect taxation. Bismarck wanted more money for military and other purposes so that the imposition of a revenue tariff suited his book. But although the economist Friedrich List (1789-1846) had formulated a theory justifying protection, free trade was an integral part of the Liberal tradition and since 1870 Bismarck had depended on the Liberals for his majority in the *Reichstag*.

The events of 1870–1 had realised the national aims of the German intellectuals and middle classes who formed the mainstay of the Liberal Party. The question for the following decades was how far they would remain content with what had been achieved and how far they would continue to want their constitutional aims realised as well. There were of course a number of Germans whose interest in Liberalism had been primarily due to a belief that only in a liberal state could Germans be united. When Bismarck demonstrated the contrary, they yielded to an uncritical admiration of his achievement and ceased to look for further reform. The process was justified ideologically by the theory that individual personal liberties and local self-government really mattered more than parliamentary and ministerial arrangements. The introduction of laws to secure these between 1872 and 1883 was claimed to have given Germany its own form of Liberalism; the authoritarian State (*Obrigkeitsstaat*) had been replaced by the State in which law reigned supreme (*Rechtsstaat*), assigning to each citizen his obligations and rights. The theory contributed to the general thesis of a specifically German solution to the problems presented to Central Europe by the political and economic innovations from the West.

The introduction of tariffs led to the left wing of the National Liberals breaking away to form (in due course) the Progressives, but the bulk of the party accepted the new policy and continued to give general support to Bismarck and (on the whole) to his successors. He might thus seem to have achieved considerable success in consolidating German society. Not only had his Empire proved able by the time of his resignation to survive for two decades but Conservatives, Liberals and Catholics had all come to accept its basic principles. Moreover, the future was to reveal a surprising degree of readiness on the part of the industrial workers to do the same.

Much dissatisfaction, however, remained. The Empire had not brought the degree either of external influence or of internal harmony which many had been foolish enough to expect of it. This dissatisfaction expressed itself in two directions.

On the one hand the Conservative-National Liberal alliance which increasingly emerged as the ruling class of the new state succumbed to dreams of national aggrandisement and talked of the need for Germany, having established herself as a European Power, to claim her rightful place as a world leader. The professors and journalists who were so strongly represented among the National Liberals, instead of demonstrating how much the victories of 1866 and 1870 had owed to superior political dexterity and better military organisation, not only invented a legend that Prussian hegemony had been predestined all along but engaged in a dangerous perversion of logic. They treated the fact of German success as evidence that German culture and talent were superior, deducing not merely the possession of a right to dominate but also an assurance of victory in the future. Treitschke said openly that a nation had to overestimate its capacities in order to become aware of them.

Like many other social groups which gain power by a gradual process rather than a sudden revolution, the German middle classes, on reaching maturity in successive generations, tended to assimilate themselves to the standards which they found dominant instead of evolving their own. This process was powerfully fostered by many of the institutions of society, and notably the student corps in the universities and the much-prized grade of reserve officer to which the steadily-growing appetite of the army for manpower made the admission of well-to-do bourgeois essential. Just when the special conditions which had shaped Prussia were beginning to lose their relevance, the traditional Prussian virtues were taken over, often by people from other parts of Germany, and exaggerated to the point of distortion. Compassion became taboo; charity and tolerance were too easily condemned along with it. Violence was exalted and little awareness shown for its effects on other people. Courage turned into a contempt for modesty and common-sense, self-reliance into a disdain for all who did not belong to the warrior caste, discipline into a demand for unquestioning obedience, patriotism into a lust for domination. The law that material resources are useless without a will to use them became a faith that all things are possible to the obstinate. Such an outlook was a hangover from the mediaeval glorification of war and the military virtues. Applied in a totally different environment, it was not only to prove a menace to Germany's neighbours but was seriously to mislead its practitioners about the realities of the world.[1]

Unfortunately this was not all. For besides the people to whom the Empire had brought success and power, even if in inadequate quantities, there were many to whom it—or, strictly speaking, the economic and social changes accompanying it—spelt failure and the need for change. Whereas in the pioneer industrial countries, the innovations stretched over several generations, reducing the risk that individuals with particular skills would find themselves obsolete in mid-career, the higher tempo which Germany as an imitator was able to achieve proved a mixed blessing. While it certainly accelerated her rise to Great Power status, it did so at the cost of multiplying internal tensions. A number of people, particularly small men, found the world going against them and instead of adapting to it, preferred to decide that it had taken a wrong turning. Among them were some who had got through a university education only to find themselves unable to gain the status of a professorial chair. The school-teaching to which they were instead reduced gave them a chip on their shoulder and a disposition to prove their ability by abstract

[1] The Prussian General Staff were pioneers in applying to war and to its preparation the systematic rationalising which underlay the Industrial Revolution. They failed, however, to apply the same yardstick to their own social and political ideas.

theorising. They lacked the alertness of mind needed to criticise the views which their intellectual training equipped them to absorb, and much high-flown nonsense was the result.

The criticisms of such people fastened not simply on the materialism of a world growing rapidly more affluent, but on the creeds which had brought this about. They denied the claims of reason, intellect, science and the critical spirit, preferring instead intuition, imagination, 'history' and faith. They rejected the view that the individual had a right to equal treatment or to freedom, preferring that an idealised élite should dictate. In short they wanted their country to break with Western Europe and return to what they regarded as its distinctive national traditions, as they considered it to have done in the Reformation and the Romantic resistance to Napoleon and French ideas.

The concessions made to Liberalism and democracy in the 1871 settlement disgusted them. The party system in particular seemed designed to create discord rather than the harmony for which they longed, the harmony which alone could make their country strong enough to recover that place in the world struggle for power which the misfortunes of its history had prevented it from taking. But since this harmony was to be a harmony on their own conditions, they rejected the idea of achieving it by discussion and compromise, preferring instead the short-cuts of emotion and autocracy. Thus there developed the idea of a community or *Volk* cemented by a common spirit because dominated by attitudes which grew naturally like plants out of its historical background and physical surroundings or *Heimat*. Where elements of the *Volk* refused to fall into line or when other *Völker* got in the way, superficial recollections of Nietzsche and Darwin were invoked to justify an appeal to force. But the general view was that a pure *Volk* would be a unanimous *Volk* so that disunity was evidence of an impurity needing to be eradicated. It was in this context that anti-Semitism became significant.

The European Jews, having for long been forbidden to own land or ply a craft, had gravitated to the towns. Their tendency towards intellectualism, possibly the result of isolation in the ghetto and absorption in Talmudic scholarship, fitted them for finance, trade and the learned professions (particularly law), the very skills which were in demand in an industrialising society. As a result they gained a social position out of all proportion to their total numbers; it was reckoned in the 1880s that, while they made up one per cent of the total population of Germany, they amounted to 5 per cent in Berlin where 25 per cent of the grammar school places were occupied by their children. The intellectuality of their outlook and ingrained instinct to expect a Messiah would probably have inclined them anyhow to the left in politics but the Liberals secured their support by advocating their emancipation. The net result was that they came quickly to symbolise to those who disliked liberal, rational, industrial society all the things which were dislikeable about it—especially as unsuccessful people are often in debt and creditors are not infrequently Jewish. By the end of the nineteenth century Lagarde, Dühring, Böckel and a number of other writers had identified the Jews as the source of Germany's weakness.

Though the peddlers of all these sorts of notions were active enough in the Second Reich, its success and social respectability deprived them of serious political influence. Moreover, although their views on several aspects of internal social policy were to prove significantly divergent from those of the ruling classes, they saw eye-to-eye on the question of extending Germany's authority abroad—a fact which must have enhanced the attractions of that theme in the rulers' eyes. All the same, their existence hung an extra question mark over the future, especially as many of them earned their living in ways which gave them a hold on youth. Indeed Germany diverged from much of the rest of Europe in that her middle-class youth, though eager for change, were looking right rather than left. This was not true of the workers who had been inoculated against Volkism by Marxism—which made all the more tenuous the prospect of ever finding a society into which both social groups could comfortably fit.

Bismarck's Foreign Policy

In 1871 Germany imposed on the defeated France a heavy indemnity, which was paid off much faster than had been bargained for, and annexed Alsace and Lorraine. Nobody thought of asking the inhabitants of these two provinces whether they wanted to become German, but then nobody had asked them in 1648 whether they wanted to become French, and German historians found no difficulty in producing justifications for the action. Bismarck later declared it to have been his constant endeavour to induce the French to forgive Sedan as after 1815 they had forgiven Waterloo, but as in his treatment of the Socialists, later kindness could not heal the initial wound, and the French leader Gambetta, who advised his countrymen to 'think of it always, speak of it never', replied to Bismarck's suggestions that France should console herself with colonial expansion by saying, 'We mourn two daughters and you offer us a regiment of kitchen-maids.' Consequently the first aim of German policy should have been the isolation of an implacable France.

This task was complicated by a less obvious result of Germany's victories. The successful creation of a new national state inevitably gave great encouragement to the other national groups in Eastern Europe which still had no states of their own. Many of these were living in the Habsburg Empire, so that any widespread demand for self-government on a national basis was likely in the long run to prove incompatible with the effective functioning and indeed the very existence of that venerable organisation. In 1867 the Magyars had secured self-government for themselves in Hungary though they constituted less than half its population. The question was how long they and the Germans left in Austria could keep the upper hand over the Czechs, Poles, Romanians, Serbs, Croats, Italians and others who made up the rest of the Emperor Francis Joseph's multifarious subjects. Moreover, many of these were Slavs who looked to Russia for support, while Russia and Austria-Hungary had conflicting ambitions in the rest of the Balkans. Germany had to avoid choosing sides between these two Empires, since the obvious remedy for whichever she rebuffed would be to seek alliance with France.

When in 1875–8 a rising in the Balkan provinces of Turkey almost led to war, Bismarck did his utmost to remain the 'honest broker' and in 1878 succeeded in getting a compromise accepted at the Congress of Berlin. But the Tsar's government resented his behaviour and made what he considered to be threats as to what it might do if on another occasion he were not more cooperative. His characteristic reaction was to negotiate a secret Treaty by which Germany and Austria-Hungary promised one another mutual aid if either were attacked by Russia and neutrality if the attack came from any other country. Years earlier he had said it would distress him 'if Prussia should seek protection from a possible storm by tying our trim and seaworthy frigate to the worm-eaten and old-fashioned Austrian man-of-war'. Yet this was precisely what he had now done in the belief that, if he ever allowed Austria to be defeated, he might be left without any ally against a Franco-Russian combination. In 1882 a further Treaty brought Italy into what was thereafter known as the Triple Alliance.

As things turned out, the Austrian Treaty became the foundation stone of German foreign policy, and was to have a considerable share in Germany's undoing. But this was the work of

Bismarck's successors and far from being his intention. He immediately set to work to repair the 'telegraph line to St. Petersburg' and in 1881 persuaded the Austrians and Russians to join in the Three Emperors' League in which each country promised to remain neutral if any were attacked by a fourth. When the League expired in 1884 it was renewed for a further three years. But in 1887 Russia and Austria were again at loggerheads over the Balkans and a further renewal was clearly out of the question. To complicate the situation, France was in a state of nationalist excitement which at one point seemed capable of leading to war with Germany.

These were the circumstances in which Bismarck took his hotly debated action of secretly concluding the 'Reinsurance Treaty' (*Rückversicherungsvertrag*, lit. Treaty providing security for one's back). This secret Russo-German agreement provided for the two countries to remain neutral if either were involved in war with a third, except for an Austro-Russian war begun by Russia or a Franco-German war begun by France. Bismarck realised that he must show some sympathy for Russian aims if he were to keep her out of France's arms. If those aims included a direct attack on Austria, he could not support them and would have to support Austria. But he made this clear to the Russians by showing them the text of the 1879 Treaty and thought that the knowledge would make such an attack unlikely. It was of course true that if Russian action in the Balkans led to an Austrian attack and if in the ensuing war Austria were to be in danger of defeat, Germany might have felt compelled to rescue her in spite of the Reinsurance Treaty. But to safeguard himself against this contingency, Bismarck had induced Italy and Britain to give undertakings which meant that any Russian move in the Balkans was likely to be opposed by them as well as the Austrians. Germany therefore might hope to escape being drawn in and had secured the much-desired promise that Russia would not take her in the rear in the event of a French attack. As he considered Germany to be a satisfied Power, his ideal was a political situation in which all the other Powers except France would need her and be deprived of the possibility of forming coalitions against her by their relations with one another. Lord Salisbury called this 'employing one's neighbours to pull out each other's teeth'.

But by the time the Reinsurance Treaty came up for renewal in 1890, the German scene had changed fundamentally. For in 1888 the old Emperor William I died at the age of ninety. His son Frederick had often crossed swords with Bismarck, was much under the influence of his wife, Queen Victoria's eldest daughter, and sympathised with Liberal ideas. His accession to the throne had long been expected to prove the signal for fundamental changes in German politics. It is doubtful whether he would in fact have had enough political skill and strength of character to put reforms through in the teeth of entrenched opposition. But the issue was never put to the test for in 1887 he had developed cancer and only reigned for ninety-eight days.

Frederick's son, the Kaiser William II, was not quite thirty when he thus unexpectedly came to the throne. He had been born with a damaged left arm which did not prevent him becoming a good shot and horseman, but put him under constant strain. For the Prussian ideal took much living up to, and a particularly high performance was expected of the ruler. The effort to prevent his disabilities from standing in his way led William to adopt a hearty toughness or an exaggerated air of self-importance which was out of keeping with his real character. But to complicate matters, he had had held in front of him in the nursery not only the pattern of the Prussian Junker but also that of the liberal English Gentleman. He reacted, like any young man of spirit, against the attempts of his determined and domineering mother to impose her standards upon him, yet to his dying day they exercised a fascination which he could never for long resist. The desire to be the Englishman—and to win applause from the British —was alternating all the time with the desire to be the Prussian and to win applause from the Germans. The tension between the two, superimposed on his physical defect, and upon the tensions already inherent in German society, is the ultimate key to his character, taut, restless, impetuous, lacking the self-confidence which comes with integration. From his mother also he inherited a strong constitution, a quick enquiring mind, a keen intelligence, which was continually at the mercy of his strong emotions, a pre-occupation with himself which left him insensible to the views of others, and an inability to judge character. The creation of a new national state of 50 million people in the centre of Europe had caused a fundamental shift in the balance of power and what Germany needed was a balanced and cautious ruler who would hold his people back from provocations and check their inclinations to overestimate their power. They could scarcely have got anyone worse qualified for the task !

Characters such as William and Bismarck were bound to collide, and the constitution of the Chancellor's own devising had given the last word to the Emperor; as Lord Rosebery told

Bismarck, 'he was hoist with his own petard'. The decisive clash of personality and method came in the spring of 1890 and found expression in no less than six issues at the same time. The most prominent of these was the question of how to handle the Socialists who in the *Reichstag* elections succeeded in winning more votes than any other party (though, owing to the way constituencies were arranged, they did not get a proportionate number of seats). The Kaiser was anxious to win a favourable reputation by propitiating them with kindness : Bismarck was contemptuous of people whom he described as 'dizzy with humanitarianism' and wanted to stiffen his earlier legislation. One thing led to another (the details are of secondary importance) and Bismarck sent in a six-page letter of resignation drafted with more attention to effect than to accuracy : the Kaiser kept it to himself, publishing only his own reply which managed to suggest that the old man had forced his departure on a highly unwilling master for reasons of health. Bismarck was seventy-five and all too inclined to let his animosities get the better of his judgment : on the various questions at issue with William, he was as often wrong as right. Indeed history might well have commended his dismissal if the policies which he refused to adopt had been consistently followed by his successors. As things were, it probably only antedated nature by a few years.

Questions of foreign policy hardly figured in the episode, though this was not the impression which Bismarck later sought to convey. But in the ensuing confusion and before a new Foreign Secretary had been appointed, the decision not to renew the Reinsurance Treaty got taken, rather to the Kaiser's regret. The new brooms did not properly understand what Bismarck had been after and felt that the intricacies of his policy were beyond them. Moreover, they were deeply suspicious of the Russians and thought that secret treaties with St Petersburg constituted hostages to fortune. There was considerable, if superficial, attraction in the argument that Germany needed henceforward to conduct a 'peaceful, clear and loyal policy' which could not create the impression of leaving her formal allies in the lurch. Yet within seventeen months of the non-renewal a French naval squadron visited Russia, the Tsar stood to attention while the band played the revolutionary *Marseillaise* and a Treaty was signed pledging France and Russia to act in concert in the event of a threat to peace. The very contingency which Bismarck had been most anxious to prevent was thus allowed to come to pass.

Germany Becomes an Industrial Leader

One of the chief purposes of the first chapter was to explain wny Germany was late in starting her industrial development. This was still further delayed by the disturbance of Napoleon's wars and by the continuing lack of unity. It was not until the mid-1860s that German output (in terms of real product per person per year) reached the level which Britain had achieved in 1830. Britain for example had vastly improved her roads in the later eighteenth century and her industrial development could get under way before she built her railway system. In Germany little was done to the roads before 1815 and railway-building went hand-in-hand with the growth of productive capacity. By 1870 only a third of the railways had been built, compared with two-thirds in Britain. At the same date 60 per cent of the population of England and Wales were living in towns, whereas the German figure was only 36 per cent. But these factors meant that growth, once it began, was all the more rapid, and it was naturally stimulated by the achievement of unification, which brought the introduction of a common currency and of the metric system. Between 1871 and 1914 the population of the Reich rose from 41 million to 67 million while production accelerated fairly steadily, whereas that of Britain slowed down. Britain continued to be the richer of the two countries and the one with the bigger national product, both absolutely and still more (since the German population was 30 per cent higher) per individual. But until 1914 Germany was catching up fast.

When Germany appeared on the world economic scene, the second phase of industrialisation was beginning. In the first, the key industries had been textiles, coal-mining, iron-founding, railways, and ship-building, and most of the vital inventions had been British (largely because at that stage the demand for British products grew so fast that manufacture by traditional methods could not keep pace with it). But in the second phase, where the key industries were steel, electricity, chemicals, optical goods and the internal combustion engine, many of the inventions were German, as the names Daimler, Benz, Diesel, Zeiss and Siemens testify, while two of the relatively few British innovations, the Gilchrist-Thomas process for steel-making and Perkin's discovery of aniline dyes, were mainly developed in Germany.

The explanation of this contrast is complex and the relative importance of the various factors is still open to dispute. The British were slow to realise that technological improvement is a continuous (though not necessarily a steady) process and that, to keep pace with it, equipment may have to be scrapped before it is worn out. This involves a high rate of investment and saving, but the British financial system was principally directed to channelling savings of individuals into investment overseas. The banking system was well adapted to providing industry with short-term funds but did little to provide long-term capital which manufacturers were mainly expected to find from their own resources. This meant that there was no great volume of money in search of profitable methods of investment at home; if there had been, the incentive to innovate might have been greater. German banks by contrast not only acted as the main deposit for individual savings but regarded it as their job to provide industry with fixed capital by lending out these savings and preferred ventures near at hand over which they could keep watch. The attraction of overseas lending was further reduced by the fact that German domestic rates of interest seem to have been nearly twice as high as British. Thus although, as far as can be ascertained, the German rate of total investment was not much behind the British (and after about 1900 exceeded it), a significantly higher proportion was spent at home.

Britain therefore preferred to bring down costs by getting cheaper raw materials and food (the price index fell from 119 in 1873 to 70 in 1896) rather than by improving the efficiency of her production methods, whereas the Germans, who still had most of their productive equipment to install, concentrated on providing the most up-to-date. Thanks largely to her overseas investment, Britain was still able to make good profits by selling established products in new markets overseas and thus had less incentive to develop new products, whereas Germany, starting from a position of comparative disadvantage against an established competitor, had to make her way by the superiority of her products and the vigour of her selling methods. Between 1880 and 1913 British exports roughly doubled, even after allowing for changes in the value of money. Thus although there were slack moments in the late '80s and mid '90s when British manufacturers became concerned about the competition of Germany (which was already the second biggest exporting nation), their business was usually expanding too fast for the threat to be either a source of serious worry or a stimulus to innovation. What they failed to notice was that world trade as a whole was expanding faster than their share of it. For that share fell between the years mentioned from 38.2 to 30.2 per cent, whereas the German figures rose from 17.2 to 26.6. Thus the British were able to imagine that they were going from strength to strength at the same time as the rest of the world considered Britain's power to be on the wane.

In their anxiety to find foreign markets for their rising output, the Germans showed some interest in colonies, in the somewhat ingenuous belief that since countries with colonies were wealthy, colonies must bring wealth. In 1884–5 Germany acquired colonies in Africa and the Pacific, four times as large as herself, but found them expensive and unrewarding. Indeed if they had been more attractive, other people would have acquired them earlier. The disappointment gave birth to resentment that the parcelling out of the more valuable parts of the world should have been carried through while German attention was still absorbed at home. Pride may have led Britain to exaggerate the economic benefits which she derived from her Empire. Yet thanks to her luck and enterprise and to the effort and expenditure which she put in, she undeniably found in her colonies useful markets and sources of cheap supplies to an extent which Germany never did. But what the Germans failed to see was that, if they were to invest abroad the same proportion of their national income as Britain did (and, like Britain in South America, they could have done so without having political control of the areas), they could soon have enjoyed many of the same advantages, although the consequential reduction in home investment might have reduced their competitive power.

Another reason for Germany's industrial progress lay in her output of trained manpower. In 1863 Prussia alone had over 66,000 pupils receiving secondary education whereas in England the comparable figure was 16,000 : Germany had 13,500 undergraduates at universities, Britain 3,500. Below the top level, Germany had a sound system of technical education; Britain practically none. Moreover, Britain, besides her home needs, had to govern and develop a growing number of overseas possessions, whereas not only was Germany free from this obligation but many of the most attractive posts in her government machine were closed to Catholics, commoners and Jews. The result was a higher level of education among businessmen and industrialists; a scientific outlook combined with a national inclination towards diligence to produce a more systematic approach to the problems of manufacturing and selling as well as a tendency to mistake the trees for the wood. Technologists had a high status and considerable attention was paid to them.

Moreover, the combination of advantages which Britain enjoyed encouraged the belief

> that an Englishman could expect to obtain a much larger real income and to live much more luxuriously than anyone else; and that if he chose to shorten his hours of work and take things easily, he could afford to do it. Many sons of manufacturers . . . worked shorter hours (than their fathers) and exerted themselves less to obtain new practical ideas.[1]

What was more, a certain amount of the money made in industry, instead of being ploughed back, was put into landed estate; Germany was by no means the only country where a new class on securing power adopted uncritically the standards which it found dominant in existing society! But in Germany too the standard of living rose, almost doubling (g.n.p. *per capita*) between 1870 and 1910, while hours of work fell. The population grew by over 50 per cent and the proportion living in towns rose by 24 per cent. Since there was little industry east of the Elbe (except in Silesia) this involved a shift in the balance of population towards the west which has continued fairly steadily over the past century. Many eastern landowners found themselves short of agricultural labour and, at some risk to national security, filled the gap with immigrant Poles.

Britain, with ever-increasing quantities of raw materials and foodstuffs to import, not only preferred to aim at reducing their cost but realised that their producers would be likely to spend the money which she paid for them on buying her own manufactures. She was therefore prepared between 1880 and 1932 to let her farmers go to the wall and to stand the risk of foreign manufactures competing in her home market. The resulting agricultural depression meant that labour was relatively plentiful so that another spur to innovation was absent. All that Joseph Chamberlain achieved by proposing a return to tariffs in 1903 was a split in his own party. Germany was perhaps slow to recognise the benefits which she gained from Britain's persistence in remaining a free market; many of her purchases of tropical goods, for example, could be financed by triangular trade and paid for by sales of her manufactures to Britain.

The structure of German society, however, made it natural that she should prefer to protect her landowners and her 'infant' industries, to the detriment of her living standards and of her

[1] Alfred Marshall, *Memorandum on Fiscal Policy in International Trade,* 1903.

relations with Russia, who was in consequence deprived of an outlet for her grain. Even in the home market German industrialists preferred regulation to competition; cartels and other agreements to fix prices and share out orders were widespread. Entry into many occupations and trades was strictly regulated. German firms as an average were bigger than British; power was more concentrated. Not only were the railways and most energy-producing companies publicly owned but a certain number of coal-mines and iron-foundries as well. Thus the balance of social forces in Germany and the tendency towards a managed society meant that the disposition of her economic resources was more influenced by political considerations than was the case in Britain where indeed the reverse tended to apply. The political leadership during this period was, however, itself torn between exerting the newly-acquired national power at home in Europe and doing so overseas in the rest of the world. Its pressure was not therefore sufficient to affect basically the general preference of industry and finance for building up home strength. Had any other policy been followed, a resistance such as Germany put up against heavy odds between 1914 and 1918 would have been unthinkable. But as an industrial nation she inevitably became dependent on certain imports from overseas and the failure of her political leaders to keep Britain out of the enemy camp meant that in the end this weakness was fatal.

Internal Affairs under the Kaiser

The major internal problem between 1890 and 1914 was the struggle as to how far the German political system should be adapted to the industrial changes just described. The pace of social change accelerated and increasing numbers of people acquired an occupational status and a real income in advance of that enjoyed by their parents. They looked for this to be reflected in a greater say about the running of the country and until this was accorded them inclined to support the parties of the left, particularly the Socialists, whose votes rose from 1.4 million in 1890 to 3 million in 1903.

But though the Socialist threat to the established order might seem to be increasing, other forces were operating in the reverse direction. The German educational system may have made it virtually impossible for workers to rise into the ruling class but it did help them to gain technical skills and so move into the lower middle class, while the rising standard of life had a similar effect. With their new status they acquired the petty bourgeois virtues of industry, frugality, good citizenship and moral restraint which do not as a rule make men into revolutionaries. The various social measures introduced by Bismarck were beginning to have a delayed effect. These tendencies were even more marked where the leaders were concerned. The party functionaries, enjoying a regular salary, had no incentive to put it at risk. With much justification they believed their gains to be largely due to good organisation and concentrated on making it even better, at the expense of their interest in ideology. They were not only reluctant on general grounds to do anything which might provoke renewed repression but unwilling to risk the confiscation of the considerable charitable funds which had been built out of subscriptions. It was from their ranks that Deputies were chosen to represent socialism not merely in the *Reichstag*, but still more in state parliaments and municipalities (where in not a few cases there was a Socialist majority); the practical experience so obtained was as usual a brake on radicalism. Given a little encouragement from the government, the success and prosperity achieved by the Second Reich seemed to be in process of inducing the Socialists to follow the example of the Liberals and Centre by becoming integrated into the existing structure of society.

Government encouragement, however, was not forthcoming. The benevolent intentions towards the workers which the Kaiser had professed in dismissing Bismarck did not survive long against the influence of his entourage, though admittedly he did not reimpose the restrictive laws. The orthodox view was that the introduction of universal suffrage for the *Reichstag* had been a disastrous mistake and during the nineties there was much talk of a *coup d'état* to reverse it. But neither the ruler nor his more responsible advisers ever had quite the nerve to embark on such a challenge to public opinion and the reactionaries gradually became resigned to living with something which they could not alter. But this made them all the more insistent on maintaining the 1871 distribution of constituencies for the *Reichstag* (which favoured country districts), the three-tier Prussian suffrage, the open voting which went with it, and the tariffs on grain which were its economic counterpart. In 1908 the Progressives brought into the Prussian Parliament a proposal for universal suffrage (which Baden had introduced in 1904 and Bavaria in 1906) and William was induced to say that he intended the voting system to 'undergo an organic development'. In 1910 a modest measure to give effect to this actually passed the Prussian Lower House, only to be thrown out by the Upper one. The sole way of over-coming their opposition would have lain in a massive creation of peers, and from this both the Kaiser and his Ministers shrank. Nothing effective was done about the franchise till October 1918.

In face of such obstruction the Social Democrats split into three sections. On the one hand the left wing argued that nothing short of a revolution would break down the resistance and bring to the working classes their due position in the State. They therefore resisted the demand of the right wing for the Marxist revolutionary programme of the party to be watered down into a campaign for reform by constitutional means. The leadership, straddled between the two extremes, concentrated on holding the party together; this they succeeded in doing by maintaining the letter of the programme and departing from it in practice. The Party Congress of 1903 rejected revisionism and that of 1906 the use of a general strike to enforce political demands. The dilemma of the Socialists was that to get support outside the working class, they needed to show their moderation but, even so, could not be sure of getting enough support to succeed by peace-ful means.

The justification offered by the ruling classes for their inaction was that any reform was bound to weaken those who could be relied on to stand up for national interests and bring to greater influence those whose loyalty was questionable. A country sur-rounded by so many enemies was thought unable to run risks of this kind, especially as the process of carrying reforms through would shake society to its foundations, possibly even resulting in civil war and foreign intervention. Indeed any discordant opinion tended to be looked on as unpatriotic since weakening the nation. It is highly questionable whether this sacrifice of liberal to national values was justified, even in the interests of the German people. For on the one hand the absence of any effective challenge to the ruling élite fostered the prevalence of a high-handedness, an over-emphasis on force and a disregard of world opinion which resulted in Germany's capacities being exaggerated and her downfall thereby produced. And on the other the refusal to trust the lower classes was hardly calculated to encourage the spirit of unity on which the nation must depend for its survival if it should ever get into what proved a long war. In 1911 a Colonel Ludendorff, on becoming head of the mobilisation section of the War Office, called attention to the fact that the German army was not big enough to carry out the tasks assigned to it in the strategic plan (largely because only 52 per cent of the available recruits were actually called on to do military service, as against 82 per cent in France). But the increases needed to be effective could not have been fully achieved without bringing in as soldiers, and still more as officers, men whose origin and political views led them to be regarded as unreliable. Although the Chancellor, Bethmann Hollweg (1909–17), was more ready to provide money for the army than for the navy, the army leaders refused to take as many men as they could have had.

But whereas the army ever since the days of the *Landwehr* had regarded popular movements with suspicion, those responsible for bringing to fulfilment the Kaiser's dream of a strong navy were more adroit. Instead of being connected, like the armies, with individual states, the navy was a national affair and appealed to the younger generation who were tired of hearing from their elders about Germany's great victories on land. Rather than seek to cut down the *Reichstag's* authority over naval finance, Admiral von Tirpitz laid before it in 1899 a building programme which seemed superficially to make sense and backed the plan with an up-to-date propaganda campaign. Pressure groups like the Navy League (largely financed by the steel barons whose interest in building battleships was natural), the Colonial League and the Pan-German Union gave their aid, and the *Reichstag* lent themselves to the policy with enthusiasm, thereby doing much to rehabilitate themselves in the Kaiser's eyes. But in 1895 Tirpitz had given as a main justification for Germany becoming a world Power the argument that such 'a new great national task and the economic benefits which went with it would provide a good antidote to sophisticated and unsophisticated Social Democrats'.[1]

Undeniably the desire to distract attention from internal tensions was a major reason why the ruling classes appealed to national sentiment and encouraged the oscillation between admiration and jealousy in the German attitude to Britain to polarise in a negative hostile direction. Nor is there any doubt that the bulk of the German people gave their support gladly and blindly to the policy of national aggrandisement.

The trend of internal events could not however be arrested for long. The Social Democrats lost ground at the elections of 1907, only to recover sensationally in 1912 when they became the strongest party in the *Reichstag*. As the strength of the Conservatives and National Liberals waned, the government came more and more to rely for support on the Centre; an attempt to dispense with this support between 1907 and 1909 broke down because of

[1] E. Kehr, *Das Primat der Innenpolitik*, p. 165.

the Conservative refusal to make the concessions needed for keeping the support of the Progressives who were the only possible alternative. But the Catholics in Germany no longer consisted overwhelmingly of landowners and peasants. Catholicism had always been strongly represented in the Rhineland and Silesia which had become major industrial districts. Both priesthood and political leadership realised the need to give evidence of social enlightenment if they were to keep a hold on their followers. As long ago as 1879 some Centre supporters in the Rhineland had alarmed Bismarck by working with Social Democrats and in 1895 the Centre had joined with Progressives and Social Democrats in the *Reichstag* to prevent him being congratulated on his eightieth birthday. The results of the 1912 election gave a majority in the *Reichstag* to a similar coalition. In 1914 an incident provoked by military high-handedness in Alsace led to a motion amounting to non-confidence in the Chancellor being passed by 293 votes to 54. But the result was precisely nothing. The government made no appreciable alteration in its policy and when the Social Democrats proposed to force its hand by refusing it money, the Centre took the view that Germany's external situation made any such course impossible.

Another result of this situation was to rule out the possibility of doing anything effective to solve the second main problem of the period, which lay in the Kaiser's slapdash, spasmodic and inconsistent interference in policy, combined with what one of his subjects described as the 'undergraduate impetuosities' leading only too often to 'rhetorical derailments'. A particularly bad example of this occurred in 1908 when he gave to the London *Daily Telegraph* an interview which could hardly have caused wider or graver offence abroad as well as at home if that had been its deliberate intention. Even the Conservatives joined in demanding that something should be done to check William's 'personal rule'. Yet as long as the Chancellor and Ministers were chosen by and depended for their tenure of office on the pleasure of the Emperor, he could not easily be denied a voice, and often a decisive one, in their policy. But if Ministers were not to be appointed by him, what other source was there except the *Reichstag*, which would inevitably have chosen party leaders? It was a widely-held dogma of the time that a parliamentary system of government was too dangerous a thing to introduce in a country with enemies on two fronts, where no single party would be strong enough to have an absolute majority and where so much depended on co-operation between Federal and State systems. But could a state in such a situation afford to have enemies on both sides? And was it not storing up trouble for the future to refuse education in the responsibilities of government to party leaders if there was any chance that sooner or later their assumption of such responsibilities would become inevitable?

The Road to War

The conclusion of the Franco-Russian Alliance in 1891 did not cause the alarm in Berlin which might have been expected, in spite of the extent to which Russia thereafter came to depend on French loans. For at this period the chief enemy of both parties to the Treaty was not Germany but Britain who was finding her dominions distinctly too far-flung through the variety of the disputes they involved her in. In 1898 her traditional antagonism to France reached a head in the Fashoda crisis when the two countries seemed for a moment on the brink of war. Russia's activities in Central Asia were watched with much alarm from Whitehall and Delhi for fear they would spark off a fresh mutiny in India, while Russian ambitions in the Far East were thought capable of starting a scramble to divide up China. The struggle with the Boers united almost the whole of Europe against the British, so that the telegram of congratulation which the Kaiser at the prompting of his Ministers sent to Kruger after the Jameson Raid in January 1896 met with general applause on the other side of the Channel. By contrast, Russia's absorption in Asia distracted her attention from the Balkans and until her defeat by Japan in 1905 her relations with Austria-Hungary were almost cordial.

This situation lulled those responsible for German policy into thinking that the British, and not themselves, were the people in a tight corner. They doubted whether Britain could come to terms with France and they were convinced that, if she did, the result would be a breach between France and Russia. British policy was, however, coming into the hands of men, who, themselves fearing and disliking German behaviour, considered their attitude to be widely shared in Europe. The result was that when on two or three occasions between 1898 and 1901 the officious zeal of subordinates led each of the two governments to think that the other was seeking an alliance, neither felt there need be any urgency about exploiting the opening. The Germans were doubtful whether negotiations would lead to an agreement but certain that the mere act of initiating them would put an end to the

Russian friendship on which they fondly imagined they could count. Germany in their view 'could only exact compensation comparable to the immense risks it was taking if England had a more accurate, that is to say a more modest, opinion of its performance'.[1]

Lord Salisbury, who was far from convinced that Britain needed allies, said that the Germans asked too much for their friendship. Each side distrusted the other and each thought that, by waiting, it could secure better terms later. The alternative method of reaching agreements on individual problems was tried over China, the Portuguese colonies and the South Seas but did more to divide than to draw together because each side, with some justice, came to suspect the other of sharp practice in negotiation.

The episode had more results than appeared on the surface. Before it began Britain had been uncommitted, standing on the whole nearer to the Triple than to the Dual (Russo-French) Alliance. When it ended there was not a single Minister left on the British side inclined to start any further attempt at drawing the links closer. With few people in responsible positions prepared to argue the case for friendship, popular animosity had free rein and the Press and public on both sides saw to it that any act capable of arousing suspicion did so. An underlying divergence of will was becoming steadily more obvious and neither side was prepared to make the compromises which would have been the pre-essential to cooperation.

Britain's first step to relieve the pressure on her was to conclude in 1902 an alliance with Japan. The Germans welcomed this as being certain to embroil her with Russia and probably with France : in fact it held the ring while the Japanese, more to Britain's surprise than Germany's, beat the Russians and precipitated an attempt at revolution in St Petersburg. Before this result was evident, the British had responded to a French suggestion that the two countries clear up the points of difference between them. In April 1904 this was done in a series of agreements centring round the exchange of a free British hand in Egypt for a free French hand in Morocco. At this some of the German leaders took fright and decided that, while Russia was incapable of action, the opportunity must be seized for showing the French how dangerous it could be to disregard Germany. Morocco, where the French had been deliberately trailing their coat, was chosen as the stage for this drama, and the Kaiser was

[1] Holstein, quoted in Eckardstein: *Lebenserinnerungen und Politische Denkwurdigkeiten*, II, p. 282.

sent in April 1905 to show the flag at Tangier. But confusion of purpose and a loss of nerve at the crucial moment led to the affair being mishandled; at the Conference of Algeciras in the following year the Germans found themselves virtually alone and emerged almost empty-handed. Instead of disrupting the Anglo-French entente, they had consolidated it and even precipitated military conversations which had the effect of committing Britain morally, though neither formally nor publicly, to come to France's aid in the event of a German attack. The coalition against Germany which had always been Bismarck's nightmare was steadily taking shape as a reaction to her own policies.

Instead of learning from their mistakes, the Germans repeated them over Russia. An attempt by the Kaiser in 1905 to take advantage of the Tsar's embarrassments and talk him into an alliance by personal diplomacy collapsed as soon as the project was referred to their respective Ministers. This should have shown how deeply Russia was committed to the opposite camp, if only by reason of her need for French finance, and the commitments were increased two years later when Britain copied her procedure with the French and made another series of agreements removing outstanding difficulties. Then in 1908 the Austro-Hungarian Foreign Minister with little reference to Berlin outwitted his Russian opposite number in a secret deal over the Balkans : Austria annexed two Turkish provinces which she had been occupying for thirty years while Russia found that the other countries on whom her *quid pro quo* depended were not prepared to give it to her. The Germans tried to be clever and, in the guise of a friendly mediator, forced the Russians into a corner, thereby enabling them to attribute to German intimidation the climb-down which they would have had to make anyhow. They did not forget their humiliation or forgive the authors of it, while the British and French realised that, to keep Russia's friendship, they must be prepared to offer some support to her interests in the Balkans. Thus the bonds grew tighter on each side, and the stock of international willingness to compromise was depleted.

Moreover, the British were growing slowly but steadily perturbed about the character and objectives of the German naval pro-gramme. In so far as a navy was desired as more than a badge of Great Power status, its expansion was undoubtedly started in order to have an instrument for putting pressure on Britain. But this concept dated from the turn of the century when Britain was thought to have many enemies, so that an extra navy considerably smaller than her own could still constitute an inconvenient threat. By 1907 the international situation, as a result of German behaviour, had completely changed. Yet all suggestions that the Germans alter their course were met with emotional tirades from the Kaiser and his subordinates about constitutional necessities and the rights of nations to behave as they wished. The Germans were obsessed with the idea of becoming a world instead of just a European Power; they refused to recognise the folly of challenging the major naval Power on the sea at the same time as they tried to impose their will among their neighbours on land. They not only did much by their obstinacy to ensure that, when war came, Britain joined in against them. They spent vast sums of money (and compelled Britain reluctantly to spend more) on a fleet which in the event proved to be incapable of use in an effective way. The motives for their behaviour are hard to understand or excuse—even in their own interests. But it must be remembered that they always expected a land war to be a short affair after which they could turn to the sea-fight with the whole resources of the continent behind them.

In 1911 the French decided that they must increase their hold on Morocco and their Prime Minister, behind the backs not only of the British but also of his colleagues, tried to insure against German objections by offering concessions. But the German Foreign Secretary decided that negotiations would go better if he got his claim staked out before the other side had realised theirs. He therefore persuaded the Kaiser and Chancellor to send a gunboat to the port of Agadir. The British were (with some justice) afraid of a deal being done behind their backs which might even start off a Franco-German reconciliation. Lloyd George therefore made a warning speech at the Mansion House which the Germans took as a threat to themselves and the French used as a justification for resisting German demands. After four months of negotiation France emerged with exactly what she wanted in Morocco and Germany with some relatively small but strategically useful bits of land in Central Africa. The German public, which had been led to expect much bigger things, was highly indignant and put most of the blame on the British, who in exchange acquired the almost certainly unfounded conviction that only their government's firm action had stopped Germany from attacking France. British arrangements for sending an expeditionary force to France in the event of war were made rather more formal, though no binding commitments to do this were given. The whole episode, which provides an object-lesson in how diplomacy should not be conducted, left all the countries involved less ready to be conciliatory in future.

Yet during the next two years a series of upheavals in the Balkans were prevented from leading to a war between Austria and Russia, largely because Germany was prepared to hold back the former while Britain did the same to the latter. In Germany, however, the conviction was growing that unless the Habsburg Empire was before long allowed to achieve some striking success, it would disintegrate in face of agitation and subversion on the part of the subordinate nationalities and in particular the South Slavs who were receiving aid and encouragement from the independent Kingdom of Serbia on the other side of the south-eastern frontier. Even if the process of collapse did not of itself start a general war, Germany could not afford to see the Danube basin pass into hostile hands since she would then be left without allies in face of a generally hostile world. It is true of course that Germany need have had no fear if she had been ready to follow what had been Bismarck's policy for his last twenty years of office and remain content with what she already possessed. But the essence of the German attitude was that the resources which their country had come to command during the nineteenth century entitled them to a larger say in world affairs than other countries were prepared to accord them. They were not therefore willing to go on giving way even if that meant fighting a war (which was, after all, the traditional method of adjusting the boundaries and rights of states to meet changes in their relative resources). The German government had come reluctantly to the conclusion that a war with Russia in support of Austria was inevitable sooner or later, while the General Staff estimated that the chances of winning it would grow worse the longer it was put off. If the conduct of Germany's affairs is open to criticism, such criticism should concentrate not on the course which was taken in face of the 1914 situation so much as on the misjudgements and overestimates of strength which had allowed that situation to grow up.

The murder of the Habsburg heir to the throne, Archduke Franz Ferdinand, by a Bosnian Serb in Serajevo on 28 June 1914 was thought in Berlin to provide Austria-Hungary with an opportunity such as might never recur for disciplining Serbia with the sympathy of the world behind her. Accordingly when the Vienna government enquired in Berlin what the German attitude would be, it was assured that whatever it did, it could count on full German support. The danger of a war spreading was realised but it was hoped for a variety of reasons that Russia might not choose this occasion for a fight.

The Germans, however, had assumed that the Austrians would strike quickly while the shock caused by the murder was still vivid. But despite German pressure the Austrians delayed for nearly a month before delivering an ultimatum so stiff that it was intended to be rejected. The Serbs disconcertingly agreed to almost all of it within the time limit of forty-eight hours so that when the Austrians none the less broke off relations, declared war, and bombarded Belgrade (even though they were not going to be ready to cross the frontier for another seventeen days), the sympathies of the world began to change sides. The British government pressed the Germans to join with them in acting as mediators, on the precedent of the Balkan wars, but Bethmann Hollweg, the German Chancellor, showed great reluctance to act on the suggestion, possibly because he wanted to allow the Austrians room to secure a clear prestige success. By the time he changed his mind, Russia had mobilised and it was too late.

For General von Schlieffen, the Chief of the German General Staff, in considering some twenty years previously the problem of how to fight Russia and France simultaneously, had decided that, since Germany could not withstand a long war against both Powers and since a quick decision was unlikely to be reached on the vast plains of the East, the most hopeful strategy would be to throw as many divisions as possible against France and try to knock her out, leaving the Austrians to hold up the Russians for six weeks until this had been done. But one of the factors which made this strategy possible was the fact that Germany could mobilise her army much faster than Russia. This advantage would be lost unless both mobilisations began simultaneously and therefore the German generals could not afford to wait and give mediation a chance. The military timetable took over.

Nor was this all. The German plan of attacking first in the west assumed that either France would declare war on Germany or that it would not matter if Germany were openly the aggressor. To complete the predicament, the General Staff had decided that the Franco-German frontier proper was too short and too well defended to make practicable a break-through across it. Instead a strong right wing was to make a wide encircling sweep through Belgium which was to be invited to give passage to German troops; if it refused it was to be overrun, in defiance of a Treaty which Prussia had signed in 1839, guaranteeing its neutrality. Although three German Chancellors, including Bethmann, had known of this plan, nobody ever challenged it. Jagow, who was Foreign Secretary in 1914, had in the previous year pointed out that the violation of Belgian neutrality was bound to bring in Britain but as nobody could think of an alternative which met the requirement of offering a quick victory (something which it is still hard to do even today!), and as in a six-week war Britain would not have time to make herself felt, the plan was left unaltered. At one time there had been an alternative for an offensive eastwards but this had been allowed to get out of date, as unnecessary. Germany (like Britain but with less excuse) had planned for only one strategic contingency and when the crisis came, had to put that plan through regardless of the political and psychological repercussions which its application in the actual circumstances might have.

Under the constitution the Chancellor had no control over the military machine. Responsibility for ensuring that the military and civilian sides of the government were coordinated rested with the Emperor. Kaiser William had never realised what the job implied, let alone tried to tackle it. Moreover, by brusquely rebuffing any attempts by civilian Ministers to show interest in or express opinions about military matters, he had stacked the cards against their questioning the political implications of the generals' plans. The damage which Germany did to her own cause in the eyes of third parties by the way she began the war sprang directly from the whole character of her society.

The attention of the world and particularly of the British, French and American publics fastened on the fact that it was in all cases Germany and Austria-Hungary which had taken the initiative in declaring war and Germany which had broken a promise by making an unprovoked attack on Belgium. The German public, however, were encouraged to treat this as a technicality. They were led to believe it was Russia, France and Britain which were to blame, having allied together out of jealousy to encircle Germany and frustrate her legitimate growth. They were told that she was inspired by no lust of conquest but, for the sake of holding what she had, was seizing her sword with a clean hand and a clear conscience. From this initial difference of view much recrimination was to follow, once the war was over.

The War of the Three Gambles

At the end of August it looked as though the first great German gamble was going to succeed and that the campaign of 1914 would end as quickly as those of 1866 and 1870. But Moltke, nephew of the victor of the earlier wars and now himself German leader, had always been worried about the problem of controlling effectively the much larger numbers of men who would be under his command. Early in September the appearance of a gap between two of his formations on the Marne led him to lose his nerve and order what he thought to be a tactical retreat. In fact, however, the war of manoeuvre was not to be resumed in the west for over four years and the two opposing armies settled down to dig trenches all the way from the sea to the Alps. A couple of brilliant victories by Hindenburg and Ludendorff over the Russians could not conceal the fact that the war was going to be a long one and therefore one for which Germany was ill-prepared.

Things also went wrong at sea. The Germans had assumed that the British fleet would institute a blockade close to the eastern shores of the North Sea and planned to attack it piecemeal in the hope of whittling down its superiority until a general action could be undertaken on terms not too unfavourable. But a month before war began the British had decided to take advantage of the accidents of geography and institute a 'distant' blockade at the Straits of Dover and between Norway and John O'Groats. Instead of having the British fleet at the mouth of the Elbe, the Germans found that they could only get at it by themselves making a risky journey across the North Sea. To make matters worse, the British disregarded an International Agreement of 1909 which they had never ratified and instead of applying their blockade only to munitions, extended it to all kinds of foodstuffs and materials. A time therefore could be foreseen when, unless the blockade was somehow broken, the people and cannon of Germany would be starved into submission. The British fleet never succeeded in winning a clear victory—but it did not need to win one, merely to avoid getting beaten.

What were the Germans to do? A compromise peace based on a return to the pre-1914 situation would have been regarded by the Allies as tantamount to defeat since it would have been an open acknowledgement that their ten million fighting men were inadequate to bring down the six million of the Central Powers. Nor had they any intention of playing into enemy hands by winding up one war and thereby giving the Germans time to prepare for the next. On the other hand, the whole reputation of the German élite was at stake in the war which but for their attitudes might never have come about. They could not hope to maintain their privileges if they returned from the battlefield empty-handed and weakened by casualties.

Moreover, that overestimate of their own strength which had done so much to involve the Germans in the war continued to delude them while they fought it. The majority of people, even in responsible positions, had little idea of the real situation; the public were never told the truth about the opening battles. The belief was general that their country would gain by her struggle, which was to bring her 'break through to world power'. The out-break unbridled many ambitious tongues and imaginations which had till then been reined in for fear of frightening Germany's neighbours. Although she was represented as only fighting in self-defence there was widespread agreement that as a compensation for having to do so once, and as a security against having to do so twice, she was entitled to 'guarantees'. Germany's exact war-aims varied from time to time in accordance with the strategic position (which meant that 'the more we win the further off does peace get'). But until late in 1918 most or all of Belgium, the Longwy-Briey basin with its valuable ores, Poland, the Baltic states, exten-sive indemnities and colonial concessions were constant items. Behind these demands loomed the wider dream of bringing the whole of 'Middle Europe' from Antwerp to Odessa under German control. Such greed not only removed any inclination to make terms which the Allies might have considered[1] but prevented Germany from getting neutral opinion on her side by a show of moderation. Yet for long the only people inside Germany to challenge this megalomania were the despised Socialists.

If a compromise peace was ruled out, the alternative was to resume the original strategy of securing an overwhelming victory on one front so that all available resources could then be con-centrated in the hope of doing the same on the other. To this the first three years of fighting were in effect devoted and, in spite of a certain dispersion of effort being caused by differences of view as to which front offered the best chances of a knock-out blow, success came in 1917 with the collapse of Russia. The liberal régime which gained power there in February of that year was in half a mind to keep on fighting. To get them replaced by people more cooperative, the German government gave the Bolsheviks a quarter of a million pounds and enabled Lenin to return from Switzerland. But before this opportunity of supping with the devil presented itself, the effects of the blockade had brought Germany

[1] It is in fact highly doubtful if the Allies would have accepted anything which the Germans would have been prepared to offer.

close to desperation while Austria-Hungary was in an even worse condition. Something had to be done to break Britain's stranglehold and the only course which offered any prospect of achieving this was unrestricted submarine warfare. Indeed, this could have been tried earlier if Germany had formed her navy with light craft and submarines rather than with the battleships that she dared not use.

But by the time sufficient U-boats had been built to give them a chance of being effective, it had become clear that their unrestricted employment would almost certainly bring the United States into the war on the Allies' side. A dreadful and much resented choice presented itself between risking the loss of the war by failure to press home a submarine blockade of Britain and making such an attack effective at the risk of provoking American intervention and so losing the war. The issue was argued between the High Command and Bethmann Hollweg in an atmosphere of mounting emotion in the autumn of 1916. An attempt to avoid a decision by getting the Americans to act as mediators between the belligerents broke down through the German refusal to name any precise terms. The soldiers and sailors, who grossly underestimated the implications of an American entry into the war and the speed with which these would take effect, claimed that they could force England to her knees before a single American soldier could land in Europe and early in 1917 they got permission to try their luck. But this second gamble met the same fate as the first. Britain, though hard pressed, found adequate means of defence against the submarines just in time, the United States declared war in April and their first troops reached France in July.

The same month brought a political upheaval inside Germany. At the beginning of the war the Socialists had given the lie to the accusations of the right by voting unanimously for the war credits. But the left wing had never taken kindly to this policy and the example of Russia now led to their breakaway. The party leadership, afraid of losing control, felt obliged to adopt as their official policy the demand of the Petrograd Council of Workers and Soldiers for a 'peace without annexations or reparations'. Bethmann had sought to retain the loyalty of the masses by inducing the Kaiser to make an indefinite promise about reforming the Prussian voting system. To the great indignation of the right, the Socialists pressed for prompt action in both directions and Erzberger, the Centre leader, supported them with a speech which for the first time gave the German public some idea of the true war situation. The coalition of Centre, Progressives and Socialists again asserted itself to pass through the *Reichstag* a resolution which, after recalling the 1914 claim that 'Germany had no lust of conquest', demanded a negotiated peace and international conciliation.

The next steps threw a revealing light on German conditions. Hindenburg and Ludendorff, who since 1916 had held the High Command, declared that Bethmann had lost their confidence and that they could no longer work with him. The leaders of the right-wing parties agreed, while those of the majority wanted him replaced by someone more flexible and open-minded. He therefore made up his mind to resign. But the parties still could not bring themselves to insist on the Chancellor being a man of their own choice and indeed would have precipitated a major crisis if they had done so since the High Command would undoubtedly have refused to accept or listen to the kind of man they would have chosen. After a frantic search for a new Chancellor who would be acceptable both to the soldiers and the parties, a nonentity was installed in the post. He made common cause with the High Command and the Peace Resolution was watered down by 'interpretations'. The truth was that the reactionary and nationalist groups in Germany, embodied in Hindenburg and Ludendorff, had taken the management of civilian as well as military affairs into their own hands and nothing short of force was going to get them to relinquish it. Unfortunately for their country, the force had to be applied by their enemies.

For a moment, however, all energies were bent on taking advantage of the Russian decision, after the Communist October Revolution, to stop fighting, and on concentrating all available forces for a final effort in the west before the Americans could really make themselves felt. Yet to win decisively they had not only to conquer in the field but to break the blockade and for this they had to be able to count on getting all they wanted in the way of food and raw materials from Russia. Nor could they resist the temptation of exploiting the fact that they appeared to have Slavs at their mercy. In the Peace of Brest-Litovsk they imposed terms so harsh as seriously to impair Germany's right to expect merciful treatment herself later, and in the process of failing to extract the corn, oil and ores which they wanted, tied up a million soldiers whom they were to need badly in the west. For although the offensive in March 1918 began by making quick progress and nearly broke the Franco-British line, it gradually ground to a halt without quite achieving this. Later attempts at renewing it met the same fate and when in July the Allies counter-attacked with a growing superiority of arms (including tanks) behind them, the fighting morale of the German troops at long last broke. At the end of September the High Command told the Kaiser that they saw no alternative to asking for an armistice on the basis of President Wilson's 'Fourteen Points'. Germany had lost her third gamble.

One of these points, however, was 'the destruction of every arbitrary power that can separately, secretly and of its single choice disturb the peace of the world'. And the victorious Allies made clear that they regarded the power which had hitherto guided the destinies of the German people as included within that description. On the day on which the Kaiser ordered an armistice to be sought, he announced that 'men who possessed the public confidence' were to take a larger part in the rights and duties of the government. The Chancellor was made responsible to the *Reichstag,* Deputies were allowed to become members of the Cabinet without resigning and authority over the armed forces was transferred from the Emperor to the Minister of War. Parliamentary government thus came to Germany as an expedient conceded by a bankrupt régime rather than as a right insisted on by the people. Responsibility for this with all that it later implied must rest on the numbers and obstinacy of those in Germany who sympathised with and supported the right.

Surprisingly enough the first democratic Chancellor, Max, was a Prince even though Baden from which he came was the most liberal of the German states. But before he had taken over, consternation had been caused among the party leaders when a spokesman of the High Command revealed the true military situation to them. For four long years the German people had held out with amazing tenacity against unfavourable odds; a great part of the credit for this result was due to the fidelity and competence of their Civil Service. But it was the hope of making their country great which had kept them going. Once the knowledge spread, with very little preparation, that success was not to be had, they not unreasonably asked why they should go on enduring cold and illness and hunger. The number of people who wanted a radical recasting of society was small. But as long as the only group which would offer a quick peace was the extreme left wing, others who did not share their social views would listen to them, as had happened in Russia. Prince Max's Cabinet seemed too implicated in the past and failed to get on quickly enough with the job of liquidating it. Austria stopped fighting, sailors mutinied in Kiel, a Workers' Republic was proclaimed in Munich. On 9 November the Berlin workers went on strike and the garrison fraternised with them. Prince Max handed over power to a government of Social Democrats and Progressives under Fritz Ebert who had once been a saddler, and in a moment of excitement tinged with panic, one of its members proclaimed a Republic. At headquarters in Spa the Kaiser was persuaded to abdicate and next day sought refuge in Holland.[1]

On 11 November a delegation led by Erzberger signed an armistice whose severe terms were designed to put out of question any attempt at renewing the conflict. But that was the last thing which the mass of the German people wanted to do and much was to happen before they changed their minds. The achieving of this result had, however, cost the lives of some thirteen million people.

[1] The other German princes followed his example. When the King of Saxony was advised to abdicate by a delegation in top hats and frock coats, he replied in his broad accent, 'Eh well, mayke yer mook yerselves' and added, 'Luvly repooblicans you be'.

Chapter 3

First Attempt at Democracy

The Revolution that never Happened

ON THE NIGHT of the Kaiser's departure Ebert as head of the new government sat at the Chancellor's desk in Berlin and contemplated his problems. Germany seemed to be heading for chaos; the system that had been held together for so long by such great efforts ceased to function as soon as the will to make the efforts departed. External failure threatened to reverse the social integration which had been achieved since 1871. There was a danger that separatist movements in the different states might undo Bismarck's work of unification. Everywhere the soldiers and workers were forming themselves into Councils (which in Russia were called 'Soviets') and hoisting red flags. Those in the capital were talking in wild terms and it was natural, though incorrect, to suppose that the same held good throughout the country. The Spartakists, as the left-wing Socialists called themselves, clearly intended to follow the Russian example and, by seizing the leadership of the councils, precipitate a social revolution. But Ebert had no intention of being the German Kerensky. He and his immediate colleagues were democrats before they were Socialists. Long years spent in trying to establish parliamentary government in Germany had accustomed them to think in terms of order and fairness; their first instinct was to let the German people as a whole decide on its future by a free vote. Their chances of putting through their ideas, however, depended on the force at their disposal. What attitude was the army going to take?

There lay in front of Ebert a telephone giving direct access to Spa. Suddenly its bell rang. Ebert lifted the receiver and heard the voice of Hindenburg's deputy, Groener. The armistice terms which he had just received were such that a strong government would be needed to carry them out. They required the German army to withdraw to the east side of the Rhine within a month; any troops left on the west side would be made prisoners. To do this so fast was a major administrative task which strengthened the soldier's instinct for giving high priority to the maintenance of rank and discipline. Would the new government back the generals in this or would it seek to undermine their authority? The men at the two ends of the telephone needed one another and out of the conversation a working alliance was born.

The next few months were to contain many anxious moments. There was more than one rising in Berlin and extremists held power in Munich with scarcely a break until May 1919. Gradually the new government gained the upper hand. But in doing so it put itself into the hands of the military. Moreover, since many of the rank-and-file sympathised with the workers, while the temporary soldiers hurried back to civilian life, the term 'military' meant the regular troops, the officers and the people with no obvious peace-time job. Some of these, after their regular units were disbanded, were formed into special groups called *Freikorps,* and used to protect the eastern frontier. They all tended to be strongly imbued with the autocratic traditions of the Empire and hostile to the idea of government by the people. And what was true of them went for much of the rest of the administrative hierarchy, the Civil Service, the courts of justice, the universities and the Church. The people staffing these organisations carried on under the Republic very much as they had done under the Empire. They found themselves compelled to serve under a changed class of master but this did not compel them to change their views. The landlords and the industrialists were left with their property intact.[1]

The left-wing Socialists, some of whom[2] in December 1918 founded the German Communist Party, were only too conscious of these facts. True to their Marxist training, they argued that the political revolution would not be effective unless as in Russia it was accompanied by a social one which deprived the old élite of the economic basis for their power and substituted new leaders committed to the new system. But any attempts to do this would have precipitated a civil war which the left would have been unlikely to win. For by contrast with Russia, the German army was intact, the middle classes were more numerous and more reactionary, the workers were better integrated in society and the suspicion of novelty habitual to peasants was not outweighed by hunger for land. The German proletariat was in no position to set up a dictatorship and any attempt to do so would probably

[1] Two changes which the Republic did introduce were to require almost all children to spend four years in common primary schools and to require all would-be officers to start off with a few months in the ranks.
[2] Including a certain Wilhelm Pieck.

have precipitated a military *coup d'état* followed by Western intervention. It would have been far from easy to find enough trained men to run the country without drawing on people whose allegiance to democracy was shaky. But this has not prevented the growth of a left-wing tradition that a great chance was lost. The fighting of 5–15 January 1919 in which majority Socialists allowed the army and *Freikorps* to suppress a rising by the Berlin workers and to murder their leaders Liebknecht and Rosa Luxemburg, has been called 'German democracy's Battle of the Marne'. Yet the defeat of the left did not dispose of their question as to whether a political revolution by itself could be successful, and indeed, by sowing dissension among the opponents of the right, reduced the chances of this proving possible.

The Imperial *Reichstag* had adjourned after enacting the constitutional changes in October 1918 and was never called together again. The new government drew its original authority from an assembly of the Soldiers' and Workers' Councils and subsequently got the same body to support the convening of a National Assembly, elected by universal suffrage. To mark a break with Prussian traditions and to escape the influence of the capital, the Assembly met in Weimar and between February and July 1919 drew up a constitution for the Republic. For this the black, red and gold flag (the colours of 1848) was adopted in place of the Imperial black, red and white (to the great distress of good monarchists).

A proposal to abolish Prussia was defeated and Germany was divided up into nineteen units along traditional lines, which were called 'Lands' rather than 'states'. The abolition of its three-tier franchise[1] turned Prussia from a stronghold of reaction into one of socialism. The powers of the Federal government were strengthened, particularly in finance and military affairs. The *Bundesrat* was replaced by a *Reichsrat*, composed of delegates of the *Länder* governments, but acting as a Second Chamber of the legislature with limited delaying powers. The chief of State was to be a President, chosen by popular vote for seven years; he was to sign treaties, command the armed forces and appoint the Chancellor and Ministers, who, however, had to have the support of (but not necessarily belong to) the *Reichstag*. The President could also dissolve the *Reichstag* but not more than once on the same grounds. An article later to become notorious gave him power to take emergency action (which could be cancelled retrospectively by the *Reichstag*), 'if public security and order was materially

[1] See p. 35.

disturbed or endangered'. No attempt was made to define more closely how the existence of such a situation was to be identified.

The new *Reichstag* was to be elected every four years by universal suffrage (including votes for women) and proportional representation, so that each party was to obtain one seat for each 60,000 votes that it received. This system meant that people voted for a party rather than for an individual. It resulted in a very accurate representation of opinions, but encouraged the multiplication of separate parties. Much of the blame for the political situation which subsequently developed in the Republic tended to be placed on it. But in fact all it did was to exaggerate rather than counteract a position which was bound to cause trouble and which had been foreshadowed by the election to the National Assembly itself. The Communists boycotted the occasion and the Independent Socialists only won 22 seats. But the Social Democrats themselves only obtained 163 out of 421. Thus they were unable to form a majority without the support of the Centre (89 seats) or the German Democratic Party (as the former Progressives, with 74 seats, renamed themselves). Further to the right came the German People's Party (the former National Liberals, 42 seats) and the German Nationalist Party[1] (the former Conservatives, 22 seats). Thus the group which had formed the opposition under the Empire came to power under the Republic but the formation of each government was going to involve negotiations between the various parties to ensure it enough support, while the middle- and working-class representatives who habitually engaged in such negotiations were flanked both to the left and right by groups whose loyalty to the régime was questionable. The Republic's chances of success depended on being able to strengthen the centre at the expense of the extremes. It would be doomed if affairs so developed as to encourage the reverse process. In 1920 and again in 1922 the Socialists under left-wing influence went out of office rather than work with the People's Party. This was hardly a good omen.

Moreover, the former ruling classes underwent a searing experience. At the outset and at short notice, they had the bottom knocked out of their view of life and expectation of the future. Then for months they lived in conditions which they can hardly be blamed for comparing with the beginnings of the French and Russian Revolutions. A community which traditionally set great store by order and discipline persuaded itself that the foundations

[1] So generally called but strictly the German National People's Party.

of those qualities were being undermined. Small wonder if enthusiasm was lukewarm for a régime under which this could happen!

Peace without Honour

Most Germans considered that they had agreed to make peace on the basis of President Wilson's Fourteen Points. But four of these points did not directly concern Germany at all and five stated, in general terms but with the almost inevitable 'weasel words', broad principles on such matters as open diplomacy, the freedom of the seas and the removal of economic barriers. Another called for a free, open-minded and absolutely impartial adjustment of all colonial claims, in which the interests of the populations were to have equal weight with the equitable claims of governments. The remaining four called for the evacuation of all Russian, French and Belgian territory, the restoration of damage in France and Belgium, the restoration of Alsace and Lorraine to France and the erection of 'an independent Polish state which should include territories inhabited by indisputably Polish populations and be assured a free and secure access to the sea'.

The Treaty presented to a German delegation at Versailles on 7 May 1919 had been arrived at not by open diplomacy but behind closed doors, and it was handed over for comment rather than negotiation. But it cannot be said in its treatment of Germany clearly to have violated any of the actual 'points'. For all her colonies to have been taken away from her was perhaps hardly an 'impartial settlement' and there was room for dispute about the character of the population in some of the territories handed over to Poland. But these were partly adjusted through plebiscites and in any case details of this kind were only marginally responsible for the storm of indignation which broke out in Germany when the terms became known. What was felt to be involved was not so much the interpretation of any particular text as the violation of the spirit expressed by Wilson in a number of speeches about the form which the peace should take. Instead of the old methods of power diplomacy, justice, generosity and the wishes of individuals were supposed somewhat naïvely to be going to prevail. The Germans had thought also that, by adopting a democratic form of government, they would get a mild peace. When it came to the point, Germany was presented with a demand for the handing over of 27,000 square miles in Europe and 6 million people, for the amputation of East Prussia from the rest of the country (so as to afford Poland access to the sea through West

Prussia) and for rigorous reparations (in security against payment of which the whole country west of the Rhine was to be occupied for fifteen years). Both reparations and occupation were only extensions of the terms imposed on France in 1870 and in fact represented modifications of what had originally been proposed by the advocates of a 'hard' peace. But this was not noticed by the uninformed observer.

On the pretext that it was needed to provide a legal justification for the peace terms, a clause had been inserted in the Treaty attributing to Germany and her allies exclusive guilt for the outbreak of the war. This was a subject on which there was, and was long to remain, a wide difference of view between ordinary men on the two sides of the wartime fence. The average German was slow to admit that the allegation contained any truth at all and bitterly resented it. Moreover, the Germans knew that Allied propaganda had made a great impact on neutral opinion by denouncing them for exalting might above right—but considered that this was precisely what was now being done to them. The shock of having the implication of losing the war brought home to them would have been a bitter experience at the best of times. But their resentment was intensified by the belief that they had been tricked by hypocrites.

For the time being, however, the nation was helpless. Groener reported to the government that armed resistance was out of the question (though not all his subordinates agreed with him). Bitter protests and elaborate arguments only secured from the Allies marginal changes in the terms, coupled with an ultimatum to sign or take the consequences which would have included the occupation of the Ruhr and a renewal of the blockade (hitherto only partially lifted). The Socialists and Centre reluctantly decided to advocate signature and obtained a majority in the National Assembly against the votes of all the parties to the right of them. Refusal to sign might well have precipitated chaos and national dissolution. On the other hand it might have been preferable to what inevitably became signature in bad faith, with a widespread if undeclared intention to escape as quickly and as fully as possible from the fulfilment of the terms. Defiance might have brought the Allies more quickly up against the permanent realities and, by showing them the limits of their power, have served Germany's interests better in the long run. But belief to the contrary did not imply treachery to the nation and the men who took the difficult decision hardly merited the attacks which they suffered later and which amounted in the case of Erzberger and the Jewish Foreign Minister Rathenau to assassination.

Large numbers of the German people had been so schooled to believe in their country's superiority that they were unable to reconcile themselves to the fact of its defeat. Some dreamt of repeating the national rising against Napoleon, forgetting that in those days it had been France and not Germany which was isolated. Others set themselves to 'organise sympathy' abroad, which in time they did with considerable success. The tendency to reject the verdict of war received powerful encouragement in November 1919 when Hindenburg, in giving evidence to a *Reichstag* committee, endorsed the view (fathered on an 'English general' who has defied all later attempts at identification) that the German army was 'stabbed in the back' by the inability of the home front to hold out. The Republic, in other words, owed its existence to cowardice and treachery.

With the example of Prussia's resistance to Napoleon in mind, the Allies had insisted on the German army (henceforward known as the *Reichswehr*) being cut down to a long-service force of 100,000 men, on the General Staff being suppressed and on the use of tanks, aircraft and certain other weapons being prohibited. They called for the demobilisation of all troops in excess of this figure and the efforts to comply brought the government into collision with the *Freikorps*. In March 1920 an order by the Allied Control Commission requiring the dissolution of two of these bands led them to march on Berlin and endeavour to set up a right-wing government under a Pan-German farm-inspector called Kapp. General von Seeckt, the officer responsible for organising the new *Reichswehr,* had not been unaware of what was in train but had taken no steps to prevent it. He now said that 'we cannot conduct a field exercise with live ammunition between Berlin and Potsdam'. Only when the action of the trade unions in calling a general strike made it clear that the rising would fail did he allow the army to intervene.

The trade unions' action represented a temporary lapse into radicalism forced on their leadership by the discovery that the rank-and-file, and in particular the Berlin metal-workers, were turning to the left. The same motive led the unions, after the rising was over, to present the Cabinet with a number of demands for a new and more democratic Minister of Defence, for a greater say in policy and for closer democratic control over the *Reichswehr*. These demands were first watered down and then, when the emergency was over, forgotten. Had they been successfully enforced, the subsequent history of the Republic might have been altered. But enforcing them might well have precipitated a head-on collision with the *Reichswehr* who for their part insisted on the resignation of the Minister of Defence because 'no member of the government which had supported the general strike could ever regain the confidence of the Armed Forces'. The relatively small number of officers who had taken a decided line against the rising (including the Chief of Staff) were victimised and Ebert was prevailed on to draw the teeth of a *Reichstag* Committee of Investigation. The bands which had made the rising were first sent to suppress the striking workers in the Ruhr and then after a decent interval became the nucleus of the new German navy. The new Minister of Defence was a monarchist who appointed von Seeckt Chief of Staff and connived with him to set the *Reichswehr* effectively free from parliamentary control. Hence the effect of the civilian victory was to turn the armed forces to the right and to deepen the suspicions between them and the Social Democrats.

So far from helping German democracy to take root, the Allies had only been kept from annexing the whole area west of the Rhine by the promise of an Anglo-American guarantee and were left empty-handed when this was invalidated by the refusal of the U.S. Senate to ratify the Peace Treaty. Suspecting with justification that the *Reichswehr* were trying to get round disarmament, the Allies refused the republican government any latitude over keeping extra forces to maintain order. Disregarding both the basic principles of economics and Germany's internal problems, they treated any requests for postponing the payment of reparations as attempts at evasion. Mounting disagreement on this score led the French and the Belgians in January 1923 to occupy the Ruhr and redouble their efforts to get separatist governments set up in the parts of Germany which they already occupied. This step, from which the British dissociated themselves and to which the German people as a body replied by passive resistance, cost its authors in all ways more than they gained by it. Moreover, it gave a final blow to the German economy.

Instead of paying for the war by higher taxes, the Imperial government had met the cost by internal loans which it intended to make its enemies pay after their defeat. When instead those enemies won (and required Germany to pay for the debts which they themselves had incurred to one another) the result was to alter fundamentally the relationship between money and goods, so that by 1919 the Mark was only worth a third of its pre-war value. Heavy compensation and pension payments and occupation costs increased government expenditure whereas the dislocation of civilian life reduced revenues. Although industrial activity in Germany recovered between 1920 and 1922, the need to pay reparations upset the balance of payments and by June 1922 the Mark's value had dropped to one per cent of 1914. The French suspected the German government of having deliberately facilitated this inflation in the hope of proving that reparations were impossible. If their suspicions were right they went the best way about making the proof conclusive! In 1923 inflation got completely out of hand and for all practical purposes the currency became valueless. Manufacturing output fell to almost half the 1913 level.

At this point though only by slow degrees reason began to prevail. The mass of the German people realised that passive resistance would have to stop but so widespread was the feeling against surrender that, to secure support for the decision, a 'Great Coalition' Cabinet from Socialists to People's Party was formed under Stresemann who until 1918 had been among the most chauvinistic leaders of the National Liberals. The Communists had for the last three years been alternating between a policy of outright revolution and cooperation with parties further to the right of them, not so much to bring about changes constitutionally as to draw members of those parties into their own ranks. They now, under instruction from Moscow, decided that the moment for action had come. Saxony had always been a red stronghold but though the Socialists and Communists had a majority in the *Land* Parliament, the Socialist leaders under pressure from their national headquarters had refused to allow the Communists into the Cabinet. The local rank-and-file now insisted on reversing this and a left-wing Ministry including Communists was formed. Much the same occurred in Thuringia.

On the opposite wing, Nationalists in Prussia and Bavaria were also considering a rising to overthrow the Republic and prevent a surrender being made to the French. Some of those in Bavaria wanted as well to restore the Wittelsbach monarchy and the degree of independence which the *Land* had enjoyed until 1919. The southern conspiracy included Ludendorff, who had become a nationalist crank, and a thirty-four-year-old Austrian agitator called Adolf Hitler, whose National Socialist German Workers' Party (N.S.D.A.P.) was beginning to find its feet; Kahr, the special commissioner appointed by the Bavarian government to handle the crisis, and Lossow, the district commander of the *Reichswehr*, were implicated to a lesser extent. Seeckt, afraid that the army might be called on to put down a rising, was considering a military dictatorship. Stresemann, seeing the Republic threatened simultaneously from left and right, proclaimed on 26 September a state of emergency and gave to the War Minister many of the powers which Seeckt had been thinking of seizing. The district *Reichswehr* commander in Saxony was authorised to proclaim a state of siege, depose the Cabinet and install a Reich commissioner. The Socialists at national level supported this action; thanks to their votes and in spite of the fact that Nationalist and Communist Deputies made common cause against him, Stresemann was able to get *Reichstag* endorsement for his emergency measures.

These included the discarding not only of passive resistance but also of the old currency. A new one was substituted based (in theory at least) on the total value of German real property. This change favoured people who owned things at the expense of those whose wealth had taken the form of money; debtors came off better than creditors. A number of people who had done well during the inflation managed to keep their profits. The new *Rentenmark* worked because the Germans were ready to believe in it. But a lasting psychological blow had been dealt to thrift and confidence.

In Bavaria manoeuvrings continued for some time between Seeckt, Lossow, Kahr, Ludendorff and Hitler. When Seeckt decided that a military dictatorship was impracticable, Kahr and Lossow felt compelled to suspend their own plans. But they did so with reluctance and Hitler thought he could force their hand. He was, however, disillusioned on 8-9 November when, after proclaiming a revolution in their presence in the *Bürgerbräukeller*, he was made by Ludendorff to march his followers through the city, only to be shot down by the police. He turned his subsequent trial into an occasion for propaganda and when condemned to six months imprisonment in a fortress used it to write *Mein Kampf*. The kid gloves with which the government had handled the Bavarian situation contrasted so markedly with their vigorous action in Saxony that the Socialists withdrew their support from Stresemann who resigned the chancellorship at the end of November to become Foreign Minister in a new Cabinet headed by the Centrist Wilhelm Marx. Two months later the Socialist leaders in Saxony, in defiance of their followers, joined in a Cabinet with parties to their right and succeeded for five years in frustrating all rank-and-file efforts to make them keep different company.

The Republic thus survived the emergency, though for some time its continuance and the continued unity of Germany had been a matter of touch and go. The next contribution to consolidation was to come from the Allies. Before Stresemann resigned, he had already secured their consent to the examination of the reparations problem by a group of technicians and so completed the essential steps towards a long-term settlement.

Precarious Fulfilment

The Dawes Plan (so called after the American Chairman of the Committee which drew it up) laid down what seemed at last to be a realistic programme for reparations payment in the following years, provided for sufficient international control of the German economy to ensure that the programme could be maintained and backed up the whole arrangement by an international loan. Elections in France and Britain had brought more liberal governments to power at a timely moment, since it enabled the introduction of the new Plan to be linked with a gradual French withdrawal from the Ruhr. Even so, the acceptance of the Plan was bitterly opposed in Germany by the Nationalist right, though in the end just enough of them voted for it to get it through.

In February 1925 President Ebert died, having been to the last the target of bitter and undeserved attacks. At the first election for his successor, none of the seven candidates (who included Ludendorff) came anywhere near getting enough votes, and just before the second, the National Party assisted by Admiral Tirpitz talked Hindenburg into standing. The Communists insisted on splitting the left-wing vote and the old gentleman of seventy-eight won by a short head. For the next seven years, however, he bitterly disappointed his backers by treating his oath to the constitution seriously and listening to his Ministers even when they were Socialists.

The post of Foreign Secretary was held from 1923 until his death in 1929 by Stresemann who maintained that the only practicable course for Germany was to recover the confidence of the world by scrupulously fulfilling her commitments or at least appearing to do so, in the hope of getting the restrictions imposed on her gradually relaxed. By the autumn of 1925 he had succeeded well enough to bring about the Locarno Treaties. In these France, Belgium and Germany accepted the existing frontiers between them (including a demilitarised zone east of the Rhine) and agreed to settle all disputes by arbitration; Britain and Italy promised to come to the help of the victim if this agreement was ever violated. In the east Germany, Poland and Czechoslovakia promised never to seek to alter their common frontiers by force but the German government did not dare to defy its public opinion to the extent of formally renouncing the areas taken away at Versailles, and no guarantees were given of third-party help against aggression. The Allies promised to support German entry into the League of Nations (which followed after tiresome hitches in 1926) and to begin winding up the occupation of the Rhineland. The instruments embodying these far-reaching Allied concessions were criticised as 'an instrument of shame' by the Nationalists, among whom a former manager of Krupps and member of the Pan-German League called Hugenberg was beginning to play an influential part : he had large newspaper and film interests which he used ruthlessly to support his views. He and his like regarded the Allied concessions not as acts of generosity which deserved gratitude but as admissions that gross injustice had previously been attempted. Seeckt too disapproved of the commitments undertaken by Germany at Locarno. The *Reichstag*, however, approved the agreements by a 5 to 3 majority.

Stresemann's aims were not confined to the West and in 1925 he concluded a Trade Treaty with the Soviet Union, followed six months later by a neutrality Treaty. These pacts were a continuation of one which the two countries had signed at Rapallo in Italy as long ago as 1922 when both were being treated as international outcasts. An even closer liaison with the Russians was being built up in these years by Seeckt, who as early as 1920 had privately said that 'only in firm cooperation with a Great Russia will Germany have the chance of regaining her position as a world power' and two years later had recorded that 'Poland's existence is intolerable—incompatible with the survival of Germany'[1]. Seeckt evaded the disarmament provisions of the Versailles Treaty by building up a force sufficiently highly trained (and free of Socialists) to act as the cadre for a subsequent rapid expansion, and by getting secret facilities in Russia for trying out prototypes of the forbidden weapons. This was known to Stresemann and other Ministers but their somewhat half-hearted attempts at interference were disregarded. The suspicion which the Treaties with Russia aroused in Western Europe was in the circumstances hardly surprising.

In the second half of the 1920s the Weimar Republic seemed to be on the verge of establishing itself. Conditions were becoming more settled, industry was getting on with the job of making up lost ground and flourished in consequence, while the arts were blossoming in an uninhibited way. G.d.p. *per capita* in 1929 was 12 per cent higher than in 1913. Exports doubled between 1924

[1] F. L. Carsten, *The Reichswehr and Politics 1918–33*, pp. 68, 140.

and 1929. Net investment reached the high average figure of nearly 12 per cent. The Socialists, after being out of office at national level between November 1923 and May 1928 (though controlling a number of *Länder,* notably Prussia), made considerable gains in the 1928 elections, which showed a distinct leftwards swing. The Nationalists lost ground and the National Socialists looked insignificant. But there were still disturbing aspects. Although the abler republican leaders were well up to the level of their Imperial predecessors, a certain number of financial scandals did no good to the reputation of the new groups who had come into the ruling classes since 1918. Unemployment was considerable, exceeding 2 million in the winter of 1928–9. The elderly and cautious officials who provided too much of the Socialist leadership were at a complete loss for a remedy. Much of the prosperity was based on loans from abroad, and indeed Germany's ability to pay reparations punctually depended on the fact that she was lent a sum three times as large by America. Thirty-one parties contested the 1928 elections though only fourteen secured representation. Cabinet crises were frequent, in some cases being caused by parties insisting on their own Ministers going back on decisions already agreed. There were five governments in as many years and the bargaining needed to produce a new coalition sometimes lasted weeks.[1]

But above all there were the incessant attacks of the right wing on the policy of fulfilment, on the very existence of the Republic and on the characters of the men who were trying to make it successful. These attacks were by no means confined to the Nationalist Party and to those who wanted to restore the monarchy. The defeat, the peace terms, Allied occupation, reparations and the inflation had all combined to swell the ranks of those who regarded the entire course of German history since 1870 as mistaken. Such people now longed for a German revolution which would bring into being a new, Third, Reich based upon the application of traditional German principles to the modern situation. On the practical consequences of this application there was considerable difference of view. While many nationally-minded conservatives continued to regard communism (with which they virtually equated socialism) as the main enemy, others had picked up from the Socialists their hostility to hereditary privilege and finance capital (just as they had often picked up from the Liberals

[1] Among the people who once tried unsuccessfully to form a government was a Lord Mayor of Cologne called Konrad Adenauer.

their scepticism about Christian beliefs). Without being against private property as such, they insisted it must be used for the benefit of the community. The one point on which all alike were agreed was hostility to the Jews.

Paradoxically the Socialist gains at the 1928 elections made matters worse rather than better because they led to the leadership of the Nationalists passing into the hands of Hugenberg who made it his aim not to join in governing the Republic but to render republican government impossible. In 1929 on American initiative the Young Plan was drawn up as a final settlement of the reparations issue. The total to be paid (which in 1921 had been put at RM 132,000 m.) was reduced to RM 37,000 m. and a timetable was framed for its discharge by instalments lasting till 1988! International control of the German economy was to be lifted and the Rhineland evacuated by 1930, five years ahead of the Versailles date. Although Germany had been represented on the Young Committee by bankers and industrialists (led by the head of the *Reichsbank*, Dr Schacht), this did not prevent Hugenberg and his associates from demanding that all the Allied concessions should be accepted but all further reparation payments refused. They also called for the war guilt clause to be repudiated, although Ministers had not only issued such repudiations on more than one occasion but, to the considerable distortion of historical discussion, set up a special department of the Foreign Office to organise the publishing of refutations. The Young Plan, in spite of a Nationalist attempt to organise a plebiscite against it, was confirmed by the *Reichstag* in March 1930. Dr Schacht, however, may have scented a change in the wind and resigned in protest against his own production.

What the supporters of the 'Fulfilment' policy intended to do once the victors' controls had been fully removed is a question which it is still premature to answer with assurance. That they would have gone on paying reparations without argument for sixty years is hard to believe and they may therefore be thought to have had much the same goal as the nationalists and to have differed only in their views about the methods which were practicable. Yet their readiness to realise that Germany was not strong enough to defy her neighbours suggests that they had learnt the main lesson of the war and that even when their country had recovered her freedom, they would have sought to restrain her further demands within the limits of what could be obtained by agreement.

The Wild Men Get Their Chance

The 'Great Crash' on the New York Stock Exchange on 29 October 1929 was to prove the undoing of, among many other things, the Weimar Republic. The preceding American boom had already led to funds being withdrawn from Germany so as to win bigger profit across the Atlantic. Now injudicious speculators went bankrupt, loans were called in and orders cancelled in a chain reaction all round the world. In a process of *sauve qui peut* each government sought to secure at least its own home market for its own industry by raising tariffs. International trade and demand for raw materials shrank; prices fell and the total process was thus intensified.

This was the situation which was to give an opening to one of the most remarkable characters in history. Adolf Hitler combined a second-rate intellect with pronounced emotional instability. Born in 1889 in Upper Austria, he only came to Germany in 1913 and only became a citizen of the Republic in 1932. His mind was thus formed in Linz and Vienna during the last days of Habsburg rule when among the many and various ideas that were prevalent he seems to have had an unfailing flair for the meretricious. The Austrian Germans were at this time losing out in the political struggle and those who did not relapse into resignation or escape into cultural activities compensated for their failure by adopting the most extreme attitudes of racial nationalism and in particular a vicious disdain for the apparent authors of their humiliation—democrats, Slavs, Jews. Hitler reproduced their situation in microcosm, compensating for an initial lack of worldly achievement by belief in his mission coupled with hatred of those who failed to recognise it. Self-centred and sentimental, he was prone to violent gusts of rage and derived great emotional satisfaction from being ruthless in imagination or by proxy.

Such qualities are hardly a recipe for greatness. But to them he joined a gift, said to be often associated with dementia, of intuitively divining the mental processes of others, provided that these were not distorted by altruism. Moreover, his intense belief in his own arguments did not render him incapable of regarding them objectively as weapons for influencing people. These faculties helped to make him a most effective public speaker, entering into his audience's frame of mind, presenting ideas clearly thanks to oversimplification and swaying in the last resort by emotion rather than thought. But the same faculties made him a wily tactician, playing off one group of supporters against another and postponing for as long as possible commitments which might lose him support.

Above all he was lucky in his epoch. The advance of technology had on the one hand enabled the orator for the first time in history to speak directly to a mass audience. But on the other hand, and particularly in Germany, it had cut great numbers of people adrift from their moorings, leaving them resentful and apprehensive. A complex economic web had come into existence which only too often put the livelihood of the individual outside his own control before effective means of controlling it centrally had been devised. Hitler's audience was predominantly one of small men who alike in the professions, trade, industry and agriculture found themselves pushed to the wall by the trend in favour of larger units and continent-wide division of labour. They were bewildered in an unfamiliar situation which nobody seemed able to master and for which their self-respect made them unwilling to take the blame. The slump, coming on top of the years 1918–24, eroded the social integration achieved in Germany prior to 1914, and the only remaining banner round which there seemed a chance of rallying successfully was that of the nation. But thanks to the assiduity of studious theorists over many years, the nation had in Germany acquired special associations of which the chief was hatred of the Jews.

Intellectuals, however, are bad at working together, especially if they are second-rate, and the potential supporters of a 'German Revolution' embraced a wide variety of outlooks. Hitler came out on top because he 'mobilised disaffection'[1] by promising, with a complete lack of scruple, all things to all men. On the one hand the events of 1920 and 1923 had shown that no right-wing movement had a chance of success if the masses stood solidly against it. Yet a mass movement was anathema to those who thought national revival should be the work an an élite leadership, while the possessing classes, whose subscriptions were essential for victory, were not to be had for anything which smacked of socialism. The National Socialists like the National Liberals and the Social Democrats (and, some would say, the Christian Democrats) were faced with the problem of keeping a balance between the two elements in their title. The anti-Semitism which distinguished them from other European Fascist parties was not simply the result of passionate conviction; it was also the best means of holding the party together. If Hitler was to be believed, Germany's troubles had not been due to an exaggerated idea of the position to which

[1] D. Schoenbaum, *Hitler's Social Revolution,* p. 15.

she was entitled in the world, but to those decadent and alien elements in her population, particularly Communists and Jews, which had sapped her belief in her destiny and so enabled her external enemies to destroy her. If she could eliminate such elements and recapture belief in herself, she could regain material and psychological prosperity. It was almost the exact reverse of the truth but in the circumstances it carried conviction.

Even before the American crash the growth of unemployment in Germany had upset the financing of the relatively new system of unemployment benefits. The claims of the Socialists for the workers and of the People's Party for the employers had only with difficulty been reconciled. The Great Coalition government which had held office since the 1928 election and to which both belonged had thus been put in jeopardy. Now came the fall in world demand, the flight of foreign capital and the embarrassment of those German firms and institutions which had depended on it (especially when they had borrowed short to lend long). The inflow of dollars which had made it possible to pay reparations dried up. Unemployment rose (to reach 5 million in the winter of 1930–31 and 6 million a year later), expenditure went up, revenues fell. In the spring of 1930 the government succumbed to the task of getting agreement between its various components on a policy adequate to the emergency and on 27 March its Socialist Chancellor resigned. Some historians regard that date as marking the end of the Republic.

For the President, partly on *Reichswehr* advice, entrusted the task of forming a new government to a Centre Deputy called Heinrich Brüning. He was a devout Catholic, a brave ex-officer, an upright man, a democrat (though on the whole a conservative one), and an expert on economics. He considered that the only way to solve the problem lay in savagely deflating the economy, cutting expenditure and wages till the Budget was balanced and by slow degrees the cheapness of money revived enterprise and demand round the world. Even if this had not been at that time the generally accepted orthodoxy, Brüning himself was doubtful whether a reflationary policy of deficit financing would be feasible in a single country, especially when the country was one obsessed by the fear of inflation. Yet a deflationary policy meant a return to the hard living conditions from which Germany had only escaped five years previously, and involved a degree of disillusionment and sacrifice which might well destroy (particularly in the middle classes) the last vestiges of support for a democratic system. Indeed the problem of settling exactly how the sacrifices were to fall was clearly beyond the capacity of the parties and the *Reichstag*. A recourse to rule by the emergency article 48 was therefore envisaged from the outset of Brüning's administration by those who had helped him to power. This meant a return towards the system of the Second Reich where the Chancellor had been responsible not to the *Reichstag* but to the head of State; as soon as Hindenburg refused his signature to an emergency decree, Brüning's position would be untenable.

Not that the government ruled in defiance of the *Reichstag*. The only occasions when a majority of Deputies voted against it occurred in July 1930 and Brüning thereupon secured a dissolution. The elections in September showed only too clearly the difficulty of the situation; the Socialists and the middle-class parties (including the Nationalists) lost ground, whereas the National Socialists leapt from 12 seats to become the second strongest party with 107, and the Communists rose from 54 to 77. Henceforward the *Reichstag* was only convened at intervals. Its sittings were stormy until an extremist motion of no-confidence was put and lost, after which the Nazis and Communists left the hall; the remaining Deputies passed a few trivial laws and then agreed to a lengthy adjournment during which the government ruled by decree. Such methods were a bad advertisement for democratic institutions.

In the spring of 1931, hoping to offset internal misery by external success, the German and Austrian governments announced a Customs union between their two countries. A political union had been planned at the end of the war but forbidden by the Allies and it was questionable whether even a Customs union was compatible with the Austrian Peace Treaty (the Hague Court later decided by 8 to 7 that it was not). France at any rate was dead set against the proposal and, thanks to a recent housecleaning and devaluation, happened at the time to be in a strong financial position. By withdrawing credits, she caused the collapse of the Austrian *Creditanstalt Bank* and set off a train of emergencies through Europe. Germany came to Austria's rescue. Two months later two of the four major German banks had to be given State support. Britain came to Germany's rescue and two months later, after the break-up of the Labour government, the pound was forced off the gold standard and devalued. These dramatic developments did no good to German official finances or to the confidence of her people in their government. The damage was inadequately offset by the fact that in the hurly-burly President Hoover proposed and, after a damaging delay due again to

France, secured agreement to a twelve-month moratorium on all reparations and war debt payments.

During the winter of 1931–2 Brüning exerted himself to get this moratorium made permanent, emphasising that he could see no prospect of Germany ever again being in a position to pay reparations. To this step American agreement was essential since the other European countries only sought from Germany enough reparations to enable them to pay their war debts to America. The United States, which were themselves moving towards the financial emergency coinciding with President Roosevelt's inauguration in March 1932, were in the end to have to carry the whole loss, but the negotiations to this effect were not finished quickly enough to help Brüning. The same was true of another attempt to use his credit outside Germany for strengthening his internal position. French objections again were responsible for delaying acceptance of a proposal to remove the discrimination against Germany involved in the disarmament clauses of the Peace Treaty. It is, however, doubtful how much Brüning would really have been helped by quicker action on these schemes. What the German people wanted was work and prosperity. Mere diplomatic successes made little impression and indeed were used by the right wing as proof that more intransigent action earlier, such as they had advocated, would have been both safe and successful.

By the spring of 1932 the sands were beginning to run out. There was no sign of the economic conditions improving. The Nazis were growing in strength and boldness. Bloody collisions in the streets between their brown-shirted storm-troopers and Communists were a regular occurrence. Some senior *Reichswehr* officers and more junior ones sympathised with Nazi objectives, while others thought they could turn the storm-troopers into useful auxiliaries, and all hoped to gain influence and promotion under a right-wing government. Industrialists, with whom Hugenberg had close connections, expected such a government to cut social benefits and so make profits again easier to come by. There was a widespread demand for a strong man who would take 'strong' measures to restore prosperity. There was also considerable, though carefully fostered, nervousness about the Communist gains in votes (which never exceeded 17 per cent of the total). Many people were coming to think that a change could only be for the better. The decision lay in the hands of a monarchist aged eighty-four, whose faculties were beginning to deteriorate.

In April 1932 Hindenburg's seven-year term of office expired and the election of a new President proved inescapable. The straits to which the Republic had come were abundantly illustrated by the fact that no truly democratic candidate could be found who would have had any chance whatever of election against the rival who got the backing of the right. The only thing that could be done was (with some difficulty) to persuade the Field-Marshal to stand again. He had both Hitler and a Nationalist candidate, as well as a Communist, against him but was helped successfully back into office by the votes of all groups which had opposed his original election. But he took unkindly to this separation from his natural soul-mates, and bore a grudge against the people who had forced it on him and who now brought him under virulent criticism by insisting that he agree to prohibit the Nazi storm-troopers. Intensive intrigues developed behind the scenes in which Hindenburg's son Oskar and General von Schleicher, the *éminence grise* of the *Reichswehr*, played a large part. Much unscrupulous play was made with a plan attributed to Brüning but in fact unknown to him for settling unemployed as smallholders on bankrupt estates in East Germany; this was described as 'agrarian bolshevism' by the big landowners who had adopted Hindenburg as one of themselves. The net result was that at the end of May the President refused to sign any more emergency decrees for Brüning whose Cabinet thereupon resigned. They have been reproached for not putting up more of a fight but, without a reliable majority in the *Reichstag* behind them, a fight would have been difficult to win.

Brüning's successor, von Papen, was a Catholic aristocrat and ex-cavalry officer of considerable charm but somewhat dubious reputation and little judgement. Somebody said to Schleicher 'Papen is no head' and got the answer 'He is not supposed to be. But he is a hat.' Schleicher joined him as War Minister, with five nobles and two commoners in what became known as the 'Cabinet of Barons'. Papen had sat in the Prussian *Landtag* for the Centre but that party refused him its support and his chances of avoiding a parliamentary defeat were soon shewn to be nil : fresh elections doubled the strength of the Nazis, slightly increased the Communist numbers and decimated the middle-class parties without altering the basic situation. The stage had been reached at which the only possible alternative to admitting the Nazis to office would have been an attempt to rally against them all the non-nationalist groups (and experience showed only too clearly the difficulty of finding a policy which would do this). An attempt to run Germany on right-wing lines yet to exclude the party with the overwhelming majority of Nationalist votes made no sense and could not last. A strike by Berlin transport-workers was exploited to revive

Reichswehr fears of being called on to maintain order against right and left simultaneously. The generals could if they so desired have obtained auxiliaries by arming the *Reichsbanner*, a democratic counterpart to the storm-troopers whom it still outnumbered. This, however, would have aroused bitter criticism from the right and Schleicher preferred in December to oust Papen and take over himself as Chancellor. In further elections during November the Nazis had for the first time lost ground; their funds were sinking and their internal feuds rising. Schleicher believed he could persuade the wing led by Gregor Strasser, who were inclined to take the 'Socialist' part of their title seriously, to break with Hitler, and join the Centre and trade unions in supporting the government. But Strasser lost his nerve and left the country : Hitler reunited the party, while Schleicher's attempt to develop a social programme lost him the support of the industrialists without gaining that of the unions. If this was how Hitler was to be kept out, Brüning should never have been discarded.

By now it was not a question of whether Hitler should come to power but on what terms. The upper-class Nationalists were divided into those who did not trust him and those who trusted in their own ability to control him. He reassured the first by promising to use only constitutional methods and thwarted the second by holding out for the post of Chancellor, even though his votes and his funds showed serious signs of dropping and his more timorous followers begged him to settle for less. The initiative in the final negotiations was taken by von Papen, who felt he had been double-crossed by Schleicher and wanted his revenge. He induced a group of Rhineland businessmen to put the Nazis back in funds. On 30 January 1933 the Field-Marshal, on the theory that the Nazis must be given enough rope to hang themselves, was finally talked into making 'the Bohemian Lance-Corporal' Chancellor of the Reich, with Papen to watch him as Vice-Chancellor, Hugenberg as Minister of Economics and Agriculture and seven other Nationalists in a Cabinet of twelve. They fondly imagined themselves to have 'framed' their nominal chief. They failed to realise that with Frick as Minister of the Interior, Goering doubling the job of Air Minister with that of Reichcommissioner for Prussian Internal Affairs and the crypto-Nazi *Reichswehr* General Blomberg as Army Minister, the Nazis effectively controlled the police and the troops.

There has since been much discussion as to who was to blame for allowing the Nazis to achieve power. Only relatively few people were wholeheartedly in favour of the move, which explains why so many felt afterwards able to deny that they had ever really been Nazis. But a number of groups for various reasons had come to believe (often as the result of adroit propaganda) that such a development could be turned to their advantage, while Hitler exploited the situation with considerable skill. And on the other hand there was not really anybody left by 1933 who had both the will and the resources to put up an effective stand on behalf of democracy. The workers would not do it, as had been shewn in July 1932 when Papen turned the Socialist government out of power in Prussia; the view was taken (with some prompting from Schleicher) that, in view of the height of unemployment, a general strike would be bound to collapse. The Allies would not do it, for they would neither accelerate concessions to help Brüning nor withhold them from his successors. The Communists had been schooled to believe that a Nazi government would precipitate their own accession to power; they talked of the Social Democrats as the 'moderate wing of Fascism', only different from the National Socialists in being less extreme. The *Reichstag* was so divided as to be impotent. Army, President and Civil Service were at best fair-weather friends. Once again Germany had sacrificed liberal values to national ones, and once again the result was to be an arrogant misjudgement of national strength which led to disaster. But any fair-minded observer is bound to admit that German democracy had been tried beyond reasonable expectation of endurance.

Chapter 4

The Third Reich

The Totalitarian State

PART OF THE Nazi technique lay in never allowing their competitors a let-up or the German people a dull moment. No sooner was Hitler installed as Chancellor than another election was announced—the third in eight months. The propaganda machine, which now had full access to the radio system, was turned on in full strength and the storm-troopers, 40,000 of whom got taken on as auxiliaries by the Prussian police, were let loose in the streets. We are unlikely ever to know for certain how fire was set to the *Reichstag* building on the night of 27 February; it is just possible that the half-witted Dutchman found inside really did the job on his own. What is beyond dispute is the energy with which the Nazis exploited the opportunity. On the following day Hindenburg was induced to sign an emergency decree suspending most of the vital personal liberties, authorising the Reich government to interfere in the *Länder* and making death the penalty for a number of new crimes.

But when the elections came on 5 March, they were far from being the triumph which was represented. The Nazis won only 43.7 per cent of the poll, and were left relying on the Nationalists for a majority in the *Reichstag*; the Communists only lost 19 seats, the Socialists only two, while the Centre actually gained three. When the Assembly met, with the Communists conspicuous by their absence (since if they had attended, they would have been arrested), the Deputies were presented with an Enabling Bill which would for four years authorise the Chancellor, without reference to the President and irrespective of anything which might be said in the constitution, to issue laws on any subject he chose. This, like other Nazi methods of government, represented a considerable departure from Prussian ideas about Law and Order. But then the majority of the leading Nazis came from South or West Germany and had no particular love for Prussia. Only one Socialist Deputy (to Hitler's fury) spoke against the Bill and only the Socialists voted against it. The Centre, who could have prevented it from getting the two-thirds majority which it constitutionally required, allowed themselves to be hustled into letting it through. Hitler thus made himself a dictator by legal methods, while the *Reichstag* abdicated its functions and henceforward only met at intervals to be harangued.

'Coordination' (*Gleichschaltung*) now became the catch-phrase of the day and, as its visual symbol, the Swastika waved everywhere.[1]

The Nazis had studied closely the methods of communism, and proceeded to apply the principle that all institutions and activities inside the State must be made to serve the purposes of the dominant group. Germany, long inclined to authoritarian rule, now became totalitarian. Totalitarianism turns private enterprise and the wish for independence into treachery; the leader of the Labour Front said that the only thing left private was sleep. Moreover, as with communism, the State organisation was in all directions and at all levels matched and directed by a party unit. With this went the Principle of Leadership (*Führerprinzip*) by which decisions and appointments came downwards from the top instead of being worked out by discussion and choice from below.

Reichcommissioners had been put into a number of *Länder* after the *Reichstag* fire, but on 7 April they were replaced by Reich Governors, who were all Nazis (usually the leader of that party area, or *Gau*, which corresponded most closely to the political division). Papen found himself supplanted in Prussia by Hitler. The *Land* Parliaments were reconstituted according to the voting on 5 March. Though the traditional boundaries of the *Länder* were left unchanged, Germany thus became for the first time a thoroughly centralised state; totalitarianism could not tolerate local freedom.

So it was in almost all phases of life. On 11 March Goebbels, one of the most talented but unprincipled propagandists who ever lived, was added to the Cabinet as Minister of Propaganda. He proceeded to organise a 'Reich Chamber of Culture' which embraced all forms of publicity, culture and information. Persons who did not belong to it were forbidden to engage in any activity within its field. Papers were told what to say, even where to print the news.[2]

---

[1] The black, red and white colours recovered their place from the black, red and gold.

[2] On 16 April 1940, in the middle of the Norwegian campaign, a senior official of the Propaganda Ministry was ordered by Goebbels to warn a

A few reputable journals like the *Frankfurter Zeitung* were left a limited amount of freedom to conciliate people whose opposition might be dangerous and to impress the outside world, but it was a freedom to omit rather than one to speak out. The unions were organised in the Labour Front, farmers in the Reich Food Estate, schoolmasters in the Teachers' League, women in the *Frauenschaft*, youth in the *Hitler Jugend*, sport under the *Reichssportleiter*. University Senates were no longer allowed to choose their own Rectors but had to accept the Minister's nominees, and for the first time in its history Germany had a single Minister of Education responsible for the whole country. It also had a unified police force. The German people were thus left the choice between falling into line by joining the organisation appropriate to their work or endangering their livelihood. But those who had the choice should perhaps have considered themselves fortunate. It was not open to Communists or other known opponents of the régime, while the supposed superiority of the Aryan race led to all Jews being deprived of public positions and severely limited in their private activities.[1] The regular prisons were inadequate to accommodate the numbers detained for political reasons, and 'concentration camps' were established to hold them under Nazi control; these, although not yet slaughter houses, soon earned an ugly reputation.

The Nazi State by no means fulfilled all the expectations which had been placed on it, for the good reason that it had been represented as meaning so many different things to different people as to put out of question the possibility of satisfying them all. The leaders did not take long to realise that the qualities which had been useful in seizing control of the State were not those needed to run it. Few party members were given administrative positions in the government and fewer still were allowed to become personnel officers. Moreover, the organisation of Germany for successful war called for an intensification of the trends to large-scale industry rather than for a reversion to a society of small men. Yet on the other hand the open admission of these facts would have alienated the party members and small men whose support was necessary to give the impression of an inte-

---

local newspaper editor that he would be sent to a concentration camp if he ever again meddled in such matters of high policy as to suggest in print that a football match might be broadcast instead of a popular record equest programme.

[1] One development with serious future consequences was that of 7,758 university teachers in 1932, 1,145 had been dismissed by 1934.

grated 'monolithic' society. The solution adopted was to intensify theory—or in other words propaganda—but allow practice to diverge considerably from it, and to keep organisations and institutions in being for the sake of appearance, even on occasion to add to their number, but leave them with nothing significant to do.

Few people were wholly content. All those concerned with institutions and spheres of life which were being 'coordinated' resented (unless fervent Nazis themselves) the pressure put on them and the loss of autonomy. The great and good disliked the flattery lavished on the small man and the need to deal as on an equality with men of humble origins. The small man could not help noticing that the deeds done to remedy his grievances were a good deal less numerous than the words spoken would suggest. The lawyers and all who had been brought up to reverence the principles of the *Rechtsstaat* watched with growing concern the tendency of Nazi tribunals and judges to make their own law. The technicians and administrators were increasingly appalled by the confusion, corruption and inefficiency which Nazi methods involved, yet feared that, if they refused their collaboration, things would only get worse. Those who had looked for an improvement in the standards of public life were fobbed off with the excuse that they were being unreasonable in expecting this to happen while a revolution was still in progress. The Nazis were skilful at appearing all things to all men and much of their doctrine such as the emphasis on obedience, devotion to duty, hard work and toughness corresponded with traditions which had long been admired in Germany. At the outset many, remembering what had gone before and swayed by the insidious arguments insistently dinned into their ears, were anxious to give the régime a fair trial. Later they hesitated to turn against leaders who had so much success to show in the fields of economics and foreign relations, while later still they hesitated to stab their country in the back during a war. Time was needed for members of a legalistically-minded society to realise that resistance to the legal order might be justified on moral grounds. Thus the Nazi leaders not only succeeded in giving Germany once again the unity needed for effective action but in maintaining this for over ten years on what was seldom more than a provisional basis.

In any case an individual who was shocked by the cruelty, the violence and the denial of human rights (and far too few were) could not find much positive action to take beyond giving surreptitious aid to victims. Reliable information was hard to come by, all organisations were being drawn into the Nazi net, the police were ubiquitous, informers frequent and all channels of communication liable to be examined. Germans did not have to know exactly what went on in concentration camps in order to be afraid of getting sent to one. Any private attempt to organise mass opposition was bound to be discovered before it could reach an effective scale, while individual acts of resistance at low levels might satisfy the resisters' conscience but could have no practical effect. To any person not directly attacked, the temptation to go along with the régime on account of its redeeming features was strong. Even when it became unmistakable that Germany had got into the hands of megalomaniac gangsters who were prepared to stop at nothing, there seemed tragically little which any ordinary decent man could do about it. Large numbers of Germany's best and most gifted citizens, including Einstein and Thomas Mann, saw no tolerable alternative but to emigrate.

The problem of resistance was well illustrated by the case of the Churches. The party claimed in its programme to take 'the standpoint of a positive Christianity' and expected to 'coordinate' both Catholics and Protestants in its support with no more difficulty than it had encountered in the universities and professions. There were several considerations in its favour. The Evangelical (Protestant) Churches had always been conservatively inclined and ready to leave social as well as political affairs to the State, on which they were dependent financially. Even Martin Niemöller voted for the Nazis from 1924 onwards and welcomed Hitler's accession to power as 'the fulfilment of cherished hopes'. There was a widespread desire for the twenty-eight independent *Land* Churches to be united in a single nation-wide institution. Some theologians had flirted with the idea of a 'German Christianity' which would eliminate what were considered to be the Semitic elements in the creed and link it with the ancient German legends. A German Christian movement initiated in 1929 had won numbers of recruits among the clergy. So when the Nazis announced the formation of a national Church and ordered elections to be held for its synod, they did not really need to pack the electorate in order to get a majority which would approve the new constitution. The first clash, however, came with the appointment of the 'Reich Bishop' when the Nazis insisted on installing Ludwig Müller, an ex-army chaplain responsible for bringing Blomberg into their ranks. The hotheads demanded the abandonment of the Old Testament ('one of the most questionable books in world history'), the elimination from the New Testament of superstitions such as the 'Scapegoat and Fall theories of the rabbi Paul', the rejection of the Cross and the adoption by the Churches of the measures against non-Aryans. Although Luther had been distinctly anti-Semitic, this was too much for many pastors and in November 1933 an emergency association was formed under Niemöller which gradually developed into the 'Confessional Church'.

The struggle that then began lasted throughout the Third Reich. Numbers of pastors, among them Niemöller, went to prison or concentration camp; not a few were executed. Both sides became increasingly convinced of the impossibility of serving two ultimate masters : the *Führerprinzip* was incompatible with the sovereignty of God, just as the Gospel of human brotherhood was incompatible with the Nazi treatment of the Jews. The party abandoned little by little its effort to use the Church for its own purposes and started instead to drive it to the wall, by forbidding such of its activities as were not purely religious, and depriving it of facilities and supplies. Individual cases of defiance and martyrdom, no matter how numerous, got no publicity and could do little to arrest this process. In the first flush of enthusiasm for the new order, a number of activities, such as youth work, had been given up, while after 1939 the fear of seeming unpatriotic, the curtailments inevitable in wartime and the feeling that Germany was fighting civilisation's battle against godless communism all combined to hamstring opposition. On the other hand the party, judging it inopportune in wartime to alienate the numerous believers among the armed forces, refraining from pressing persecution to the limit.

Although German Catholics had been much less susceptible than Protestants to nationalist and anti-Semitic theories, the story with them was not radically different. The Papal Secretary of State (later Pope Pius XII) had been Nuncio in Germany from 1917 to 1930 and there acquired a profound fear of communism. The traditions of the Church inclined it to sympathise with an authoritarian rather than with a liberal régime (even though eight of the fourteen republican Chancellors had belonged to the Centre). Papen soon tempted the Vatican with the offer of a Concordat which had been long desired but ruled out as far as the Reich was concerned by Socialist opposition. The price paid for its conclusion in July 1933 was the abandonment of the Centre so that a law could be passed making the National Socialists the only political party allowed in Germany. Signature was promptly though unfairly exploited as implying Papal approval of the Third Reich. The terms, had they been kept, would have assured the Church freedom for worship, for education and for social activity.

But the Nazis treated all promises like tools, to be discarded as soon as their purpose was served, and a stream of Church protests against violations, culminating in March 1937 in the encyclical *Mit brennender Sorge* (which had to be smuggled into the pulpits) only resulted in tactics of gradual erosion being substituted for more direct methods. The existence of the Concordat made official resistance more difficult for fear of giving the government a pretext for denouncing it and made unofficial resistance more difficult through respect for the hierarchy. After 1941 the Catholic dilemma became acute, and could only be resolved by a compromise peace since either a Communist or a Nazi victory seemed bound to be won at the Church's expense.

There was, however, one institution in Germany which did succeed for a long time in putting up a successful resistance to Nazism. That was the *Reichswehr,* still Prussian-dominated; enrolment in it was once described as 'the gentlemanly form of emigration'. The exception shows that the only hope of security lay in superior and organised force. The navy, which had always been less aristocratic and more nationalist, and the air force, which owed its existence to the new régime, proved more susceptible to infiltration. Envious eyes were indeed cast upon the military sphere, and most of all by the storm-troopers under their leader Röhm. By 1934 these rowdies had largely lost their function. As soon as everything had been coordinated, there was little left to bully or break up. Opponents of the régime had mostly been arrested, or fled the country or were lying low. There were, however, more people around with well-lined pockets than the propaganda in its more radical moments had suggested was going to be the case. It was true that a number of the storm-troop leaders were living in a manner which showed much more concern for comfort than for morals or honesty. The story went that a cabaret artist was thrown into prison for saying he had actually seen a Mercedes without a *Sturmbannführer* inside it, only to get into worse trouble on his release for admitting that he had made a mistake for was it not ridiculous to suppose that there could be a Mercedes which did not contain a *Sturmbannführer*? But the brown-shirts hankered for something to do, they hankered for a second Socialist Revolution, they hankered to turn the aristocrats out of the officer corps and to convert the *Reichswehr* into a National Guard. They thought they had found an ally in General von Schleicher. They pressed the *Führer* to agree to their plans.

This was not Hitler's only difficulty. There was widespread dissatisfaction among his Nationalist allies over the way in which he had treated them as tools. As early as June 1933 Hugenberg allowed himself to be provoked into resignation. The Nationalist private army, the *Stahlhelm*, which had Hindenburg as its President, was manoeuvred into impotence about the same time. Even the vestiges of the *Freikorps* were showered with plaudits but seen off the stage. In February 1934 all monarchist organisations were banned. Many conservatives who sympathised with Nazi aims considered their methods distastefully crude. Papen found himself left increasingly on the outside. In a speech at Marburg in June 1934 with the encouragement of Hindenburg he allowed words to be put into his mouth which criticised the party's excesses and called for a restoration of the monarchy and a return to life on orderly Christian principles. When Goebbels suppressed the speech, Papen threatened to take the matter to Hindenburg. Hitler got there before him but was received by Blomberg whose demeanour was for once out of keeping with his nickname of 'Rubber Lion'.

What made the situation acute was the fact that Hindenburg's life was running out. The conservatives planned to use his death as the occasion for bringing back one of the Kaiser's grandsons as Emperor. Hitler had no intention of being edged out in this way and planned himself to be the President's successor. With the encouragement of Goering and Himmler, who was emerging as the organising genius behind the S.S. Black Guards, he did a deal by which *Reichswehr* support for such an arrangement was traded for the virtual liquidation of Röhm and his brown-shirts. Hitler's side of the bargain was fulfilled on the 'Night of the Long Knives' on 30 June 1934 and the following days when over 100 people were summarily done away with. They were by no means all storm-troop leaders but included Schleicher and another general; Gregor Strasser; Kahr, who had failed to back Hitler in November 1923; the men who had written Papen's Marburg speech, and many others who knew too much or had at some past date got in the way. One innocent music critic was shot by thugs who mistook him for someone else of the same name. Papen was allowed to escape with his life and to go off next month as ambassador to Austria. Though by no means the whole story was known at the time, the episode should have left the world in no doubt as to how Germany was governed. But the pay-off came five weeks later when Hindenburg died and all the armed forces took an oath of personal allegiance to Hitler who succeeded him as Führer and Reich Chancellor, the post of President being abolished.

How momentous the consequences of this change were to be was only gradually revealed. The generals were to be progressively disabused of the idea that their independence had been safe-guarded. It was true that they had got rid of Röhm and the S.A. which soon ceased to have any practical purpose at all. But they found that the real beneficiaries of this elimination were Himmler and the S.S. who presented a much more formidable rival. To go on with, they had bound themselves (and oaths meant much in German army tradition) to someone who was going to insist on being his own strategist. This connection was drawn closer in February 1938 when General von Blomberg inadvertently married an ex-prostitute and was forced to resign.[1] An unfounded charge of homosexuality was trumped up against General von Fritsch,[2] the man marked out to succeed him, and the way was thus opened for Hitler himself to annexe the job of Commander-in-Chief of the three services. Sixteen generals were relieved of their commands (though a number of these were called back later) and forty-four were reposted.

By the time he had finished, Hitler had about forty-two executive bodies reporting to him directly though, for reasons already given, a number of these had little to do. But his lust for taking power into his own hands was itself to prove fatal. For one thing, it facilitated his belief in his military genius which after receiving apparent confirmation was to lure him into attempting too much. But it was also part and parcel of his system of ruling. To prevent any subordinate from becoming too powerful, he divided functions up in such a way that nobody was in complete control of anything but that everyone had a rival against whom he would be keen to get the Führer's support. Thus although Goebbels was supposed to be in charge of the whole field of news and culture, Hitler imposed on him as his deputy Otto Dietrich who, as Press Chief of the party with direct access to the Führer, was largely outside his nominal Minister's control. The Foreign Office was duplicated by Rosenberg's 'Party Office of Foreign Affairs' and then more seriously by the Ribbentrop Bureau. Frick, as Minister of the Interior, struggled with Himmler for control of the police. Speer, when in charge of production during the war, had no authority over labour which was the concern of Sauckel. The Ministry of Economics had to compete with Goering as Minister for the Four-Year Plan, the army with the S.S. and so on. The system made for confusion, waste and

---

[1] It seems probable that Goering and Himmler knew about the lady's antecedents and encouraged Blomberg to dig his own grave in the hopes of benefiting themselves.

[2] The secret police persuaded a man who had been blackmailing a Major von Frisch to swear that his victim had been General von Fritsch.

lack of direction, while behind the much-vaunted façade of monolithic unity, feuds were waged as bitter as any which occur openly in democratic countries. And since there were no institutional channels to contain these rivalries, the laws which prevailed were those of the jungle. The 'Cabinet' never met after February 1938 : Lammers, as Secretary to the Chancellor, once suggested inviting the members to meet for drinks but Hitler forbade what he regarded as a dangerous idea! Decisions were taken haphazardly, wherever the Führer happened to be, with the help of whoever happened to be around at the time. Gradually Hitler lost interest in day-to-day affairs and then decisions got taken as best might be.

The situation in industry was not wholly different. The principle of leadership was applied to establish a planned economy very much on Communist lines. Each concern was told what to produce and at what price and issued with the necessary raw materials. Instead of decisions about output being taken in relation to consumer demand as expressed in prices, the demand which was effective was that backed by government order. 'Small business . . was bullied into *gleichschaltung*. Big business was bribed'.[1]

The result inevitably involved a certain amount of waste and corruption; the decisions taken by the administrators were not always sensible and, even when they were, might be upset by the industrialists or party functionaries whom they did not suit. Yet the system appeared to produce results, largely because the government abandoned the policy of deflation and spent or stimulated capital investment on rearmament, industrial expansion and public works of which the motorways (*Autobahnen*) are the most notable monument. The benefits of this expenditure were felt throughout the economy at a time when natural forces were anyhow coming into play to reverse the depression. By 1937 g.n.p. *per capita* had risen 10 per cent over 1929. Moreover, Hitler not only kept a large number of men in various kinds of uniforms but created in the Labour Service (*Reichsarbeitsdienst*) a system by which all young men between eighteen and twenty-five were required to work for six months on various projects of general benefit to the community such as afforestation and land drainage.[2] These various measures explain why unemployment fell to 3.8 million by the end of 1933 and went lower thereafter. But its reduction was an undoubted feather in Hitler's cap.

[1] Schoenbaum, op. cit., p. 130.
[2] Both *Autobahnen* and *Reichsarbeitsdienst* were ideas introduced on a small scale under the Republic which the Nazis took over and magnified.

An expansionist solution to Germany's economic ills had been ruled out under the Republic for fear of the effect which it would have on public confidence in the Mark and on the balance of payments. But under the dexterous management of Dr Schacht, who returned as Governor of the *Reichsbank* and became Minister of Economics on Hugenberg's resignation, *Gleichschaltung* was applied to the monetary system as to everything else. All foreign payments were put under control and a network of clearing arrangements negotiated with individual countries. Germany's creditors and those who wanted to sell non-essential goods to her were given the choice between taking most if not all of their payment in kind or blocked (i.e. inconvertible) Marks or going without. Some trade reverted to barter. So keen were foreign producers to find markets that many of them put up with this treatment and the frequent forecasts that Nazi policies would lead to financial ruin went unfulfilled, though foreign trade was in 1938 only about half what it had been in 1929.

Hitler's plans, however, were such as to make a trend towards self-sufficiency welcome. Germany was to be put in a position where she would never again succumb to a blockade. Among the projects for which capital was made available were the production of synthetic petrol and rubber and the exploitation of low-grade iron ore. Too much should not, however, be made of the contribution which armaments made to Germany's economic recovery. German industry was far from being put on a war footing; the equipment needed for the armed forces was turned out with relatively little dislocation of civilian production. Goering in a celebrated speech faced the German people with the need to choose between guns and butter. But this was largely ulterior decoration; in practice they got enough of both to satisfy all reasonable needs. Steps were, however, taken to reduce Germany's need for imports, even if the substitutes were more expensive or less satisfactory. This was the epoch which gave currency to the term *ersatz*.

The Bluffs that Succeeded

The restriction of Germany to her own resources was in Hitler's view only a temporary measure necessary to make it safe for her to start grabbing other people's. He had absorbed, along with the race theories which attributed to the supposed Nordic peoples a superiority entitling them to rule, the theories of geopoliticians according to which great states require to command large areas as sources of supply and markets. And to an instinctive impulse to dominate, he added the desire, widespread by that time in Germany, to humiliate other nations as a compensation for the humiliations which they had inflicted during the past fifteen years on his adopted country. The aims of the Nazis were by no means satisfied by the establishment of supremacy at home; they intended that Germany under their control should make another and more successful bid for world power. They reminded the German people that the first bid had failed because degenerate elements had stabbed the fighting forces in the back, and because the country's leaders had lost their nerve in an emergency. Seeing that these sources of failure had now been eliminated, victory could be counted on at the second attempt. Many of those who propounded such views believed too much of what they said, and were as a result prevented from making a wholly realistic estimate of Germany's long-term situation.

At the outset, however, Hitler and his colleagues were only too aware of Germany's weaknesses. The problem was to head off other countries from intervening while those weaknesses were being cured. This dilemma was exploited with great skill. Human inertia, fear of war, desire for fairness, fear of communism, international jealousies and personal vanity were played on at the appropriate moments. *Coups* were staged when public attention was elsewhere, and notably on Saturday mornings. Much was made of the wrongs done to Germany; solemn professions of pacific desires were alternated with unilateral acts of defiance. The very secrecy in which German rearmament was wrapped was exaggerated to convey the impression that she was already more dangerous than the real facts warranted. For a fair judgement on the reaction of other countries, certain considerations must be remembered. Men were widely afraid of another war, expecting it to be even more devastating than it proved. The course of events since 1918 had disillusioned them about the advantage of winning a war. There was a widespread desire to learn from history and avoid repeating what were taken to have been the mistakes of 1914, 1919 and 1923. Those who most loathed National Socialism were also the people most likely to admit that it was to some extent the product of their own country's mistaken policies. Materialist interpretations of history were much in vogue and men hoped, by adopting more generous policies, to bring Hitler to a more reasonable frame of mind, or, if that was not possible, to induce better Germans to overthrow him. Where they went wrong, of course, was in failing to understand that only superior force could deflect a man so bent on world power, that internal resistance was unlikely to occur except in conjunction with external resistance and that promises did not mean the same things to Nazis as to most men. Men of good-will were gradually to be driven to the realisation that there was no satisfactory alternative to the use of force. But by the time that happened, the amount of force needed was considerable and the experience underlying the realisation had generated a cold exasperation which boded ill for Germany.

There is little to be gained by lingering over most of the steps on the road. A conciliatory speech by Hitler on 13 May 1933 was followed in October by Germany's withdrawal from the Geneva Disarmament Conference and the League of Nations. In January 1934 the Poles, whose apprehensions had been considerable, were pleasantly surprised by the offer of a non-aggression pact, to last ten years. Not only did they fall for the bait but allowed the new intimacy which for a time followed to put into the background their more valuable links with France. Later that year, however, Hitler made his first bad mistake. In between the Night of the Long Knives and the death of Hindenburg, when matters at home were far from stable, the Austrian Nazis were allowed to attempt a rising in Vienna and murder the Austrian Chancellor Dollfuss. The job was bungled and the ringleaders captured before there had been time for aid from Germany to reach them. Whether it would have been sent in any case is doubtful since Mussolini massed troops on the Austrian frontier and gave every sign of being prepared to cross it if the Germans did so. Hitler's quick reaction showed that this was the language he understood but he for his part learnt a lesson in the importance of thorough preparation.

In March 1935 Hitler officially admitted that Germany possessed the air force forbidden her by the Peace Treaty. When the world showed little excitement over something which it had come to take for granted, he went on a week later to reintroduce conscription and announced his intention of creating an army of thirty-six divisions; the figure was fixed without reference to the generals who at that stage would have been content with a lower one. This left open the question of the fleet and Britain with considerable distaste began to prepare for a return to the days of Tirpitz and naval competition. Her relief can be imagined when she was offered a promise to limit new German building to 35 per cent of her own total, and an agreement authorising the Nazis to break the Peace Treaty up to this level was quickly concluded. The price was estrangement from France and Italy (who on Nazi insistence had been left unconsulted), and the gift to Hitler of a propaganda success as great as that involved by the Concordat. And of course the document was valueless since once the Germans felt capable of building beyond its limits, they would have found a pretext for denouncing it (as they did in 1939). All the same the German fleet was not in a position by the time war came to wage it effectively against Britain.

The winter of 1935–6 was occupied by Mussolini's Abyssinian campaign and his dispute with the League of Nations. This suited Hitler excellently for if Mussolini came out on top, the chances of the League being invoked against Germany would be small, while if the League won, Mussolini would no longer be able to protect Austria. The failure to get sanctions made effective led to recriminations inside France and Britain as well as between the two countries. Germany was thus given the opportunity in March 1936 to send her troops into the demilitarised zone along the Rhine. As long as such a zone existed, she could not undertake any action in the east without being extremely vulnerable in the west. The moment was therefore the last at which Britain and France could have intervened to overthrow Nazism with relative ease : had they marched in, the Germans could not have stopped them. But they were taken by surprise and were obsessed by uncomfortable memories of the passive resistance which had greeted the French in the Ruhr in 1923. Hitler's bluff, which had caused extreme alarm among his generals, met nothing more serious than protests. In these circumstances it would not have been surprising if, in the plebiscite which he organised, 99 per cent of the German voters who were said to have expressed their approval actually did so.

The Führer had all along realised that allies would be an asset in the process of dominating the world. There is reason to think that the ally he would most have preferred was Britain but she would not actively collaborate even if she would not actively oppose. Instead, he exploited Italy's isolation and the apparent similarity of their political systems. Mussolini was gratified and in November 1936 described the relation between the two countries as 'not a diaphragm but rather an axis' : a year later he paid a State visit to Germany. During the Spanish Civil War the two dictators, in common with Stalin, treated their signatures of non-intervention agreements as scraps of paper. If the Italians sent more troops, the Germans used the peninsula as a useful testing ground for their new weapons; they must have found the performance put up by their dive-bombers in devastating the town of Guernica in April 1937 very encouraging indeed. But the closer Mussolini drew to Hitler, the more difficult did it become for him to stand up for his interests in Austria and the Balkans. For some time Nazis had been infiltrating the Austrian administration and police; the moment of action was rapidly approaching.

On 5 November 1937 Hitler expounded to his Chiefs of Staff and Foreign Secretary his plans for the future. The Germans had the right to a greater living space than other peoples. Autarchy was impossible, dependence on overseas supplies too dangerous. Their future was therefore wholly conditional on obtaining more space in the heart of Eurasia. The history of all ages proved that expansion could only be carried out by breaking down resistance and taking risks; the attacker was bound to come up against a possessor. Two 'hate-filled' enemies, Britain and France, stood in Germany's way. Neither was unshakeable but must all the same be considered, along with Russia, as 'power-factors in our political calculations'. If he were still living, it was Hitler's unalterable determination to resolve Germany's space problem at the latest by 1943–5. The process of rearmament was already approaching completion so that thereafter her position could only deteriorate. The first target must be the overthrow of Austria and Czechoslovakia, to prevent them attacking Germany from the rear in the event of trouble in the west.

The Führer's audience was horrified, not so much at the thought of war but at the thought that the war was one which Germany might not win. Hitler, however, reacted to their doubts by removing them from their posts; this was the occasion for the already-mentioned fall of Blomberg and Fritsch. The French ambassador described the episode as a 'dry thirtieth of June'. Within a week of taking over as Commander-in-Chief Hitler summoned the Chancellor of Austria, Dr Schuschnigg, to Berchtesgaden and browbeat him into taking two Nazis into his Cabinet, one as Minister of the Interior, with a pro-Nazi as Minister of Finance. Schuschnigg was in a weak position, much like that of the German Nationalists five years earlier. His predecessor, Dollfuss, had crushed the Austrian Socialists instead of making allies of them. The police and army were so riddled with Nazis as to be unreliable. Mussolini had written Austria off. The British and French publics, unenlightened as to the strategic considerations, saw no reason why the Germans in Austria should be prevented from joining their fellow-nationals if they wanted to do so, and were certainly not prepared to adopt the only course by which this might have been prevented, namely war.[1]

Schuschnigg, however, declared that Austria would not give up her independence and then announced the holding of a plebiscite on the issue. The step forced the Nazis' hand and they answered by sending their troops across the frontier. When the plebiscite was held a month later, 99.75 per cent of the population were reported to have voted for annexation. Meanwhile the Vienna Nazis expended their passions on the city's 180,000 Jews.

It was now the turn of Czechoslovakia. Although the capture of Austria put the head of this country into the tiger's jaws, that head was protected all round by fortified mountain barriers and by a well-equipped, well-trained army of thirty-five divisions. But Czechoslovakia had inherited from the days when it was under Habsburg rule—indeed from a period even earlier than that—a weakness which was to prove fatal. In the 'Sudetenland', it contained over three million people speaking German, most of whom lived close to the German frontier. These people had not been badly treated in the democratic republic but many of them resented the loss of their old predominance and disliked being ruled by people whom they had always despised. Hitler had for long been fanning their dissatisfaction and by 1935 the Sudeten German Party which voiced the nationalist claims had become the strongest in the country. He now set out to exploit their supposed grievances, not with the object of getting these grievances alleviated but of turning the sympathies of the world, and particularly of the British and French publics, against the Czechs. In private he decided in May 1938 to 'smash Czechoslovakia by military action' before the beginning of October. When he conveyed this decision to the generals, they were once again horrified. Not only did they seriously doubt whether they had enough troops to break through the Czech fortifications but they could only obtain the troops which they did propose to use by reducing to twelve divisions those left in the west for guarding the French frontier. If the French moved (and they were bound by Treaty to come to the help of the Czechs) they could not possibly be held up. General Beck, the army Chief of Staff, was so disturbed by the prospect that he resigned his post in mid-August and worked out with a group of generals a plan to seize Hitler as soon as the order to attack Czechoslovakia was finally issued. Information about these plans was conveyed to London.

Hitler, however, welcomed Beck's departure, though he did not

[1] France at the crucial moment was in the middle of a Cabinet crisis.

think fit to make it known. He was convinced that he could bluff the Western Powers out of acting. And indeed by a chain of events stretching from the despatch of Lord Runciman's mission to Prague at the end of July, through Chamberlain's visit to Godesberg on 22 September to the Munich Conference on 29 September, this is precisely what he achieved. He was deprived for the time being, to his considerable annoyance, of the pleasure of actually marching into Prague but he secured without war the handing over to Germany of all the Sudeten German areas, with which went the Czech chances of putting up a successful resistance later. The British and French governments not only accepted this solution but took the initiative in negotiating it and forcing it upon the luckless Czechs. Their peoples, having been given little preparation for such an emergency, were deeply divided about the need to fight. They imagined themselves to be relatively in a more disadvantageous position as regards armaments than was the case. What will not be certain until the British records are opened is whether it was their expert advisers who failed to appreciate the weakness of the German military position or the Ministers themselves who disregarded their experts. If the latter, they might seem to have been taking a leaf out of Hitler's own book—but unlike him the result did not enhance their reputation.

The Bluff that was Called

For the first time since the Middle Ages, virtually all the people speaking German were now united in a state of 80 millions.[1] But what Hitler failed to realise in his natural self-satisfaction was that, as far as the British people were concerned, he had exhausted his credit and their patience. Events in the following months did nothing to make them better disposed towards Germany. In November the murder of a German diplomat in Paris by a Jew with a grievance was used as the excuse for an attack on Jews throughout Germany in which some were killed, many arrested and much property destroyed. In the past, anti-Jewish violence had mostly been perpetrated by individuals, while police and officials looked the other way; the 'Crystal Night' (so called because of the broken shop-windows) was the first large-scale operation to be officially engineered and its execution whetted unnatural appetites.

The rump of Czechoslovakia had been divided, at Nazi instigation, into three provinces. When in March 1939 two of these tried

[1] The most notable exception was the German-speaking Swiss.

to break away from the third, Dr Hacha, who had become President after Munich, dismissed their governments and proclaimed martial law. For this, he was ordered to Berlin and there compelled to advise his people not to resist the occupation of their country by German troops. The rape of Czechoslovakia so shocked the world that the seizure of the Memelland from Lithuania five days later was almost unnoticed. Although we now know that Hitler's object had all along been to take possession of the whole country, he had justified his actions in 1938 by the need to relieve the lot of the Sudeten Germans. In support of this, he could appeal to the principle of national self-determination which was supposed to have underlain the Treaty of Versailles. He had told Chamberlain that this was his last territorial demand, that he wanted no Czechs in the German state. Six months later he himself showed what many had all along suspected, that this had been merely a propaganda position. He thus demonstrated that there could be no knowing where he would stop, since nothing he said could be trusted. The reply of the British government was to promise all possible support to Poland if the Polish government found it vital to resist any threat to their independence. France was already pledged to such a course by Treaty.

Chamberlain's promise, of course, made strategic nonsense. The Polish army was bigger than the Czech but less well-equipped and the Polish frontiers were harder to defend. The only effective way to protect Poland against Germany would have been to secure for the Poles the help of the Russians, but this the British government was strangely slow to seek and the Polish government adamantly unwilling to accept. If Britain was to go to war with Germany a second time, it would have been better to do so in 1936 or 1938. But Britain's aim had been to avoid such a second war out of a belief that it might create more problems than it solved. The need to wait for a demonstration that this could not be done on any acceptable terms had outweighed considerations of strategy.

The British change of policy did not deter Hitler. Three days after it occurred, he ordered his generals to be ready by 1 September to seize Danzig and destroy Polish military strength. Yet within three weeks he made a speech in which he not merely ridiculed Roosevelt's attempts at preventing war and tore up the Polish-German Treaty of 1934 as well as the Anglo-German Naval Agreement of 1935 but declared that reports of German plans to invade Poland were 'mere inventions of the international press'. On 23 May he told the generals that Poland was to be attacked at the first suitable opportunity. Danzig, like the Sudetens, was admitted to be only a pretext. The real aim was the expansion of living space in the east as a necessary preparation for a showdown with the West. Germany's food problem could only be solved by the acquisition of underpopulated territories to which she had direct land access, while non-German populations would strengthen her labour force. The Czech experience was unlikely to be repeated. This time there would be fighting. This time too none of the generals offered any objection.

In May a formal military alliance—the so-called Pact of Steel— was signed with Italy. But the Führer had few illusions about the quality of the metal, realising that Italy's pro-German policy was mainly due to Mussolini : in the event Italy took advantage of various pretexts to avoid going to war until Germany had already won her victories. Hitler had a much larger fish on the line and finally landed it on 23 August when the conclusion of a non-aggression Pact between Germany and Russia caused a world sensation. How could a party which had always proclaimed Bolshevism to be one of its greatest enemies, which along with Italy and Japan was a signatory to an anti-Comintern Pact, bring itself to make terms with the leader of world communism? Had the Russians lost their senses for them to join hands with people pledged to destroy them?

The explanation is that the Pact with Germany was Stalin's reply to Munich. He believed in common with many other people that the real objection on the part of the British and French governments to fighting Germany was the fear that such a war would exhaust both sides and leave Europe at the mercy of communism. On such a hypothesis, the object underlying the Munich Pact was to turn Hitler eastwards so as to make it Nazism and communism which wore one another out. The weakness of this policy (if indeed it was what motivated the Western governments, and of this until records are fully opened we cannot be sure) was that, though Hitler almost certainly intended to attack Russia sooner or later, he would have much preferred to do so after putting the Western democracies out of action, so as to prevent them from taking him in the rear. But before tackling them, he wanted security against being taken in the rear by Russia (like Bismarck in the days of the Reinsurance Treaty[1]). Stalin, for his part, wanted to turn Germany westwards rather than eastwards. He thought to do this by agreeing to stand aloof while Germany invaded Poland provided that (as a secret

[1] See p. 49.

section of the Pact stipulated) he got the half of Poland which Germany did not take and so improved his frontier against Germany. The Russian government should have known how dangerous the game was, since they can have had no illusions about Nazi trustworthiness, and the British might have forestalled the Germans by clever diplomacy. Instead, they dragged their feet in a marked manner and the Russians decided to take what they could get.

With Russia's neutrality in his pocket, Hitler might have been expected to hesitate no longer. Indeed he told the generals on 22 August that his only fear was an attempt to mediate by some *Schweinhund*. Moreover, he often spoke as if he believed that when the British said they would fight for Poland, they meant it. Yet the outlook of people who persisted in such a hopeless cause clearly baffled him. He could not abandon the idea that Chamberlain was looking for a decent excuse to remain neutral and he put off the attack on Poland for a week while he tried to provide one. But the minimum British condition was the abandonment of that attack and they would not even put pressure on the Poles to accept specious proposals of Hitler's about coming to Berlin to negotiate. So the dateline of 1 September set by the military timetable arrived without anything having been settled and only when the troops were already moving did the Nazis produce and publish to the world a highly reasonable set of terms which they alleged would have been given to the Poles supposing that negotiations had ever begun. Once the Polish frontiers had been violated, the British refused to consider any proposal for mediation from Mussolini or anybody else unless Germany agreed to withdraw again. This of course Hitler would not dream of doing and so on 3 September Britain reluctantly declared war, leaving an even more reluctant France with no honourable alternative but to follow suit.

Europe at his Feet

The invasion of Poland was the first major occasion in history on which the internal combustion engine was fully exploited for military purposes. Its employment for the conveyance of troops, guns and supplies on land and in the air immensely increased the speed at which operations were conducted, occasioning the term 'Lightning War' (*Blitzkrieg*). Small wonder that the Poles, who still largely depended on horse transport, and even on cavalry, were unable to withstand it. The campaign was over before the unenthusiastic French had had time to move in the west and almost before the Russians had had time to seize their share of the spoils. In fact, they left to the Germans two more provinces of restive Poles than had been originally intended, taking instead the three Baltic states of Lithuania, Latvia and Esthonia.[1] On 6 October in a victorious speech to the *Reichstag* Hitler proposed to the Western Powers that they should make peace; the proposal was rejected by the Prime Ministers of France and Britain.

But before the latter had spoken, the Führer had ordered his generals to make plans for an attack on France through Luxembourg, Belgium and Holland. When told to be ready by mid-November, they were so alarmed as once again to consider removing him. Neither party carried out its intentions. The starting date for the operation was postponed fourteen times and the winter was chiefly remarkable for a naval action which led to a German pocket battleship scuttling itself in the South Atlantic and a bitter northern war which caused the Russians to think they had ensured the subservience of the Finns.

The coming of spring brought a dramatic end to the 'phoney war'. On 9 April German seaborne forces, with the help of a few parachutists, evaded the watch of the British navy and landed without warning or declaration of war in Denmark and Norway. Denmark was seized virtually without a struggle. Five of Norway's six ports were also taken without difficulty, but at Oslo plans miscarried. The King and Cabinet managed to get away and refused all suggestions that they should surrender. For the last ten days of April small British and French forces endeavoured to help in resistance but the Germans had gained too big a start. At the end of the month the effort was abandoned as hopeless, the King and Ministers were evacuated to Britain and Norway left to a German *Gauleiter*; the traitor Quisling, who originally proclaimed himself Prime Minister, was kicked out after only six days, though not before he had added a new term of abuse to the international vocabulary.

Then on 10 May the assault on the West was launched. Belgium, Holland and Luxembourg were entered without notice or pretext. In addition to the techniques which had overwhelmed Poland, parachutists, gliders and airborne troops were employed to create confusion and leap over obstacles such as rivers or forts. An air raid on Rotterdam killed 800 civilians while negotiations for surrender were already under way. Concern for their own

[1] Russian designs on these states had been one of the obstacles to an agreement with Britain.

neutrality had kept the Dutch and Belgian governments from having more than the most superficial contacts with the French and British and though the armies of the latter now raced forward to their aid, the effort was partly responsible for the disaster which followed.

For the Germans had calculated that the enemy would expect them to repeat their 1914 strategy by which the main weight of the attack was concentrated on the right wing and used in a wide encircling movement through the Low Countries. This had indeed been their original intention and plans for such an operation had fallen into Allied hands in January. But subsequently Hitler had adopted a new and daring scheme proposed by General von Manstein. Four days after the original invasion, when the French and British had had time to race to their left flank, a concentrated force of armoured divisions, supported by motorised infantry, fell upon the weak Allied centre, although the hilly nature of the country was supposed to make it unsuitable for tanks. Six days later the head of this column reached the sea at Abbeville. Though the Dutch had had to stop fighting on 15 May, the Belgian, British and French forces had managed to halt the German right wing east of Brussels, but this achievement was rendered futile when they were taken in the back. Indeed the German armoured column moved rapidly north, took Boulogne, surrounded Calais and by 24 May stood poised outside Dunkirk for the final kill.

At that point it was halted by Hitler, with the approval of General von Rundstedt, for what appear to have been a variety of reasons. One was to keep the tanks intact for later use against the main French army further south. The second was Goering's desire to secure for his air force (*Luftwaffe*) the credit for the final act. The third was the belief that anything left after the air force had finished could best be 'mopped up' by ordinary infantry. But finally Hitler was reluctant to bring Britain to her knees. He explained on a number of occasions that all he wanted from her was an acknowledgement of Germany's position on the continent. To destroy the British Empire would in his view benefit 'not Germany but only Japan, the United States and others'. The air force, in face of bad weather and the British fighters, fell down on its assignments and to the vast surprise of the German High Command, accustomed to think exclusively in terms of land warfare, the British succeeded in evacuating nearly the whole of their troops, the essential trained nucleus on which a new army was to be built, and the majority of the French ones. The Germans had to be content with the capture of 40,000 French troops, quantities of equipment and the surrender on 28 May of the Belgians on the orders of King Leopold against the advice of his Cabinet.

On 5 June, the morning after the last British troops were evacuated, the Germans launched the final phase of the campaign by attacking the remaining French forces further south. These were outnumbered and outclassed and were soon in full retreat. Paris fell on 14 June and three days later Marshal Pétain, the new Prime Minister, asked for an armistice. It was given to his delegates on 20 June on the same spot and indeed in the same restaurant-car as the Allied terms had been handed to Erzberger in November 1918. The German terms now were no less merciless. Not only were Alsace and Lorraine taken back but the whole of North and West France was to be occupied. Her fleet was to be demobilised and disarmed to keep it out of Britain's hands. All prisoners were to remain in German hands till the war ended (which proved a much more serious stipulation than anyone imagined at the time) and all anti-Nazi German refugees were to be handed over. Nothing was fixed about reparations—the Germans proceeded to take what they wanted from the occupied area. Mussolini, who had waited to declare war until 11 June, had only managed to get hold of a small strip of frontier territory and that was all he was allowed to keep.

Hitler had therefore succeeded in less than six weeks in an even greater achievement than the one which had eluded the Hohenzollerns. The whole of Western Europe from the North Cape to the Spanish frontier, from Memel to Trieste, lay at his feet and the lands to south-east and south-west looked likely to do his bidding. Only Britain had eluded him and nobody in Europe thought Britain could resist much longer—few even of the British saw how they could ever reverse his success. This he had brought about with the help of German enthusiasm, German efficiency and German resources—but very largely on his own intuition and against German advice. Even those of his countrymen who still disliked him felt unable to withhold their admiration, while someone who saw him at the French surrender described his face as being 'afire with scorn, anger, hate, revenge and triumph'.[1]

The Long Road Back

The Germans never seem to have contemplated that they might

William L. Shirer, *The Rise and Fall of the Third Reich,* p. 977.

have to invade Britain and had made few plans or preparations for doing so. Hitler waited for almost a month before ordering the omission to be remedied, hoping that the British would agree to negotiate. Thus it was not till mid-August that operations got seriously under way. For an invasion to succeed, the attacker had to command two out of the three elements. The Germans were supreme on land and there was nothing much which the British could do about it : the British were supreme at sea, and there was nothing much to be done about that by the Germans, who had lost heavily in the Norwegian campaign. Everything therefore turned upon the air[1] and here Goering set out to show the *Luftwaffe's* superiority; although his losses were all along heavier than those of the Royal Air Force, he might have succeeded if he had concentrated his attack on the British radar stations and control centres. But not only were the Germans slow to appreciate the importance of these : at the crucial moment their attention was diverted. A dozen German planes one night dropped bombs on the centre of London; though this was in fact a mistake, the British thought it was deliberate and retaliated by making their first raid on Berlin. Little physical damage was done but the psychological effect was considerable, for if the German victories were as complete as they were represented to be, the German capital should have been inviolable. Hitler called for retaliation and London was heavily bombed by night for a week. Then on 15 September a massive daylight attack was ordered; the R.A.F. had used the interval to recover and shot down fifty-six planes for the loss of twenty-six. The barges and other boats which the *Reichswehr* had collected in Channel ports as part of their own independent preparations for invasion had already suffered seriously from British bombing; the autumn had arrived and the weather was expected to get worse. Two days later the invasion was postponed indefinitely and on 12 October was called off until 1941.

One cannot help wondering what would have happened if Hitler had been able to start the attack on Britain six weeks earlier or had returned next year with the whole resources of Europe behind him. The invasion might well have succeeded. But Churchill's threat to continue the war from beyond the seas was not an idle one nor is it easy to believe that the United States and Russia would indefinitely have tolerated a Nazi domination of Europe—especially as the Nazis were unlikely to have known when to stop. Much recent experience shows how hard it is to go

[1] For what it is worth, this is how the author analysed the situation for himself in July 1940.

on for long ruling sophisticated peoples possessed of alien nationality against their consent and even Nazi ruthlessness might have found itself over-extended in trying to overcome this difficulty. Certainly, however, Hitler's ultimate downfall was much hastened by the fact that a free base was retained on the east side of the Atlantic, and this was due not only to his military failure in 1940 but to the decision which he had made before that failure ever occurred.

For, talking to his generals on 31 July, Hitler had said that what prevented Britain from making peace was the hopes which she placed in Russia and America. If Russia were knocked out, Japan would be greatly strengthened and America's attention absorbed in the Pacific. Russia therefore must be smashed in the spring of 1941, to make Germany undisputed master of Europe and the Balkans. But of course the idea of an attack on Russia had much deeper roots. He had frequently spoken of the Germans as a people without living space (*Volk ohne Raum*). He had said in *Mein Kampf*, 'If we speak of soil in Europe to-day, we can primarily have in mind only Russia and her vassal border states'. And Berlin had been observing with displeasure the way in which during the western campaigns Stalin had been strengthening his hold on precisely those vassal states. When Molotov, the Russian Foreign Secretary, visited Berlin in November, he was inconvenient and uncompromising : Russia's requirements were too big for Hitler to concede. At the beginning of December he set May 1941 as the date for the attack on the Soviet Union.

Russia was not the only direction in which things were going wrong. General Franco refused to bring Spain into the war and so deprive Britain of Gibraltar. Mussolini, although well on the way to being driven out of North Africa by the British, thought fit to retaliate on the German habit of acting without notice by launching in October an unheralded and unsuccessful invasion of Greece. German troops had to be despatched to stiffen both areas and it was decided that the Balkans must be secured before the Russian operation began. A popular revolt in Yugoslavia in March made this more complicated than had been expected, and though the whole area including Crete was duly secured, the diversion led to the main operation being postponed for five weeks. In the interval Rudolf Hess, Hitler's deputy, sought to put himself back in the limelight by flying on his own to Scotland in the hope of inducing the British opposition (a figment of his imagination) to turn Churchill out and make peace before their country was annihilated : he certainly succeeded in creating a nine-days wonder, not least among the German leaders, but one that was soon obliterated by other events.

The Russians got notice of the impending attack from at least four independent sources but may have decided that the warnings were a capitalist plot intended to damage their relations with Germany. Their troops were easily beaten when attacked on 22 June and the Germans got two-thirds of the way to Moscow in three weeks. The remaining third took longer but on 8 October Otto Dietrich was authorised to tell the world Press that Russia was finished. But the Russians had far more troops than the Germans bargained for, equipped with effective weapons and fighting with great stubbornness. The drive in the centre was halted for six weeks by Hitler, against his generals' advice, while the Ukraine with its vast resources was appropriated; the autumn rains set in before the capital was reached; the *Reichswehr* bogged down; the Russian winter caught it unprepared and in the open.

On 6 December General Zhukov counterattacked with troops trained and equipped to fight in sub-zero temperatures. The Germans began to give ground : their Führer, adding the job of Army Commander-in-Chief to his other functions and superseding demoralised generals in quantity, furiously forbade them to do so, but all he could achieve was to slow down the pace of retreat. He seems to have realised that outright victory was no longer in his grasp; to make matters worse, Japan's attack at Pearl Harbour on 7 December 1941 (which came as a complete surprise to Germany) brought America into the war. At the beginning of the year, Hitler had said that 'if the U.S.A. and Russia should enter the war against Germany, the situation would become very complicated'. At the stage when he was confident of beating Russia, he had sought to distract American attention from Europe by inciting the Japanese to attack Britain in the Pacific. The idea of a Pacific war, but one against America as well as Britain, was received so favourably in Tokyo that later, when Hitler wanted Japanese help against Russia, they were not willing to change targets. Their obstinacy proved disastrous. Russia's secret agent in Tokyo, Sorge, just had time before being caught to advise Moscow of the Japanese decision to strike south (rather than west) and it was therefore with confidence that the Soviet command could take troops away from East Siberia to turn the tide against the Germans.

As Hitler realised, the Germans now faced a very different kind of war from the one which they had got used to winning. For like his predecessors in 1914 he had gambled on his campaigns being short; unlike them, his gambles had come off. The equipment and munitions needed for such speedy operations could be produced at relative leisure beforehand and the losses made good at equal leisure afterwards. Many of the reserve soldiers, called up from the factory benches, got back to them again before civilians had noticed any interruption in normal supplies. Germany therefore had no need for industrial mobilisation on anything like the British scale. There was no direction of labour, less employment of women and far less shift working. The failure to knock out Russia in a single summer brought this happy state of affairs to an end. The Germans and their allies were now outnumbered on the scale of 2 to 9, so that progressively they were to be the side which found itself at a logistic disadvantage. Their methods had lost the advantage of surprise : the rest of the world was hard at work coping and copying. Belief in the invincibility of the *Reichswehr* had been shattered in front of Moscow and they had over one million casualties in Russia.

In such circumstances Hitler's readiness to take risks, which had been one of the chief explanations of his success, turned into a liability. Strain, excitement and over-confidence were beginning to tell on him; his megalomania was increasing while his physical condition deteriorated. Goering was growing lazy and incompetent; Goebbels nervous and tired. The exaltation of jungle warfare into a method of government which had distinguished the Third Reich behind its outward façade was ill-designed for the impending task of stretching output to the limit. The challenge was in fact met with considerable success : German industrial production actually reached its peak in 1944 and tank production in December of that year. Until May 1944 inferiority in size of output was largely made good by superior weapon design. The credit for this was due to Fritz Todt, the creator of the *Autobahnen*, and then, after his accidental death in February 1942, to Albert Speer. All the same, Germany could have afforded to have her production peaks occur earlier, and even as it was, *Gauleiters* and other party functionaries impeded Speer's efforts for fear of being made unpopular by the discomforts which total mobilisation might entail.

Another reason why the German people escaped serious privation till a late stage in the war was that the produce and the possessions of occupied Europe were mercilessly requisitioned to ease the life of the master race. It has been estimated that 15 per cent of Denmark's gross national product was taken to Germany without payment—and Denmark was better treated than most. France was made to pay reparations at more than four times the rate against which Germany had protested so vigorously under the Dawes and Young Plans. In addition the Germans removed 9 million tons of cereals, three-quarters of the total steel production and large quantities of textiles. Numbers of special machines were carted out of the country for use in Germany. By the end of September 1944 some seven and a half million civilians (men and women) from other countries of Europe were working as slave labourers under appalling living conditions. The persons concerned had largely been chosen by hazard; one of the pleasant customs of the S.S. was to round up people as they came out of church or the cinema! In addition 40 per cent of prisoners-of-war were employed on making munitions and other war work, in contravention of the Hague and Geneva Conventions. Some three million Russian prisoners—over half the total number—were so badly treated that they died.

German brutality was not confined to exploiting their subjects and captives with the object of winning the war. Slavs and Jews were murdered on a mass scale for the simple crime of belonging to what were regarded as inferior races. By 1940 over a million Poles had been uprooted from their homes in the provinces nearest to Germany (where they were replaced by Germans expelled from Russia or the Baltic states) and driven eastwards across the Vistula where they were left to maintain existence on starvation rations. In all, over six million Polish civilians are believed to have died violently during the war (though some of these were killed by the Russians). There are believed to have been some ten million Jews living in 1939 in the lands which came under Hitler's control. When the war ended, between four-and-a-half and six million had been exterminated, some by firing squads, others (because firing squads were too slow) in the gas chambers of concentration camps.

This is not the place to make a full catalogue of the crimes against humanity which were committed by Germans on the orders of Germans during the five-and-a-half years of war. But there are at least two reasons why the whole subject cannot be glossed over, as a bad dream. One is that the memory has inevitably affected the attitude of other people towards Germany and Germans since 1945 and especially that of the nations which received the worst treatment. Even if many of the people most responsible have been sought out and punished (increasingly, by Germans), there are still people going about their business in Germany today who took a hand in the cruelty or at least allowed themselves to be used as tools. And the second reason consists in the need to remember the Nazi record when considering any suggestion that the German nation, in battling against communism, was performing a heroic role in the interests of civilisation and that the Atlantic Powers, in allowing it to be defeated, were guilty of a fatal miscalculation. As that defeat approached, Goebbels was prodigal of such suggestions :

> Europe's political bourgeoisie is so frightened of death that it is committing suicide by allying itself out of hate and despair with a revolutionary power which cannot win without its help but which will choose a suitable moment after victory to do away with the people who have made victory possible . . . There is only one power and one idea in Europe which has enough strength and drive to stand up successfully to red anarchy and that is the National Socialist *Reich*.
>
> Our success would mean a new beginning for the world, our failure the end of the Occident.[1]

Yet the very Germans who so often claimed to have a civilising mission in their eastern borderlands, and who had one of the highest standards of education in the world, were the men who proved capable of acts such as the world has hitherto associated with barbarians like the Huns and Tartars. Civilisation is more than learning, technical skill, comfort and a preference for sophisticated methods of indulging the senses. To be sure, Nazism had no monopoly of cruelty and crudity. But to have allowed it to take the place of communism would hardly have contributed to the greater happiness of mankind.

In the 1942 campaigns, German arms swept over the frontiers of Egypt and up to the summits of the Caucasus. But in order to have the troops needed to get there, Hitler had to fill the centre of his Russian front with Hungarian, Romanian and Italian divisions; even so, he was held before he could reach either the Nile or the oilfields of Baku. And the advances which he did make proved the high-water-mark of his success. For in the autumn Montgomery defeated the *Afrika Korps* at Alamein, Eisenhower with an Anglo-American force landed at the other end of North Africa, and the Russians broke through the second-rate satellite divisions to surround the Germans at Stalingrad. At the end of January 1943 General Paulus surrendered with 91,000 men—all that were left out of 285,000; many of these might have escaped if Hitler had not fanatically refused to consider any form of withdrawal.

Just before this surrender Roosevelt and Churchill, at their Casablanca Conference, had decided to make 'Unconditional

[1] *Das Reich*, 4 February 1945.

Surrender' their terms for ending the war. Churchill a year later pointed out to Parliament that the Allies would not in consequence be bound to the German people after surrender by any pact or obligation. 'No such arguments will be admitted by us as were used by Germany after the last war, saying that they surrendered in consequence of President Wilson's "Fourteen Points". If we are bound, we are bound by our consciences to civilisation. We are not bound to the Germans as the result of a bargain struck.'[1] This attempt to learn from history has often been criticised on the ground that it prolonged the war, since the prospect of a relatively mild peace might have induced the German generals and administrators, who were becoming increasingly critical of Hitler and concerned about his consequences for their country, to overthrow him and ask for an armistice. But Churchill has also put on record[2] his view that 'a statement of the actual conditions on which the three great Allies would have insisted, and would have been forced by public opinion to insist, would have been far more repulsive to any German peace movement than the general expression "Unconditional surrender" '. Indeed by leaving the terms of surrender undefined, Roosevelt and Churchill may well have avoided committing themselves to terms harder (and not softer) than those ultimately imposed. Moreover, one of the considerations prominent in the minds of the Western leaders during the later stages of the war was their knowledge that Stalin considered them capable of making a separate peace with the Germans in order to prevent the victory of communism. They thought it by no means impossible that, in return, the Russian generalissimo would halt his forces at the 1941 frontiers and himself make his own peace. Had that happened, the task of decisively defeating the Germans without any more Russian aid might well have proved beyond Anglo-American capabilities.

But was a decisive defeat of Germany essential? Would not a lasting peace have been much more likely to result from a settlement which, while involving a change of régime, left the Germans united and sovereign within their 1937 frontiers? Supposing that there had been no failure in the detonating mechanism of the bomb smuggled on to Hitler's aircraft in February 1943, would not the world today be a different and less dangerous place? The answer would seem to depend on two interrelated factors : the possibility of getting the British and American publics to accept anything short of clear victory and the extent of the political

1 *Second World War*, IV, p. 618.
2 ibid., p. 617.

changes which could have been brought about in Germany without the compulsion of defeat. From the outset of the war the British public had been encouraged to think of its struggle in moral terms and the Americans later followed suit. Though much can always be done by skilful and prolonged presentation, there would have been deep misgivings, to put it mildly, at any solution which left in power the associates of the Nazis, let alone the Nazis themselves. But until the German armed forces had been clearly defeated, a compromise peace would have had to be a peace acceptable to the generals.

As has been seen[1] resistance to the Nazis had to centre round the army because that was the only body with any autonomy left which could provide the organisational framework essential for success. But the chief objection of the army leaders to Hitler was that they considered him to be leading Germany towards catastrophe; there was an element of truth in Osbert Lancaster's cartoon which made one of them say 'If we don't get out of this war soon, we'll be in no position to start another in ten years time'. Most of the other resistance leaders were people who had had influence or position until pushed aside by the Nazis; they naturally aimed at recovering what they had lost, but that meant putting the clock back, with minor adjustments, to 1929 or even 1913. The most thorough-going ideas for change were put forward by the Kreisau Circle round Count Helmuth von Moltke; this was not so much a resistance organisation as a group making preparations for what should follow on the Nazi downfall which they considered not only inevitable but an essential object-lesson and preliminary to a fresh start. Von Moltke was dominated by the desire to create a society in which the individual, the unofficial association and the local community would have the maximum of autonomy, a concept which, admirable as it would be, is hard to realise in a large-scale mechanised world. Such left-wing resistance groups as existed were weakened by suspicion between Communists and Socialists as well as by their reluctance to work with the *Reichswehr*.

Yet many of the institutions and ideas which characterise Western Germany today owe their form to survivors of the resistance or to like-minded people who preferred for various reasons to avoid implication in resistance. If the Allies had come to terms with the generals and their associates, how different would the face of a United Germany be today from that presented by West Germany? The answer turns on the importance to be attached

[1] See p. 102.

to the traumatic experience of indisputable defeat, and foreign intervention. The topic is one on which it would be futile to expect British and German judgements to approximate to one another, even in retrospect.

In May 1943 with the surrender of over 100,000 German and Italian troops, North Africa was lost to the Axis and in July Eisenhower's forces landed in Sicily. Mussolini was overthrown in favour of a government under Marshal Badoglio which began secret negotiations for an armistice. This was proclaimed in September at the same time as Allied troops landed south of Naples, but the Germans managed to hold North Italy and establish a front south of Rome. Mussolini was rescued, dusted and put back on his pedestal, but his image was permanently dented and the dent did not go unnoticed in Germany. In Russia a German offensive at Kursk failed and was turned by a counter-attack into a steady retreat towards the frontiers of Poland and Romania.

By this time the British bombing attacks, which had been growing steadily in strength since 1940, were making life very uncomfortable for the inhabitants of most German cities; a series of incendiary raids on Hamburg from 24 July to 3 August 1943 caused particular damage and loss of life. As bombing by daylight for a long time led to unacceptable losses and as precision bombing by night was virtually impossible, the attack had to be directed at central urban areas rather than strictly military targets. This strategy has been criticised in that its weight fell on civilians but had relatively little effect on the German war effort (though more than some of its critics have allowed, e.g. by getting fighters built instead of bombers). When initiated it of course represented one of the few ways in which Britain could strike back at Germany and the spirit which insisted on using whatever weapon came to hand was also the spirit which prevented surrender from being seriously considered. It was also until 1944 the only way the British could answer insistent Russian appeals for action in Western Europe to take the pressure away from the eastern front. And as long as the fog of war complicated the collection of evidence, the military effects of the bombing were considerably overestimated. Moreover, the British believed that the Nazis had anticipated them in its employment and though this happened to be untrue as regards London, the precedents of Guernica and Rotterdam tell against Germany. Had the full facts been available at the time, the strategy would almost certainly have been modified on grounds of efficiency as well as humanity. In particular a stop would have been put to raids such as that on Dresden in February 1945 which caused great damage, killed at least 60,000 people, wrecked lovely buildings and did little or nothing to achieve its object of helping the Russians. But in wartime the full facts never are available, while the relapse into the primitive form of relationship represented by war inevitably rouses passions and lowers all standards, which is yet one more reason against initiating its use, let alone glorifying it. It should not be forgotten that William Temple, the Archbishop of Canterbury, and George Bell, the Bishop of Chichester, made themselves very unpopular by questioning the bombing policy.

From all points of view the prospects which any level-headed German could see for his country from the autumn of 1943 onwards were such as to make urgent the question of removing Hitler, even if the Allies would not commit themselves over what would happen thereafter. But the problems involved in getting access to the target were still great, as were those of thoroughly yet secretly concerting all the steps to be taken against the rest of the leadership after the lynchpin had been disposed of. Count von Stauffenberg's attempt of 20 July 1944 failed through a combination of these reasons. The punishment of all whose connection with the conspiracy could be traced was savage and not only eliminated surprise that no subsequent attempt was ever made but raises the question whether Germany might not have gained if the task of eliminating Nazism had been left to the Allies and numerous valuable lives thus spared to help in building up a new society after defeat. But however attractive such a view may be at first sight, it disregards the lasting blot which would have been left on the German record if no risks had ever been run to get rid of the gangster régime. From this point of view what mattered was that the attempt was made, not that it failed.

The July attempt was hastened forward because the June invasion of Normandy by British and Americans under Eisenhower was threatening to bring the war in the west to a speedy end. Hitler's much-advertised V weapons gave south-east England a preview of what future conflicts might be like but came too late to affect the course of the existing one. In fact, the advance halted in September along Germany's western frontier and the attempt to seize a bridgehead at Arnhem failed. But in spite of a drive by Goebbels to mobilise the people for total war and call young and old into the National Militia (*Volkssturm*), it was clear, especially after the repulse of the German Ardennes offensive in December, that Allied progress would be resumed irresistibly in the spring. Western air superiority was such that precision bombing was at last practicable and was directed with particular effect at oil installations. As a result the German air force was partially grounded for lack of petrol while Speer's production efforts only led to more tanks being turned out than could be fuelled. The shortage was aggravated by a Russian thrust into Romania so that the Germans not only lost the use of its oil wells but in the autumn of 1944 had to evacuate the greater part of the Balkans. In August the Russians reached Warsaw but there halted for two months while the Germans annihilated the Polish insurgents who had risen in the hope of helping the Allied cause : Stalin felt strong enough to dispense with the assistance of people who were not committed to communism, thus condemning 200,000 to death. The British and Americans had to look on from a distance which prohibited effective help.

The Russians resumed their offensive in mid-winter. By now they were reaching districts like East Prussia and Silesia which had long been German and the civilian population faced a choice between flight through the snows and the hazards of capture. Goebbels increased his efforts to arouse in his audience strength through fear :

> If the German people were to lay down their arms . . . the Soviets would occupy the whole of Eastern and South-Eastern Europe, plus the largest piece of the Reich. In front of these territories . . . an iron curtain would at once come down behind which the mass slaughter of the people would take place.

But the material prerequisites for resistance were vanishing. Germany had for all practical purposes lost the two industrial areas of the Ruhr and Silesia on which its economy depended. Railways could now be bombed so frequently as to make their repair futile and even before Allied troops crossed the Rhine in March, the movement of coal and other goods was becoming impossible. Industry could no longer function and without it the armies could no longer fight.

Realising that the war was lost, Hitler tried to increase rather than lessen the damage to his country. On 19 March he gave orders for the German earth to be scorched in face of the invader, with the destruction of all installations which might help to hasten his victory. When Speer protested against denying the nation the possibility of future reconstruction the Führer burst out :

> If the war is lost, the nation will also perish. This fate is inevitable. There is no necessity to take into consideration the basis which the people will need to continue a most primitive existence.

On the contrary, it will be better to destroy these things ourselves because this nation will have proved to be the weaker one and the future will belong solely to the stronger eastern nation. Besides, those who will remain after the battle are only the inferior ones for the good ones have been killed.

Fortunately Speer had not lost the ability to disobey and, with his staff and *Wehrmacht* support, showed almost as much ingenuity in frustrating his master's wishes as he had previously done in facilitating them.

By now it was merely a question which Allied troops would reach Berlin first. The German command would have gladly helped the Anglo-Americans to do so by surrendering to them while continuing to resist in the east. But the fear of provoking the Russians was still strong enough in the west for the proposition to be firmly rejected. A few American troops in fact crossed the Elbe five days before the Russians broke in force across the Oder. But they had run well ahead of their communications while part of the American effort was switched south in the unfounded fear that the Nazis would try to organise guerilla resistance from the mountains of Bavaria. Hitler, by this time a nervous wreck, retreated to his underground shelter (*Bunker*) in the centre of Berlin and it was there on 30 April at the age of fifty-six that he committed suicide. Five days previously American and Russian forces had met near Leipzig. Seven days later Jodl, the *Wehrmacht* Chief-of-Staff who had been faithful to his master through thick and thin, signed at Eisenhower's headquarters a document of unconditional surrender for all such troops as were still fighting. This time, unlike 1918, the army could not avoid taking responsibility for the outcome of the appeal to arms.

The war in Europe was over and the Third Reich at an end. To say how many people's lives they had cost is difficult, for many extermination agencies kept no records. But twenty-five million would seem to be a conservative estimate.

In Wagner's *Ring of the Nibelungs* Wotan steals the pure and noble gold from the depths of the Rhine so as to fashion for himself a Ring which will confer world mastery. But Alberich lays the curse of death on everyone into whose possession the Ring comes. Only when the Ring is restored to the river from which it was taken can peace return to the world.

The greatest creative artist to be born in Germany in the nineteenth century based his masterpiece on an allegory only too applicable to the history of his own nation. For it is indeed the German desire for world mastery which has done so much to bring the curse of death upon the world. Twice the lust of Germans for a position which they did not have the necessary strength to achieve and which the rest of mankind would never have allowed them to retain has shaken the social order of the West to its foundations and endangered the survival of civilised life.

The main question which must therefore come to the mind of anyone studying contemporary Germany is whether the Ring has been returned to the Rhine. Has the German nation abandoned its exaggerated ambitions and is it prepared for the future to be content with a position proportionate to its resources?

Like the Rhine, however, history is moving, not stagnant. Those who seek to adapt their conduct to its lessons often find themselves as a result behaving in a way more suited to the past than to the present. The circumstances to which the German people must now adapt themselves are very different from those obtaining before 1914 or 1939. This fact is too obvious for anyone to overlook. For the German people to realise its implications is another matter : for them to accept those implications more difficult still. How far they have succeeded in doing either of these things will provide the basic theme for the rest of this book.

Part Two

Chapter 5

The Post-War Settlement 1943 – 5

Plans prior to Surrender

FOR OVER TWO years before the Germans surrendered uncondi-
tionally, the Allies had been trying to settle what was to happen
afterwards. Some things had been agreed without too much
difficulty. Americans, Russians and British, for example, all alike
took the view that the whole country must be occupied. An Allied
Control Council in Berlin was, for the time being, to replace a
German government and each of the three Powers was to be
responsible for maintaining order and for seeing that the Commission's decisions were carried out in a zone approximating to one
third of the country. A western boundary to the Soviet zone, running roughly south-east from Lübeck, had been proposed by the
British and accepted by the other two; a belated American proposal for a line much further east, which would have resulted in
three zones converging on Berlin, was never discussed internatio-
nally. A prolonged squabble between the British and Americans as
to who should have the north-west was settled in September 1944
in favour of the former. At the same time it was agreed that Berlin
should constitute a special area occupied and administered by all
three Allies, each of whom would be assigned a sector of the city.
Lastly at Yalta in February 1945 Stalin had been persuaded to
allow the French a seat on the Control Council and a zone of
occupation, which was formed out of the south-west corners of
both British and American zones and as a result shaped like an
hour-glass.

For any decisions of the Control Council to be valid, the unanimous consent of all four members was required. This put a premium
on inter-governmental agreement about the instructions given to
their representatives. The Allies saw eye-to-eye about how to impose
their will. But unless they could also reach accord about what will
to impose, they would be in danger of letting slip the unique
opportunity provided by the collapse of a totalitarian régime for
giving a new shape to almost all the institutions of society. No

great difficulty was found in deciding that National Socialism must be eliminated, its representatives removed from positions of influence and its laws annulled. Nor did anyone object to the disbanding of the German armed forces and the destruction of all military material. There was even unanimity that the future German government should be 'democratic' though events were to prove that East and West attached very different meanings to that ambiguous adjective. Where agreement ceased was over frontiers and reparations, both of them subjects crucial not only for the future life of Germany but also for the answer found to the question 'How can Germany be prevented from disturbing the world again?'

From the outset of discussions, the Russians had insisted on hanging on to virtually all those parts of Poland which they had annexed in 1939—along a frontier known as 'the Curzon Line' after the British Foreign Secretary who had proposed it in 1920 in an (unsuccessful) effort to end the fighting then in progress between the Russians and the Poles. This obstinacy had secured for the Russians the agreement first of the British, then of the Americans and finally of the pro-Communist government which was set up in Poland after the Germans were driven out. But the Curzon Line involved for the Poles, as compared with 1938, the loss of some 180,000 sq. km. containing 11.6 million people (by no means all Poles). There was general agreement that Poland should be compensated by acquisitions in the north and west at the expense of Germany; these were to go up to 'the line of the Oder,' a river which after flowing south from the Baltic turns south-east through the centre of Silesia. It thus anyhow involved the transfer of half of that province to Poland. But at Yalta the Russians had proposed that, where the Oder turns, the frontier should continue due south along the Western Neisse river.[1]

This alteration, which involved the transfer to Poland of the southern half of Silesia, was resisted by the Americans and British, Churchill in particular protesting against 'stuffing the Polish goose so full of German food that it got indigestion'. The Conference agreed that the 'final delimitation of the Western frontier of Poland should await the Peace Conference'. This decision did not, however, prevent the Russians from handing over to the Poles the whole area up to the Western Neisse (and includ-

---

[1] To be exact, the line acceptable to the West at Yalta turned south from the Oder along another river called Neisse 80 miles further to the east. But to avoid confusion the only Neisse mentioned again in this book is the western one. There seems no truth in the story that the statesmen at Yalta failed to realise that two rivers had the same name.

ing Stettin on the west bank of the Oder) soon after it had been wrested from the Germans. By such largesse (which even then only amounted to four-sevenths of what they were taking away) the Russians not only increased the distance any future German army would have to march before reaching Moscow, they ensured for the Poles the lasting enmity of the Germans, and so thought to safeguard themselves against any later risk of a Polish-German deal at their expense. What the Germans were, however, even more likely to resent was the loss of East Prussia with its memories of the Teutonic Knights; this the Russians divided with the Poles without the least attempt being made by either the Americans or British to contest the appropriation.

A question which had produced uncertainty rather than disagreement was the disposition of the rest of Germany. At various times the leaders of all three Allies had shewn an inclination to carve up this area into two or three separate states. Their subordinates had felt more doubtful: the American Cordell Hull once warned Eden that partition 'might merely create a German national slogan for union'.[1]

At Yalta, however, dismemberment was agreed in principle and a committee set up to work out the details. By the time the committee met, all three governments were beginning to have second thoughts. The Western Allies realised that there might be advantages in having a united Germany as a barrier against Russia, while the Russians may have thought for their part that one Germany would be easier to turn Communist than several. No plan of division was prepared and on 9 May 1945 Stalin in a proclamation denied that the Soviet Union intended either to dismember or destroy Germany. The idea of putting the Ruhr under some sort of international control was, however, taken almost for granted, while the French provisional government under de Gaulle demanded that in addition the Rhineland and Westphalia should be separated from the rest of Germany.

But what form was the post-war Ruhr to assume? Here one touches on the most deep-seated problem of all, where the conflict between East and West overlapped with that between 'doves' and 'hawks'. For the Western camp was divided between those who believed that the only way to stop Germany from aggression was by depriving her of the tools essential for war, and others who argued that, since the prosperity of Europe was inseparable from that of Germany, the aim must be to see that Germany got into the hands of people who would not be aggressive. The leader of

[1] H. Feis, *Churchill, Roosevelt, Stalin,* p. 221.

the hawks was, of course, the American Secretary of the Treasury, Henry Morgenthau, who threw all Western post-surrender planning into confusion by getting, during a few weeks in the late summer of 1944, the support of both Roosevelt and Churchill for his ideas. These, in addition to extensive transfers of territory to other Powers, were based upon the ease with which modern industry can beat ploughshares into swords and so involved depriving Germany of almost the whole of her heavy industry. While the 'doves' quickly succeeded in regaining ground, the episode weakened their position through a critical period during which the Americans consistently favoured toughness rather than clemency, urging the British to follow suit and thus get rid of a dangerous industrial competitor. This hardening of attitude was reflected in the directive, JCS 1067, in which was laid down the policy to be followed by the American forces on occupying Germany.

The Russian approach was different. For in their Marxist eyes Germany's aggressive tendencies were the inevitable result of her capitalist structure. The appropriate remedy was therefore not to remove German industry but to socialise it, to worry not about control of the political government but about ownership of the means of production. True, they did not talk much about such things in the pre-surrender conferences; they probably considered that to do so to the two classic exponents of capitalism would be lacking equally in politeness and point. Their less ideological though more immediate interests included, besides a German eastern frontier as far removed as possible from their own western one, as much compensation as possible for the damage which Germany had inflicted on them. Taught by the experience of reparations after 1919, they proposed to extract this compensation in kind rather than money. Factories and equipment were to be removed from Germany and taken to the victor countries; factories left in Germany were to be used to produce goods for the Allies while prisoners in Allied hands and Nazis captured on defeat were to be kept for ten years to work at reconstruction. At Yalta the Soviet government proposed that the total value to be obtained in these ways from Germany should be set at $20,000,000,000, of which their own share should be half. This proposal fitted in with the idea of disarming Germany economically : factories which had been taken away could never again be used to serve German aggression.[1] Neither the British nor the Americans opposed it in

---

[1] Morgenthau's closest associate, Harry Dexter White, had secret Communist affiliations. How far these influenced the advice which he gave has never been cleared up.

principle and the Conference communiqué said that Germany should be obliged to 'make compensation in kind to the greatest extent possible'. But who was to say what was possible? Churchill and Eden maintained that the collection of the sort of sum suggested by the Russians would render Germany destitute, that the United States and Britain would have to keep her alive and would therefore in effect have to pay part of the Soviet bill themselves. Roosevelt supported them to the extent of agreeing that the Three-Power Commission to be set up in Moscow for the purpose of working out a detailed plan should merely take the Russian figure 'as a basis for discussion in its initial studies'.

This postponement of the issue was not adroit enough to prevent the Russians from starting on the process of removal immediately they got into Germany. Over and above the official activity, individual soldiers were for some time allowed great licence to do as they chose with persons and property. Germany was full of grim stories about the excesses of Soviet troops, many of whom were no more Russian than Gurkhas are English. For, as one Russian officer remarked, 'The Red Army perished on the battle-fields of 1941 and 1942. These are the hordes of Asia whom we have whipped to war so that we might roll back the German onslaught.' To the injury of defeat there was added for the vanquished the insult of having their traditional disdain for the victors confirmed and the process did nothing to endear to the German people either Slavs or communism.

A Summer of Make-do and Mend

Germany thus fell in May 1945 into the hands of four governments who had not yet reached either agreement or final disagreement about certain vital points concerning the way she was to be treated. Further discussion of these questions at top level was accordingly urgent. A variety of reasons, however, prevented it from taking place for two months and in the 'deadly hiatus' the proposed Control Council was unable to start work : the commanders of the four armies, meeting in Berlin on 5 June, could do no more than proclaim its establishment, the division of Germany into zones and the assumption of supreme authority with respect to the country by their four governments. The precise basis of their power, along with the question of what happened to German sovereignty after unconditional surrender, was for some time thereafter regarded as a merely academic question of interest to legal theorists : it later proved to have political implications.

This gap in the joint handling of Germany, though probably inevitable, was unfortunate, occurring as it did at a time when every day called for decisions to be made. Since there was no machinery for making decisions applicable to Germany as a whole, they were made individually by each army at various stages down its chain of command and thus inevitably four patterns grew up which did nothing to ease future harmonisation.[1]

The policies followed in the American and British zones had been largely worked out by the joint Anglo-American staff before Supreme Headquarters were dissolved in July. They therefore bore some resemblance to each other though the Americans (who were busy bending their energies to the defeat of Japan) were in more of a hurry than the British to get on with decentralisation, disarmament, denazification and democratisation. The French and the Russians, however, had their own ideas of how to go about things; these were followed with rather more ruthlessness and a good deal less attention to fairness and uniformity.[2]

To have ruled Germany on a uniform basis during those months would anyhow have been difficult, for the havoc played with the transport system during the final stages of fighting, along with the inertia accompanying defeat, had removed the previous German drive to keep wheels moving. The territory was fragmented into small districts and in particular the basis of interchange between town and country was undermined. The Nazi government had financed the second war much as the Imperial government had financed the first. Taxes were raised to a smaller extent than in Britain or America and over two-thirds of the war's cost was met by borrowing : the volume of money in circulation increased about five times. The inflation which would naturally have resulted was held in check by rigid controls over prices and wages. Defeat then destroyed the confidence of the population in currency. The Russians helped on the process by printing vast quantities of notes (on plates provided by the Americans) and distributing these to their troops, many of whom had not been paid for weeks. Those like farmers who were lucky enough to have surplus supplies of essential commodities sought and found ways of holding on to them or exchanging them for things rather than

---

[1] Allied occupation had been in gradual process of territorial extension ever since September 1944, which in itself increased this tendency.

[2] A German once said: 'The British like us but don't always notice that we are there; the Americans like us but treat us like badly-behaved children; the French hate us on equal terms.'

for cash. This tendency combined with the lack of transport to produce a supersession of the ordinary channels of distribution.

Not that Germany was as seriously damaged by the war as its outward appearance suggested. Thanks to the ruthless way they ran Europe, the Germans had until 1944 been growing fat at other people's expense. The bombing and the fighting had done great social damage, particularly to private dwellings, but underneath the rubble of factories, much of the machinery was intact or capable of fairly easy repair. The amount of irretrievable damage to plant was estimated at 15 to 20 per cent. The obstacle to recovery lay more in dislocation than in destruction.

The dislocation involved supplies, accommodation, transport, finance and ideas. But above all in the early days it involved people. Seven million members of the German armed forces surrendered to the British and Americans; they had to be rounded up, disarmed, and either held for trial or dispersed to their homes. A number of Allied prisoners-of-war and just over half the six million foreign workers had to be repatriated. For the remainder, mainly Poles, Balts and Ukrainians, homes which were under Communist rule had lost their appeal. Some ten million Germans who had evacuated the bombed cities sought to return, if only to discover what had happened to their property. A considerable number more had fled westwards in face of the Russian advance. And no sooner had the Poles, Czechs and Magyars thrown off German control than, remembering the way in which the Nazis had exploited the German colonies in their midst, they began to expel the members of those colonies and send them back to Germany proper. The most notable of these groups were the 3 million Sudeten Germans who now had to take the consequences of having in 1938 put loyalty to Germany above loyalty to the state in which they lived; the refusal of the restored Czech government to risk the same thing ever happening again may have been drastic but was certainly intelligible. What was more, the Poles administering the parts of Germany east of the Oder-Neisse line started turning out the inhabitants (8.8 million in 1939) since they needed this area to provide fresh homes for their own people who were being expelled by the Russians from east of Curzon Line. There was every prospect of the population of Germany being swollen in a short time by over ten million extra people.[1] How in these circumstances

[1] In May 1939 the population of Germany within its 1937 frontiers had been 58.8m. In spite of 4m. or more deaths due to the war, the population of 'Potsdam' Germany in October 1946 was 65.2m., divided as follows: British zone 22.35m. US 17.25m. French 5m. Russian 17.35m. Berlin 3.2m.

the country could be deprived of most of its industry was a question which began increasingly to be asked.

The immediate task was seen, in the west at any rate, to consist in getting everyone provided with a sufficient minimum of shelter and food to prevent revolution, starvation and disease. To do this, communications had to be patched up and essential transport made possible; above all, the harvest had to be got in. But the German administrative system was in collapse. The Nazi leaders had made themselves scarce and although a remarkable number of officials remembered having sufficient doubts about the Third Reich to justify an assurance that they had never been Nazis, it was a tricky question how far they could or should be believed. If a literal interpretation were given to everything which the Allied leaders had said about rooting out Nazism, practically nobody who had held office during the previous twelve years (including lawyers and teachers) could be allowed to keep it—though quite how the country could then be run was obscure. In these early days, however, the question of who could be used had mostly to be settled locally off the cuff by men with a jaundiced view of German history and a rudimentary command of the German language. For the time being, there were narrow limits to the amount which Germans on their own could do. The Allies might proclaim that their aim was to control rather than to govern, but they alone possessed the organisation, the prestige and above all the power to dispose of internal resources and gain access to external ones. For anything to happen, the officials of the military governments had to have a large hand in it.

The number of practical tasks pressing to be done and the complete obscurity about the form of the new state provided the British with a welcome excuse for giving politics a rest, whereas the Americans set up a hand-picked government in Bavaria as early as May. Things were very different in the Russian zone where a picked and trained group of ten German Communists led by Walter Ulbricht had been brought from Moscow early and set to work. To the surprise of almost everybody, including some of themselves, they did not immediately set up a Communist régime but made great play with 'anti-Fascist' Committees in which anyone who could claim to have opposed the Nazis was encouraged to join. When it came to choosing the new local officials the character of each district was taken into consideration as well as technical qualifications; only the first deputy mayor, the personnel officer and the education officer had to be Communists. 'The result must look democratic, but the reins must really be in our own hands'.[1] In keeping with this policy, the registration of the Communist Party on 25 June was quickly followed by those of the Social Democrats, Christian Democrats and Liberal Democrats. Early in June, after the arrival of Wilhelm Pieck from Moscow, the zone was divided into five 'Lands' and in each a coalition government established. Why the Russians should have preferred 'People's Democracies' of this kind is not altogether clear. They probably realised that there was no hope of setting up a government for the whole of Germany on a Communist basis and calculated that by bringing in other parties to a system where they themselves controlled the key positions, they stood the best chance of gradually extending their authority throughout the country.

Although the division of Germany into zones of occupation was announced on 5 June, it did not come fully into effect for another month. Until that time, the troops of the three main Allies remained where they had been when fighting stopped. The western boundary of the Russian area thus ran along the Elbe instead of at a distance varying (except in the extreme north) between 50 and 150 miles west of that river, while on the other hand the whole of Berlin was under Russian control. Churchill, who had regretted the halting of the Western armies short of Berlin, was reluctant to give up the extra territory until it could be seen how much attention the Russians were going to pay to Anglo-American wishes on frontiers, reparations, the supply of food from East to West Germany and various other matters at issue in Austria, Poland and the Balkans. But the Americans considered, and were before long able to quote Marshal Zhukov in confirmation, that the Russians would insist on previous agreements about zonal boundaries being honoured before they would allow the West access to Berlin or Vienna, get the Control Council working, or indeed come to the conference table at all. Moreover, Russian help and American troops from Europe were both wanted to polish off the war against Japan and neither would be available if a show-down was precipitated at this juncture. Accordingly on 12 June President Truman agreed to withdraw his forces and Churchill reluctantly concurred. The move, finally made on 1 July, has since on occasion been condemned. But if it had not been made, the many difficulties which were to follow with the Russians and which certainly would not have been lessened by the breach of faith, would have been widely blamed on Western intransigence. There are times, of which

[1] W. Leonhard, *Die Revolution Entlässt Ihre Kinder*, p. 358.

this seems one, when a policy must be followed to its logical end in order to demonstrate to the public that its results are unsatisfactory and so obtain the general consensus of opinion needed for a radical change.

As an integral part of the bargain, American and British troops moved off on 1 July to take over the sectors allotted to them in Berlin, where the royal suburb of Potsdam was due to be the scene of a Summit meeting between the Allies on 16 July. The whole idea of a jointly-occupied city two-thirds of the way across the Russian zone was unprecedented. Its adoption reflected not only the wartime assumption of the Americans that cooperation with the Russians would be much the same as with the British but also the belief that, in a Germany which was to be treated as a unity, boundaries between zones would only be significant for the quartering of troops and not for government. In the negotiations which led to the agreements on occupation plans signed on 12 September (for Germany) and 14 November (for Berlin) 1944, the Soviet representatives had insisted that the presence of British and American troops as an integral part of the occupation and administration of the city carried with it all necessary facilities of access. But the Civil Affairs Division of the American War Department had prevented this principle from being spelt out on paper in advance, for fear of being committed to arrangements which might in the event prove inconvenient. The task was therefore left for the military commanders to perform when the time came, though the precaution was not taken of briefing those commanders about possible snags. When they met on 29 June to carry out their remit, Zhukov refused to grant his Western colleagues two out of the three railways, one out of the two highways and one out of the three airfields for which they asked. Moreover, he made clear that what they did receive would come as a privilege rather than a right, while he passed over in silence their request that all traffic be free from Customs control and military (but not police) search. Faced with the need for an immediate decision and reluctant to hold up by haggling the Allied arrival in Berlin, not to mention the Summit conference, the American and British generals contented themselves with what they could get, merely reserving the right to reopen the matter in the Control Council (unaware that in it the Russians would have a veto). Partly to save time, partly to leave elbow-room for future discussion, they did not even get any written confirmation of what had been agreed. They imagined that they had merely the rights and interests of their own troops to consider. Only when they met ten days later to settle how the city should be ruled were they faced with a Russian demand that supplies of food and coal for the Western sectors must be obtained and brought from the Western zones : only later still did the question arise of how far and under what conditions German persons and goods possessed rights of movement between the city and the West.[1]

Much subsequent argument has flowed from the failure to get the Western rights of access to Berlin clearly defined at the outset. The Civil Affairs Department certainly has a great deal to answer for. Against the generals the case is less clear. The cost of being intransigent might have been considerable and the existence of an agreed document would at best have impeded rather than prevented the Russian inclination to make trouble. In the last resort the Western presence in Berlin rests not upon written texts but on the power which is deployed in its support.

The Potsdam Conference

In the meeting which took place at Potsdam between 17 July and 2 August 1945 the Americans and British were at a certain disadvantage. It was barely three months since the inexperienced Truman had succeeded Roosevelt. He naturally hesitated to break away from his predecessor's determination to work with the Russians, and refused Churchill's suggestion of preliminary discussions with the British for fear of thereby antagonising Stalin. Moreover, the British general election was so timed that the Conference had to be interrupted as it neared its climax while the British delegation went home for the poll to be declared, and when they came back the leaders were Attlee and Bevin rather than Churchill and Eden. Attlee had admittedly attended the Conference from the start and both had belonged to the War Cabinet but according to Churchill this did not prevent them from taking their places 'without any serious preparation' and 'unacquainted with the ideas and plans' which their predecessors had in view.[2]

Finally although the French were to join in the Control Council and occupation, a deaf ear was turned to General de Gaulle's persistent requests for a seat at the conference table, largely because at the crucial moment he chose to make himself difficult in south-west Germany, north-west Italy and Syria.

[1] The one railway line allowed to the Western Allies proved inadequate for moving the supplies for the civilian population because one of its two tracks had been taken off to Russia ! Consequently the Russians were forced to allow empty trains to return along a second line. In November the Control Council increased the number of air corridors westward to three.

[2] Churchill, *Second World War*, VI, p. 582.

The meeting was not a Peace Conference and was in no position to dictate a Treaty to the leading enemy state, since Germany had no government. Instead the conclusions were given to the world in a 'Protocol of Proceedings', drawn up somewhat hastily in the closing hours : such a document was not felt to need ratification either by Congress or Parliament. Thirteen of its twenty-one sections, amounting to about two-fifths of its total space, did not concern Germany. Those which did dealt with Political and Economic Principles to govern Germany's treatment : Reparations : Disposal of the German Navy and Merchant Marine : East Prussia : Poland's West Frontier : War Criminals and the orderly transfer of German populations. Of these it was again Reparations and Frontiers which caused the most trouble.

The Political Principles, based on an American draft, were agreed to without much argument. Germany was to be completely disarmed and demilitarised and kept in that condition : even clubs and bodies such as veterans' associations were to be abolished for fear they should nourish the military tradition. The National Socialist Party and all organisations and institutions connected with it were to be dissolved; all Nazi laws which provided the basis of the régime or established discrimination on grounds of race, creed or political opinion (though not any other legislation passed since 1933) were to be cancelled. All members of the Nazi Party who had been 'more than nominal participants in its activities' were to be removed from office, while leaders and high officials were to be interned and war criminals brought to judgement. A significant clause laid down that 'so far as practicable' the German population throughout the country were to be treated uniformly. Preparations were to be made for the eventual reconstruction of German political life on a democratic basis, particularly by the encouragement of democratic political parties and the introduction of self-government from local councils upwards. Subject to considerations of security, freedom of speech, Press and religion and the formation of trade unions were to be permitted. For the time being, no central government was to be established, though five or more central administrative departments were to be set up, which were intended to execute policies laid down by the Control Council throughout the country as a whole. One of the objects of the occupation was declared to be the convincing of the German people that they had suffered a total military defeat and could not escape responsibility for the inevitable suffering and chaos which they had brought on themselves.

The Economic Principles, again based on an American draft,

were more contentious but principally in their relation to reparations. Of Morgenthau's ideas little was left beyond an injunction to restrict to Germany's peacetime needs the production of metals, chemicals and other items essential to a war economy, whereas 'primary emphasis' was to be given to the development of agriculture and peaceful domestic industries. The economy was to be decentralised and decartellised, but Germany was to be treated as a single economic unit, common economic policies were to be established, and essential commodities equitably distributed between the various zones so as to produce a balanced economy and reduce the need for imports. To the fullest extent practicable, the Germans were to be made to administer their own controls.

Productive capacity, even if for peaceful purposes, could be removed as reparations. But a separate clause laid down that sufficient goods and services were to be produced and maintained as, after meeting the needs of the occupying forces and displaced (non-German) persons, 'were essential to maintain in Germany average living standards not exceeding the average . . . of European countries' (excluding the U.K. and U.S.S.R.). Much subsequent discussion has started from the assumption that Germany was here promised standards equal to the European average and it is hard to see what other effect the words 'essential to maintain' could have been intended to have. But although the American directive to their commander forbade him to do anything which might support living standards in Germany *higher* than those in surrounding countries, and thus supports the idea that a standard equal to the rest of Europe was in mind, the inclusion of the words 'not exceeding' in the Potsdam text is out of line with this interpretation and virtually has the effect of depriving the statement of any meaning at all! To complicate matters further, yet another clause laid down that:

> Payment of reparation should leave enough resources to enable the German people to subsist without external assistance. In working out the economic balance of Germany the necessary means must be provided to pay for imports approved by the Control Council in Germany. The proceeds of exports from current production and stocks shall be available in the first instance for payment for such imports.

As regards reparations there was general agreement that these were to be obtained by 'removals', presumably of plant. No reference was made in the Protocol to the requisitioning of future production and the Americans were under the impression that the Russians had agreed to abandon this source. The crucial issue was the amount of plant which might be removed. The Russian action in taking equipment out of their area without waiting for it to be valued led to an American proposal that each occupying Power should primarily draw its reparations from its own zone. But the Russians had been promised half the total amount, whereas only 40 per cent of the available plant was estimated to be in their zone. To honour the pledge, therefore, they had to be allowed a sixth of the surplus established in the west.[1]

This arrangement left undefined the total of plant and output to be removed from the four zones taken together. Stalin and Molotov tried hard to secure acceptance of the figure which they had used at Yalta[2] but the Americans and British made clear that they would break off negotiations rather than name any figure at all. Instead, the Control Council was left to work out how much productive capacity Germany could spare in the light of the other economic terms—a solution which gave crucial importance to the way those terms were phrased, and thrust into the foreground a difference of approach between East and West. The Americans were afraid of being made to bear the cost of keeping Germany going. They therefore insisted that she must have enough capacity left to pay for essential imports and that the first call on her export earnings must be the payment of those imports. The Russians took the opposite view. First call on Germany must be the payment of her obligations and her imports must be restricted to what she could afford after those obligations were met. Otherwise a disproportionate share of the cost of Germany's war was likely to be paid by Russia. The two views could of course have been reconciled if both sides had been in agreement about the level at which the Germans should live or in other words about the importance of German prosperity to the rest of Europe. On this subject American thinking had for a time under the influence of Morgenthau been close to Russia but by the Potsdam Conference was rapidly drawing away from it because to them a prosperous Europe would mean a Europe which did not need support, whereas to the Russians a destitute Europe would be all the readier to turn Communist.

Concessions, however, are not made gratuitously, especially in

---

[1] In practice they were given a quarter in return for renouncing claims to a share in German external assets. For three-fifths of this share they were to pay in food and raw materials.
[2] See above, p. 138.

negotiations with Russians, and Stalin's desistance from having a total figure set on reparations (along with his consent to the admission of Italy to the United Nations) was only purchased as part of a package deal which included a Western concession on frontiers. The Americans had come to Potsdam disposed to give Poland even less generous frontiers than the 'line of the Oder' mentioned at Yalta. But when the West complained about the way in which the whole area up to the line of the Oder-Western Neisse had been turned over to the Poles and the German inhabitants expelled, they were met by a bland assurance that all the Germans had fled of their own accord so that the area would remain an uncultivated desert unless resettled by Poles. Accordingly the Americans, with the reluctant concurrence of the British, decided to make the most they could out of accepting what they felt themselves powerless to prevent and agreed that, though the final delimitation of Poland's western frontier should await the peace settlement, the Poles should be allowed to administer the whole area up to the Oder-Neisse except for the part of East Prussia round Königsberg which was to be transferred to Russia.[1] The Foreign Ministers and the Control Council were given the task of trying to arrange with the Polish, Czech and Hungarian governments for the expulsion of their German inhabitants to be slowed down until it could be conducted in an orderly, if not humane, manner.

The Conference was thus able to disperse with the appearance of agreement. The agreement, however, proved to have several serious flaws. For one thing, the French were not a party to it nor was their acceptance of its terms made a precondition of their admission to the Control Council. This put them in a position to block the establishment of central administrative departments, to which they objected because they wished Germany to be broken up into small states. This obstruction, when coupled with the unwillingness of the British and American governments to override it, meant that there was no German channel by which the decisions of the Control Council could be transmitted to such lower-level German administrations as did exist or were formed. The gap had to be filled by the Allied commanders. Consequently the zonal boundaries acquired a political significance which they were not originally intended to have and for which they were imperfectly designed. On the other hand the failure to create a unified German administration may well have saved the Western

[1] Technically this transfer also was to require confirmation at the peace settlement but the Western Powers pledged themselves to support it there.

Powers from having to cope with one which was Communist-dominated.

Secondly, the common economic policies which the Control Council was required to establish were not defined and their establishment was made dependent on the agreement of all four occupying Powers. Such agreement was more readily forthcoming for destructive purposes such as disarmament than for positive ones. Where it was not achieved, progress in reconstruction was either paralysed or improvised in four distinct directions; even where it was reached, scope for diversity of interpretation was given by a clause allowing account to be taken, 'where appropriate, of varying local conditions'. In such matters as denazification and education, the most that the Control Council succeeded in doing was to bless and to throw an appearance of harmony over measures already being taken in the various zones. Both the French and the Russians went on their preferred paths with little more than a genuflection to the resolutions of Berlin. The only denazification action of any consequence carried through on a quadripartite basis resulted from American insistence that the chief available Nazis should be dealt with by judicial process rather than disposed of in a summary way. This led to the trial in Nuremberg of Goering and twenty-two other members of the Nazi hierarchy who had fallen into Allied hands. After ten months' hearings in which much highly illuminating evidence was brought to light, eleven were condemned to death, seven imprisoned and three acquitted.

This tendency to divergence might have been reduced if reparations had been handled, in the way originally intended, as a joint concern instead of zone by zone. To have prevented the Russians from acting as they chose would at the best of times have been difficult but in fact they were left largely free to do so. Moreover, the failure explicitly to rule out at Potsdam the taking of reparations from current production (clearly envisaged at Yalta) proved a loophole of which advantage was quickly taken. Thus the concessions which the West thought they had obtained by yielding over frontiers proved largely illusory. What is more, the mirage of an early 'Peace Settlement' at which the Western frontiers of Poland would be 'finally delimited' has proved a source of misunderstanding. As East-West relations acquired acrimony, more and more weight was placed on this, the only saving clause in a surrender which American and British (not to mention German) opinion came to consider an error of judgement. The myth has grown up that at Potsdam the West refused to consider the Oder-Neisse line instead of in fact virtually conceding it. Many Germans have even allowed themselves to believe that what was contested was not merely the area between the Oder and the Western Neisse but the entire 1937 frontiers of their country. They have thus been able to escape from the conviction that territorially at least they suffered a total military defeat and have to bear its consequences.

Early in the morning of the day on which the Potsdam Conference was due to open, a flash of blinding intensity lit up the desert of New Mexico. The news of the first successful explosion of an atom bomb was 'casually mentioned' by Truman to Stalin eight days later. 'The Generalissimo seemed pleased rather than surprised'; his agents had undoubtedly told him what was afoot even if they had not reported the actual occurrence. The effect on the Conference is hard to detect; the Americans did not become noticeably more uncompromising or the Russians more conciliatory. Undoubtedly, however, the event made itself felt during the following months. The Russians neither asked nor were invited to share in the secret. Instead they withdrew more in themselves as though the added doubt about the practicability of getting their own way only emphasised the desirability of doing so. And the task of rebuilding Russia must have looked more formidable than ever when they realised that, to remain a Great Power, they must forthwith set aside the extensive resources needed to give them a bomb of their own.

For Germany also the explosion had implications which were more profound than appreciated. Even if quadripartite control were to prove temporary, the loss of territory and wealth imposed at Potsdam must seem to render the manufacture of German bombs almost out of the question and so finally put paid to dreams of a 'breakthrough to World Power'. But the bomb decisively underlined the effect of modern weapons in making war so lethal as to cause all participants more loss than gain and thus to become unthinkable except as an act of desperation. But with war ruled out, any attempt to reverse the Potsdam settlement, except by mutual consent, must also be ruled out. Yet paradoxically the fear of such an attempt being made by a Germany in control of nuclear arms was to complicate all subsequent efforts at relaxing European tension.

Chapter 6

Towards Two Germanies 1945 – 8

THROUGHOUT the winter of 1945–6 the Economics Directorate of the Control Commission, putting the horse after the cart, laboured to spell out what the broad conclusions of the Potsdam Conference would mean in concrete terms. 'A difficult task was not made easier by such distractions as a Russian insistence on discussing, for almost an hour, the question whether rabbit meat, nuts and berries should be included in the food resources of Germany, even while admitting that no figures on them were available.'[1] By the end of March they had managed to agree on the shape which German industry should hence-forward assume. Fourteen of its branches, including the manufacture of heavy machine tools, radio-transmitting equipment, primary aluminium, synthetic rubber and ball-bearings, were to be prohibited altogether; such plant in these branches as was not required for reparations was to be dismantled. Twelve more branches, including heavy and light mechanical engineering, basic chemicals, commercial vehicles and precision instruments, were to be limited to a percentage of pre-war output varying between 11 and 80 : here again all plant surplus to requirements was to be dismantled. The crucial industry in this sector was steel and here a stiff battle was fought between the British and the Russians with the French and Americans in between; the figure finally agreed allowed for an output only slightly larger than Germany before the war had needed for miscellaneous uses in light industry. In all, 1,636 factories were to be dismantled in the U.S. and U.K. zones. In spite of the confiscation as reparations of Germany's merchant marine and overseas assets and so of the cessation of the invisible income flowing from them, the balance of trade was on paper to show a surplus by 1949. But this assumed that the money earned in pre-war days from the exports of heavy industry would be replaced by sales of coal and consumer goods, although

[1] B. U. Ratchford and W. D. Ross: *Berlin Reparations Assignment,* p. 159.

the total output of these was still expected to be below the 1938 level. No allowance was made for the loss of output involved in shifting resources from one industry to another, for that caused by the loss of territory in the east, or for the need to maintain a population swollen by refugees. No attention was paid to lack of stocks or to probable adverse shifts in the terms of trade. The German standard of living was to be reduced to 74 per cent of the pre-war average, which happened to be the figure reached in 1932, the slump year paving Hitler's way to power.

The publication of this plan served to bring home forcefully to the British and American publics the nature of the policy to which their leaders had committed them and the reactions were not surprisingly emphatic. But by this time it was becoming notorious that much of the output of the Eastern zone was being taken off to Russia without payment. This was a breach of the Potsdam provisions that Germany was to be treated as a unit and that the proceeds of exports from current production should be available in the first instance to pay for imports. None of the foodstuffs which had been wont to flow in peacetime from the East (and particularly from East Prussia and the areas occupied by the Poles) were reaching West Germany; in the chaos of the time there was little surplus to come, though there might have been more if the Russian authorities, to undermine the economic position of the landowners, had not increased the confusion by introducing in August 1945 a programme of land reform. Consequently the population of the U.S. and U.K. zones, far from self-sufficient at the best of times, were being kept alive on a subsistence diet by $1\frac{1}{2}$ million tons of food imports at the expense of the American and British taxpayers. Ministers as well as people began to ask indignantly why they should sacrifice scarce foreign exchange and forego increases in their own rations in order to help out the people who had caused all the trouble. What they were in reality doing, of course, was indirectly to help out the Russian people who had done so much to win the war, but this was neither appreciated nor explained. Seen in retrospect, one of the anomalies of the time is that the Americans, who were to spend so much on helping the Germans, never offered a reconstruction loan to the Russians. But the Russians did not (after Yalta) ask for any such thing, would probably not have accepted the conditions which the Americans would have been likely to attach and by their unilateral and abusive methods did much to deter their former allies from making any offers at all.

Thus at a Foreign Ministers' meeting in Paris in April 1946

Molotov revived the demand for $10 milliard reparations and said that reparations payments must 'naturally' include goods out of current production. He also brushed aside proposals designed to facilitate the treatment of Germany as a unity, with centralised handling of imports and exports. His minions in the Control Council, along with the French, followed suit until in exasperation the American Commander, General Clay, suspended deliveries of plants from the U.S. zone which had been allocated to the Russians as reparations. This step evoked an indignant assertion that, as there was nothing wrong with taking reparations from current production, Clay's behaviour was illegal and due to the sinister influence of capitalist circles in the United States. The Russians went on for another seven years taking up to a quarter of the gross national product of their zone and the West never found an effective way of stopping them.

The cessation of reparations deliveries highlighted the problems of the West German economy but did little or nothing to resolve them. Essentially they consisted in an ill-conceived programme of dismantling and the exhaustion of stocks, coupled with a complete loss of faith in the currency. In point of fact, reparations from the Western zones reached only 5 per cent of industrial capacity, fell chiefly on industries which in terms of 1938 requirements (though not 1958 ones) were over-equipped and cleared the ground for the later installation (with government subsidy) of fresh and more modern equipment. As the plants taken away were not often of any use to the new owners,[1] the policy was productive of neither serious damage nor benefit. But considerable faith in human incompetence would have been required to foresee this and during the time when the precise effect of the policy was in doubt (and this was much prolonged by the endeavours of the administrators to be methodical and fair all round) great alarm and acrimony were caused. Nobody was going to put much effort into stepping up the production of a factory as long as there was still a possibility that it might be picked on for dismantling by the high gods in Berlin or Brussels.

Yet for more factories to have been functioning would have aggravated the problem instead of easing it. For manufacturing involves the steady consumption of materials and once the stocks

[1] This may not be true of certain early removals. The electricity generating plant which the French took from Mannheim to Caen probably enabled services to be restored in the Normandy town more quickly than would have at the time been possible in any other way. But the Russian emphasis on reparations from current production probably developed because they had found how unsatisfactory it was to remove plant.

available in Germany at the end of the war had been used up, there was nothing to replace them. The modern economic system has come to take for granted the existence of innumerable 'pipe-lines' through which goods in various stages of elaboration are con-tinuously moving from primary source to ultimate consumer. Germany had been depending upon pipelines which sucked goods out of occupied Europe, with little regard to local needs. These needs, however, recovered top priority the moment that German power was withdrawn. Consequently there would have been few goods available to flow to Germany even if communica-tions had remained intact. The only continents with substantial resources to spare lay overseas, primarily in America, and to these not only did new channels of supply have to be organised but the problem of payment had to be overcome. Germany could not pay because she could not produce, but before she could produce, she must be able to pay. About the turn of the year 1945-6 General Clay was told by his economic chief that 'we must have $100 m. to finance essential imports other than food if we are to succeed.'[1] And not only did Germany need gifts or credits enabling her to buy abroad and so get the machines restarted, but somebody in a position of authority had to do the buying for her. For all European countries were queuing up to restock them-selves and the defeated enemy, if on her own, was likely to come last in the line.

Coal vividly illustrated the difficulties. All Europe was short and Britain, a traditional source of supply, had none to spare. The countries which Germany had occupied, and particularly France, insistently demanded that her output should be used to alleviate their needs. As coal exports would earn valuable foreign exchange, there was good reason in Germany's own interest for making them and some were in fact made. But as German production was down to about a quarter of pre-war, these exports left little for German industry, transport and utilities, and virtually nothing for domestic use. Owing to lack of coal, the steel industry could not achieve even the output permitted under the Allied Plan and without steel other industries, including coal, could not raise their output, while crop yields were held down by lack of basic slag as fertiliser. The occupation authorities, particularly in the British zone where most of the coal was produced, were taken to task by the liberated countries on the one hand for not exporting more coal, and on the other by the Germans for exporting so much.

For the people of Germany were too much obsessed with their

[1] Lucius D. Clay, *Decision in Germany*, p. 196.

own plight to absorb information about conditions outside their frontiers. This did not mean that their outlook remained unchanged by defeat. During the closing stages of the war (and probably over a still longer period) the proportion of 'hard core' Nazis and of active anti-Nazis would seem to have been roughly balanced at 10 per cent alike. Twenty-five per cent had been believers with reservations, 40 per cent unpolitical conformists and 15 per cent passive opponents. The hard core was now in internment or concealment, aware for the most part that their only hope was to lie low and trust to time bringing a reaction. The reservations of the next category had swollen to obliterate uncomfortable thoughts about what they had approved, and some indeed may have been genuinely convinced that ideas which could lead to such disaster must have been mistaken. Along with the conformists, they were ready to go along with the new order even if they were more inclined to criticise its shortcomings than to appreciate the reasons for them. 'They did not realise how much of their own mental furniture was involved in a condemnation of Nazism and they had neither the stamina nor the mental equipment to conduct a revaluation.' [1]

The anti-Nazis, both active and passive, were in a more difficult position. The perpetual fear of arrest and the self-control needed to avoid trouble had in many cases been replaced by profound searchings of heart about the validity of German values, an obsession with the problem of guilt and a conflict between remorse and patriotism. To admit to mistakes and make recompense might be regarded as surrendering the national case and justifying Allied policy, while nobody could be sure that in a few years 'collaboration' with the victors might not prove as much a cause for reproach as it had just become in liberated Europe. Many of the most positive minds emerged scarred by their experience in the Third Reich. To their resentment of the Allied refusal to make resistance easier by modifying the demand for unconditional surrender, there was now added disappointment that so much responsibility was kept in Allied hands, so little preference shewn to those who had proved by their acts that they were worthy of confidence. In the long run this Allied caution, born largely of uncertainty, paid dividends, since it postponed the danger of a reaction and saved many valuable democrats from damaging their usefulness by an over-eager association with the victors. In any case, those who wanted to assume responsibility were for a year or two in a minority. Most Germans wanted

[1] M. Balfour, *Four-Power Control in Germany, 1945–6*, p. 60.

nothing better than to recover their breath and collect their thoughts—indeed much of their time was absorbed in securing the essentials of life. Once again, the integrating processes in Germany had been put into reverse by failure.

Such circumstances hardly encouraged a revival of political life. But parties had been given leave to organise themselves in the Western zones by September 1945 though they did so at first under close supervision and on a local basis. The most notable innovation was the foundation, as in several other Western countries, of a party which sought to rally all the forces in Germany that were both anti-Communist and anti-Nazi under the positive slogans of religion and democracy. The Christian Democratic Union combined Protestants with Catholics (thereby differing markedly from the old Centre) and heirs of the National Liberal tradition with a pronounced radical wing. The Liberal or Free Democratic Party sought to inherit the anti-clerical *laissez-faire* tradition of the German middle classes, while the Social Democrats and Communists both based themselves on organisations which had maintained a precarious underground existence during the Third Reich. The Lower Saxon *Land* Party, originally founded to reactivate Hanover's past independence, gradually extended the range of what it sought to resurrect.

Two arguments were prevalent in favour of the left-wing parties working together. One was that if such a front had existed in 1933, National Socialism might have been kept from power. The other was to be found in the general agreement that the essential step towards eradicating the aggressive authoritarian influences from German society lay in bringing the means of production under communal control. The chance which had been allowed to slip in 1919 must this time be seized; land reform and the nationalisation of the basic industries must not be confined to the Russian zone. One of the main reasons why the Socialists were impatient with the Allied refusal to put power in German hands was that the accomplishment of this process was thereby delayed. But to one of the Western Powers nationalisation was a dirty word and though the British Labour government was engaged on just such a programme at home, the precarious state of the U.K. economy made it too dependent in Germany on American help for diametrical opposition to be practicable. By mutual agreement therefore the issue was shelved until the Germans could decide it for themselves.

This compromise solution may appear to be justified by subsequent events, since when the West Germans did come to decide, their verdict was unmistakably adverse. It would therefore seem that, as in 1919, a thorough-going programme of socialisation could not have been carried out and maintained without political dictatorship. Once again Germany had to choose between socialism and democracy. On the other hand there is no doubt that the political climate of Germany immediately after 1945 was much more radical than it subsequently became. An early election would almost certainly have given a majority for socialisation and experience elsewhere suggests that there are limits to the extent to which this, once carried through, could have been reversed. What must, however, be doubted is whether cooperation between Socialists and Communists would have lasted long enough for socialisation to be carried very far. For soon the animosities which had weakened the German left all through its history began to reassert themselves.

The policy of the Russian government towards and the conduct of the Russian troops in Germany were proving a serious obstacle to the popularity of the Communist Party and the workers in all zones turned increasingly towards the Socialists. Ulbricht and other Communist leaders in the Russian zone sought to turn this awkward development to their advantage by launching the idea of a single anti-capitalist party and in February 1946 induced the executive of the Berlin S.P.D., led by Otto Grotewohl, to vote for the fusion of their party with the Communists in a new Socialist Unity Party (S.E.D.). Two days later, however, a mass meeting of Berlin Socialists declared against the union and at the end of March Socialists in the three Western sectors of the city were encouraged by Socialist leaders from West Germany to poll a vote of 82 per cent against the merger. What the Socialists in the Russian sector may have thought remains unestablished for the authorities refused to allow their opinion to be tested and the fusion was forced through. When six months later municipal elections were held throughout Berlin under quadripartite supervision, the S.P.D. led in all twenty of the city's boroughs, whereas the S.E.D. got less than half the number of votes, trailing behind the C.D.U.

Thus began a process in which the S.E.D. received steady favouritism in the areas under Russian control, and increasing difficulties were placed in the way not only of the S.P.D. but of the two other middle-class parties as well. Since the S.E.D. cut no ice in the Western sectors of Berlin and did not exist in the Western zones, the development created a major distinction between the two halves of Germany. The division between radical and moderate which had existed between the Marxist and Lassallean wings when the Socialist Workers' Party was founded in 1875; which had given rise to the gap between revolutionary theory and revisionist practice in the years before 1914; which had led to the breakaway of the Independent Social Democrats in 1917; and which had produced the rivalry between S.P.D. and K.P.D. throughout the Weimar Republic now took on geographical form. One part of Germany under Russian direction put socialism before democracy; the other, under Western influence, reversed the priorities.

Western Germany was also witnessing the gradual evolution of a federal structure. The Americans as early as the summer of 1945 confirmed the right of Bavaria to form a distinct political unit and brought into being the new 'Land' of Greater Hesse. The need to provide the French with a zone combined with American communication requirements to divide the north of both Württemberg and Baden from the south, though, whereas the French kept their pieces distinct, the Americans joined theirs to form a composite *Land*. The enclave of Bremen, given to the Americans as a port, formed another *Land*. The heads of the governments nominated to run these four *Länder* were already meeting regularly by October and elections for *Land* Parliaments (*Landtäge*) were held in June 1946. In Bavaria they led to a majority for the Christian-Socialist Union (as the local version of the C.D.U. was called), in Hesse to one for the Socialists and in Württemberg-Baden to an indecisive result.

In the British zone four *Länder* were set up during the second half of 1946, in the light of advice from Germans serving on a Zonal Advisory Council. Hamburg and Schleswig-Holstein formed natural units and Lower Saxony a convenient combination of several smaller ones. The remainder of the zone presented more of a problem but one which was solved in July 1946 by the amalgamation of most of two Prussian provinces into the *Land* of North Rhine-Westphalia, with a population as large as the Netherlands. This move was variously attributed to a desire to head off French claims on the Rhineland and Russian demands for a share in governing the Ruhr, to a wish to join the industrial complex of the Ruhr with its agricultural hinterland, and to anxiety to deprive the Socialists of an almost certain majority by bringing in more conservative areas. Certainly no serious Anglo-American objection was raised when in January 1947 the French proclaimed a Customs union between their country and the Saar, while North Rhine-Westphalia was the only British zone *Land* in which the

Socialists did not emerge as the strongest party when elections were held in April 1947, though even there the C.D.U. came a good deal short of an absolute majority.

Apart from the Saar, the French zone consisted of South Baden, South Württemberg-Hohenzollern, and Rhineland-Palatinate; elections in May 1947 showed a C.D.U. majority in all cases. Meanwhile the Soviet zone was divided into five *Länder* (though this was to prove a transient arrangement). As a net result, Germany became organised in seventeen units which, while still varying from the 11.8 million of North Rhine-Westphalia to the 226,000 of Bremen, were on the whole better balanced than ever before. The vast preponderance of Prussia had been eliminated even before the Control Council in February 1947 passed a law bringing that state's existence formally to an end. The responsibilities assigned to the *Länder* governments and subordinate authorities by the British and Americans were later to form broadly speaking the basis for the division of powers between federal and *Land* governments under the Federal Republic.

By the time that *Länder* governments had been elected, however, a considerable change had come over the whole administrative structure of Western Germany. For the problem of repriming the German economic pump could not be indefinitely deferred, yet could not be solved within the boundaries of a single zone. Apart from the difficulty of treating as a separate unit something never designed for that purpose, the Americans, who alone were in a position to provide the wherewithal, were only prepared to risk their money in a unit which had a prospect of proving viable. The British, themselves dependent on American support, could not for much longer afford to go on spending £80 million a year in support of an area with a population half their own total. Consequently in July 1946 the American Secretary of State, James F. Byrnes, offered to merge the United States zone in economic matters with that of any other Power willing to join, and before the end of the month the British had accepted. The Russians and French tried to make conditions and found themselves left out in the cold. A complicated organisation was set up to run the merged zones, with six boards in four different places, each supervised by a Committee of Ministers from the eight *Länder*. In addition a Joint (U.S.-U.K.) Export-Import Agency was established and provided with a fund of $121 m. The proceeds of German exports (which in 1947 amounted to $225 m.) were used in the first place to pay for imports of essential raw materials; until this account showed a surplus, the occupying Powers not only

1. About the year 1300 this figure was placed in the porch of Freiburg Münster to symbolise the temptations of the world. A major theme of this book is the attitudes of the German people to those temptations.

2. The Rider of Bamberg, 1235.
(For notes, see p. 321)

The Western and Eastern Faces of Germany.

3(a) Cologne Cathedral (begun 1248) in 1854
3(b) The Castle of the Master of the Teutonic Knights at Marienburg, 1280.

(For notes on both pictures, see p. 321)

4. The Knight, Death and the Devil: Albrecht Dürer, 1513.
(For notes, see p. 321)

5. The temptation of St Antony: Mathis Grünewald, 1515.
(For notes, see p. 322)

6. The Great Elector: Andreas Schlüter, 1696–1709.
(For notes, see p. 322)

7. The Rathaus, Landsberg-am-Lech: Domenicus Zimmermann,
1720. It was while in prison at Landsberg after the Munich rising
of 1923 that Hitler wrote *Mein Kampf*.

8. Maria Immaculata: Josef Anton Feuchtmayr, *c.* 1760.
(For notes, see p. 322)

Two nineteenth-century artists recreate Germany's past.

9(a) Hermann's Tomb: Caspar David Friedrich, 1813.
9(b) Frederick the Great's Flute Concert: Adolf Menzel, 1852.

(For notes on both pictures, see p. 322)

The Kaiser William I Memorial Church, (West) Berlin.

10(a) As built by Schwachten, 1891–5.

10(b) As restored after war damage 1959–61.

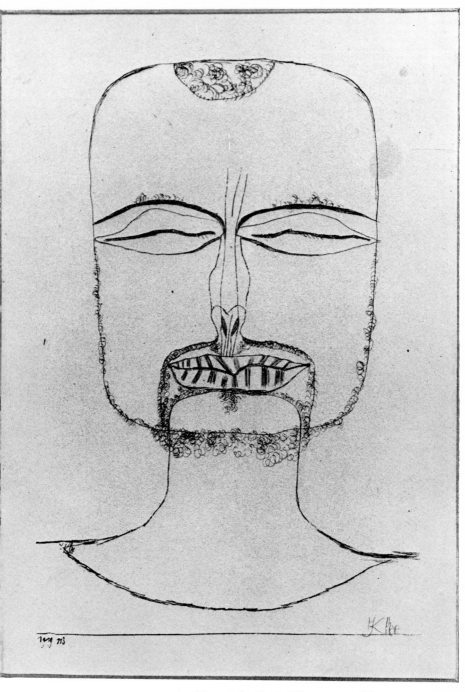

11. Self-portrait 'Lost in Thought': Paul Klee, 1919. Klee was born and died in Berne but lived in Germany from 1906 to 1933.

12. Students' Hostel at the Bauhaus, Dessau: Walter Gropius, 1926. A building which has been copied all over the world.

13. The Flame: Ernst Barlach, 1934.

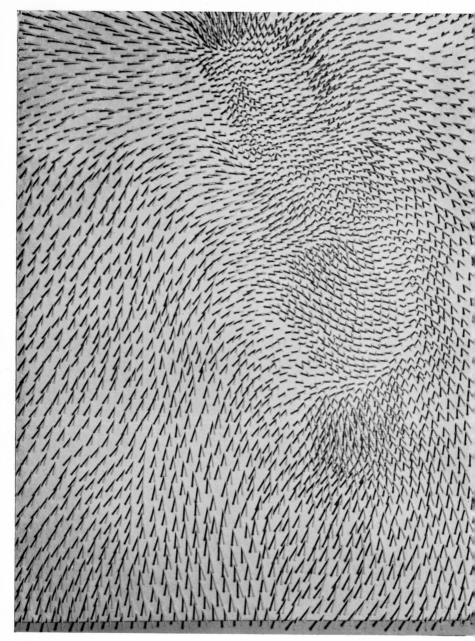

14. Organised structure: Günther Uecker, 1963. The pattern is made by nails driven into a white board and illuminated.

15.   The Philharmonia Concert Hall, West Berlin: Hans Scharoun, 1960–63.

16. The Rhine at the Lorelei Rock.

Between Koblenz and Bingen the Rhine, which the poet Arndt (1769–1860) said should be 'Germany's stream, not Germany's frontier', flows through a deep gorge. At its narrowest and fastest, it turns a sharp corner, where the number of accidents gave rise to the legend of a beautiful girl who sat on top of the 'lure-rock' (*Lore-lei*) and distracted the attention of pilots with fatal results. The story was developed by the romantic poet, Clemens von Brentano (1778–1842) and then made the subject of a poem by Heinrich Heine (1797–1856). Set to a traditional melody, this has become well-known and made the spot a godsend for tourist agencies.

In 1840, when there was a scare of a French attack, the poet Schneckenburger wrote a rousing song with the refrain

> 'The Fatherland can trust the line
> Of sentries watching on the Rhine'
> (Lieb Vaterland! Magst ruhig sein,
> Fest steht und treu die Wacht am Rhein!)

The difficulties of navigation do not prevent the Rhine (not to mention the railway and road on each bank) from being one of the world's busiest channels of communication.

made up the deficit but bore the entire costs of the foodstuffs and other imports needed to prevent 'disease and unrest'. A Joint Procurement Committee in Washington made sure that the needed goods were there to be bought. As Byrnes said in a speech at Stuttgart on 6 September, 'Germany must be given a chance to export goods in order to import enough to make her economy self-sustaining. Germany is part of Europe and recovery in Europe, and particularly in the states adjoining Germany, will be slow indeed if Germany with her great resources of iron and coal is turned into a poorhouse.'

German recovery = European recovery

It had been fundamental to Morgenthau's arguments that Germany was *not* necessary to Europe, and to Russian arguments that reparations must have priority over the German standard of living. The Byrnes speech was a landmark because it explicitly rejected both points of view, clarifying the ambiguities of the Potsdam wording in a sense that the Russians were unlikely to accept. And whereas hitherto an early American withdrawal from Europe had been taken for granted, Byrnes announced his country's intention to remain as long as the occupation lasted. Thanks to their insistence on taking reparations from current production, the Russians found themselves denied any influence over developments in West Germany while if the American policy succeeded, the prospects of German Communists gaining control there would vanish away. But through Soviet spectacles this change was seen as the result of international capitalism rehabilitating the economic system which had produced Fascism and recreating the danger of a German onslaught on the Communist world. A feeling of betrayal and alarm combined with an awareness of weakness to make them hold more firmly than ever on to what they had and refuse concessions. A meeting of the Foreign Ministers in Moscow in March 1947 coincided with the announcement of the 'Truman Doctrine' by which America pledged her active support to all free peoples resisting subjugation by armed minorities or outside aggression. Molotov combined a renewed bid for $10 milliard reparations with a demand that the fusion of the zones be cancelled. As he offered little in return, his attitude convinced the new Secretary of State, General Marshall, that the Russians were stalling in the hope of time being on their side and all Western Europe soon going Communist.

Russia and views on Germany

The attempt to carry over into peace the wartime alliance with Russia had cost a year's delay in the reconstruction of Europe between the dissolution of Supreme Allied Headquarters on 11 July 1945 and the fusion offer exactly 365 days later. The effects of this delay became painfully prominent when the winter of 1946-7 proved exceptionally cold. The waterways which play so large a part in German transport froze over; the roads and railways were still in too precarious a state to carry the displaced traffic. Supplies had for long been so short that everything was distributed as soon as it arrived; when it failed to arrive there were no stocks to fall back on. Rations could not be honoured, power stations ran out of coal, factories closed. But the crisis was not peculiar to Germany. All over Western Europe countries were running out not merely of supplies but of the foreign exchange needed to buy them. In France, the Low Countries and Italy production, which by a great effort had been brought within sight of pre-war levels, stopped expanding. In August 1947 the British attempt to make the pound convertible had to be cancelled after most of the laboriously negotiated U.S. loan had been paid out in thirty-six days. In August, the French government suspended all dollar imports except coal, cereals and other essentials : in September the Italian government stopped purchases even of coal and oil.

Such was the background against which General Marshall made on 5 June 1947 his speech at Harvard announcing that if the countries of Europe could agree on a combined plan for recovery, the American government would finance it. The task of reconstruction had proved much bigger than anyone had foreseen; now at last there was a prospect of it being tackled on an adequate scale. Bevin for Britain grasped at the offer, and Bidault for France followed suit. But at a conference in Paris at the end of the month and after frantic consultations with Ulbricht and Grotewohl, Molotov insisted that the money must be given to individual countries to dispose of as they thought fit. To this the Americans were not prepared to agree and it was clear that, to win their agreement, any joint scheme must be aimed at the restoration of free trading conditions incompatible with the operation of a centrally-controlled economy. The Russians accordingly walked out of the discussions and compelled other East European countries to do the same. Sixteen Western countries then proceeded to draft a four-year programme which was accepted by Congress during the winter and began to operate in mid-1948. In this programme the provision of aid to Western Germany formed an integral part, whereas Eastern Germany was excluded by the Russian reaction.

But before Western Germany could be set fully on the path of recovery, two further steps were needed and for neither was

Russian agreement likely to be forthcoming. First of all the totally artificial position of currency in Germany had to be altered. As has been seen[1] the German government's policy during the war had put a greatly increased amount of currency in circulation but had by price and wage regulations barred most of the ways in which it would naturally have got spent. The occupation authorities continued the price and wage controls but could do little to reduce the volume of currency beyond imposing drastic nominal taxation when what was wanted were incentives. Money ceased to be of any importance and the legal channels of trade were less and less used; goods were exchanged either in barter or at exorbitant sums on the black market. Cigarettes in particular proved a form of payment which was both convenient and utilitarian. Evasion of the regulations became respectable, while bribery and other demoralising practices flourished. The widespread realisation that a reform must come increased the reluctance to hold currency and too much of what was manufactured got hidden away until the reform had been announced. The volume of money available had to be brought more in line with the volume of goods available, either by raising the prices of the goods or by reducing the value of the money. But the Russians insisted on being issued with some of the plates for the new notes and left to do their own printing; in view of what had happened with the occupation currency, the other Allies would not agree. The introduction of the reform was virtually impracticable without a central bank of issue and there was little prospect of such a bank being able to function on a quadripartite basis when one of the participants held economic views diametrically opposed to those of the others. Moreover, Communist and capitalist ideas of who should be the main sufferers in any monetary reform were widely at variance. Discussions of the subject in the Control Council got nowhere. An ugly choice grew inevitable between jeopardising the success of the other recovery measures and deepening the breach between the two halves of Germany.

Though there could only be one answer to this question, the giving of it was eased by developments in another direction. For some time, and particularly since the 'Great Freeze' of 1947, it had been growing apparent that, if the Germans were to make anything of their country, they must be allowed more say in its control. They had recovered much of their interest in life since the low point of 1945 and lost much of their respect for their masters, to whose misjudgements, rather than to the hard logic of the

[1] See above, p. 140.

world situation, they attributed the fact that conditions seemed
to be getting worse instead of better. But political responsibility
meant setting up a central government and when the Council
of Foreign Ministers met again in London in December 1947 it
became clearer than ever that the minimum Russian price for
such a step would be a free hand over reparations and the can-
cellations of the measures so far taken in the West. After the
Council had adjourned indefinitely, the Americans and the British
decided to shut another of the doors hitherto left open and give to
the economic machinery of 'Bizonia' the political character which
they had so far carefully withheld from it. The French had been
led by their opposition to a central German government to turn
down the fusion offer in 1946 but they were induced to think
again by the prospect that their zone, if it remained on its own,
would not get any Marshall Aid. They accordingly agreed to
attend a London conference in the spring of 1948 and there somewhat reluctantly consented to merge their zone with the other
two, bring West Germany as a whole into the Organisation for
European Cooperation (O.E.E.C., the body set up to run the Marshall Plan) and allow the West Germans to start drafting a constitution. The Russians were not long in replying. On 10 March
1948 the coalition government in Prague was replaced by a
purely Communist one. Ten days later Marshal Sokolovsky walked
out of the Control Council in Berlin and from 1 April increasing
restrictions began to be placed on personal travel between West
and East Germany. The episode of four-power control was in
effect at an end, although its formal winding up was to take a
further fourteen months.

Many mistakes were undeniably made by the Western Powers
during the occupation of Germany, since the period was one in
which the world situation made satisfactory solutions of communal problems even more difficult to attain than usual. The
positive achievements of the episode are too often lost to sight.
Amid conditions which could easily have given rise to civil war
or epidemic disease, both were avoided, and when all the world
was hungry, the number of Germans whose deaths could be
directly attributed to starvation was insignificant (though weakness due to lack of food certainly increased the susceptibility to
other diseases). This result was not due to luck but to hard work
and generosity. The Americans had given $11,300 m. to Europe
before the Marshall Plan so much as came into operation, while
U.S. relief agencies spent $29 m. from private sources between
1946 and 1948. Owing to the need to divert food to Europe,

rations were shorter in Britain in 1947 than at any time during the war. The Germans were wont to say that the demand for total surrender carried with it the assumption of total responsibility. The principle is open to argument but it is one on which the Anglo-American record can stand up to examination.

But what of the attempt to change Germany and provide the world with some guarantee against renewed aggression? Did this not rest on the highly improbable assumption that conquerors with such very different views on politics and society would be able to prolong into peace the cooperation forced on them by the needs of war and agree on how to coerce the Germans instead of competing for them? And even assuming that East and West had agreed on what will to impose, is not the very attempt to impose outlooks and change minds misconceived? Not only does the overt attempt provoke a natural resistance. Ideas and institutions are so clearly interconnected and so largely influenced by the total character of a culture as to make isolated changes inadequate and wholesale ones impracticable. Transplantation of practices evolved in other surroundings seldom prove satisfactory and often produce quite unexpected results. It is tempting to condemn as a waste of effort the whole policy misleadingly labelled 're-education' (and thereby prejudiced at the outset) and to condemn along with it the entire process of 'denazification'.

Any such judgement would, however, be unhistorical and excessive. Unhistorical because it is absurd to suppose that after a war such as that of 1939-45, when success had been won after immense effort and sacrifices, the victor peoples would have given power to leaders who said 'There is nothing we can do to prevent this from happening again'. To have argued in the middle of the war that Nazism, or at any rate German nationalism, could not be 'rooted out' would have played straight into the hands of those demanding a vindictive peace. The idea of helping Germany to change itself deserves to be judged as an attempt at providing a constructive alternative to a purely penal solution. Moreover, once it had been decided to insist on 'unconditional surrender', the Allies were almost bound to march into Germany and, once there, were almost bound to stay until the elements of order were restored since the Germans were clearly without the means needed to do this for themselves.[1] This inevitably made the views of the

---

[1] Even if unconditional surrender had not been demanded, the Nazi downfall might have led to civil war inside Germany which in turn might have led to Allied troops entering the country.

Allies influential, even decisive, in settling what was to replace the self-liquidated Third Reich.

If ever a country was crying out for a clean slate and a fresh start, it was Germany in 1945. One does not have to be a sociologist to realise that no slate can ever be completely clean and no start completely fresh. But at least the Germans were forced to reconsider all their ideas and all their institutions, something which certainly cannot be said of 1919. Of course any attempt to force anything on anyone can be counter-productive, but this possibility was not altogether unfamiliar to those who were in Germany with the occupation forces. In the process of that occupation, many changes *were* made and many new ideas rendered familiar—more than would have been likely to do so if the Germans had been left to themselves. Just as in the economic field Western officers were busy re-establishing old connections and inaugurating new ones, so in the realm of the mind those responsible for 're-education' saw their task as being to repair the links with Western culture which the Nazis had done their best to destroy and make it easy for Germans to discover fresh ways of thought and action. By no means all the changes endured, by no means all the ideas won acceptance. But at the best an effort was made to forestall a defensive reaction by relying on reasoning and collaboration rather than compulsion.

Certainly people's minds cannot be changed to order and the possibility of leading the Germans to a new view of the world depended for any chance of success on securing the cooperation of Germans who could not be tarred with the brush of collaboration. But there were many Germans who rejoiced in the opportunity of access to new ideas. There were also many who were as worried as their enemies by the excesses of their nation and who, without necessarily accepting the outsider's diagnosis, were concerned to find a remedy. A good deal was done to help such people into positions of influence : to do more might perhaps have been counter-productive. Not all those to whom responsibility was given were successful but many have been. It is too early to pass judgement on the degree to which their influence will prove enduring and effective. But what changes the character of societies must after all be the example of individuals.

The reverse process of trying to drive out of public life all who had participated 'except nominally' in the fallen régime may have been carried too far and conducted too slowly. But to conclude that nothing of the sort should ever have been attempted is again unhistorical and runs counter to the general interest. To suppose that at the end of the war which was proclaimed to be directed 'against the evil things', a war which ended by the uncovering of the concentration camps, public opinion would have allowed bygones to be bygones is to ignore human nature. To claim that war justifies any kind of conduct no matter how criminal is to canonise human fallibility; as with British bombing, to understand is not necessarily to endorse. Among the people who would have been most critical if the Allies had stooped to anything of the kind were the very Germans whose opinions were most important for the future.

If more imagination had been used in working out the practical implications of pledges indignantly made during the war, the scale of the operation would have been reduced; the Nazi Party had numbered some 8 million members with another 4 million in associated organisations and to drive out of public life a fifth of the population is not a practicable proposition. There would have been great advantage in a procedure which gave those moderately compromised without being accused of inhumanities a chance to work their passage back by payment in money, kind or labour to a fund for reconstruction and compensation rather than detention. But a major difficulty was the need for the Allies to be seen to be acting justly, since this called for the collection of evidence and the application of judicial principles, all of which takes time. Until each individual had been tried, a procedure which sacrified justice to simplicity and speed threatened to allow too many of the guilty to get off too lightly. But as this happened in any case, there would have been much to be said for any solution which enabled Germans to work off the feeling of shame (and often of guilt) which many felt even when inhibited by patriotic feeling from openly admitting it.[1]

At the start of the occupation, many people were to be heard saying that, to be effective, it would need to continue for twenty or even fifty years, and indeed, for force to give ideas time to take root, it may have to go on being exerted over a period of that length. From this standpoint the experiment was condemned to futility before it was fully under way as a result of the need to secure

[1] One misconception which seems well on the way to becoming accepted as established fact is that the Allies regarded the German people as collectively guilty for the war and the Nazi crimes. To the best of the author's knowledge, no such charge was ever formulated by any responsible Allied statesman, though less responsible subordinates may on occasion have talked more wildly. What was said was that the German people were collectively responsible in the sense that a people cannot escape the consequences of deeds done in their name by a government which they did not prevent from coming to power. But responsibility does not imply moral stigma.

German cooperation against the Russians. But even supposing that the Russians had not become a menace, the Control Commission could not have gone on governing Germany for much longer than it did. There are narrow limits to the possibility of ruling a developed industrial country as though it were a colony, especially in an epoch when colonies all over the world were demanding and being granted the right to self-determination. Once the Germans had recovered the will to control their own destinies, the only alternative to letting them do so would have been a descent into repression, sabotage and mutual recrimination. Indeed the only reason why such a descent did not take place in the west may have been the stimulus to cooperation which both rulers and ruled found in the Russians. The occupation was bound to be an interlude and might have been better used if this had been recognised from the outset.

Above all, the interval of external control afforded the Germans time to sort themselves out. The Weimar Republic had been handicapped from its birth by the conditions under which it had to start work. A new German régime after 1945 could not wholly avoid the association with failure which has been one of the chronic handicaps of democracy in Germany. But by postponing the assumption of responsibility for three or four years, the chances of fairly soon achieving a reasonably creditable record were enormously increased. The cards were stacked so heavily against the occupation being satisfactory that the new German government did not have to be very successful in order to seem an improvement on its predecessor!

Chapter 7

Crisis and Miracle 1948–9

Currency Reform and its Consequences

THE WITHDRAWAL of the Russians from quadripartite discussions and the decision of the French to conform removed the obstacles to a reform of the currency. On 20 June 1948, according to a plan decided on by the Allies with German advice, the old Reichsmark was made valueless in the three Western zones and replaced by the Deutsche Mark. Everyone was immediately allowed to exchange 40 of the old Marks for 40 of the new ones but to get any more had to produce old currency or bank deposits. The original intention had been to change these at a rate of 10 : 1, but experience showed that this would not reduce the volume of money sufficiently, and the rate was therefore reduced to 100 : 6.5. All debts, however, were paid off at the 10 to 1 rate so that creditors came out well. Existing securities of the governments, municipalities and public corporations in corporate hands were replaced on a much smaller scale by new government obligations with the object of bringing the assets of the banks nearer to their (greatly diminished) liabilities. Practical effect was thus given to the national bankruptcy in which the Third Reich had involved Germany. Banks were also given new, but scaled down, reserves in the form of deposits with a new central bank of issue, the *Bank Deutscher Länder* (which in 1957 became the *Bundesbank*). The note circulation was fixed at DM 10 billion, a figure which the occupation authorities pledged themselves to observe in order to give the population faith in the new currency. The degree of devaluation gave Germany a level of costs which was relatively low by comparison with other similar economies and therefore favoured German exports.

As in 1923 the reform bore hardly on those who held their savings in money rather than in goods, though to some extent this was made up for by the relatively light taxation with which they had been let off during the war. The original intention had been to make a 'levelling of burdens' (*Lastenausgleich*) an integral part of the reform so that those who came off best would be forced to help those less fortunate. But the Americans insisted that the devising of such a readjustment must be left to the Germans, and four years of argument were needed before a final measure could be agreed on. But whatever the social effects may have been, economically the reform came at exactly the right time and, after several nervous moments, proved highly successful. A sufficient volume of goods was beginning to emerge from the factories for there to be something to buy and the capacity to produce more was available. The initial issue of the new currency was small enough to leave everyone short of money and therefore reversed the previous situation by making cash more sought after than stocks. Goods which had been hoarded were unloaded, the shops filled up and the black market disappeared overnight. For some time past the German people had been ready to exert their habitual industry but had lacked any incentive to do so : they now set to work with a will. Much of the credit for the amazing change has with considerable justice been given to this response and to the population's readiness to trust the new currency. Less spectacular was the part played over the preceding months by the Allies in building supply lines and providing many of the supplies out of their own pockets. It was, however, equally essential to the result and deserves not to be forgotten. As so often in looking back on a joint operation, each partner tends to give prominence to its own contribution.

The Western Allies had not intended to extend the Currency Reform to their sectors of Berlin and on 18 June wrote to the Russians expressing the hope that a single currency could be agreed for Germany as a whole. Their only condition was that it must be handled as a completely quadripartite measure. But the Russians, who had just dealt another blow to cooperation by walking out of the quadripartite *Kommandatura* governing the city, turned the offer down. Marshal Sokolovsky announced that banknotes issued in the Western occupation zones of Germany would not be allowed to circulate in the Soviet occupation zone nor in Berlin which, in contradiction to the 1944 agreements, he described as being 'part of the Soviet occupation zone'. The Western move obviously caught the Russians unprepared since they had no new currency notes ready. But, although money is less vital to a controlled economy than to a free one, and although measures against private enterprise in earlier years had done much to reduce the volume of money circulating in their zone, they clearly could not tolerate for long a situation in which a unit was worth ten times as much on the East side of the zonal boundary as it was on the West side. Consequently they improvised on 22 June a somewhat less drastic measure of their own, sticking stamps on the old notes to show the new values. These they sought to make valid throughout Berlin. But the Western authorities feared that if the currency in their sectors was to be the same as the East yet different from the West, the trend of trade would soon be the same direction. Accordingly, on 25 June they declared that both East and West Marks would be valid in West Berlin. The ratio between the two established itself in free exchange as 1 to 2 but quickly altered to 1 to 4.

There were cogent reasons why a reform of the currency could not be postponed much longer but its introduction on a tripartite basis provided the Russians with too good an opportunity for them to let pass. Declaring that the Western action was illegal, the Soviet authorities on 24 June extended to freight movements between Berlin and Western zones the restrictions which had already been applied to movements of people.[1] They reckoned correctly that this step caught the West at its most vulnerable point. As has been seen[2] the circumstances of the American and British entry into Berlin had left them without any written definition or even confirmation of their rights of access. This precarious position had been aggravated by the acceptance in July 1945 of the Russian demand that the supplies of food and coal for the Western sectors must come from the Western zones (though it is arguable that the Russians would in the long run have been in a stronger position if they had made the Western sectors rely on the East for both supplies and markets). Although the possibility of an interruption to communications had been at intervals the subject of speculation in Berlin, no attempt at planning for the contingency had been thought worth while; stocks were limited and in some public services such as electricity the Western sectors still depended on the Eastern. The Russians therefore had some justification for thinking that they had the Western Allies in a corner, facing a choice between three courses, all unpleasant. Russian superiority in conventional forces was overwhelming so that any attempt at pushing columns through by road involved the risk of defeat and a Soviet advance to the Rhine which could only be countered by the tremendous sanction of the atom bomb—and there were at that time no bombs outside America and no direct means of striking at Russia from America. Otherwise the only alternative

[1] See p. 164.
[2] See p. 144.

to the second course—a humiliating withdrawal from Berlin—
appeared to be acceptance of Russian terms; the chief of these
would involve the halting of the steps already in train to give back
self-government to West Germany. For there can be no doubt that
what most of all worried the Russians was the prospect of the re-
emergence of a Germany which would be strong, dissatisfied and
anti-Russian.

There were, however, three routes into Berlin which were
authorised by a quadripartite document and to close which was
impracticable unless the Russians took the initiative in using force.
These were the three air corridors from Hamburg, Bückeburg and
Frankfurt. Nobody imagined that a city of $2\frac{1}{4}$ million people
could be kept supplied for long by air but no other expedient was
available and even if surrender to the Russians could be postponed for only a few weeks, the delay might give time for working
out some sort of settlement. But the Russians imagined that they
held winning cards and in negotiations during the early autumn
showed themselves intransigent. By then the 'Air Lift' was getting
under way and functioning well enough to suggest that, provided
enough planes could be made available, it would afford the
Western Powers a means of escape from the corner in which they
had found themselves. The question was whether the necessary
rate of one plane every two minutes could be kept going
throughout the winter.

The credit for answering that question successfully belongs not
only to Western technology and its practitioners but also to the
population of West Berlin, under their mayor, Ernst Reuter, who
showed themselves ready to bear considerable privations, notably
in the lack of heating, light and work, so as to avoid falling under
Communist rule. Fortunately the weather was relatively mild;
had it been such as to make flying impossible for many days on
end, things might have become desperate. In three ways also the
Russians refrained from pushing their advantages home. After one
of their fighters had caused the crash of a British airliner, they
did not persevere in harassing Western planes, whereas by slowing
down the timetable they could have materially reduced the amount
supplied. They never withdrew their representative in the quadripartite Air Control centre regulating traffic to and from the city.
And although one of the radio beacons used in guiding aircraft
was situated in the Russian sector, it was allowed to go on functioning unimpaired. What may well have prompted this caution was the
knowledge that, though they had atom bombs in the making,

the explosion of the first one would not take place till three or four months after the blockade ended.

For once the winter was over and the decision not to press matters to extremities had been taken, the Russians stood to gain nothing but unpopularity by continuing the blockade. Moreover, a counter-blockade instituted by the West on the movement of goods to the Soviet zone was starting to pinch. Feelers were secretly put out through the Russian representative at the United Nations, and on 4 May 1949 the world learnt with some surprise that the blockade was to be lifted. Eleven days later the four Foreign Ministers met in Paris to find a permanent settlement for Berlin, but after arguing without result for nearly a month, decided to leave the future legal position of the city as ill-defined as it had been before the blockade began.

Certain vital changes had, however, taken place, some of which were irrevocable. In August and September 1948 the Communists organised spontaneous demonstrations in front of Berlin's town hall in the Soviet sector, and councillors from the Western sectors were thereby prevented from reaching meetings; when a meeting did finally take place, it was invaded by the crowd and forced to stop. As the police for the area refused to intervene, the majority of the Council decided to transfer meetings to the British sector. In accordance with the constitution (which had received quadripartite blessing), they called new elections for December. In the Western sectors, where the S.E.D. was forbidden by their own leaders to take part, these resulted in almost a two-thirds majority for the S.P.D. In East Berlin, however, the Communists declared the old mayor and standing committee deposed, replaced them with their own people and saw to it that the elections resulted in a S.E.D. victory. The divided city thus obtained two governments, neither of which recognised the other.

But the consequences of the blockade were not confined to Berlin. In July 1948 the Labour government agreed to make British airfields available for squadrons of American B29 bombers, along with the atomic bombs which these machines carried. The West thereby acquired the capacity to deliver nuclear weapons behind the Iron Curtain. By November, ninety such aircraft were stationed in Britain, and after the blockade ended, they were not withdrawn. For the Russian policy had led the West to take a fresh look at its arrangements for mutual defence, with the result that a Canadian suggestion made in April 1948 was a year later realised and the North Atlantic Treaty Organisation created. By the N.A.T.O. Treaty the American government, with the approval of Congress, joined the alliance which Britain, France and Benelux had concluded in the previous year. The Truman Doctrine of the previous year was expanded into the first U.S. commitment ever made in peacetime for taking military action in the event of an attack on any part of Western Europe; the size of American resources, and the immense superiority in nuclear ones, meant that their accession transformed the alliance, even although it may only have formalised a situation which already existed in practice. The Russians could no longer have any excuse for not realising that Western Europe was under the American nuclear shield. Germany, it is true, was still outside the alliance but the feeling of common fate which had been engendered during the blockade between the people of Western Germany and their nominal masters created a psychological situation which was bound before long to be given formal expression. The Russians had achieved the opposite of their intentions and had brought into being a bloc which was once described, with a backward look at the war, as 'The Allies and their Associated Enemies'.

Economic Reform

On the Sunday on which the Currency Reform was introduced, the German Director of the Economic Administrative Office for Bizonia went to the microphone and promised to the German people the removal of all but a bare minimum of the multifarious controls existing on prices, wages and supplies. The name of the man responsible for this step was Ludwig Erhard. He was not being quite as rash as might appear, for the sectors kept under control involved such things as bread, milk, meat, electricity, coal and steel which influenced much of the rest of the economy, while wage control was retained until the autumn. But to cut in this manner through the whole complex of restrictions which the occupying Powers had inherited from the Nazis was enough to unnerve many of the Control authorities, and great strength of mind was needed to push the change through. But the Americans had a soft spot for anyone who, not content with arguing in favour of free enterprise, was actually prepared to practise it, while the idea commended itself to the Germans because it would reduce the opportunities for Allied interference.

In the second half of 1948 industrial production rose by 50 per cent and in the following year, by a further 25 per cent. By 1953 average living standards were higher than in 1938, while in the fourteen years following 1950 the gross national product trebled.

In 1958 Germany passed Britain to become the world's second largest exporter and by 1961 was the third largest industrial producer. What is perhaps more surprising is that Germany's net balance of foreign trade on current account showed from 1951 to 1964 an uninterrupted surplus, occasionally of high proportions. No wonder that people talked about an 'economic miracle' and that the prestige of Dr Erhard rose to great heights. In reality, however, the phenomenon was due to the happy coincidence of a large number of factors, not all of them likely to last. In the euphoria of the moment, this fact tended to be overlooked and the assumption was too easily made that, because the policy of a 'Free Market Economy' had proved brilliantly successful in a particular situation, it would continue to bring equally good results indefinitely. For this reason an analysis of the main features in the West German economy of 1948 is important for an understanding of subsequent developments and particularly those since 1962.

(a) Reference has already been made to the part played by American and British aid in the reconstruction of West Germany. But what should not be forgotten is that the European Recovery programme (to give 'Marshall Aid' its official title) came into full operation within a month of the Currency Reform and that in the course of the next four crucial years Germany was the fourth largest beneficiary, receiving in all $1·389 m. (about a tenth of the total). Without these dollars to draw on for vital purchases, the German balance of payments over the period 1948–51 would have caused even more anxiety than it did. Moreover, Marshall Aid meant that Germany was recovering in the middle of a continent doing the same; each stimulated the other.

(b) German industrial equipment was, as mentioned, less seriously affected by the war and the reparations programme than might be supposed, while both processes literally cleared the ground for re-equipment, often with the help of a government subsidy which in other circumstances would have been considered illicit. Some firms which might not otherwise have modernised their plant and products were thus forced to do so.

(c) The loss of the lands beyond the Oder-Neisse as a source of food supply has often been considered a great disadvantage for Germany. But in fact these areas were relatively uneconomic producers by comparison with extra-European sources, and had only been saved from drastic readjustment by tariffs. As soon as Germany could find the exports with which to pay for substitute imports of food, she stood to gain by the switch.

(*d*) In the years following 1945 many people had been unable to see how Western Germany could ever support the vast addition to her population caused by the inflow of refugees from the East. And indeed, as soon as many nominal jobs were made uneconomic by the Currency Reform, unemployment rose to 2 million and did not fall below half a million till 1955, while the provision of housing for the newcomers (coming on top of the need to replace the destroyed and damaged houses of the pre-war population) did prove a major burden on the economy. On the other hand the presence of a plentiful supply of labour (and one which was being continually replenished) removed what was to prove one of the chief hindrances to growth in other, more stable countries. Moreover, the additional labour, having left its roots behind, could easily be moved to where it was needed (though in practice many new firms established themselves in country districts where refugees happened to have congregated).

(*e*) Germany is often considered to have gained because her economy was not burdened until the mid-fifties by any defence expenditure of her own but only by the costs of her occupiers (which were fixed until 1952 without reference to her). These did not include any expenditure falling outside the country but for some time they took up a proportion of her resources comparable to the defence outlays of many other countries; in 1950 they amounted to 37·5 per cent of her budget and 4·6 per cent of her g.n.p., while in 1951 the figures rose to 42·6 per cent and 6·4 per cent respectively. It was only after the expansion of the economy got under way that they fell, to 27 per cent and 3·5 per cent in 1953. This burden was, however, counterbalanced by the considerable amount of military expenditure made directly or indirectly in Germany by foreign governments which was *not* charged to the occupation costs. Between 1955 and 1964 Germany's cumulative net balance on government invisibles (mostly military) was favourable to the extent of £2,600 m.[1]

(*f*) The German people as a whole are industrious and methodical by tradition and training. Their standard of education has long been high so that they make an admirable labour force for an industrial country. Supplies of skilled management talent were ample, not least from highly trained General Staff officers forced to seek fresh jobs as the result of disarmament.

(*g*) Patriotism, extensive unemployment, lack of funds (as a result of Currency Reform) and the fact that in Germany their

[1] A. Maddison, *How Fast can Britain Grow?* Lloyds Bank Review, January 1966, p. 9.

membership had never been anything like complete all combined to keep the trade unions from making exorbitant demands. Union structure had been reorganised after the war (partly at British prompting) in such a way as to reduce inter-union rivalry and demarcation disputes, while German labour has never been able to establish the principle of the closed shop. The British had in 1947 given the workers a considerable say in the management of the coal and steel industries ('Co-determination'); the extension of this principle to the rest of industry was under discussion and might have been prejudiced if the unions had made themselves awkward. For all these reasons, demands for wage increases remained moderate, while production was not disrupted by strikes. The failure of a 24-hour general strike in November 1948 reinforced this trend which was one of the most important elements in the whole situation.

(h) Nearly everyone in Germany had suffered some material loss or had come down in the world. Consequently almost everybody was prepared to work hard and anxious to make money in order to rebuild his capital and provide himself with fresh security. German society, like Germany itself, was starting again from zero and could use all its resources to build up instead of facing the British problem of how to make greatly reduced resources stretch to maintain an established position. Sacred cows were comparatively rare and vested interests on the defensive.

(i) Thanks to the restraint of the unions, wages remained at a relatively low level and salaries did the same, amounting (1950–60) to only 47 per cent of the g.n.p. as compared with 58 per cent in Britain. Although both showed a steady rise over the years, the rates were for long slower than the growth in output. Thanks to the general desire to rebuild personal positions, the propensity to consume was the lowest in Western Europe. The rate of saving was high while the profits of firms were ploughed back in fresh investment instead of being distributed in wages and dividends. Private consumption only accounted for 59 per cent of the g.n.p. as against 65 per cent in Britain (1950–60). The demand for consumer goods, being limited, could largely be met by home production, and by the hoarded stocks which Currency Reform brought on to the market. Imports of such things remained relatively restricted.

(j) The government exempted overtime from tax and gave considerable premiums to savers. Taxes on the higher income brackets were relatively unprogressive. Considerable inequalities in income were thus tolerated and even encouraged, while the ability of the successful to save was increased.

(*k*) As will be seen in the next chapters, the new political system quickly established itself on a firm basis and the growing prosperity combined with the relative stability of prices to create confidence in the future in spite of the Communist threat on the very boundary of the country. The general mood was such as to encourage investment.

(*l*) Thanks to all the factors mentioned, the rate of investment was high. Gross domestic capital formation rose between 1950 and 1960 by 157 per cent in real terms, as compared with 46 per cent in Britain. Total fixed investment at home during the same period absorbed 21.9 per cent of the gross national product, as compared with a British figure of 16.6 per cent. Counterpart funds under Marshall Aid were used for investment to remove particular bottlenecks identified as holding back expansion.[1] But as saving was also high, this rate of investment did not lead to serious inflation or price rises.

(*m*) A frequent result of high investment is an increase of demand for imports so that the national trade figures are thrown into deficit, as Britain knows to her cost. Why did this not happen in Germany? One answer is that in the early years it did. Until March 1951 Germany was in serious deficit, especially in the European Payments Union where she exhausted her credit quota by December 1950 and had to be granted a further $120 m. of which she used three-quarters in the next two months. The situation was aggravated by the rapid rise in world prices resulting from the Korean war and the action of German importers in buying unusually large quantities immediately in order to avoid having to pay higher prices later. It was also aggravated by the cuts in import quotas ('liberalisation') which all the members of the Organisation for European Economic Cooperation had agreed to make. The German position led for a time to considerable criticism in O.E.E.C. where it was argued that the Germans were making other people pay their way for them in order to avoid damaging their own interests. Great pressure was put on Erhard to reimpose import quotas and tighten credit. His view was that such measures

---

[1] Under the Marshall Plan, the United States provided dollars with which European governments could buy goods on world markets. The governments passed on the goods to private citizens who, to prevent the import from being deflationary, paid for them in domestic currency. American approval was needed for the uses to which European governments put these 'counterpart funds'. Britain used most of hers for reducing debt, as her productive equipment was already being worked to the limit.

would merely hold back production just as it was getting under way, and invite retaliation against German exports. He also argued that at a time of rising prices it was better to hold goods rather than money. At the end of February 1951 he was driven to suspend liberalisation and tighten credit but just at that moment Germany's balance of payments took a turn for the better. By the end of May she had repaid all her special credit and some of her previous debts. From that time forward she moved steadily into a stronger creditor position and Erhard's reputation soared higher than ever. The explanation seems to have been threefold :

i. The heavy German purchases of raw materials at the start of the Korean boom led to stocks being built up, after which imports could be reduced. Moreover, once the peak of the boom was passed, prices fell as quickly as they had risen so that the bill for subsequent imports was even lower. Germany's buying policy was initially expensive but thereafter paid off.

ii. In spite of the large amount of replacement needed inside Germany, factors already described kept within limits consumer demand and consequently also limited the imports to which such demand gave rise. The extensive efforts made by the Nazis during the 1930s to render Germany self-sufficient had some permanent effect in limiting the need for imports.

iii. The rearmament programme set going throughout the Western world by the Korean war called above all for finished manufactures, and particularly for modern types of machinery. As these were just the types of machinery which Germany's reconstructed industry was well equipped to supply, external demand for German goods soared. Even apart from Korea, the world's need for goods to replace those which would normally have been installed between 1939 and 1945 was still unsatisfied, while the steady liberalisation of trade, the pursuit by governments of inflationary policies of full employment and the requirements of backward countries for development all combined to keep demand for manufactures high.

In an economy such as Germany's in which foreign trade absorbs a relatively high proportion of output, buoyant exports are of particular importance since it is their course which principally gives manufacturers confidence about the long-term prospects of demand. But the view taken about the future course of demand is the chief factor in influencing the readiness of manufacturers to invest and on investment above all depends an economy's rate of growth. With output expanding rapidly, productivity is also likely to rise, thanks to economies of scale and generally improved organisation, thereby reducing costs and increasing still further competitiveness on foreign markets. In addition, the return obtainable on investment is likely to rise, making it more attractive in comparison to other uses of money and hence stimulating it.[1]

The essence of the German 'miracle' was that at a time when world demand was high, German industry found itself with spare capacity, the right products and relatively low costs, so that exporting was easy and profitable and hence popular. Once this export-led expansion got under way, the prospect of making profits attracted investment into export industries whose growing earnings made it easy to pay for all the imports which increasing manufacturing of export involved. The pool of unemployed, continually refilled by migrants from East Germany, for a long time prevented shortage of labour from constricting output. Thanks to the high rate of investment, production grew at a rate which allowed for ample increases in prices and wages without inflation. The exchange rate remained favourable (in spite of being devalued less than most other European currencies in 1949) and the costs of most of Germany's competitors rose faster than hers did, so that she could afford increases without pricing herself out of the market. All in all, she was for a time in the exceptionally fortunate position of finding herself in a 'virtuous' spiral.

(*n*) Neither the old Reichsmark nor the new Deutsche Mark was a reserve currency and Germany was not under any obligation to provide other countries with capital. Indeed the authorities put up interest rates so as to check home demand with the result that, in spite of the big export surplus, capital flowed *into* rather than *out of* the country. Owing to the lack of institutions needed to make foreign investment easy, not to mention the caution engendered by having had her holdings abroad twice confiscated for reparations, Germany was to be slow in burdening her balance of payments with heavy capital movements abroad. Even today her total overseas investments, at DM 8.5 billion, are about one-twentieth the size of Britain's—and her income from them of course proportionately lower. A relatively generous agreement made by her creditors in 1953, before the full extent of her prosperity became evident, enabled her to pay off by moderate instalments the debts inherited from the Weimar Republic and those incurred since 1945.

(*o*) In times of slump, governments are blamed for much that is not their fault; in times of prosperity, the reverse occurs. For this reason the part played by official policy in producing

[1] See W. Beckerman, *The British Economy in 1975,* Chapter II.

Germany's success story has been left to the end so as to emphasise the number of other factors involved. But undoubtedly government actions contributed in many ways to the total result. Some have already been mentioned, such as the provision of subsidies to help replace bombed or dismantled equipment and the exemption of overtime earnings from tax.[1] Between 1950 and 1955 exports were stimulated, in violation of G.A.T.T. rules, by certain taxes being refunded in respect of them. Measures taken to stimulate internal competition may have contributed to improvements in product design. The abolition of import quotas was originally imposed on Germany by O.E.E.C. but in the mid-1950s the government went further and deliberately made unilateral cuts in a number of tariffs with the double object of encouraging exports and depriving inefficient domestic manufacturers of a sheltered life in the home market.

These, however, are not the government actions commonly given credit for the German achievement. Many, particularly in circles where official interference with industry is disliked, have attributed this achievement first and foremost to Erhard's courage in removing controls and giving freedom to private enterprise. There is undoubtedly something in this. Thanks to cartels and other restrictive agreements, as well as to the chronic itch of an authoritarian government to regulate, Germany had never known an economy in which market forces were really allowed free play. And by 1948 the controlled economy had got into a strait-jacket which distorted its natural shape. Initiative was being held back and resources used unprofitably. Their more rational allocation is unlikely ever to have been achieved by central government direction. Nobody knew the direction in which the horse would naturally choose to go and in order to discover the answer, it had for a time to be given its head. This, however, does not prove that it is always a good thing in the contemporary world for horses to be allowed to stray wherever they wish.

The second government policy for which much credit has been claimed is the deflationary policy of the Finance Ministry and *Bank Deutscher Länder* in restricting credit and holding down the monetary supply in a world where a desire for full employment

---

[1] There was for long a widespread belief among British industrialists that the success of their German competitors was due to 'improper' and secret government aid. Not only have extensive enquiries failed to reveal anything beyond the aids mentioned here (and other schemes parallel to those available in Britain such as ECGD). They have shewn that German industry for long believed exactly the same thing about 'secret aid' to British industry!

was producing a steady trend to inflation. Undoubtedly those policies did help to check home demand and encourage exports. A tendency of consumer prices to rise in the early months was also nipped in the bud. But when so many other powerful factors were working in the same direction, a contribution from monetary policy was probably superfluous. During the earlier years, however, the German leaders may well be excused for lacking confidence that non-monetary forces would do the trick; the importance of Germany earning her way in the world was great enough to justify them in wanting to make assurance doubly sure.

Whether they were wise to go on depressing demand for as long as they did is more questionable. Once a country has paid for all the imports it needs, the only virtue in continuing to expand exports lies in the hope of living more easily later or in having reserve resources to draw on if things go wrong. But there is a limit to the extent to which monetary reserves can be built up without causing grave trouble to the other countries from which those reserves are drawn. Hence a country which wishes to be a persistent creditor must in the long run be prepared to become as well a persistent investor abroad. For Germany there were built-in obstacles to such a course. There would therefore seem to have been all the less reason why the West German people should not have been allowed to become prosperous even faster than they did, even at the cost of some inflation. But whereas memories of the 1919–39 period caused British and American policies to be dominated by fear of unemployment, the same and even more recent memories caused German policy to be dominated by fear of the currency losing its value.

Chapter 8

The German Republics are Founded
1948 – 9

The Western Parties Jockey for Position

THE FIRST time that Kurt Schumacher, the Social Democrat, ever encountered Konrad Adenauer, the Christian Democrat, was at a meeting of the German Advisory Council for the British zone in March 1946. The one is believed to have said to the other, 'Every objective observer will admit that the S.P.D. is the largest party with the greatest future and will remain so.' At the time the prognostication was made, most people in Germany (though not Adenauer) would have agreed with it. Yet within four years Adenauer was to enter on a tenure of the Chancellorship lasting fourteen years, whereas Schumacher's party was destined to wait twenty years before taking office and only do so after he himself had been dead for fourteen.

The outstanding reason why expectations were thus falsified is of course the quarrel between the Atlantic Powers and the Soviet Union. This cut the country in two and completed the process by which the north-east and centre of Germany, including nearly all the lands which Prussia had held before 1815, were lost by the West. At the end of 1937, Germany had covered 470,000 square kilometres. One hundred and eighteen thousand square kilometres of this had been taken in 1945 by the Russians and Poles, and 104,000 sq. km. were in the Soviet zone. The area lost was not only predominantly Protestant but under the Weimar Republic had included many Socialist strongholds. Although the remaining 248,000 sq. km. (about the same area as Great Britain and Northern Ireland) still contained more Protestants than Catholics, it was almost bound to find its centre of gravity in the Rhineland and south where Catholicism predominated and social antagonisms were on the whole less keen.

The division of the country was of course not merely geographical but ideological as well, and the increasing imposition of a Communist system in the East produced in the West a reaction to the disadvantage of the left wing generally. Many Americans regarded 'pinks' as no more than a sub-species of 'reds' and although the Socialists had the sympathy of Britain's Labour government, supporters of that government were not numerous among officials controlling the British zone while Britain's difficulties at home limited her ability to push her views abroad. In proportion as order and prosperity returned to Germany, the more conservatively-minded of her citizens, recovering their nerve, advanced the line of the last ditch in which they were prepared to die, and proposals for which they would have been glad to settle in 1945 became out of the question four years later. All these influences caused the Socialist tide to ebb in the West before power had been put back into German hands, and once again the party was to pay dearly for its fidelity to democracy.

Personal factors, however, also affected the result. Kurt Schumacher was a Prussian from the eastern borderlands who had dedicated his life to the Socialist cause without ever occupying a position which gave him practical experience in government. Having lost an arm in the first war, he had disdained in 1933 to seek safety in exile and had as a result spent ten years in concentration camps. Though the iron certainly entered into his soul, he was never one to sit on the fence. Such was his faith in his creed that as a subordinate he was inevitably a rebel and as a leader inevitably a tyrant. Before political parties had been authorised to operate above local levels, he had managed to convene a meeting of Socialist leaders in Hanover and assert his authority. He it was who chiefly prevented the Berlin S.P.D. from accepting Ulbricht's proposals for fusion[1], thereby saving the party in the West from Communist infiltration but wrecking the chances of left-wing unity. By a great effort of will-power he overcame the physical damage which had been done to his body but what he could not remedy was the rigidity which had been imposed on his mind. He tried to apply to the Germany of 1950 the outlook which he had acquired in the Germany of 1930. He persisted in believing that a proletarian revolution was imminent and showed great bitterness towards the Americans (though circumstances made him work most of it off on the British) for preventing it from taking place (as he believed, out of capitalist prejudice). The C.D.U. he regarded as a refuge for anti-democratic reactionaries and refused to consider cooperation except on his own terms. In particular he demanded neutrality in politics from the clergy and once described the Vatican as 'the fifth occupying power'. Thus he

[1] See p. 158.

ended by alienating almost all the people whose help he needed, and damaging a cause for which there was more to be said than he allowed to appear.

Prominent among his mistakes was his underestimation of his C.D.U. antagonist. Konrad Adenauer was a seventy-year-old veteran of the Centre who during the Weimar period had distinguished himself as Lord Mayor of his birthplace, Cologne, had become a member of the Prussian State Council and had once been considered for the post of Chancellor.[1] So downright a personality and so convinced a Catholic was incapable of getting on with the Nazis; he was dismissed from his post and retired to cultivate his roses and his taste for wine.[2] In 1945 he emerged again and was reinstated by the Americans as Lord Mayor, only to be dismissed by the British six months later and forbidden to take part in politics. The nominal reason was alleged dilatoriness in reconstruction; the real cause is more likely to have been obstinacy in dealing with the military authorities, coming on top of agitation against his reactionary views by Socialist emigrés. Though there was some truth in the latter charge, it could have been made equally well against a number of other people who were being admitted to positions of responsibility. If, in addition to ex-Nazis, 'reactionaries' and Communists were to be barred from office, there would have been practically nobody left—except of course Schumacher—to run the country.

The long-term effects of the dismissal were considerable, not so much because it prejudiced Adenauer against the British (the episode left on the whole lack of enthusiasm rather than ill-will) but because it removed him from the ranks of Allied-appointed administrators at a crucial moment and, as the ban on his political activity was soon lifted, enabled him to devote his time to precisely such activity. Before little more than a month was up, C.D.U. executives from all parts of the British zone were in January 1946 called to a meeting to decide who should represent the party on the Zonal Advisory Council. While the rest of those present were hesitating how to begin, Adenauer characteristically sat down and said 'As I am the senior person present, you will no doubt wish me to take the chair'. (He also arranged for the meeting to be held in a monastery, where the food was, for those days, unusually

[1] See p. 86.
[2] Some have found it significant that Adenauer should have been a drinker of wine rather than beer, the produce of South Germany rather than that of North. If there is anything in this, it is relevant that Bismarck was much addicted to Black Velvet, a mixture of champagne and stout.

good, so that everyone was in a good temper!) Nobody saw fit to challenge this assumption of authority which he promptly used to rule that, as the meeting had been called to choose representation for the British zone, only those officially invited to attend in that capacity (many of them picked by Adenauer himself) could participate in the discussions. Hermes from Berlin was forced to leave the room while Schlange-Schöningen, the other main aspirant to the post of chairman, was a refugee from Pomerania who lacked supporters in north-west Germany. Adenauer thus had no difficulty in getting himself confirmed as chairman—a position which he lost no time in exploiting. The various *Land* parties in the zone were forbidden to correspond with outside bodies except through the Zonal Party Headquarters. His main rivals were the groups in Berlin (from which he kept away) and South Germany. To hold them off until he was ready, he procrastinated over the formation of a federal party organisation and in fact no such organisation came into existence until over a year after he had become Chancellor. The Russians aided him by denying authority in the areas under their control first to Hermes and then, at the end of 1947, to Kaiser and Lemmer, thus making it less and less possible to claim that the party must be centred on Berlin. The southerners were kept in play until the moment was ripe for a deal. But most remarkable was the way in which the wily old man contrived to neutralise Karl Arnold who throughout this period was C.D.U. Minister-President of North Rhine-Westphalia, Adenauer's own *Land*!

There was more to these manoeuvrings than a personal struggle for power. The same climate of thought which encouraged the expectation of Socialist predominance had encouraged the more Socialist wing of the C.D.U. with which the union leaders Kaiser, Lemmer and Arnold were particularly associated. The community of the future was generally assumed to involve widespread socialisation, and favour to the small man. A planned economy was expected to remain essential if Europe was to make the best use of her scanty resources. The Ahlen programme of the party, adopted in February 1947, centred round the idea of a 'semi-public economy'. 'The new structure of the German economy must start from the realisation that the period of uncurtailed rule by private capitalism is over. The mere replacement of private capitalism must however also be avoided.'

Adenauer had agreed to the Ahlen programme (which at the time of its formulation possessed considerable electoral appeal) but had no love for it. He was biding his time until a good word for capitalism might become fashionable again. Kaiser in December 1946 had supported Bevin's plan to socialise the Ruhr: Adenauer insisted that a decision on this must be postponed until the German economy was free. General Clay had used this argument to suspend the socialisation clause of the Hesse constitution even after it had been approved in a referendum, and when in the summer of 1948 the *Landtag* for North Rhine-Westphalia passed, against the advice of Adenauer and the votes of the C.D.U., a bill nationalising the coal mines, the British military government insisted that the matter must be held over till it could be considered at national level.

In this situation the Bizonal Economic Administration acquired key significance. In June 1947 this institution[1] was reorganised and an Economic Council established to control it. On this Council both the C.D.U. and the S.P.D. possessed an equal number of representatives; thus neither party could dominate it in isolation. The C.D.U. would probably have been prepared to work with the S.P.D. but Schumacher, who controlled the S.P.D. delegation without belonging to it, refused to cooperate except as a dominant partner. He not only insisted on the directorship of the economic branch being given to a Socialist but refused into the bargain to 'buy' this appointment by relinquishing to the C.D.U. three of the eight Economics Ministries which his party monopolised in the *Länder* of the American and British zones. The result was that the C.D.U. joined forces with the Free Democrats and the German Party (as the Lower Saxon *Land* Party had been rechristened) and so excluded Socialists from the administrative board altogether. Moreover, in March 1948 the first man appointed as the Director of Economics resigned and was replaced after long discussions by a professor whom the Socialists and the Americans had eighteen months earlier discharged from the post of Bavarian Minister of Economics. This was Ludwig Erhard and although he as yet belonged to no particular party, his appointment and the success of the policy to which he committed himself were of crucial importance for the more conservative wing of the C.D.U.

Like Schumacher, Adenauer kept clear of the Economic Council but many of the C.D.U. delegates to it were his friends, notably the Cologne banker Robert Pferdemenges. Adenauer could be just as pertinacious as Schumacher but was far more adroit. Possessing something of Bismarck's flair for distinguishing the possible from the desirable and anticipating how other people would react, he would never have overplayed his hand in the way Schumacher did.

1 See p. 160.

For an old man, he could be remarkably quick-witted and these gifts combined with a not inconsiderable intelligence to make him more than a match for his rivals and opponents. He once confessed to occasional doubts about the justice of God when he considered the narrow limits which had been set to human wisdom compared with the unlimited opportunities allowed to folly. As a Catholic Rhinelander, he had grown up under Prussian administration in the full flush of enthusiasm for a Germany at last unified. As a result his local loyalties were tempered by awareness of the advantages brought by belonging to a large centralised state, while his genuine national patriotism was widened by recognising a European tradition. Nationalism in its more radical form repelled him as brash, unintelligent and uncivilised, but he could understand its appeal to people concerned for the welfare of their country. By temperament and training an autocrat who preferred 'yes-men' to colleagues with ideas of their own, he knew that effective leadership depends on men being managed rather than intimidated. An unrepentant individualist, he had a lively sense of responsibility for the welfare of others while submission to an authoritarian Church had taught him that individual ends must be sought in and through social organisation. This mix of qualities explains why he became a rallying-point for post-war Germany. Aided considerably by luck, he gave Germany seventeen years of prosperity and order in which democracy for the first time in the country's history became associated with success. It remains to be seen whether this breathing-space will have made easier or harder the adjustment of a divided Germany to a world where appeals to force are self-defeating.

The Drafting of the Basic Law

The Anglo-American-French conference in London in the spring of 1948[1] finally agreed on four documents. The first authorised the convening in Germany of a Constituent Assembly to 'draw up a democratic constitution which will establish for the participating states a governmental structure of federal type which is best adapted to the eventual re-establishment of German unity at present disrupted and which will protect the rights of participating states, provide adequate central authority and contain guarantees of individual rights and freedom'. The second called for a re-examination of the boundaries of the Länder. The third set out in general terms the powers which the Allies proposed to reserve to

[1] See p. 164.

themselves after the creation of a German government. The fourth (withheld from the Germans for the time being) set out the criteria by which the Military Governors were to decide whether the constitution produced by the Constituent Assembly was acceptable.

The body to which these documents were directed was not the Economic Council but the Ministers-President of the eleven *Länder* in the Western zones, who at two meetings in 1947 had sought to establish their claim to speak for the German people. They consisted at this time of five Socialists, five Christian Democrats (one being Arnold) and one Free Democrat. But when they met at Koblenz from 8 to 10 July 1948, a fortnight after the beginning of the Berlin Blockade, they rejected the idea of calling a Constituent Assembly to draft a constitution as prejudicial to the chances of re-establishing German unity. This attitude owed much to the influence of Schumacher who, in his anxiety to secure something so vital to his party, still hoped to persuade the Communists to cooperate on his own terms. Instead, the Ministers-President proposed to make temporary arrangements on a democratic basis with a temporary executive and a document formulating the rights of the occupying Powers, since the absence of any such definition was a matter of great concern to many Germans. The Military Governors were highly surprised to find an offer which had been decided on after many heart-searchings made the subject of arguments; General Clay described the attitude as a 'catastrophic disregard of the total European situation'. In the end, however, and after two more meetings, a more constructive outlook prevailed and it was agreed to convene a 'Parliamentary Council' to draft a 'Basic Law': the Allied proposal to confirm this law by a referendum was dropped in favour of ratification by *Landtäge*.

The party leaders had not been consulted over this decision but it was from the parties rather than from the *Länder* Cabinets or the Bizonal Administration that were drawn the majority of the sixty-five members of the Parliamentary Council which met at Bonn on 1 September. Each *Landtag* elected one representative for every 750,000 of population with an extra one for any remainder over 200,000. The political parties were represented in proportion to their strengths in the *Landtäge*. This arrangement gave the C.D.U./C.S.U. and S.P.D. 27 members each, the F.D.P. 5 and the German Party, Centre and Communists 2 each. As the votes of the three last were seldom all cast on the same side, the F.D.P. often found itself able to exert decisive influence. Schumacher was laid up with serious illness from March 1948 to April 1949 and could only direct the S.P.D. delegation from his sickbed, whereas Adenauer was chosen as President of the Council and set promptly to work at reducing the influence of the Ministers-President over its proceedings : they were not invited to take any part and no particular attention was paid to a draft constitution which they had had prepared. A first draft of the Council's own document was ready by the end of the year and, after further discussion and revision, presented to the Military Governors on 13 February 1949. On 2 March they replied objecting to certain compromises laboriously achieved by the German parties, and the whole matter went back into the melting pot. The Germans imagined themselves faced with a choice between giving way on certain contested points and risking an Allied rejection of the whole document.

Early in April the three Foreign Ministers meeting in Washington authorised the Military Governors to make concessions, but knowledge of this decision was on American insistence held back from the Germans for over a fortnight. Finally word of it was leaked by the British to Schumacher who was thereby encouraged in his inclination to stand firm, at the moment when the Christian Democrats were reluctantly reconciling themselves to surrender. The leak forced the Military Governors' hands; the Foreign Ministers' message was published; a final compromise was reached; the text of the Basic Law was agreed by the Parliamentary Council against a minority of twelve on 8 May (simultaneously with the lifting of the Berlin Blockade), approved by the Allies four days later and brought into force on 23 May 1949. Only the Bavarian *Landtag* refused to accept the Law, arguing that it gave too much power to the central government but, as they agreed to accept it as valid if the other *Länder* did so, they were considered to have shouted 'No' but whispered 'Yes'. An election was held on 14 August and the first Federal Parliament met on 7 September.

During the various discussions there were three main questions at issue. The first and biggest concerned the respective powers to be allotted to the Federal and *Land* governments, especially in matters of finance. The Socialists and the F.D.P. were in favour of far-reaching centralisation, the Bavarians, the Ministers-President and the Military Governors by contrast wanted the central government to be relatively weak. The C.D.U./C.S.U. was split, with its left wing inclining to the Socialist position, and Adenauer had to fight for a compromise by arguing that a bad Basic Law was better than no Basic Law at all; he bitterly resented being outdone by the Socialists on this very issue by virtue of their backstairs information. The second and related issue concerned the Second Chamber. The Socialists and the British zone C.D.U. including Adenauer favoured a Senate elected by the *Landtäge* in relation to party strength and proportional to *Land* population : the southern C.D.U./C.S.U. and the Centre and the German Party fought vigorously for a *Bundesrat* (Federal Council) made up of delegates from the *Land* governments. At the crucial moment a deal was made by which the Socialists withdrew their opposition to the Council form in return for a reduction in the powers which it was to have over legislation, only to find at a later date that a provision giving the *Bundesrat* power to veto any legislation which affected the *Länder* made it much stronger than anyone had allowed for.

Voting procedure in Federal elections was not laid down in the Basic Law but in a separate document prepared by the Parliamentary Council. There was a widespread belief that the Weimar method of proportional representation had been largely to blame for the failure of the Republic, and in consequence many favoured the British system of election by a simple majority in single-member constituencies. Objection had, however, been raised to this in discussions about some *Länder* constitutions on the ground that, in the conditions of Germany, it would lead to one party being represented out of all proportion to its strength. As a result a compromise was evolved which the Parliamentary Council adopted. The 484 seats in the first Federal Chamber were to be divided into two parts : for the first, Deputies would be elected by simple majority in 242 constituencies of roughly equal size. But every voter would have two votes; second votes were to be collected *Land* by *Land* and each party allocated as many seats as it was entitled to by its proportion of the votes.

The Military Governors, who would seem to have been worried by the provision for proportional representation, denied that the Parliamentary Council was competent to decide how the Chamber should be elected. This task they wished to be left for each *Land* Parliament to settle individually, though the plan prepared by the Parliamentary Council might be taken as a guide. The Germans not unreasonably replied that such an arrangement would cause confusion and controversy. The only concession offered was the adoption of a complicated method of reckoning proportional votes known as the d'Hondt procedure. The Governors then tried to induce the Ministers-President to insist on modifications but only two were effected. The proportion of seats to be directly elected was raised to 60 per cent, while, as a safeguard against splinter parties, seats were to be denied altogether to any party which could neither win a single constituency nor obtain at least 5 per cent of the votes in any one *Land*. The Law as thus amended was promulgated by the Governors, only to provoke protests from German politicians who feared that their parties would lose by it.[1]

The Parliamentary Council had included representatives of West Berlin and the Council's intention was to make West Berlin into a twelfth *Land* of the Federal Republic. The news of this intention produced a protest from the Russians and the Western Powers, anxious to do nothing which might give the East a pretext for further assaults on the city's freedom, insisted that the proposal in its original form be dropped. Instead representatives of West Berlin were allowed to sit, but not to vote, in the *Bundestag*. In 1950 it was agreed that West Berlin should be governed by a constitution of its own with a House of Deputies and Senate, but the House of Deputies was allowed to adopt such laws of the Federal Republic as it saw fit, subject always to reserved powers of control by the Allied Commandants. The articles of the Basic Law defining the relationship between the Federal government and the *Länder* were to be taken as a guide for the Federal government's relations to Berlin in as far as this was found necessary to avoid confusion.

The Basic Law

The Basic Law opens with a preamble saying that it has been decided on by the German people in eleven named *Länder* (i.e. excluding the East and Berlin) inspired by the wish to preserve their unity as a nation and a state and to serve the peace of the world as a fully qualified member of a united Europe, in virtue of their power to make a constitution with the object of giving their political life a fresh form for a transitional period. Nothing is said about either the occupying Powers or the *Land* governments authorising the German people to take this step which is thus tacitly claimed to rest upon an inalienable right inherent in the people. Such a claim corresponds to Adenauer's thesis that the Allies were wrong by international law in interpreting unconditional surrender to mean a complete transfer of government authority into their hands. The preamble goes on to state that the inhabitants of the 'Lands' concerned were acting for all those

---

[1] The electoral procedure has undergone several minor modifications since 1949. For a description of the present system and of the d'Hondt procedure, see Annexe, p. 301.

Germans who were prevented from taking part, and to proclaim as a task of the entire German people the realisation of the unity and freedom of Germany in free self-determination. These sentences have been interpreted as implying that the Basic Law would have to be amended before any Federal government could recognise another government as entitled to rule over Germans in any other part of Germany.

The first chapter of the Law consists of nineteen articles defining fundamental rights. The opening article proclaims the dignity of man to be unassailable and says that in consequence the German people recognise certain inviolable and inalienable human rights as the foundation of every human community, as well as of peace and of justice in the world. This wording neatly evades the question whether these rights exist prior to the state or, as the classic German view maintained, are derived from it, thus precluding the individual from claiming any rights against it. There follows, however, an article inserted at a late stage in the drafting, which says that these rights may only be encroached upon pursuant to a law. Moreover, article 19 says that such a law must apply generally, must name the basic right and the article of the Basic Law protecting it and must refrain from infringing the 'essential content' of the right. These limitations bar the police and courts from interfering with rights by virtue of a supposed power given them by natural or customary law to maintain public order or security. This police power was used even under the Weimar Republic to justify considerable interference with private freedom, especially where 'public morals' were supposed to be involved.

The third article provides for equality between the sexes, a radical departure for many Germans. The Parliamentary Council gave a chilly reception to the idea when it was proposed by the Socialists but yielded reluctantly to a storm of letters from indignant women. Discrimination on account of sex, descent, race, language, nationality, origin, belief or political or religious views is also forbidden. Other articles provide for freedom of expression (though freedom of teaching is not to justify disloyalty to the constitution), of assembly, organisation, communication and movement. Articles protecting marriage and the right of parents to decide on the religious education of their children were put in to meet the wishes of the Christian Democrats, although education is strictly a *Land* rather than a Federal responsibility.

The Socialists wished to include a right to strike but dropped the proposal when its opponents pointed out serious difficulties of interpretation; the Free Democrats for their part did not press a proposal to forbid the 'closed shop'. The Socialists also wanted a clause providing that anyone who abused his rights of ownership should forfeit them, but were assured (almost certainly in error) that this was secured by an article depriving of his rights anyone who used his right to freedom of speech for campaigning against the free democratic order. An attempt was made by the German Party to ensure that anyone whose property was expropriated should receive 'adequate' compensation, but such a question-begging adjective was kept out.

The next chapter of eighteen articles deals with the relationship between the Federation and the *Länder*. At all lower levels of government there are to be representative bodies based on general, direct, free, equal and secret voting. Black, red and gold were again to become the republican colours. An important article provides not merely that the internal organisation of political parties must conform to democratic principles but condemns as unconstitutional parties which by their aims or the behaviour of their members set out to influence (*beeinträchtigen*) or set aside the free democratic order. Another article authorises the Federal government to part with sovereign rights in so far as this may be involved by member-ship of a system which seeks to preserve peace by mutual collective security or to secure peaceful and permanent order in Europe. At the time of drafting, no proposal to admit Germany to any such organisation was under official discussion so that the clause came close to foreshadowing a claim. Actions were declared unconsti-tutional which threatened to disturb the peace of nations or lead to a war of aggression. Unless otherwise provided the *Länder* are responsible for the execution of national authority and the fulfil-ment of national tasks, though Federal Law takes precedence over *Land* Law. Foreign relations are declared a Federal matter. If a *Land* fails to carry out duties imposed on it by the Basic Law or other Federal laws, the Federal government can, with the approval of the Federal Council, step in. Provision is made for boundary changes between the *Länder*; the only use so far made of this has been the amalgamation of the three states of Baden, Baden-Württemberg and Württemberg-Hohenzollern[1] into a single *Land*.

The third chapter (12 articles) deals with the Federal Assembly (*Bundestag*). Anyone over twenty-one is entitled to vote in elections to it, and anyone over twenty-five to be elected. It is chosen for four years and there are provisions to ensure that it is both called together and (ultimately) dissolved. Ministers need not belong to it

[1] See p. 160.

but have the right to attend all sessions (including those of committees, of which one for foreign affairs and another for defence are statutory) and must do so if summoned. Deputies enjoy the usual immunities and are paid (about £2,300 per annum). Officials who wish to stand as candidates are entitled to go on leave during elections and, if successful, during their period of office.

The Federal Council (*Bundesrat*) is disposed of in 4 articles. Consisting, as already mentioned, of representatives chosen by the *Länder* governments, it provides the forum in which Federal and *Land* officials can work out (largely in committees) problems affecting their respective spheres of responsibility. The *Bundesrat* now contains forty-one members, five each from *Länder* with populations of over six million (North Rhine-Westphalia, Bavaria, Lower Saxony, Baden-Württemberg), four each from *Länder* with populations between two and six million (Rhineland-Palatinate, Schleswig-Holstein, Hesse) and three each from those with populations of under two million (Hamburg, Bremen, the Saar). This allocation of seats represents a compromise between the Socialists who wanted all *Länder* to be equal (which would have given them 18 seats to a C.D.U. 15) and the other parties who wanted representation to be proportionate (which would have given the C.D.U. 25-8 seats to a S.P.D. 19). The votes for each *Land* have to be cast as a block. Though officials can represent Ministers at the committee stage, votes are only valid in plenary sessions if cast by a Minister.

The approval of the *Bundesrat* is required for a wide range of legislation on the ground that it affects in one way or another the affairs of the *Länder*. Where such approval is not required, the Council is still entitled to vote against legislation. If it does so by a simple majority, the vote can be overridden by a similar vote in the Assembly. Where the Council's adverse vote is carried by a two-thirds majority, the Assembly must in turn produce a two-thirds majority to give the law validity. But before things get to this stage, differences are usually ironed out by a conference between representatives of the two bodies.

The fifth chapter of 8 articles deals with the Federal President who is elected by a Federal Convention consisting of the members of the *Bundestag* and an equal number of *Länder* representatives chosen by the *Länder* assemblies on the basis of proportional representation. This arrangement represents a reaction from the Weimar constitution, where the President was elected by direct popular vote. It is one of the points at which the framers of the Basic Law showed a distrust of the masses. This is further displayed in the requirement (taken over from the constitution of 1871) that with four exceptions every act of the President requires the counter-signature of the Chancellor or responsible Minister to be valid.

Perhaps the most important chapter (of 8 articles) concerns the Federal Government which is to consist of the Chancellor and Ministers. The Ministers are appointed by the President on the nomination of the Chancellor. The Chancellor himself is elected by the *Bundestag* without debate on the proposal of the President (here acting on his own authority). If the person proposed does not obtain a majority of votes, the *Bundestag* can within a fort-night propose its own candidate who, if he obtains the votes of over half the Deputies, must be appointed by the President. If this does not happen, a fresh vote must be taken immediately the fort-night is over. If anyone then receives the votes of more than half the Deputies, the President must appoint him; if nobody fulfils this condition, the President has to choose between nominating the man who got most votes and dissolving the *Bundestag* (again on his own authority). To deprive a Chancellor of office, the *Bundestag* must not merely vote by a majority against him but must at least forty-eight hours previously name a successor, whom the President is then compelled to appoint. This 'vote of constructive no-confidence' was taken over from the constitution of Baden-Württemberg where it was devised by an American historian of the Baroque; it is intended to obviate the situation where two extremes unite to eject a Chancellor of the centre, without being able to agree on the policy which should be followed instead. If a Chancellor asks the Assembly for a vote of confidence, and fails to get one, he can (article 68) demand within three weeks from the President a dissolution of the Assembly and fresh elections. His right to do this lapses, however, if the Assembly before dissolution can agree on an alternative Chancellor. If the Chancellor does not want a dissolution (as was the case in 1966 when Erhard fore-saw that an election would go against the C.D.U.), the President can, given the approval of the *Bundesrat* (which is to say, of a majority of the *Länder* governments), declare a law passed as a matter of emergency even against the votes of the *Bundestag*. This procedure can be repeated for six months but cannot thereafter be resorted to again as long as the Chancellor concerned holds office. Laws, however, which amend or otherwise affect the Basic Law cannot be passed in this way. Inside the Cabinet, the Chancellor is given the responsibility of deciding the general principles of policy to be followed, within which each Minister is responsible for running his department on his own responsibility. Clashes between

Ministers on this basis are decided by the Cabinet. This arrangement represents a compromise between a Presidential Cabinet of the
American type and the collective responsibility of Ministers on
the British pattern. How it works in practice depends on the
personalities of both the Chancellor and the remaining Ministers;
Adenauer frequently interfered with his subordinates, whereas
Erhard was often unable to make his come to heel.

For a long time there were no Junior Ministers. This considerably reduced the patronage available to, and so the power of,
the government. Moreover, it not only laid an exceptionally heavy
burden on the single Minister in each department (especially if,
as is often the case, he has to spend much of his time representing
the country in Brussels or other international gatherings) but also
involved the State Secretary or senior Civil Servant of the department in many activities such as answering Parliamentary questions
which in Britain would be considered political. Accordingly a
tendency grew up for Ministers to bring into their departments
State Secretaries who share the same political views. In 1967, however, the coalition government decided to appoint 'Parliamentary
State Secretaries' to the Chancery and six other departments with
a view to improving contact between the political and administrative worlds.[1]

The remaining five chapters and 77 articles of the Law deal in
considerable detail with the passing of legislation, and its execution, and with administration, justice and finance. There are three
broad types of legislation :

(a) Exclusive, i.e. where the *Länder* can only legislate if a
Federal law gives them express authority to do so. In this field
come nationality, freedom of movement, currency, weights and
measures, Customs and trade treaties, railways, air travel, post and
long-distance communications; rights of Federal officials, commercial law, criminal police; Foreign Affairs (after 1952) and
defence (after 1954).

(b) Concurrent, where the *Länder* can legislate in so far as the
Federal government makes no use of the powers given to it in
fields where legislation, to be effective and avoid clashes, must

---

[1] German commentators made what can only appear to a British observer
as extremely heavy weather over this innovation, chiefly on the ground that
it would restrict the functions of the existing State Secretaries to administrative matters. To those accustomed to a politically impartial Civil Service,
this might seem a good thing. Germans, however, are sceptical as to whether
political impartiality in the higher grades of the Civil Service is possible.
Their State Secretaries have always been more politically active than British
Permanent Secretaries, and indeed were until 1918 virtually in the position
of Ministers.

extend to more than one *Land*. The Basic Law lists twenty-three subjects for such legislation, most of which relate to law and economics though matters like infectious diseases and rules for road and sea transport are also included.

(*c*) Other, where *Länder* are free to legislate as they choose subject to the Basic Law.

The position is, however, complicated by the fact that, in accordance with German tradition, much Federal legislation is in practice administered by the *Länder*. The Federal government supervises this process and has power to issue general regulations as to how it shall be done which, provided they obtain the approval of the *Bundesrat,* are binding on the *Länder*. Other matters, however, such as Finance, Railways and Posts, are administered by federal authorities scattered through the country. The Ministers-President in the first instance only allowed for 3,225 established Civil Service posts in the Bonn offices and although this number has since multiplied, the proportion of the Civil Service at the centre remains relatively small.

In the financial field the Americans horrified the German administrators by proposing that both Federal and *Länder* governments should be free to levy the same kinds of taxation. Instead, an elaborate division was made, on lines traditional in Germany, by which the proceeds of certain taxes (mainly indirect) were to go to the Federation and others (including property taxes, driving licences and the beer tax) to the *Länder,* while revenue from income and corporation tax was to be divided between the two on a stated percentage, the adjustment of which has proved a standing bone of contention. A further elaborate compensation arrangement, requiring the approval of the *Bundesrat,* evens out the burden between the relatively rich and the relatively poor *Länder*. The net effect of the whole arrangement is to make German financial affairs complex and inelastic since the Federal government is often not legally able to make its decisions effective without securing the agreement of the *Länder*. A further complication is added by the absence of anything corresponding to Standing Order No. 82 of the British House of Commons, according to which increases in expenditure can only be proposed by a Minister; the responsibility for seeing that finance is available to cover the proposed expenditure is instead laid upon the *Bundestag's* Finance Committee.

Responsibility for ensuring that the Basic Law is observed and, more particularly, for delimiting the constitutional spheres of the Federation and *Länder* is laid on the Constitutional Court of Karlsruhe. (This is distinct from the Federal High Court in the same city which is the last instance of appeal for non-constitutional cases.) Appointments are made alternately by the *Bundestag* and by the *Bundesrat* from a list drawn up by the Federal Ministry of Justice : this includes not only Federal judges but other people with legal training who have made a name for themselves in politics, administration or the universities, since only a quarter of the seats on the courts are filled by professional judges. Besides reviewing legislation, the court deals with complaints from individuals who consider that rights guaranteed to them by the Basic Law have been infringed. But on the major issue of the Federation's right to legislate in the concurrent field, the court is not entitled to do more than examine alleged abuses of discretion; it may not challenge the need for a particular piece of legislation.

Amendments to the Basic Law require the approval of two-thirds of the members of the *Bundestag* and two-thirds of the votes in the *Bundesrat*. No amendment is, however, admissible which alters the federal character of the State, the rights of the *Länder* to cooperate in legislation, the democratic basis of the State or the human rights recognised in the opening paragraphs.

The Basic Law represented a determined attempt to learn from experience and was a good deal more down to earth than the Weimar constitution. Its framers sought to provide against the paralysis of the legislative parties by the inability of the Assembly to agree, against the consequent resort on a lasting basis to government by emergency decree, against the growth and agitation of anti-democratic radicalism and against the victory of anti-democratic forces in a single *Land*. Critics have alleged that, had it been in force in the early 1930s, it would not have prevented Hitler from coming to power. The present document would, however, seem to give more opportunities than did its predecessor to anyone who was prepared to defend the kind of system which it instituted —and that must remain a principal test of any paper formula. But of course the problems of today are not those of thirty years ago and how far the Law will help to the solution of these is still hard to judge. Most forms of government are satisfactory when times are prosperous. The real test lies in how much they do, when troubles come, to magnify or reduce divisions of opinion and to facilitate or impede the taking of decisions.

Germany Gets Governments Again

The Parliamentary Council had formed life pleasant in the small and relatively undamaged university town of Bonn and when the time came to choose a capital for the Federal Republic, felt that it had many advantages over Frankfurt, which although more important, was for that very reason badly bombed and full of Americans. The popular story is that Adenauer got Bonn chosen because he happened to live close by, but a more likely explanation of his advocacy is the fact that Schumacher preferred Frankfurt and, after the advantage which the Socialist leader had gained over the question of standing up to the Military Governors, the C.D.U. leader was in search of an issue on which to reassert his authority. But the alleged Schumacher statement that 'the selection of Frankfurt would be a defeat for the C.D.U.' which played some part in getting the C.D.U. to vote for Bonn, is said to have emanated from the fertile brains of two newspaper correspondents who were in love and wanted money to set up house. Another factor which played a part was the argument that Bonn would be easier to abandon than Frankfurt if Berlin ever became available. Such are the reasons why the new state came to acquire as capital a 'Federal village' where 'either it is raining or the climate makes you sleepy or the level-crossing gates are shut'. The choice underlined the character of the Federal Republic as a West European state under strong Catholic influence.

The election on 14 August 1949 brought the C.D.U./C.S.U. 139 seats, the S.P.D. 131, the F.D.P. 52, the Bavarian Party and the German Party 17 apiece, the Communists 15 and others 31. In the light of these figures, the Socialists were inclined to a 'Great Coalition' with the C.D.U., as were the left wing of the C.D.U. and the politicians from the south-west *Länder* which were mostly ruled by coalitions of this type. The Ministers-President also favoured a Great Coalition which they guessed would leave them more power. Adenauer on the other hand was on bad personal terms with Schumacher but was pleased with the results which had followed from C.D.U./F.D.P. cooperation in the Bizonal Economic Council. Indeed the C.D.U. had largely fought the election on the economic policies of Erhard (who had only recently joined the party) but these aroused little enthusiasm in the groups favouring a Great Coalition. Adenauer would seem to have inclined instinctively towards the more conservative solution of a 'Little Coalition' with the F.D.P. and the German Party which would not only be anti-Socialist but would be sufficiently far to the right to deprive any more reactionary groups of most of their allure and so reduce the danger of anti-democratic elements exploiting their social status to turn the bureaucracy and professional classes against the Republic. He must also have seen that his own influence in his own party would be greatest if he could act as a balancing factor between two divergent wings, and that he would be more likely to hold this position in a Little Coalition since in a Great one he would himself belong to the right wing. Moreover, in a Little Coalition the C.D.U./C.S.U. would be the dominating partner.

His behaviour in these circumstances was characteristic. A week after the election he held at his home a tea-party for a hand-picked group of 25 C.D.U. members including those on whom he thought he could count and those on whom he felt he would need to count. Arnold, although C.D.U. Minister-President of the *Land* in which the conference was held, was not invited to it. Kaiser, on the other hand, was a key figure who at an early stage was talked into supporting the Adenauer solution. Some of the opponents of this course made the mistake of quitting the meeting early and left the way open for the impression to be created by adroit handling of the journalists waiting at the gate that the gathering had come down in favour of continuing the grouping which had proved so effective in the Economic Council. Soon afterwards Adenauer secured the support of the F.D.P. by promising his backing for their leader Theodor Heuss as President of the Republic, and of the C.S.U. by promising in a similar way to back Ehard, the Minister-President of Bavaria, for the chairmanship of the *Bundesrat*. By the time the rank-and-file Deputies of the C.D.U. got to Bonn, they found that the die had been virtually cast.

Only at the outset did these carefully calculated schemes break down. In the election for the chairmanship of the Federal Council the delegation from North Rhine-Westphalia voted not for Ehard but for their own leader Arnold, who was in consequence elected. The C.S.U. were furious and, if an acceptable clerical candidate such as Schlange-Schöningen had been standing for the Presidency, would probably have voted for him, since Heuss was too liberal for their tastes. But Schumacher, refusing to contemplate any 'bourgeois' candidates, had insisted on standing himself with the result that he lost to Heuss on the second ballot. Heuss then nominated Adenauer for the Chancellorship and on 17 September the Assembly met to vote on the proposal. It was carried by one vote—Adenauer's own! He told his followers that they must contrive to hold office for eight years.

Earlier planning had contemplated eight Ministries—Finance, Economics, Justice, Interior, Labour, Transport, Food and Agriculture, and Posts. Adenauer added Ministries for *Bundesrat* Affairs, All-German Affairs, Refugees, Housing and the Marshall

Plan. A disarmed Germany naturally had no Defence Ministry and as long as Foreign Affairs consisted of relations with the Military Governors (who now became civilianised as High Commissioners), they were kept in the hands of the Chancellor himself. Adenauer thus had thirteen posts to distribute, of which five went to the C.D.U., three to the C.S.U., three to the F.D.P. and two to the German Party. Three of the C.D.U. Ministers, including the key figure of Erhard at Economics, were Bavarian born. Kaiser was made responsible for All-German Affairs but found it to be a back-seat. The C.D.U. left wing, along with those members of the party who were prominent in the *Länder* governments, and the staff of the Bizonal administration were largely passed over. Except for Kaiser, the Cabinet included nobody who had offered serious opposition to Adenauer's wishes. It soon fulfilled its promise of proving an obsequious body.

Meanwhile those in charge of the Russian zone had been following step by step behind the West. In March 1948 an executive body of 400, the People's Council, was set up by a People's Congress and in March 1949 (during the blockade) approved the constitution of a German Democratic Republic (D.D.R.). In May 1949 a third People's Congress was elected on a single party list, and this in turn elected a second People's Council. This in the month following Adenauer's assumption of office constituted itself a Provisional Popular Chamber and commissioned Grotewohl to form a provisional government. The Russians retained their grip upon the new Republic's territory but followed Western example to the extent of converting their military government into a Control Commission.

Chapter 9

Rearmament and the Restoration of Sovereignty 1949–55

Saar and Ruhr

THE CREATION of a German government logically implied the end of foreign rule and the Western occupying Powers had therefore agreed, as an integral part of the deal, to change the Control Commission into a High Commission and give written definition in an 'Occupation Statute' to their rights and obligations towards the new German authority. The High Commissioners at one stage intended to deliver the Occupation Statute to the Federal government in a solemn ceremony and suggested to Adenauer that he should formally present his Cabinet to them at the same time. He, however, demurred : an 'Occupation Statute', though an improvement on the situation in which the Germans had no defined rights, was still in his eyes a disagreeable document and its presentation no occasion for festivities. The High Commissioners therefore decided to hand over the Statute on 21 September 1949 in a formal but private ceremony on the Petersberg above Bonn.[1]

They would stand together on a carpet while Adenauer waited in front of them and listened to an address by their French Chairman, Monsieur André François-Poncet. After the speech was over, Adenauer was to step on to the carpet and be given the document. When, however, Adenauer entered the room, François-Poncet took a step forward to greet him. The German saw his opportunity, went towards the Frenchman and so brought himself on to the carpet before the speech had begun. The incident well illustrates the way in which the new German Chancellor exploited every opening given to him for extending the scope of the powers which the Allies had granted. In yielding to one of his demands during the negotiations soon to be described, the American High Commissioner was to say, 'All right then. This is now the 122nd concession we

[1] The Petersberg was the hotel in which Neville Chamberlain had stayed during the Bad Godesberg talks with Hitler in 1938.

have made to the Germans'. Nobody could complain that the Allies were committing the frequent mistake of 'too little and too late!'

Yet at the same time fairness demands a tribute to the extent to which Adenauer worked with the Allies and tried to meet their wishes. There were no doubt two main reasons for this. One was that the basic Allied policy of resisting Russia and integrating Western Europe coincided with his own desires and his ideas of what was good for Germany. But in addition he believed, as Stresemann had done before him, that cooperation was likely to release Germany from her limitations and penalties more rapidly than resistance would do. This attitude involved him in a considerable amount of criticism, particularly from the Social Democrats; Schumacher once taunted him in the *Bundestag* with being the 'Federal Chancellor of the Allies'. But the High Commissioners in the ceremony on the Petersberg had given an unmistakable hint that early changes in the Occupation Statute would be possible if the German government observed their side of it. The Statute itself talked of revision in twelve to eighteen months. The Chancellor, however, lost no time in driving home the argument that, if the Allies really intended to develop West Germany as a prosperous member of the European Community, further demolitions of factories made no sense. The truth was that Allied policy, as so often where several countries are working together, was evolved not so much as a logical whole but as a compromise between different points of view. The transition from the policy of holding Germany down to that of building her up had therefore to be gradual and while it was in process, contradictory things were quite capable of happening at one and the same time. Yet a policy which is patently inconsistent is not easy to defend and by his pressure on this weak point Adenauer not surprisingly obtained quick concessions.

Another sore point concerned the Ruhr. Talk of 'internationalising' this area as a security measure was of long standing and the British had put both the coal and steel industries under public control. The Foreign Ministers, in agreeing to hand the government of Germany back to its inhabitants, had sought to allay the fears which this step aroused by including in the package a Ruhr Authority. This body was to include representatives of America, Britain, France and the three Benelux countries, along with a German. It was to allocate the coal, coke and steel output of the Ruhr between the German home market and exports while it was also authorised to fix prices, quotas and transport arrangements. Such an interference with liberty, which was moreover to last until a peace treaty was signed, aroused much resentment in Germany and indeed the Authority would probably have belied its name if the German government and public had chosen to thwart it. Much pressure was put on Adenauer to refuse to nominate a German member. He, however, took a wider view. The very first time he spoke as Chancellor to the High Commissioners at the Petersberg ceremony, he expressed the hope that the Ruhr arrangement would gradually grow into an organisation embracing the basic industries of other countries besides Germany, with an underlying hint that otherwise it could not last. Moreover, he realised that in this field the decision rested in the hands of the French since it was their desire for security which lay behind both the Authority and the dismantling policy : they too would be the people with the most to contribute, after the Germans, to any organisation of Europe's basic industries. To win their confidence was imperative and the best way of doing so would be to take part in the Ruhr Authority instead of boycotting it.

There was, however, another apple of discord between the two countries in the shape of the Saar, the area with the second largest exports of coal in Europe. France had tried to get possession of it in 1919 but had only obtained control over the mines; the actual territory had been placed under the League of Nations, and had then returned to Germany after a plebiscite in 1935. Immediately on occupying it in 1945, the French had made it into a separate *Land* and set about detaching it from the rest of their zone, since their industry was vitally dependent on its coal. On 21 December 1946 a Customs union between the Saar and France was proclaimed and the area was given a separate currency in the following June. Elections in October 1947 gave an 87 per cent majority to parties favouring independence from Germany and close association with France. In March 1950 the resulting government was induced to sign a convention giving France a fifty-year lease of the Saar mines. While the Americans and British did not much like these proceedings, they preferred tolerating them to meeting French wishes about the Rhineland and Ruhr. The Germans resented the French behaviour and argued (as events were to show, with justice) that the election results did not represent the considered wishes of the population. Moreover, Adenauer with the full support of the S.P.D. enunciated over the Saar a doctrine which had even more significance when applied to the East, namely that the Allied declarations of 5 June 1945[1] had left unaffected the continued existence of Germany as a state within the frontiers

1 See above, p. 139.

of 31 December 1937 (i.e. before the annexation of Austria and Czechoslovakia) and that no part of that area could be legally and permanently transferred to another state unless the government of a free and united Germany gave its consent.

German feelings were therefore very mixed when the suggestion was made in Strasbourg that the Federal Republic and the Saar should simultaneously become associate (rather than full) members of the Council of Europe which had been set up in May 1949 and had held its first meeting the following September. On the one hand German ability to attend meetings would be a step forward, yet for the Saar to obtain the same treatment might imply an admission that the valley was no longer in any sense German territory. In the end the whole complex of outstanding problems were brought together in the Petersberg Agreement of 24 November 1949 between the High Commission and the Federal government. Germany accepted the offer of association with the Council of Europe and agreed to take her seat on the Ruhr Authority. The Saar also became associated with the Council but there was general agreement that a final settlement of the area's status could only occur at a Peace Conference. The German government was allowed to open consulates (but not Embassies) abroad and send its own officials to the O.E.E.C. (instead of being represented by the High Commission). Dismantling for reparations, although not completely wound up for another two years, was reduced to a very small scale. Responsibility for decartellisation was transferred from the Commission to the Republic and the size of ships permitted to German builders was increased.

To obtain so many concessions within two months of the entry into force of the Occupation Statute was a distinct score for Adenauer, though the opposition preferred to concentrate on what he had given rather than on what he had won. Gradually too his longer-term calculations began to work out.

The more far-sighted French statesmen were coming to realise that the chances of pushing through the policy towards Germany advocated by de Gaulle and Bidault after the war were, in face of the American and British determination to rebuild that country, virtually nil. France needed dollars too badly to withhold her cooperation from the Anglo-Saxons and if Germany was to be allowed to recover, she must be prevented from swinging into hostility to France. In both countries there was a widespread desire, nourished by the mutual experience of defeat and occupation, to end an antagonism which had done so much to disturb the peace of Europe. With this went a belief that such an ending could only be achieved inside the framework of a closer European association. Moreover, France needed both German coal and an outlet for some of the steel, surplus to her domestic requirements, which an ambitious investment programme had just put her in a position to produce.

Such was the background which led on 8 May 1950 to the receipt by Adenauer of a letter containing a proposal for a Franco-German Coal and Steel Community, signed by the French Foreign Minister Robert Schuman, himself a Lorrainer who had been born in Luxembourg. As Schuman was well aware, his Plan fitted so closely to Adenauer's desires as to be certain of a sympathetic reception from the German government.[1] It was a first step towards integrating Europe, and reconciling France with Germany; it got rid of the Ruhr Authority, nullified the main advantages of the Customs union between France and the Saar and restored to Germany some measure of international equality. The Allied governments promised to lift the ceiling on German steel production as soon as the Community was in being. The idea of having to compete with the Germans without tariffs or quotas and on equal terms frightened the French steel industry, although a German industrialist, whom Adenauer was soon to make Minister of the Interior, described the Plan as 'an effort to overcome the difficulties of the French steel industry'. The Social Democrats attacked the proposal on the ground that it would continue Allied controls in a new form and make reunification harder, but they were fighting against the tide and did not have the trade unions behind them. Within six weeks of Schuman's dramatic proposal, negotiations were opened to give it concrete shape. The Benelux countries and Italy accepted the invitation to join in, though Britain held aloof, and on 18 April 1951 Adenauer for the first time left the territory of the Federal Republic to sign in Paris the Treaty establishing the Community. Before he did so, however, he insisted on Schuman exchanging with him letters by which the French government recognised that German signature did not imply definitive acceptance of the Saar's status.

The Defence of Western Europe

Discussions on the Schuman Plan had hardly begun when the whole world picture was transformed by the launching of a

[1] Adenauer received notice of the Plan over twenty-four hours in advance of Britain who was only informed on the eve of the Press Conference at which it was made public (see article by Ulrich Sahn in *International Affairs*, Vol. 43 No. 1, January 1967).

Communist attack on South Korea which they had been given ground for believing to lie outside the range of American strategic interests. Reinforcements, nominally under the United Nations flag but in practice consisting as to 85 per cent of American troops, were rushed to the victim of this aggression and quickly succeeded in carrying the war into Communist territory. The result in November 1950 was the entry of Chinese troops into the fighting and the prolongation of the war for nearly three years.

Not unnaturally, though not necessarily with justification, the Communist initiative made many statesmen consider the possibility of its being repeated in other continents and look anxiously to their defences. In such a survey, the West's weakness in Europe leapt to the eye. Since the Hiroshima explosion, the West Europeans had in effect been relying on American nuclear predominance to keep the Russians from risking a forward move. In the summer of 1950 there were in effect only four properly equipped divisions in Western Germany, whereas in East Germany or within easy call the Russians had 175. Not only was Russia known now to possess her own fission bombs, even if in far fewer numbers than the U.S., but the Korean experience emphasised how unsatisfactory it was to rely on so devastating a weapon to meet all types of warlike situations. There was a widespread agreement that the West must greatly improve its strength in 'conventional' weapons if its determination to resist aggression was to be made 'credible' to the East. A production programme was set in hand which led to the prices of raw materials first rocketing and then, once the peak of demand was past, sharply relapsing; as has been shewn[1] the switchback nearly wrecked the German economy but in the end proved its salvation. An integrated staff was brought into being under N.A.T.O. and in December 1950 General Eisenhower assumed office as Supreme Commander of Allied forces in Europe. By July 1951 the number of divisions in Germany had been raised to some fifteen. But it was clear that even this strength would still be no match for the Russians.

None of the N.A.T.O. countries was prepared to dislocate its economy and cut its living standards so as to divert into the armed forces the manpower needed to match the Russians in numbers. This was not entirely due to selfishness. Both Britain and France had many of their forces tied down by commitments outside Europe; America could only finance the rearmament of others as long as she was prosperous herself. No country could become poorer without risking political upheavals which would

[1] See p. 179.

play into the hands of the Communists. Only one alternative solution was in sight and that was to rearm the Federal Republic. At this stage her productive capacity or technical skills were of secondary interest, except for the need to keep them out of Russian hands. What the West wanted was men to fight. Ever since 1947 the War Department in Washington had been pressing for such a policy; now at last they succeeded in overcoming the political objections of the State Department. At a N.A.T.O. meeting in New York in September 1950 Dean Acheson, the American Secretary of State, made it clear that his government's willingness to remain in Europe was contingent on agreement to rearm Western Germany as a matter of urgency.

The proposal met on all sides with considerably less than enthusiasm. Many Europeans were deeply disturbed at the thought of giving arms back to a nation which had in the past put them to such brutal and destructive purposes. A Germany equipped with nuclear weapons was a particularly unpleasant thought. A wave of pacifist revulsion, partly spontaneous, partly the outcome of Allied indoctrination, had swept through Western Germany itself. There was little eagerness to provide the West with cannon-fodder. The catch-phrase of the time was *ohne mich* or 'include me out'. Rearmament would imperil the economic revival, increase the risk of Germany becoming the first theatre of any East-West clash and above all reduce the likelihood of reuniting the Federal with the German Democratic Republic, especially as the Russians had already increased the para-military 'People's Police' in the D.D.R. to 55,000 and equipped them with tanks and artillery. Yet these dangers would not necessarily be avoided by remaining disarmed. And the plain facts remained that the rearming of Germany was the price demanded by the Americans for assistance which the Western Europeans considered essential, and that the Germans were therefore themselves in a position to demand concessions as the price for their consent.

The influential groups of enthusiasts for European integration saw in this situation an opportunity of carrying their aims a large step closer to realisation. In August the Assembly of the Council of Europe, with the encouragement of Churchill, called for the formation of a European Army, subject to democratic control. On 24 October 1950 Monsieur René Pleven, the French Minister of Defence, followed the example of his colleague Schuman and proposed to the French Parliament the creation of 'a European Army attached to political institutions of a united Europe', with a European Minister of Defence.

Adenauer had repeatedly assured the Allies that he did not want
to see Germany rearmed, though he also lost no opportunity of
emphasising to them how insecure and exposed he considered
the Federal Republic to be. He had pressed for authority to
establish a Security Corps to match the People's Police and hinted
that if anything more was to be done it should be inside a European framework. Shortly before the N.A.T.O. meeting he indicated
that, if an international West European army were to be formed,
he would be ready to contribute a German contingent. But at the
same time he made it clear that the price of this contribution
would approximate to the complete restoration of German sovereignty : the German troops must be on a footing of equality with
those of other countries.

On 19 December the Foreign Ministers of America, Britain and
France agreed in principle to the idea of a German defence
contingent, and negotiations began to work out what the Pleven
Plan would mean in practice. The Occupation Statute was revised
in March 1951, eighteen months after its inauguration, to restore
to Germany, among other things, control of her foreign policy,
and German civilian and military representatives took part on a
footing of equality in the discussions about the European Defence
Community (E.D.C.). These lasted for well over a year and the
Treaty of Paris which embodied their result was not ready for
signature till May 1952. It proposed a Community with integrated
staffs and forces, though the maximum size of a homogeneous
national unit was raised in the course of discussion from 4,000 to
13,000. The idea of a Defence Minister was dropped in favour
of a Board of nine Defence Commissioners, supervised by a
Council of Ministers from the participating states, with an
Assembly elected (at the outset) by national Parliaments and a
Court to decide disputes. The board would prepare a common
budget which would need to be approved by the Council (unanimously) and the Assembly. Once that process was complete, each
member state would be legally bound to pay its contribution. The
Assembly was required within six months of the coming into force
of the Treaty to work out plans for a democratically elected
Assembly as one component in a federal or confederal Europe.

Parallel with these discussions there went on others between the
Federal Republic and the occupying Powers. They produced as
preliminary results a declaration of 9 July 1951 bringing to an
end the state of war between the negotiating parties and on 14
September 1951 a resolution favouring the inclusion of a democratic Germany on an equal basis in a Community covering

continental Europe. They were, however, held up by arguments about the repayment of German debts and the status of the Saar. The French wanted not only British membership of the Defence Community but British and American guarantees of protection in case a rearmed Germany were ever to quit the E.D.C. Not only the British Labour government but, to the surprise and disappointment of the continentals, Churchill's Conservative government which took its place in October 1951 refused to go more than a limited way to meet these wishes. All the same, a Treaty was laboriously worked out and was ready for signature in Bonn on the day before that of Paris. It restored German sovereignty, cancelling the Occupation Statute, and winding up the High Commission. Arrangements were included for the continued stationing in Germany of Allied troops as a matter of mutual security, and for the reassumption of powers by the Allies in the event of an emergency (until the Germans worked out suitable crisis plans of their own). The Americans, British and French retained their status as occupying Powers in Berlin, which was to remain outside the Federal Republic, but promised to consult the government of the Republic about the use of their rights in the city. An important article provided that an essential aim in the common policy of all four states would be 'a peace settlement for the whole of Germany freely negotiated between Germany and her former enemies. The final delimitations of the boundaries of Germany must await such a settlement'. Pending its conclusion, all four states would cooperate to achieve, by peaceful means, their common aim of a unified Germany enjoying a liberal-democratic constitution like that of the Federal Republic and integrated within the European Community.

The two Treaties of Paris and Bonn were complementary and it was provided that the second would only come into force when the first did. Moreover, although both had been signed, both required ratification by the Parliaments of the states concerned.

In Germany ratification was never seriously in doubt, and Adenauer had pressed ahead on his way with little reference to his colleagues and almost none at all to the *Bundestag*. His Minister of the Interior, Heinemann, who owed his position principally to his influence in the Evangelical Church, resigned on anti-militarist grounds but proved easily expendable.[1] More serious was the opposition of the Socialists led by Schumacher and, after his death in August 1952, Ollenhauer. The Socialist objec-

[1] He later joined the Social Democrats and came back to office in December 1966 as Minister of Justice in the 'Great Coalition' Cabinet.

tions were not based solely on dislike of rearmament but on the belief that the best hope of German reunification lay in cooperating with the East rather than in combating it. Adenauer's reply, which was much influenced after November 1952 by President Eisenhower's Secretary of State, John Foster Dulles, was that the only thing which the Russians understood and would yield to was force, so that the best prospect of reuniting Germany lay in building up the strength of the West until it was great enough to 'roll back the Iron Curtain'! As he put it in a speech in March 1952 :

> The aim of German policy today as yesterday is that the West should become strong enough to conduct reasonable conversations with the Soviet Union. We are firmly convinced that if we continue in this path the moment will not be too distant when Soviet Russia will declare itself ready for reasonable negotiation.

This attitude was based on bad psychology; men, more particularly when organised in states, do not readily yield to force unless it is overwhelming. And in the conditions of the 1950s, especially after the first Russian explosion of a fusion bomb in August 1953, the West clearly had no prospect of building up a force of the required preponderance. Though they may have had the advantage of a higher standard of living, the East had a higher standard of dying. From the point of view of German internal politics, on the other hand, there was much to be said for Adenauer's policy of integrating the young German democracy as closely as possible into the West and thereby making it as hard as possible for an aggressive anti-Western nationalism to develop again. Moreover, this policy, which met so well the wishes of the most powerful nation in the world, was far more likely to result in a prosperous Germany than either an attempt to remain neutral would have done, or coordination with the controlled economies of the East. A break with the United States might also have halted Germany's progress towards the recovery of sovereignty and equality. But such was the importance of the refugees in German political calculations, and such the emphasis which the German people had been encouraged to place on reunification, that the Adenauer policy could not be sold to the public on its genuine merits alone. For it to be accepted, they had to be given misplaced hopes of what it would produce in relation to the East. How far this deception was conscious on Adenauer's part is hard to tell : the common assertion that he, as a Rhinelander, cared little for reunification is hard to sustain in the light of his Memoirs. But there were some prices which he was not prepared to pay for it.

There is, of course, a valid excuse for the line he pursued even accepting that reunification should have been the major consideration. This is that, at the period in question, no other alternative policy was available which would have brought about reunification any faster, and yet given the reunited Germany any chance of being a democratic state. Now three months before the two Treaties were signed the Soviet government, who were clearly extremely concerned at the prospect of a vengeful and armed Germany once more arising, sent to the other occupying Powers two notes which purported to contain terms for a Peace Treaty to bring about German reunification on a neutral and democratic basis. These notes, which certainly arrived at a rather late stage, cannot be said to have been seriously considered. Instead they were regarded as a sign that the policy of negotiating from strength was beginning to yield results and, if pursued, would result in still more conciliatory offers. The Allies argued that they should not therefore allow themselves to be deflected from their purpose by what was obviously a delaying bid. The Allied reply insisted that free elections were a necessary preliminary to a Peace Treaty and negotiations bogged down in argument as to which should come first. Was this reaction justified or was a real chance of settlement missed?

The Russian proposals provided for a guarantee of democratic rights to the German people so that all in Germany could enjoy the rights of man and the basic freedoms. All democratic parties and associations were to be allowed freedom of activity, including liberty to meet, publish and decide their own internal affairs. Organisations inimical to democracy and to the maintenance of peace were not to be permitted. Civil and political rights were to be available to all former members of the armed forces and to all former Nazis other than those serving sentences for war crimes. There were to be no limitations on economic activity and Germany was to be free to join the United Nations. She was to have such national armed forces of her own as she needed for defence, and was to be allowed to produce arms, though the quantity and type of these were to be prescribed in the Treaty setting up the arrangement. But she was to promise not to enter into any kind of coalition or military alliance directed against any state which had fought her between 1939 and 1945. All Allied forces were to be withdrawn within twelve months and all foreign military bases on her territory to be destroyed.

At first sight nothing could sound more reasonable, even though the organisations to be assured freedom were obviously going to include the Communist Party. Perhaps too the presence of big and undefined words like 'peace-loving' and 'democracy' might rouse the suspicions of those who remembered the controversies which had flowed from different interpretations of similar words in the Control Council. The Russian offer may well have been seriously intended. But it involved so many opportunities for dissension and delay that its acceptance might have meant the West finding themselves after five years or so back where they had started from in 1947–9. The proposal was obviously put forward to prevent the Federal Republic from binding itself to the anti-Communist bloc and could only have been accepted by someone willing to take the risk of a reunited Germany coming under the control of the pro-Communist bloc. For German production and man-power could make too much difference to the balance of power for either side to trust the other at that stage to let them remain genuinely neutral. The reunification of Germany may well have to wait until such trust is forthcoming. An act of faith was not, however, to be expected from an elderly man who was not only a convinced European and anti-Communist but had staked his political reputation on a policy which involved binding his country to the West. By the time the offer was made, things had gone so far that a much higher bid would have been needed to make a reversing of engines seem justifiable to those responsible for Western policy. And so high a bid would have been regarded by the East as prohibitively expensive.

The East Germans answered the Bonn and Paris Treaties by establishing a security belt along the inter-zonal frontier and ending except at a very limited number of points the relatively free local traffic across it which had existed until then.

Disaster and Recovery

The attitude of Germany towards the European Defence Community could be decided by the obstinacy of a single individual but more was unfortunately needed to bring the Community into being. The Treaty signed in Paris in May 1952 needed six ratifications to take effect; it only received five. The inroads which the proposal made on national sovereignty, though designed to allay French fears of Germany, proved more than the French could bring themselves to accept. They were at this time torn apart by failure to hold Indo-China, by the beginnings of trouble in North Africa, by financial difficulties and internal dissensions. The Gaullistes and other right-wing parties, whose votes were needed to protect the franc, were opposed to any surrender of sovereignty; the Communists would not support a measure so unwelcome to Russia. American threats of an 'agonising reappraisal', especially when accompanied by what was thought to be inadequate support in the Far East, were counter-productive. Stalin died, the war in Korea was wound up, the international climate improved. Laniel succeeded Pinay as Premier and Mendès-France Laniel; Schuman was replaced as Foreign Minister by Bidault. Mendès-France attempted to get the Treaty modified so as to apply only to forces stationed in Germany, but as the Federal Republic would then be the only signatory whose forces were entirely absorbed in the Community, such a change involved discrimination and proved unacceptable. The prospects of obtaining a majority for the Treaty in the French Parliament were so slight that its presentation kept on being put off. When finally it came up for debate in August 1954, there was nobody to fight its case with enthusiasm and a large majority accepted a motion agreeing to postpone consideration indefinitely. The country which had sponsored the idea had ended up by turning against it; Adenauer's plans appeared to be in ruins.

Throughout the debate the right-wing French opponents of the Treaty obstinately refused to face the consequences of rejection, arguing as though the position would revert to what it had been prior to May 1952. But although the Treaty of Bonn was only supposed to come into force when the Treaty of Paris did, the world had too easily taken the ratification of the latter for granted. For over two years the Western occupying Powers had been treating West Germany, and West Germany had in fact been behaving, as a sovereign state, except that it had halted its preparations for raising armed forces. Here was a clock which could not be put back. The French had professed themselves nervous about the E.D.C. for fear of it being dominated by Germany : they had as a result created a position where there was little except good faith to prevent the Germans rearming in total independence free of all controls.

The blame for this predicament was, however, as widely laid on Britain as on France since the resolute British refusal to join the Community or give binding guarantees was said to have swung the balance against French participation. Though it is hard to believe that British aloofness was more than a contributing factor, it was Britain which now came to the rescue with an initiative that in

October 1954 led to the evolution of Western European Union, an organisation of sovereign states rather than a move to a supranational plane. A Secretariat replaced the proposed Commission and the Assembly (though empowered to take certain decisions by a two-thirds majority) was only allowed consultative powers. Britain undertook to keep four divisions and a fighter force on the continent till A.D. 2000; this was little more than had been offered in connection with E.D.C. and in practice troops from the four divisions were taken away within three years, but for the moment it satisfied the somewhat shame-faced French.

In some respects W.E.U. was an extension of the Brussels Alliance which Britain, France and Benelux had signed in 1948.[1] But that alliance had been directed against the possibility of resurgent Germany and not only was this animus now removed, but Germany and Italy were admitted to the Union. German entry to N.A.T.O. was also agreed upon, while she for her part announced the right to manufacture on her territory (though not that to acquire or control) atomic, bacteriological and chemical (A.B.C.) weapons. Moreover, she undertook never to have recourse to force to achieve reunification or the modification of her frontiers. In return the Americans, British and French recognised the government of the Federal Republic as the only German government 'freely and legitimately constituted and therefore entitled to speak for Germany as the representative of the German people in international affairs'. They went on to reaffirm that a peace settlement for the whole of Germany freely negotiated between Germany and her former enemies, which should lay the foundations of a lasting peace, remained an essential aim of their policy. The final delimitation of the frontiers of Germany must await such a settlement (a standpoint which was widely taken in Germany to involve agreement that failing such delimitation, the legal frontiers of Germany remained those of 31 December 1937). Germany was to raise a contribution to N.A.T.O. of 500,000 men (the size of the *Reichswehr* when Hitler reoccupied the Rhineland in 1936) but would not maintain a separate General Staff.

An awkward corner had been turned and an agreed basis found for German rearmament inside an organisation covering Western Europe as a whole. The controls which could in consequence be exercised over the Federal Republic were undoubtedly less close and detailed than those which would have been established in the E.D.C. But much has happened since 1954 to suggest that the

[1] See above, p. 174.

concept of the E.D.C. involved a degree of cooperation and surrender of sovereignty for which the nations of Western Europe are not yet ready so that even if it had come into being, its working might have disappointed the hopes of its protagonists.

Meanwhile the people of East Germany and particularly of East Berlin had on 17 June 1953 been provoked by their government into rising against their harsh conditions of life. The resources of the Ulbricht régime were completely inadequate to cope with the situation and armoured Soviet divisions were brought in to restore order, with some loss of life. The rebels may have imagined that the West would come to their aid and indeed some Western propaganda gave them an excuse for doing so. But even if the West had been prepared to act (which is highly unlikely), the episode flared up too suddenly and subsided too quickly for help to have been effective. Instead the Western Allies sought to exploit Soviet embarrassment by pressing the question of German reunification and in January 1954 a Conference of the four Foreign Ministers was held in Berlin to discuss the problem.

It was on this occasion that Mr Eden (as he then was) produced his Plan for reunification and the conclusion of a Peace Treaty. The process leading to these events was to start with all-German elections under provisions to ensure that these would genuinely be 'free' (in particular the supervising commission was to take decisions by majority vote which would mean the Soviet Union being outvoted). They further insisted that a reunited Germany must be free to make what alliances it chose, confident that it would opt for the West. Not unnaturally the Russians shied away from proposals which could only work out to their disadvantage. They insisted that measures be taken to prevent the elections being influenced by militarists and monopolies and that the first step should be a conference between the two German governments, to draft an electoral law. They also suggested that all occupation forces should be withdrawn and Germany neutralised. The West was unprepared to yield on neutrality for the sake of unity; the East was in the weaker position and for that reason less able to make concessions. The question of what counter-concessions could be extracted from the Communists in return for a Western concession on neutrality remained unexplored.

In the autumn of 1954, alarmed by the agreement on W.E.U., the Russians tried again, putting out proposals which seemed to come much closer to the Eden Plan, until in February 1955 an interparliamentary congress on the German question at Warsaw proposed the virtual acceptance of the Plan subject only to a guarantee of German neutrality by the principal nations concerned (including the U.S.). This gesture immediately preceded Malenkov's replacement as Chairman of the Soviet Council of Ministers by Bulganin, and the one has sometimes been thought to have contributed to the other. Certainly from this moment on, the Russians became as unprepared to compromise as the West already were.

Molotov gave a warning that signature of the Paris Agreement would make reunification impossible for a long period. In the following May, shortly after the Agreement came into force, the Warsaw Pact established a military alliance clearly intended as a counterpart to N.A.T.O. All the states of Eastern Europe including the D.D.R. joined the system. An additional obstacle to reunification proved to have been created in that the Russians henceforward chose to treat it as primarily an internal German affair which must be dealt with in the first instance by direct conversations between the two German governments. The Bonn government, however, absolutely refused to recognise the legitimacy of the régime in East Germany, let alone negotiate with it.

Chapter 10

Adenauer's High Noon 1955 – 61

Prosperity at Home

'Germany will blossom as never before. Her destroyed land-scapes will be rebuilt with new and more beautiful towns in which happy people will live. The whole of Europe will partici-pate in this upsurge. Once more we shall be friends with all nations who are of good will. Together with them we shall let the deep wounds heal which disfigure the noble face of our continent. In rich cornfields the daily bread will grow, banish-ing the hunger of millions who are needy and suffering today. There will be plenty of work and out of it as the deepest spring of human happiness there will come bliss and strength for all.'

THIS REMARKABLE vision of the Federal Republic in the 1950s dates from the dark days of February 1945. Its idyllic word-painting was intended by its author to show the Germans what they might hope to achieve by victory. That Dr Goebbels' dream should instead have been realised in the wake of defeat is not entirely due to Russian policy, for it would be ungrateful to suppose that the generosity of America was exclu-sively inspired by the wish to save Europe from communism. The liberal trade policies which resulted in the creation of such bodies as the International Monetary Fund, the World Bank and the General Agreement on Tariffs and Trade date from the days of the Russian-American honeymoon. Yet it was these policies and institutions which made possible the widening markets that dis-tinguished the post-war world. And without these markets it is hard to see how there could have come into existence the 'virtuous circle' on which German 'export-led' prosperity rested.[1] No comparable openings had existed since the years before 1914 and it was equally long since Germany had made comparable efforts in foreign markets. The West German share of world trade in manu-factures rose from 7 per cent in 1950 to nearly 19 per cent in

[1] See p. 179.

1959, which had been approximately its level (allowing for partition) in 1913, whereas for 1937 the figure had only been 16.5 per cent. The consequence was that Germany's export surpluses became positively embarrassing. So far from needing to conduct an 'export drive' the government was under permanent pressure to get the favourable balances reduced since their accumulation inside the country could not but have an inflationary effect.

One solution to this problem was found in the removal of import quotas and the lowering of tariffs. Germans were thus able to live better and more cheaply. Arrangements were made to pay off all Germany's outstanding debts. Another step was the Treaty concluded in 1952 by which West Germany undertook to pay Israel DM 3,000 m. to be used in compensating Jews whom the Nazis had driven out of Europe; a further DM 450 m. was made available for the same purpose in other countries. From 1953 onwards, increasing sums were made officially available in the form of loans at low rates of interest for the benefit of developing countries until by 1962 annual expenditure on this head was running at about the same rate as in Britain. Nearly all this expenditure came back to Germany in the form of orders but while it thus increased the income of manufacturers and workers, it did not necessarily add to Germany's material resources as much as its use in other directions might have done.

None of these measures proved adequate and in March 1961 the Mark was revalued upwards by approximately 5 per cent. Devaluations of currency have been distressingly frequent but this deliberate move in the opposite direction was almost unprecedented. The step was strongly opposed by the *Bundesbank* which would have preferred to see the rest of the world devalue instead, and by industrialists who feared that selling abroad would become harder and competition at home from imports fiercer (as it was intended to do and indeed has done). The truth is that, to make an international monetary system function smoothly, a country in a persistent creditor position must either readjust its price levels in relation to the rest of the world, or must get rid of its surplus by lending abroad (and by going on lending for as long as the surplus continues). This Germany failed to do in adequate measure : in comparison with her foreign investments of DM 8,500 m. (1966) her cumulative surplus over the period 1951–61 amounted to DM 24,000 m. There were three reasons for this failure. Two have already been mentioned—the relative lack of institutional machinery and the confiscation twice over of Germany's foreign assets. The third was the vast amount of capital needed in Germany itself for reconstruction, especially in the early years. By 1964, 8 million houses had been built (as against 4.8 in Britain). By 1967 over half the dwelling units in West Germany were post-war. Over half of the cost was in effect borne by the public authorities either in the form of loans or of tax remissions so that the necessary funds could be raised without having to put up interest rates to a level which made rents prohibitively high. Similar tax remissions encouraged individuals and firms to plough back large parts of their earnings into development. The government is estimated to have been responsible for 43.5 per cent of total net investment between 1948 and 1957.

Thus the background to the Germany of the 1950s was one of great and growing prosperity, a situation all the more gratifying because it was unexpected. For the first time in German history democratic government came to be associated with success and the world owes to Adenauer and Erhard a considerable debt for having proved that such a conjunction was possible. A preoccupation with material well-being absorbed the country, illustrated by the story of the girl who answered a quiz by saying that the two books to have had the most influence on her life were her father's cheque book and her mother's cookery book. Nor was it only the rich who profited, in spite of some appearance to the contrary and of the frequent assertions of foreign critics. Germany had led the world in devising social insurance and a generous if somewhat haphazard system of social security was now built up until the German people were in this respect the best cared for in the world. In particular a scheme was introduced in 1957 for 'dynamic pensions' which would rise or fall automatically with changes in the standard of living. Although much of the finance for these services came from contributions by employers and workers, the amount spent by the State trebled between 1950 and 1962, while Land and communal governments spent even more. A not surprising result was that the level of taxation also became as heavy as any in the world though less severe on the highest income groups than is the case in Britain, the U.S.A. and Scandinavia.[1]

The victims of the war, including those on whom the Currency Reform had borne hardly, were not forgotten when the benefits of prosperity came to be distributed. After a temporary measure in 1949, a Law for the Equalisation of Burdens was passed in 1952. This combined a capital levy, capital gains tax and levy on mort-

[1] Appendix Table VII.

gages, intended to amount to 50 per cent; from the fund thus created a variety of compensation payments were to be made. Obviously, however, it was impossible to raise so large a levy at one blow and arrangements were made to spread its collection over twenty-seven years, though loans were raised on the strength of the initial contributions so as to allow the hand-outs to anticipate the income. In the interval, much has changed. Values have risen, reducing the effective burden to 10–20 per cent, while some of the beneficiaries have made good on their own and others have passed beyond the range of human help. By the end of 1964, however, benefits totalling over £5,000 m. had been distributed to communal enterprises of social importance as well as to individuals. Another law in 1953 made the handling of refugees into a Federal rather than a *Land* matter, so that all should receive comparable treatment, irrespective of where they had come from or of what part of Germany they had gone to. A law passed two years earlier provided for the payment of compensation to those who had suffered at Nazi hands, as well as for their reinstatement in office or pensioning in accordance with the rank which they would have reached had they not been dismissed.

Considerable comment was, however, aroused both inside and outside Germany by the fact that this last law was accompanied by another passed under heavy pressure from the organisations representing Civil Servants and ex-members of the armed forces. Article 131 of the Basic Law had called for legislation to regulate the position of all who had been in public service on 8 May 1945 and had since been removed from office for reasons not laid down in the service code. This was now interpreted to require the re-instatement in office at their former rank of all except those actually serving prison sentences as a result of the denazification procedure. Every second senior Civil Servant in Germany in the early 1960s had worked for the government under the Third Reich. Any who had passed the age for retirement were awarded their normal pensions, as were all who had belonged to the armed services before 1935. This single act undid much of the work achieved by the occupying Powers (already considered by many to have been inadequate) of eliminating from positions of responsibility men who had shown by their attitude to Nazism that they could not be relied on as friends of democracy or humanity. Their replacements, often victims of Nazism, had in many cases to make way for them. Among the people so reinstated was, for example, Wilhelm Harster who as head of the Security Police in Holland had sent 100,000 out of the 140,000 Dutch Jews to their death in Auschwitz and elsewhere. When he returned to Bavaria in 1955 after serving a twelve year sentence (reduced to eight years) in Holland, he was put back in his old post as *Regierungsrat* in Bavaria and afterwards promoted. (He was, however, subsequently put on trial.) Between December 1949 and June 1950, twenty-three ex-Nazis were recruited into the Ministry of Economics. In March 1952 thirty-nine out of forty-nine senior officials in the Foreign Office proved to have been Nazis. A grotesque situation was disclosed when, as a result of publicity from Poland and Russia, it emerged that the Baden-Württemberg government had in 1958 appointed to the Directorship of the Central Office for the Investigation of Nazi Crimes a man whom they knew to have been a stormtrooper and party member.

This was not all. For one thing the Civil Service unions were able to frustrate most of the half-hearted measures taken by the occupying Powers to reform the administrative corps, by widening the area of recruitment in terms both of class and intellectual background. The system was re-established by which to a far higher extent than in Britain preference was given in the filling of senior posts to those who had paid for their own grammar-school and university education and had then passed an examination in law. Currently over half German senior officials are by training lawyers. This disregard of modern ideas about training for management is likely to prove costly in the next few decades.

Adenauer in addition showed himself curiously insensitive to the undesirability of employing in high office people whose record under the Third Reich had been unsatisfactory. His 1953 Cabinet included as Minister of the Interior Gerhard Schröder who had been a party member, as Minister for Refugees, Theodor Oberlander who had belonged to the S.S. and as Minister of Transport Hans Christoph Seebohm, a prominent protagonist of the Sudeten Germans who was later to define Germany as including all areas where Germans had ever settled and make many similar utterances without being seriously reprimanded. Among the Civil Servants put in charge of departments were Hans Globke (the head of Adenauer's personal staff) who, although not a Nazi, had written the official commentary on the Nuremberg racial laws; Friedrich Karl Vialon who after the war denied ever having heard of mass murders of Jews when an administrator in the Baltic states, only to be confronted later with his own signature on decrees about the disposal of the belongings of Jews earmarked for extermination; and Franz Thedieck who in occupied Belgium had been responsible for liaison between the German administration and the

S.S. Evidence was produced to show that none of these people had really behaved as badly as their critics (particularly in East Germany) suggested. But even if the evidence was true, it does not dispose of the argument that the impression created by such tolerance was bad.

The tolerance, however, was undoubtedly deliberate. The Chancellor was sufficiently a German and sufficiently a conservative to have a good deal of sympathy with the attitudes of old-fashioned nationalism. Moreover, he realised that, if such elements in the nation were cold-shouldered by the new régime, they would turn against it. One of the reasons for the failure of the Weimar Republic has been seen to be the hostility, amounting to disloyalty, of many who had formed the pillars of society under the Hohenzollerns. It was important that this should not happen again. The passage of time and the terrible demonstration of what exaggerated nationalism led to might be expected to lessen the danger in some measure. But if estimates based on interrogation were right in putting the number of hard-core Nazis at the end of the war at 10 per cent of the adult population, this would have meant the presence of about 4 million such people in Germany. Related to this is the figure of 12 million members of the Nazi Party and affiliated organisations. Again the 8 million or so refugees and expellees in the Federal Republic were all potential recruits for radical policies. To give the C.D.U. a character which enabled it to appeal to such people was not merely shrewd political tactics (though undoubtedly this aspect was not lost on Adenauer). It was also calculated to keep within limits the growth of parties further to the right. Critics who attack the policy as cynical and reactionary leave out of account the political realities in Germany. This is perhaps the most fundamental problem in German history as seen from a liberal viewpoint. How do you run a liberal democracy if the supply of competent and convinced democrats is inadequate? There can be no doubt that as a result of Adenauer's policy a number of people who might otherwise have sabotaged the democratic experiment were induced to tolerate it until its very success made them think it might after all have merits. Moreover, the changes which were bound in time to come were all the more likely to be in a leftward direction when the starting-point was so far to the right.

The satisfaction of the German people with the general policy of their government was convincingly demonstrated in the elections of 1953 when the C.D.U./C.S.U. won 243 of the *Bundestag's* 487 seats. Adenauer, however, preferred to keep his former allies of the F.D.P. and German Party in the Cabinet, so as to maintain a united anti-Socialist coalition. He even brought in the Refugee Party which had developed out of the Union of Expellees and Dispossessed (B.H.E.) established in Schleswig-Holstein in 1950; this had obtained 27 seats in the election. Two of their members were given seats in the Cabinet. In 1955, however, the rank-and-file of the party grew restless and complained that insufficient attention was being paid to their interests. Their two Ministers offered to resign but were without much difficulty persuaded to stay and, along with six other Deputies of the party, joined the C.D.U. in the following year. In the 1957 election the rump party obtained no seats at all.

In 1956 it was the turn of the Free Democrats to be riven with dissension, caused by developments in North Rhine-Westphalia. The story behind these throws light on several characteristics of German politics. Little love has been already seen to have been lost between Karl Arnold, the C.D.U. *Land* Minister-President, and Adenauer who particularly objected to Arnold's policy of finding a majority in coalition with the S.P.D. After the *Land* elections of 1950 had failed to give any party an absolute majority, Adenauer tried to prevent Arnold from reforming this coalition, and even to force him out of office : at one stage the remarkable spectacle was seen of the Minister-President boycotting the meetings of his own party, at another of the Federal leader ordering the *Land* leader, in face of all his followers, to 'resign or be faced with the charge of deception'. The only concession, however, that Arnold would make was to get his majority by coalescing with the archaic Centre Party (only extant in this *Land*) instead of with the S.P.D. This grouping lasted until the *Land* elections of 1954 when Arnold was forced to follow Bonn in taking the F.D.P. as his ally.

By 1956, however, elements in the F.D.P. were growing tired of playing second fiddle to the C.D.U. and a group of 'Young Turks' in North Rhine-Westphalia decided to break away and form a coalition with the S.P.D. Arnold was forced out of office and soon afterwards died; he was a man who might with advantage have played a larger part on the German political stage but for the fact that too many non-Germans were anxious to see him do so. Many of the fifty-two Federal Deputies of the F.D.P. decided to follow the North Rhine example, but their four Ministers felt no inclination to resign their seats in the Cabinet, and sixteen other Deputies followed the ministerial example. This group of twenty, led by Franz Blücher, the Vice-Chancellor, formed the Free People's Party (F.V.P.) which a year later joined forces with the German Party. The remainder under Thomas Dehler went into opposition. Two years later the S.P.D. chose to fight the North Rhineland elections on the issue of nuclear weapons[1] and lost heavily, after which the former C.D.U./F.D.P. coalition was re-established.

Among minor parties without representation in the *Bundestag*, some attention was attracted by the Socialist Reich Party, a right radical group centred in Lower Saxony, and the Communists. The first of these was, however, declared by the Constitutional Court in 1952 to contravene the article of the Basic Law forbidding parties which sought to alter the democratic character of the State : the second suffered the same fate, on the initiative of the Federal government, in 1956. There were some who thought it a mistake, particularly with the Communists, to drive them underground where their weakness could not be demonstrated.

The C.D.U./C.S.U. contested the 1957 elections with great vigour and spent over £3 m. (five times as much as the British Conservatives in the general election of 1955) in support of the slogan 'No experiments'. An analysis before this election suggested that there were in the Republic 8.5 m. firm C.D.U./C.S.U. supporters and 3.25 m. lukewarm ones, 9 m. firm S.P.D. supporters and 3.25 m. lukewarm ones, one million firm supporters of the minor parties and 2 m. lukewarm ones, with 3 m. voters undecided. In the event most of the lukewarm and undecided voters (many of them women) would seem to have played for safety with the result that Adenauer received an even greater majority than before in the highest poll ever known in Germany (except for 1933), while the Refugee and Centre Parties disappeared from Federal politics. Two members of the German Party continued as Ministers, but in 1960 they, along with seven Deputies, went over to the C.D.U., the remainder joining up with the Refugee Party to form the United German Party.

The year 1957 saw Adenauer at the height of his prestige. His success presented a serious problem for the Socialists. Their party was taking an active share in several *Land* governments, notably Greater Hesse, Hamburg and Bremen, as well as West Berlin, and it was at this level that their ablest administrators such as Brauer, Kaisen and Willy Brandt were deployed. On the Federal plane, however, so firmly did the C.D.U./C.S.U. appear to be in the saddle that the S.P.D. looked like being condemned to permanent opposition, which in a democratic state is tantamount to slow

[1] See p. 235.

extinction. The prospect caused the intellectual leaders of the party, in particular Herbert Wehner, Fritz Erler and Carlo Schmid, to insist that their programme must be drastically revised to take account of the Welfare State and the Communist threat. This meant not merely committing the party to the support of the free democratic order—that, after all, had been the Socialist position for many years—but also ending the identification of the party primarily as a working-class and Marxist body, which sought the public ownership of key industries. Prosperity was bringing nearer to completion a social process which had been intermittently under way since 1933, and giving to the workers an outlook hitherto characteristic of the middle classes. Unless the party could be made not merely compatible but positively attractive to such an outlook, it would have small hope of picking up the essential marginal votes needed to give it a majority in the Federal Republic. Moreover, the time had come to realise the growing affinity between the party and the increasing social awareness shewn by many members of the Churches; to this the materialism of Marxist doctrine was an obstacle. Finally, the party saw no alternative but to face the fact that Schumacher's opposition to Western integration had been a costly mistake. In 1957 the Socialists voted for entry into the Common Market and in June 1960 Wehner, speaking in the *Bundestag,* announced the party's acceptance in its broad principles of Adenauer's foreign policy. Meanwhile the new look of the party had in 1958 found expression in the Godesberg Programme. The key slogan in the economic field had already been coined by Professor Schiller, 'Competition as far as possible—planning so far as necessary.'

The dilemma of the Socialists is one familiar to left-wing parties, especially in times of prosperity—how far to sacrifice principles for the sake of gaining power. Adenauer did not simplify their task by campaigning on the thesis that a vote for socialism was a vote for Communist victory. The reasons for the Socialist action are easy to understand, and certainly some refurbishing of their image was necessary. Yet the wisdom of their actual course is not beyond question. They were confronted during the 1950s with one of those situations in which events seem to play into the hands of a particular party; in their case the advantages of their opponents were increased by Schumacher's miscalculations. In such a situation there are two alternatives. One is to adapt proposals to events, in which case some extra votes may be won, but at the cost of becoming virtually indistinguishable from the party in power. The other is to stick to old principles, reinterpreted as far as basic changes in the situation may make necessary, and hope that in due course the tide of events will turn. Since any policy, no matter how successful, is likely to have drawbacks as well as advantages, such a turning is in the long run inherently probable. But adopting this line assumes that the party as a whole will have the patience to wait for the long run. As the waiting period may consume the effective life-time of a political generation, such patience is often not forthcoming.

There were, as will be seen shortly, weaknesses in Adenauer's policy. It was not bringing reunification and the prosperity was less assured than appearances suggested. The Socialists were perfectly right in criticising these two aspects though they would have done better to hammer at long-term weaknesses instead of prophesying rapid disaster, because when such disaster did not arrive, their criticisms recoiled on their own heads. In reformulating their policy, in the 1958 Godesberg Programme, they did not of course abandon criticism. But the total effect was to emphasise their similarities with, rather than their differences from, the C.D.U./C.S.U. They thereby set themselves on a path which led logically to the acceptance of office in 1966 as the junior partner of the C.D.U. rather than on one which might, perhaps at a still later date, have made them a senior partner. They also, by leaving the Republic without a genuinely radical party, created a danger of a breakaway to the left. Although they gained votes after the change, they might well have done this in any event through growing public disenchantment with the C.D.U.

For by 1957 Adenauer was eighty-one and, though still remarkably lively for his years, was growing ever more autocratic and high-handed. His success in managing the German people led him to believe that any change of leader could only be for the bad. Various possible successors were considered, notably Krone, Etzel and Brentano, but given no real chance to show their paces and then discarded. Particular difficulty was caused by Adenauer's fixed and, as events proved, fully justified belief that the most successful of his assistants, Ludwig Erhard, was too genial and unsubtle for the post of Chancellor. He therefore determined to ditch him if he possibly could.

In 1959 an opportunity seemed to present itself. Theodor Heuss had for ten years filled the post of Federal President with a good sense, impartiality and humanity which deservedly earned him respect and affection. The Basic Law laid down that a President could only be re-elected once; Heuss characteristically refused to allow the Law to be modified in his favour, so that a successor had to be found. Adenauer tried without success to talk Erhard into taking on the job, and was then induced to announce his intention of standing as a candidate himself. But he also made remarks in public and private which suggested an intention to exert more political influence in the position than Heuss had done, and to secure the succession to the Chancellorship for Etzel rather than Erhard. Considerable opposition was at once evident to a step which would undo much of Heuss's achievement by bringing the Presidency back into party politics. The party flatly refused to consider Etzel for the succession and Erhard flatly refused to refrain from standing as a candidate, while close study of the Basic Law seems to have convinced the 'Old Man' that the President might not after all prove to have the amount of power necessary for him to carry through his plans. He therefore withdrew his candidature as abruptly as he had announced it, proposing instead Herr Lübke, his Minister of Agriculture. Although Lübke was duly elected, the impression was inevitably given that a substitute candidate, and one too with strong party affiliations, was good enough for the Presidency, so that the episode as a whole did Adenauer's reputation no good at all. His waning prestige was further damaged by developments in the field of foreign policy.

Intransigence Abroad

A minor casualty of the French failure to ratify the E.D.C. had been the idea of using the Community's existence to settle the question of the Saar. Instead, the Paris Agreement included a Franco-German deal by which the Saar, until the conclusion of a definitive Peace Treaty, was to be administered as an international territory under a European Commissioner responsible to W.E.U. The population were asked to confirm this imaginative and conciliatory arrangement but were also given the option of returning to Germany. Times had changed since the bleak days after the war when an overwhelming majority had voted for close association with France. Life in prosperous West Germany had recovered its attractions to such an extent that two-thirds of the electorate thought it preferable to becoming a guinea-pig for a federated Europe. There was nothing for the French government to do but *faire bonne mine au mauvais jeu* and at the beginning of 1957 the Saar became the tenth *Land* of the Federal Republic.

The summer of 1955 was eventful. In July the leaders of the U.S.A., U.S.S.R., Britain and France held at Geneva the first summit meeting since Potsdam. The chief problem was German reunification, on which neither side was prepared to depart from its prepared position. The West tried to persuade the Russians that, as N.A.T.O. was essentially a defensive alliance, West Germany's inclusion in it was an obstacle rather than an encouragement to aggressive German militarism. The Russians saw only that West Germans were being rearmed (as East Germans had already been). Neither bloc was prepared to take the risk of its part of Germany falling under the control of the other bloc. The East was not willing to give German opinion a really free opportunity of expressing itself; the West was not willing to see whether German neutrality could be genuine. Consequently neither the Summit nor a Foreign Ministers' conference which followed it in the autumn achieved in this field anything more than sterile argument. What the meeting did do was to reveal to each side that the other realised what an atomic war would mean and had no intention of starting one if it could avoid doing so. Though few at the time appreciated the implications of this discovery, it was to be fatal to the policy of reunification through strength.[1]

In the following month Adenauer, against the advice of his experts, decided to try his own hand at negotiating and accepted an invitation to visit Moscow. On arrival, he proposed two subjects for discussion with his hosts—reunification and the return to Germany of German prisoners-of-war still in Russian hands. He made no progress whatever on the first and for a limited verbal undertaking on the second had to agree to the establishment of diplomatic relations between the Federal Republic and the Soviet Union. To prevent such recognition from being interpreted as implying West German recognition of the 1945 territorial arrangements, he insisted on the Russians accepting from him a note stating that this was not so though even then the Russians, in publishing the note, added a statement that joined issue with it. The prisoners—or some of them—later came back, but two days after Adenauer left, a D.D.R. delegation arrived to conclude a Treaty which gave sovereignty to their government and authorised it to enter into diplomatic relations with other states.

Adenauer's chief justification for making this somewhat unhappy excursion had been that, as reunification was a matter for the four Powers rather than for the two Germanies, the Federal Republic must have direct contact with the Russians. But by his action he

[1] The first paragraph of the Geneva communiqué did however admit that the states represented at it had a common responsibility for German reunification. This was considered of importance as rebutting Soviet suggestions that reunification was a matter for the two Germanies.

had created the danger that other states would follow the Russian example in recognising and establishing diplomatic relations with the D.D.R. as well as with the Federal Republic. To counter this the Bonn government established in December 1955 the Hallstein Doctrine[1] according to which recognition of the D.D.R. by any state would be regarded by the Federal Republic as an 'unfriendly act', since it would involve recognition of the division of Germany into two states for which (in Bonn's eyes) there was no legal justification. When in 1957 the Yugoslav government accepted a D.D.R. legation, the Federal Republic broke off diplomatic relations, nor did it, until February 1967, establish such relations with any of Russia's allies in view of the fact that they possessed relations with the D.D.R. The main target of the 'Doctrine' has been the non-aligned states of Asia and Africa and there can be no doubt that, supported by Bonn's considerable programme of aid (which owes a good deal to such political calculations), nearly a hundred states have been dissuaded by it from recognising the D.D.R. On the other hand it gave to any neutral state which wished to extort concessions from Bonn a convenient handle for doing so in the shape of a threat otherwise to come to terms with the rival.

West Germany did not rest content with the Hallstein Doctrine but proceeded, with that methodical thoroughness which is such a notable national characteristic, to draw all possible consequences from the theory that their neighbours to the east had no right to exist. For one thing, use of the term 'Deutsche Demokratische Republik' was turned into an action tantamount to treachery : if employed at all, it was always prefaced by the adjective 'so-called' and as a rule the term 'Russian Zone of Occupation' was substituted for it. Indeed in many nationalist quarters the favourite description of that section of the country was 'Middle Germany' with the obvious implication that the areas taken over by Russia and Poland within the 1937 boundaries still constituted 'East Germany'. The usage can hardly be said to have contributed to realistic thinking in West Germany or to international confidence in the peaceful intentions of that state.[2]

A more constructive development also began in the summer of 1955 with the decision taken by the Foreign Ministers of the Coal and Steel Community, meeting at Messina, to set up a Com-

---

[1] Called after the then State Secretary of the Foreign Office, shortly to become President of the Commission of the European Economic Community. In fact the doctrine was formulated by Wilhelm Grewe.

[2] The West German state calls itself the Federal Republic of Germany rather than the German Federal Republic, to emphasise its claim to be the sole legally constituted government.

mittee under a 'political personality' (who proved to be M. Spaak of Belgium) with the task of working out detailed proposals for closer European integration in the economic field. This initiative led to the scheme for a European Economic Community which achieved concrete realisation twenty-one months later in the Treaty of Rome (25 March 1957). The elaborate provisions of the Treaty combined respect for the rights of member states with an inexorable advance to a situation in which decisions on such matters as tariffs, commercial and economic policy and agricultural prices would be taken out of their hands. Once signed, the Treaty allowed for no going back. It has sometimes been described as a compromise between German industry and French agriculture: this is too sweeping, but it was largely a bargain between Germany and France and represented in many ways the culmination of Adenauer's policy. Germany was henceforward to be mixed in to the rest of Western Europe in a way which would be difficult to unscramble. When critics suggested that the course might prove an obstacle to reunification, the habitual answer was that, on the contrary, only in the context of an integrated Europe would reunification become possible. The statement, however, is an article of faith rather than a demonstrable proposition : the future has still to show whether it or its opposite prove true. A minor advantage of the Treaty was that it enabled the vexed issue of German decartellisation to be transferred to a European plane. At such a level the question whether a single German firm or combine held too big a share of the market changed its character since in the future such a firm must expect to withstand competition on level terms from similar giants in other E.E.C. countries. The job of seeing that these giants did not in turn concert to fix prices or share the market was made the responsibility of the Community (though West Germany has its own legislation against restrictive practices, introduced by Erhard against the wishes of industry).

Meanwhile the Federal Republic had in 1956 put in hand the recruitment and organisation of the armed forces needed to fulfil its obligations as a member of N.A.T.O. With the example of the Weimar Republic in mind, great precautions were taken to ensure that the new troops should be loyal to the democratic state : these largely corresponded with current thinking about the kind of man needed in a modern technological army. The soldier was to be the 'citizen in uniform' : drill would be reduced to a minimum, instruction would be given in civics, while everyone from general to private would be free (as the constitution required) to join a trade union ! A significant blow to traditional attitudes was given by the requirement that mufti was to be worn off duty. Full authority over the armed forces rests in peacetime with the civilian Minister of Defence and in time of war with the Chancellor, while the Defence Committee of the *Bundestag* was given permanent status. A civilian Personnel Committee was set up to go into the record of each senior officer before appointment and the *Bundestag* was given power to nominate a Defence Commissioner with the job of watching over the maintenance of parliamentary control, investigating alleged infringements of basic rights and acting as a sort of Ombudsman for any member of the forces who felt himself aggrieved. The first few choices for this office were not wholly happy and the safeguards, taken as a whole, are so thorough as to make it a question whether they may not in due course provoke a reaction by impeding military efficiency : they have already undergone some modification. Relations between government and *Bundeswehr* are, however, very different from what they were under the Weimar Republic.

The original target had been to have 95,000 troops under arms by the end of 1956 and 270,000 by the end of 1957. Long before these dates, however, complications had set in. The aim of the N.A.T.O. allies had been to raise in Germany the men whom they were not themselves prepared to spare from their peace economies.[1] But as the Economic Miracle got under way the prospect of some 500,000 men being removed from the German labour market began to fill German industrialists with alarm. While there was some doubt whether the weapons needed to arm the *Bundeswehr* (which at this stage would have to be largely imported) could be paid for without either inflation or massive U.S. help, the real fear was that an artificially-induced labour shortage would make it impossible to hold wage claims in check. As the Ministry of Defence under Theodor Blank proved deaf to their representations, the bosses turned elsewhere and found a more receptive ear in the Minister of Nuclear Power, Franz-Josef Strauss, an exceptionally intelligent butcher's son and ex-bicycling champion who was working his passage to the top of the C.S.U.

As early as November 1955 Strauss was publicly attacking his colleague Blank's arrangements. In July 1956 the *Bundestag* Committee on Defence, whose chairman belonged to the same party as Strauss, cut out of the draft bill for raising conscripts the figure stating the length of time (eighteen months) which they were to serve. In mid-September 1956 the C.S.U. leaders laid down principles of rearmament which hardly squared with those of the

[1] See above, p. 208.

government, and at the end of September the Budget and Defence Committees of the *Bundestag* combined to cut out of the Defence Estimates the provision for equipping all units with tanks. Adenauer's majority was not such as to let him dispense with C.S.U. support, and in October he replaced Blank by Strauss. The new broom immediately cut down the numbers to be raised to 76,000 at the end of 1956 and 120–135,000 twelve months later. By the end of 1958 only 180,000 were to be in service, of whom only 45,000 needed to be conscripts. Conscription was reduced to twelve months and it gradually emerged that the final target was to be 350,000 instead of 500,000 and even this level was not to be reached until 1961 (or as far as the navy was concerned 1963).[1]

The apprehension of the industrialists were thus allayed. The Federal Republic had paid the rest of N.A.T.O. back in their own coin, refusing in turn to allow her economy to be disrupted and her prosperity checked by the need to compete with the Russians in numbers. Nor was this all. The reduction in numerical strength could only be justified if the fire power of the remainder could be increased. Just at this stage technological advances in the construction of nuclear weapons enabled them to be made in small sizes and used much as artillery. American and other strategists, convinced both by German developments and by the response of the rest of N.A.T.O. that the original target of ninety-six divisions could never be realised, argued that the use of such 'tactical' weapons offered the only means short of full-scale atomic war by which the West could hope to offset Communist superiority in men and conventional weapons. German industry saw in this development the possibility of manufacturing under licence a wide range of modern weapons and thereby gaining not merely profits and government help with research but also 'know-how' which could be turned to effective civil use. Strauss on occasion argued that, as Western Germany was on a footing of complete equality with her N.A.T.O. allies, the *Bundeswehr* must get nuclear weapons. The Americans, however, insisted that while all troops should be equipped with means of firing such weapons and trained in their use, the actual war-heads must remain under U.S. control —and American theatre commanders were bound to refer to the President before authorising the bomb to be used. There was soon every sign, however, that an attempt by the President to withhold his sanction would have thrown the entire defence arrangements of the West into disarray. The paradox of course is that the case for rearming Germany had rested on the need to match up to the Russians in conventional weapons; as things worked out, German rearmament was accompanied by a decision to abandon for all practical purposes the idea of defending the West conventionally, while the danger of a deliberate Russian attack was becoming steadily more questionable.

But a N.A.T.O. decision, taken in December 1957, to authorise the use of tactical nuclear weapons in Central Europe unleashed a flood of controversy. For, though smaller than bombs delivered by aircraft or missiles, they were clearly going to be extremely destructive, and the knowledge that the West was equipped with them would almost certainly (and in practice did) lead to the East following suit. Any incident on the East-West frontier, whether provoked deliberately or by accident, would be capable of escalating rapidly into a situation in which atomic weapons devastated considerable areas, and the areas most likely to be devastated lay in Germany. The result was a German clamour for the stationing of such weapons on German soil to be forbidden, reinforced on the part of many past victims of Germany by a clamour against putting such lethal weapons under any circumstances into the hands of German soldiers.

Adenauer and Strauss refused to make any concessions to this outcry. According to their arguments the knowledge that tactical nuclear weapons were available would in itself be enough to prevent incidents from occurring. When fifteen distinguished scientists from Göttingen University pressed that Germany should renounce all use of nuclear weapons, Adenauer disparaged them in public, while he was able to quote in his own favour a strong statement by General Norstad, the American N.A.T.O. Commander. A vote in favour of nuclear arms was forced through the *Bundestag* in the spring of 1958, largely by the argument that such a step was vital to German and European security; when the S.P.D. put their opposition to the test in elections in North Rhine-Westphalia in July, they were decisively defeated.[1]

Yet though the issue inside Germany had been settled, the fears of Germany's neighbours remained. The Communists were nothing loth to stoke the fires of disquiet, which they may reasonably be thought to have felt themselves, and the period saw a proliferation of plans for the creation of a nuclear-free or even armament-free zone in Central Europe. Adenauer and Strauss poured scorn on any

[1] See p. 226.

such suggestion especially when it was accompanied by proposals for a fresh approach to reunification initiated by direct talks between the two German states. They persuaded the Americans to treat the overtures as mere devices to stop the introduction of nuclear weapons into N.A.T.O. and were rewarded by accusations that their own ultimate aim was to make Germany a nuclear Power in its own right. Each side showed itself suspicious that the other would somehow evade its undertakings about disarmament, would use provisions for inspecting the genuineness of disarmament to carry out espionage or subversion, and would manage to exploit a disarmed zone for its own purposes. The question whether disarmament should precede or follow reunification also provided a fruitful source of dissension. The actions of both sides had built up an atmosphere of distrust which virtually precluded agreement and there is no point in trying to chronicle negotiations which were virtually doomed from the start. Mutual obstinacy had led to an impasse.

Unfortunately the East could not afford to let things go on as they were. Conditions in the D.D.R. had admittedly improved since 1953. Reparations were stopped in 1954, and occupation costs ceased to be levied after 1959. Food rationing was given up in 1958. The Republic was in process of becoming the biggest producer and exporter of manufactured goods among all the Communist satellites and was at last being paid for its deliveries, even if at low rates. Gross national product rose above the 1936 level (though long after it had done so in the West and chiefly as a result of increased output of capital goods). In 1958 personal consumption *per capita* at last rose above the pre-war level. But by that time it was half as high again in the West and the contrast between the two economies, when combined with the Communist limitations on personal freedom, provided a strong incentive to migration. Over the nine years from 1952, an average of around 600 people crossed the boundary to the West on every day of every year, the total loss coming to over 2 million. And it was mainly the young, the active, and the skilled who left. No state can face such a brain drain and survive. The policy of combating communism by making the West strong and prosperous was succeeding only too well. Its fallacy lay in supposing that countermeasures could not be devised against it.

In August 1957 the Soviet Union was reported to have launched a missile with an atomic warhead. In the following October came the first 'Sputnik' which gave evidence of a capacity to carry such a warhead from Warsaw to Washington in twenty minutes and

guide it with enough accuracy to destroy a target as limited as
the Capitol. The revelation impaired the credibility of the American threat to meet Soviet aggression in Europe with atomic
weapons, since such an act was henceforward going to invite
similar retaliation on America. There was, moreover, for some
time concern, which later proved to be unfounded, over a temporary American inferiority or 'missile gap'. The Russians would
seem to have decided to exploit their temporary advantage by
pressing for a European settlement. They made no response when
Adenauer on three occasions in 1958 secretly suggested the application to the D.D.R. of the neutrality formula which two years
before had made possible the restoration of Austria's independence.
Instead, Khrushchev in November 1958 made a threatening speech
in which he said that the time had come for the signatories of the
Potsdam Agreement to [sic] 'renounce the remnants of the occupation régime in Berlin' (which had not in fact been mentioned at
Potsdam) and thereby make it possible to create a normal situation
in the 'capital of the D.D.R.' (a description incompatible with the
agreements which actually had been made as to Berlin). Seventeen
days later his underlings followed this up by a more accurate
but equally sinister note saying that the Russians regarded the
pre-surrender agreements regulating the status of Berlin[1] as obsolete. It then proposed that West Berlin should be made into a
demilitarised free city under Four-Power guarantee and threatened
that unless the West accepted such a solution within six months,
control over communications between the city and West Germany
would be handed over to the D.D.R. authorities. Apart from the
fact that to get into the city thereafter would involve the West in
giving practical recognition to the D.D.R., the D.D.R. authorities
could be expected to act more provocatively than the Russians and
the chances of an armed clash would thus become distinctly
greater.

The Western Powers replied in effect that their right to be in
Berlin derived from the same pre-surrender agreements as gave the
Russians a right to be in Germany at all, and could not be ended
by unilateral repudiation. The Soviet Union was not entitled on its
own initiative to transfer its responsibilities to another government,
let alone to one which its co-signatories did not recognise. No doubt
was left about the intention of the West to maintain its position in
Berlin, if necessary by force. This show of firmness, which was
accompanied by expressions of readiness to discuss Berlin in the
wider context of Germany as a whole, had its effect. After

[1] See above, p. 144.

pressure had been put on Mr Mikoyan during a visit to the U.S.
in January 1959 and after argument had been deployed by Mr
Macmillan during a visit to Moscow in the following month, the
Russians began to abandon the time limit and in May the four
Foreign Ministers met in Geneva.

Whereas the Bonn government were delighted with the three
Western Powers for standing firm, they were distinctly less
enthusiastic over the idea of negotiations. Reunification was becoming so improbable that they attached ever-increasing importance
to Western pledges of support for it and deprecated any overtures
which might suggest a willingness to compromise. Macmillan's trip
to Moscow earned him a black mark in Adenauer's books, while
German faith in America was never the same after the retirement
and death of John Foster Dulles in 1959. The British and
American leaders were, however, under considerable pressure from
their publics, which, while ready to protect West Berlin and West
Germany against Communist encroachment, were much less concerned than the Germans about reunification, and insistent that
West German opposition to negotiation should not result in a
slide towards atomic war.

The Foreign Ministers' Conference lasted for four months and
at one stage seemed on the verge of agreeing to something. Their
failure to reach an interim agreement about Berlin was principally
due to disagreement as to whether, at the end of that period and
failing a final settlement, Western rights in the city were to continue until reunification or lapse. In the autumn Mr Khrushchev
visited the U.S. and agreed with President Eisenhower that another
attempt to reach agreement should be made, without a fixed time
limit. But the Summit meeting at which this was to be set in
train was delayed by de Gaulle's dislike of top-level discussions and
when it was finally convened in Paris in May 1960 was torpedoed
by Khrushchev, presumably because he saw no prospect of emerging
from it with any solution which his colleagues at home would
tolerate. Thereafter he refused to negotiate as long as President
Eisenhower was in office, and the whole question smouldered till
May 1961 when, meeting President Kennedy in Vienna, Mr
Khruschev revived his threats and again talked of time limits.

Kennedy, on taking office, had initiated a radical re-examination
of N.A.T.O.'s strategic plans. For he shared widespread fears that
the West had been preparing for the wrong kind of emergency.
A deliberate attack in strength by the East on the West, the spectre
of the early '50s, was coming to seem more and more unlikely.
What were probable were minor probes or border raids, either

deliberate or caused by misunderstandings. Yet if these were met at the outset by tactical nuclear weapons, as Western thinking proposed, there seemed a real danger that the situation would quickly though unnecessarily get out of hand, through escalation. The Kennedy administration set out to develop the theory of the flexible response, which called for the presence of sufficient ground forces, equipped *and trained* to fight on conventional lines, to hold an attack until its true scale and object became clear. The efforts to raise N.A.T.O.'s conventional forces were not notably successful but in the late '50s the Russians reduced their strength in Eastern Europe and it was not unreasonable to suppose that as a result the number of divisions in Western Europe would suffice to make a Communist attack from immediately available forces a risky business.

The new policy was, however, unwelcome to Adenauer, Strauss and German industry. Not only did it undermine the Ministers' position with their home public, to whom they had multiplied assurances that tactical nuclear weapons were essential, but it also seemed to involve abandonment of defence in forward areas for defence in depth, which was likely to make the whole of the Federal Republic east of the Rhine into a battle-ground. Moreover, in their view the certainty of nuclear retaliation could not be removed without increasing the temptation to risk a probing raid. Adenauer, as a veteran of the Cold War, would have agreed with Bismarck's view that 'Russia must be treated like bad weather until things are different'. He considered Kennedy a brash young man who was mistaken in preferring politics of movement for those of stone-walling.

During the weeks succeeding the Vienna meeting, however, Kennedy took the lead in combining firmness with conciliation. American troop strengths in Germany were increased and the German government announced its intention of raising the strength of the *Bundeswehr* to the original target of 500,000. But at the same time the West made clear that negotiation would be possible if the Soviet Union would accept the freedom of West Berlin, the principle of free access to West Berlin and the maintenance of the Western garrisons as a guarantee of these freedoms. Significantly nothing was said about reunification.

The Soviet leadership would seem to have concluded that the West was not to be cajoled or intimidated and that, as any physical attempts to exert pressure were likely to be met by force, they could not be risked. Something, however, had to be done to stop the exodus from East Germany which in the crisis atmosphere had risen to unprecedented heights. Panic signals from Ulbricht resulted in a quick decision to adopt the only practicable solution in sight. On 13 August 1961 a wall began to go up hermetically sealing East Berlin from the rest of the city. On 22 August West Berliners (as distinct from West Germans) were barred from entering the Eastern sector without passes, and as the West Berlin authorities refused to allow these passes to be issued in their side of the city, traffic came to a halt. Henceforward there was to be little refuge for the German consciousness from an extra obtrusive symbol of the country's defeated and divided condition.

The people, and possibly the government of West Germany, were disillusioned to find that their Western Allies took no steps to stop Berlin's Wall from being built, though it is hard to see what could have been done without risking all-out war. The free world, however, regarded the building of the Wall as an act of unprecedented and inhuman barbarism. But such a reaction is ingenuous. Not merely does it overlook the probability that the alternatives would have been harsher and more dangerous. It overlooks the alternatives because it assumes that an opponent who is conventionally regarded as ruthless and materialistic will act out of character by remaining inactive when pressure is applied to a foundation of his system. Sixteen years of tedious and unproductive negotiation should surely have made clear how loth the Russians would be to relax their grip on the parts of Germany which they had won.

Chapter 11

The Erhard Epilogue 1961 – 6

JUST OVER A month after the building of the Wall, on 17 September 1961, West Germany went to the polls. The growing disillusionment with Adenauer was reflected in the loss by the C.D.U./C.S.U. of twenty-eight seats, which involved into the bargain the loss of their absolute majority. The German Party, which had been their coalition partner till its split in 1960, fared even worse; it lost all of its 17 seats and so disappeared from Federal politics. Many people inside and outside Germany had hoped that the venerable Chancellor would take the occasion to retire. There were those in his own party who wanted to see him replaced by Erhard, because although they thought Erhard would make a bad leader (as he did), they reckoned for that reason on being able to get rid of him more easily than Adenauer and so open the way for one of themselves. But Erhard refused to be a party to such intrigues or put himself up against Adenauer, while Adenauer, on whom such calculations were by no means lost, regarded the situation as so serious and so many of his colleagues as unreliable that on the very next morning he announced his intention of continuing in office. To do so, however, he needed the support of a second party. The chief gainer from the C.D.U.'s lost seats had been the F.D.P. but it owed this success in large part to a promise by its leader Dr Mende not to join in any coalition as long as Adenauer remained at the helm. The alternative solution of a 'Great Coalition' with the S.P.D. had adherents in many quarters but its opponents inside that party on this occasion carried the day. In the end after seven weeks of bargaining, in the course of which Brentano was replaced as Foreign Minister by the more conciliatory Schröder, a C.D.U./C.S.U./F.D.P. coalition emerged, Mende atoning for his rash commitment by forswearing office. A promise was, however, extorted from Adenauer that he would retire in 1963 at the latest.

The building of the Wall did not end the Berlin crisis which continued to simmer for another eighteen months. Kennedy made

241

clear that he was still ready to discuss solutions which did not impair the fundamental determination of the West to protect West Berlin : as a result, he went a long way towards alienating the West Germans without quite conciliating the Communists. At one point Grewe, the German ambassador to the U.S., felt compelled to appeal to the article in the 1954 Paris Treaty by which the West had committed itself to seeking a freely negotiated peace settlement for the whole of Germany; at another, great offence was taken in Bonn when Washington suggested making concessions to the East and in Washington when Bonn sought to torpedo the move by deliberately leaking the American proposals. Grewe himself had later to be removed on account of incompatibility with Kennedy and his Secretary of State, Dean Rusk. Relations improved slightly as East and West measured up to the confrontation which was finally precipitated in October 1962 over Cuba. The demonstration that Kennedy was not to be intimidated earned him almost universal respect in Germany. The crisis had clear implications for Russian policy regarding Berlin and Germany : that Khrushchev had learnt them was suggested when on 16 January 1962 he told the East German Party Congress that the problem of the German Peace Treaty was not what it had been before the defensive measures (including the building of the Wall) were taken. Thereafter, for the time being at any rate, the chief Russian aim seemed to be to prick sleeping dogs with nothing more than tintacks.

Since the death of Dulles and more particularly since the election of Kennedy the United States administration had given Adenauer little encouragement for pursuing his hitherto unyielding line. His disillusionment with the country which he had made one of the two main foundations of his policy inclined him to pay all the more attention to the other and goes far to explain the friendship which was struck up from the autumn of 1958 onwards between himself and de Gaulle. The General's previous record towards Germany can hardly have disposed the Chancellor in his favour. His hostility to the E.D.C. and, as was to become evident, to the supranational conception of the Common Market might have been thought to show a radical difference of approach. Moreover, de Gaulle as early as March 1959 committed the sin, usually regarded in Germany as unforgivable, of saying that present frontiers (including presumably the Oder-Neisse line) must be maintained. But both men were elderly, both Catholic, both inclined to behave as autocrats; their homes were within two hundred miles of one another. Each of the two combined a respect for tradition with an astute eye for political advantage. De Gaulle could have no hope of realising his ambitions for Europe, involving as they did the reduction of American influence, unless he could secure at least one powerful ally, and in her current mood of disappointment, Germany must have appeared a more likely recruit than Britain. Another factor which could be counted on to work in the same direction was Adenauer's well-known desire to end Franco-German animosities for good and all. The Germans may well have appreciated that France's reasons for disliking America were by no means the same as their own. But the French policy of building up Europe as a 'Third Force' must have appeared to Adenauer to offer a chance of maintaining towards the East the unyielding line which seemed otherwise doomed by the withdrawal of American support.

For the rest of the period covered by this chapter, two alternative schools of thought contended inside the West German government for the control of foreign policy. The one, represented by Adenauer, Brentano, Strauss, Grewe, Baron von Guttenberg and others, denied that there had been any fundamental change in Russia's desire for world revolution, and therefore sought to maintain with as little alteration as possible the attitudes of the Cold War. But they now sought to achieve this object in association with France rather than America and by building up a 'Europe des patries' which, although composed of states still essentially sovereign, would cooperate sufficiently to overcome the inadequacies of sovereign states in the modern world, notably as regards the possession of nuclear weapons. The other school, of which Erhard and Schröder were the protagonists, argued that for the foreseeable future Germany must continue to depend for her defence on American nuclear might and that to maintain American goodwill some (but not too many) concessions must be made to the American desire for a reduction of East-West tension. If Erhard's tenure of office had been more auspicious as a whole, he and Schröder might have been able to make their views prevail. But as it was, they had to make so many concessions in order to carry the party with them as to remove any real chances of success. Thus the 'Peace Note' which they circulated to all friendly Powers in March 1966 was far too cautious to make any cuts in the Eastern ice. But the German Gaullistes for their part were frequently embarrassed by the unwillingness of their patron to consider any German interests which did not suit him.

The S.P.D. attitude corresponded to that of Erhard but was more adventurous. It was well expressed in a speech made to a

Protestant conference in 1963 by Egon Bahr, Willy Brandt's Press officer and policy adviser :

The American strategy for Peace can be expressed by the formula that the Communist domination has got to be transformed rather than superseded.

The first consequence of applying the Strategy for Peace to Germany is that the policy of all or nothing has got to stop.

Today it is obvious that reunification is not to be a once-for-all affair but a process with many stages and many pauses.

There is no need for us to be handicapped by our refusal to recognise the Zone as a lawful state. This goes without saying and without serious challenge.

Our first concern must be with human beings and with the exploration of every conceivable and defensible means of improving their situation. An improvement in material conditions in the Zone must lead to a relaxation in tension.

Such a policy can be summed up in the phrase 'Nearness will bring change'.

Herr Bahr's attitude was regarded by the 'hard-liners' of the C.D.U. as incapable of arousing any response on the part of the East and therefore as involving a gratuitous display of weakness.

This background helps to explain the commotion caused in Germany towards the end of 1962 by the 'Spiegel Affair'. *Der Spiegel* is a weekly paper which combines the format and style of the U.S. *Time* with the news-sense of the British *Daily Mirror*; it has performed in the conditions of post-war Germany the useful function of forcing on public attention issues and scandals which politicians preferred to keep wrapped up. On several occasions it had spotlighted actions by Franz-Josef Strauss of distinctly questionable propriety, even though he afterwards explained them to the satisfaction of the *Bundestag* majority. They included a report that on one of the crucial nights of the Cuba crisis the Minister of Defence had been the worse for drink. At almost the same time *Der Spiegel* published an article on the performance of the *Bundeswehr* in N.A.T.O. manoeuvres which claimed that at the Minister's instigation so much attention had been given to the use of tactical nuclear weapons as to impair the efficiency of conventional training.

Over a fortnight later police raided the office of *Der Spiegel* and the homes of some of its senior staff, on the pretext that there had been a leakage of vital defence secrets. Eleven arrests were made; that of Conrad Ahlers, the author of the article, was effected by the Spanish police, at the request of the German Embassy, while he was on holiday at Malaga. Rudolf Augstein, the paper's publisher, was kept in jail for fourteen weeks.[1]

In the subsequent controversy both Adenauer and Strauss at first attempted to minimise their parts, only to have it demonstrated that both had told lies to the *Bundestag*. In particular the telephone call to the Madrid Embassy was shewn to have been made by Strauss himself, though he has recently claimed to have been acting directly on the Chancellor's behalf. Adenauer, who on the whole despised his Cabinet colleagues, recognised in Strauss something of the flair for political manoeuvre on which he prided himself; he is less likely to have recognised as a further common characteristic a blind spot for the feelings of others. He would probably have liked to keep the offender in his Cabinet but was precluded from doing so by the F.D.P., one of whose Cabinet representatives, as Minister of Justice, had by Adenauer's orders been left in the dark in a matter directly involving his Ministry. Adenauer's first expedient was to dismiss the two senior officials who had done as they were told but this did not suffice to stop the F.D.P. Ministers from resigning in a body, and indicating that they were no longer prepared to serve with Strauss. Before they returned, the Cabinet had to be reconstructed, Strauss had to be dropped and the Chancellor had to confirm his intention of retiring in 1963. The F.D.P. Minister of Justice was not, however, forgiven for his refusal to help in hushing up the injustice done to him; he was left out of the new Cabinet and repaid his party for letting him go by joining the S.P.D. Meanwhile in the middle of the dispute the people of Bavaria had gone to the polls and voted for the return to office with an increased majority of the C.S.U., which had in the previous spring chosen Strauss as its chairman.

Hardly was the Cabinet reconstructed than Adenauer in January 1963 visited Paris to put the coping-stone on to his policy of reconciliation by signing a Franco-German Treaty of Friendship.

---

[1] The proceedings against Augstein and Ahlers were given up in 1965 for lack of evidence. But in August 1966 the eight judges of the Supreme Constitutional Court divided equally on the issue whether the action taken by the authorities had or had not constituted a violation of the Basic Law. When the Great Coalition took office four months later, with Strauss as Minister of Defence, the S.P.D. insisted on Ahlers being made Deputy Press Chief. Meanwhile in 1964 Strauss had brought an action against Augstein for saying in a *Spiegel* article that he reeked of corruption. The court of first instance found for Strauss and the verdict was strengthened on appeal in August 1966, though in a judgement open to a number of serious criticisms.

The auspiciousness of the occasion was somewhat impaired by its occurrence mid-way between the Press conference at which de Gaulle questioned the qualifications of Britain for joining the Common Market and the meeting at Brussels in which the British application for membership was finally on French insistence suspended. In retaliation the *Bundestag*, when ratifying the Treaty, insisted on adding a preamble which reaffirmed the German desire to maintain the Atlantic alliance and strengthen the European Community by the inclusion of Britain. Had Adenauer made his signature of the Treaty conditional on British entry, as some of his colleagues wished, much might have been altered. But the development and maintenance of Europe was always his first priority, while for Britain he had had at best respect, never affection. He tells in his Memoirs how de Gaulle, at their first meeting, quoted an American saying that Britain was like a rich man who had lost his fortune but did not yet realise the fact. Moreover, British attitudes towards disarmament, nuclear-free zones and a compromise with the East smacked altogether too much of appeasement for his tastes, while Macmillan's Nassau Agreement about Polaris submarines made less than no contribution to the new German objective of a nuclear force over whose operations the Americans would no longer possess a decisive veto.

The Nassau Agreement was conceived as a step towards the creation of an International Multilateral Force which would satisfy the growing demand inside West Germany for access to nuclear weapons without actually putting the control of such weapons into German hands. But the plan, which owed its origin to political rather than to military considerations, was suspect to the 'German Gaullistes' by very reason of its limitations and was much reduced in its attractiveness by the refusal of the French to have anything to do with it. Kennedy came to Germany in the summer of 1963 and improved relations by his reaffirmation of America's commitment to European defence and by a memorable speech in the Frankfurt Paulskirche where the 1848 Parliament had gathered. Khrushchev told an East German audience that the President of the U.S. was competing with the President of France in courting the old German widow, and expressed the hope that the widow would not become conceited. But the suspicions of the C.D.U./C.S.U. right wing were soon afterwards revived when the Russians suddenly decided to accept a proposal for a ban on nuclear testing which had been under discussion between them and the Americans for many months. The Treaty was signed by Russia and America on 5 August and all other states invited to adhere; China and France were the most notable abstainers, but the D.D.R. hurried to subscribe and there were those who suggested—happily in vain—that for West Germany to do the same might be taken as *de facto* recognition.

This was the juncture at which Erhard succeeded Adenauer who, however, remained Chairman of the C.D.U. and a member of the *Bundestag*. Far from endeavouring to ease his successor's task, he did not hesitate to make known his views about the policy of the new government, and at an early stage a remark that 'I can no longer endure the miserable talk of relaxation' began to make the rounds. Schröder was retained as Foreign Minister by Erhard and inaugurated a 'policy of movement', the chief feature of which was the development of trade with, and the establishment of trade missions in, the five Communist satellites whose recognition of the D.D.R. made impossible under the Hallstein Doctrine the establishment of full diplomatic relations. In the documents effecting this development, the terms offered by the Federal Republic were said to apply throughout the currency area of the Deutsche Mark; this formula evaded the controversial question of the Republic's right to act on behalf of West Berlin.

A similar evasion was resorted to at Christmas after the D.D.R. government had offered to allow citizens of West Berlin facilities for visiting relatives in the east part of the city. A representative of the Berlin Senate at the last moment negotiated an arrangemen which, rather than use names with implications which one or the other side could not recognise, opened with an admission that the two negotiators had been unable to agree on how to describe their respective areas, superior authorities or positions! The Bonn government disliked the concession but lacked the courage to veto a step which could bring happiness to so many, and almost a million people passed through the Wall. The arrangement was repeated in 1964 and 1965 but grew more and more unpopular with the hawks in Bonn who not merely feared that the very act of negotiating with D.D.R. officials might be exploited as involving recognition but also that any steps which eased the evils of partition might weaken the determination to abolish it completely. The D.D.R., observing this, thought that they saw an opportunity of putting the hawks at variance with the doves and when the 1966 negotiations started, insisted on spades being called spades. As a result no agreement was reached and no visits exchanged.

The virtual cessation of traffic between the two sides of the city was not merely a human tragedy. It called into question the functions which during the 1950s the Western side had been performing of show window, listening post, reception centre and propaganda factory. Moreover, with the ending of replenishment from the East, West Berlin's labour force fell over the years 1961-7 by 80,000, while every third person is a pensioner. In a few years' time therefore the free city is likely to become remarkable in the Western world for its freedom from congestion—but the alternative of stagnation may prove a doubtful blessing! Although the Federal Republic has continued to give subsidies of one kind and another worth over £200 m. a year, so as to make it possible for industry in the city to remain competitive, there have been signs of a drift of work, talent and control to Western Germany. The beleaguered bastion of liberty shows signs of degenerating into a dead end!

Erhard and Schröder remained faithful to the Atlantic alliance and their relations with France sadly failed to realise the hopes aroused by the Treaty of Friendship. But the difficulties in their path multiplied. Prospects of the I.M.F. coming into existence grew dimmer. The only substitute talked of was the creation of a new N.A.T.O. Committee to concert nuclear strategy on which West Germany was to have a permanent seat. America's attention and resources became increasingly absorbed by the Vietnam war and after Kennedy's assassination, few initiatives were taken in Europe. America's expenditure on aid had combined with a deteriorating trade balance to create an overall deficit, and the outlay on Vietnam made this even more serious. Britain had for some time been endeavouring to make the Federal Republic choose between contributing more to the cost of maintaining British troops in Germany or seeing their numbers reduced, and now the Americans, in search of economies, adopted the same line. De Gaulle made increasingly clear his determination to wreck N.A.T.O. which had for so long been the sheet anchor of German defence policy. In the summer of 1965 his high-handed attempt, in defiance of the Rome Treaty, to reshape the Common Market more to his liking added another ground for dissension, since the West Germans stood firm in solidarity with the Italians, Benelux and the E.E.C. Commission. The policy of seeking reunification through a relaxation of tension, instead of the other way round, seemed productive of problems rather than results.

Nor was foreign policy the only field in which things were going wrong. In the economic field much had changed since the early days of the miracle. Many of the initial advantages had faded away. Although the German defence budget in 1964 only absorbed 5.5 per cent of the g.n.p. as compared with 7.0 per cent in

Britain, the change was all the same considerable from the situation in the middle fifties. People who had rebuilt their fortunes no longer felt the same need for effort. Workers who had tasted the pleasures of the affluent society grew eager for the money and leisure needed to make more of them. The building of the Berlin Wall, by stopping the flow of workers from the east, made labour for the first time really scarce, in spite of great numbers of immigrant workers from Southern Europe. The German trade unions began to demand and obtain annual wage increases of the order of 7 per cent, whereas the annual growth in productivity was dropping towards 3 per cent and the growth in production to 2 per cent. (These were the actual figures for 1960.) German output per worker was in 1964 10 per cent higher than in Britain but over the five preceding years German wages had risen by 65 per cent and British by only 23 per cent. Rising costs began to make things harder for the exporter who had not in any case been helped by the revaluation of 1961. In 1965 West Germany had a deficit on current account of DM 6,500 m. (as compared with the British figure of £412 m. in 1964). And whereas Britain expects to cancel out her traditional deficit on visible trade by a surplus on invisibles (though many of her present troubles are due to inability to do so any longer), Germany reckons to need a visible surplus of DM 7,000 m. to offset the expenditure of her tourists, the remittances of her foreign workers and her payments in aid to developing countries.

The deficit was not confined to foreign trade. In the prosperity of the 1950s, a readiness had developed to quiet the complaints of pressure groups by handing out public money. Pensions had been made up on a lavish scale, subsidies given to encourage building and saving, the unnatural economy of Berlin had been bolstered up, compensation had been paid to all affected by the war, uneconomic industries had been kept in being, like textiles, coal-mining and shipbuilding. The fact that some of these expenditures had been sensible did not prevent them from being costly. Such generosity at the expense of the taxpayer was not confined to the Federal government : many social services in West Germany are the responsibility of the *Land* governments, others that of the cities and the communes, and extravagance was just as noteworthy here. Moreover, the division of powers under the Basic Law, and in particular the allocation of tax revenue, made it impossible for the Federal government to control total public expenditure even had the desire to do so existed. As the 1965 election approached, the largesse became more lavish than ever;

a particularly untimely step (not unknown in Britain in similar circumstances) was a cut in income tax. The praise accorded to the 'Social Market Economy', by making 'planning' a dirty word, discouraged people from asking how the Budget was going to be balanced or what levels of expenditure would be involved in future years by commitments already entered into.

Curiously enough, the election campaign of 1965 did not lead to any real debate on the problems facing West Germany in the fields of economic and foreign policy. The government were too fundamentally divided to encourage discussion, while the Socialists, fighting under the leadership of Willy Brandt, seem to have feared that talk of the need to economise or suggestions of a more conciliatory policy towards the East might lose them votes. They hoped to win victory merely by promising to do the same things as the government but do them better. Their gain of twelve seats fell far short of their expectations, whereas the C.D.U./C.S.U. who had been afraid of losing ground, actually returned three seats stronger. The real losers by eighteen seats were the F.D.P.; no other parties gained any representation at all. Although there was once again talk of a 'Great Coalition' (principally by people who wanted to get rid of Erhard) the Chancellor insisted on keeping the F.D.P. as his coalition partner and with their help beat off attempts to bring back Strauss (now leader of the C.S.U. in the *Bundestag*) into the Cabinet and to evict Schröder from the Foreign Ministry.

In the succeeding twelve months, however, things got worse rather than better. Dissatisfaction mounted with the lack of progress over reunification. The 'German Gaullistes' remained opposed to gratifying American desires for relaxation by direct approaches to the D.D.R., but their resistance to all forms of relaxation grew increasingly difficult to reconcile with their advocacy of close cooperation with France and the development of an independent Europe, since de Gaulle showed himself almost as anxious as the Americans to improve relations with the East. The choice open to West Germany was therefore no longer seen as one between rigidity and movement but between the Socialist solution of trying by negotiations with the rulers of the D.D.R. (short of formal recognition) to secure minor alleviations for their population and the official preference for trying by negotiations with other Communist states to isolate and undermine the rulers of the D.D.R. It became increasingly clear, however, that Erhard was too kindly, too much of a technical expert and too little of a politician for

him to impose his authority on his colleagues.[1] He did not dare
to threaten resignation because he knew that many would have
been glad to see him go. Consequently German policy remained
one of 'little steps' because Ministers could not agree in what
direction to make big ones.

Much the same story was repeated in economic affairs. The
Budget for 1966 showed a considerable deficit. Various proposals
for savings had no practical result and even the expedient of
forming five Ministers into a *Streichquintett* to strike out proposals
for expenditure came to little for the Ministers affected by the cuts
succeeded in getting the Cabinet to cancel most of them; party
discipline was not strong enough to prevent the representatives
of pressure groups from getting other economies rejected when
they came before the *Bundestag*. The *Bundesbank*, which had
been so constituted as to be beyond the government's control,
proved a further source of embarrassment; in its alarm over
rising prices it pushed interest rates up until industry became
reluctant to borrow. The consequent fall in capital expenditure
was all the more serious because the house building boom showed
signs of ending, as demand became satiated. For the first time
for many years, unemployment began to rise and business confidence was shaken. The early symptoms of a crisis were unmistakable. They even induced Erhard to overcome his objections to
attempts at guiding the economy and allow his Economics Minister
Schmücker to introduce a Stability Bill giving the government
powers to accelerate or slow down the rate of expenditure at *Land*
and local levels as well as centrally. The project, however, evoked
numerous objections, not least from the *Länder* governments, and
it bogged down in *Bundestag* debates.

When a *Bundestag* Deputy dies, or retires, his place is filled
automatically by the next available name on his party's list for
election by proportional representation;[2] there are thus no by-
elections. As a result, it is elections for *Land* governments which
in Germany perform the role of recording changes in public
attitudes towards the government. In July 1966 such elections fell
due in North Rhine-Westphalia, and in them the S.P.D. came
within two seats of winning an absolute majority. This was an omen
which the C.D.U. could not afford to disregard. Dissatisfaction

---

[1] His State Secretary was described, on the analogy of the Ministry for
Help over Development (*Entwicklungshilfe*), as responsible for help over
decisions (*Entscheidungshilfe*).

[2] See above, p. 101 and also Annexe, p. 301.

with Erhard ceased to be confined to political opponents and personal enemies; even for those who had hitherto supported him, he began to seem more a liability than an asset. The F.D.P. in particular began to worry whether in their electoral position they could afford to be associated much longer with a discredited régime. But article 67 of the Basic Law (Constructive Vote of No-Confidence) makes any Chancellor difficult to dislodge, and all the obvious C.D.U./C.S.U. aspirants for the succession had determined enemies. A double manoeuvre was needed at the end of October 1966 to evict Erhard. In the first place the rank-and-file of the F.D.P. Deputies insisted on their Ministers vetoing Cabinet proposals for balancing the Budget by higher taxes; they hoped by this means to force the C.D.U./C.S.U. into facing fundamental policy decisions. The rank-and-file of the C.D.U./C.S.U., led by Strauss, saw their chance and, by insisting on their Ministers standing firm, provoked the F.D.P. members of the Cabinet into resignation. Though Erhard tried for a time to weather the storm, there was general agreement that a new Cabinet would have to be formed, with a new Chancellor. But who should compose it?

The urgency of the situation was underlined by elections in Hesse on 6 November and Bavaria on 23 November. Not only did the F.D.P. lose ground in both, being completely deprived of representation in the Bavarian *Landtag,* but the right-wing National Democratic Party (which had obtained no seats in the 1965 Federal elections) made striking gains, polling 7.9 per cent of the votes (with 8 seats) in Hesse and 7.4 per cent (with 15 seats) in Bavaria. Some voters were losing patience with democracy.

The first step towards the resolution of the crisis was taken when the C.D.U./C.S.U. decided, largely on the initiative of Strauss, to bypass all the more obvious rivals for the succession and call back to Bonn, as its candidate for the Chancellorship, Dr Kurt Georg Kiesinger, a former Deputy who, after Adenauer had dashed his hopes of becoming Foreign Minister, retired to his native *Land* of Baden-Württemberg as its Minister-President. The most obvious objection to his appointment was that he had not only joined the Nazi Party in 1933 but remained a member, even if a relatively inactive one, throughout the Third Reich; this at least seemed to justify a charge of conformism, and thereby to impair the good impression created by his post-war record.

Both the C.D.U./C.S.U. and the F.D.P. regarded with distaste the idea of working together again. The character of the new government was thus made dependent on the preference of the

S.P.D. While they still differed on many issues from the C.D.U./ C.S.U., the gap between the two parties had been narrowing ever since the Godesberg Programme, while the Socialists could not be said to see altogether eye-to-eye with the leaders of the F.D.P. The greatest objection to a 'Little Coalition' lay in the fact that it would only have had a majority of six, and the loyalty of some members of the F.D.P. right wing was far from assured.[1] In a 'Little Coalition' the main responsibility would have rested with the S.P.D. and they were afraid of being discredited, on at last achieving office, by failure to discharge it effectively. Yet, if they refused office altogether, they were afraid of being condemned for shunning responsibility. They also feared that, in face of a S.P.D./F.D.P. government, the C.D.U./C.S.U. would move away to the right and criticise Ministers for lacking patriotism, as under Weimar. There was also a good deal in the argument that only a Great Coalition would be strong enough to overcome the difficulties facing the new government abroad and restore business confidence at home.

For all these reasons, under the strong promptings of Herbert Wehner, but against the inclinations of many ordinary party members, and to the disillusion of the young, the S.P.D. Deputies came down at the end of November 1966 in favour of a Great Coalition. The C.D.U./C.S.U. were delighted with a solution which spared them the unpleasant necessity of giving up office, even though a spell in opposition may well have been what their party most needed. Under Kiesinger as Chancellor, Brandt became Foreign Minister, Schiller Economics Minister, Strauss (who had recently signed on for post-graduate studies in economics at Innsbruck University) Finance Minister, Schröder Defence Minister and Wehner Minister for All-German Affairs. The wits, on the British analogy of 'Mr Butskell', talked of the 'Kiesebrandt' Cabinet.

With the accession to office of the Great Coalition, German

[1] The British experience of 1950–1 and 1964–6 has been invoked to show that the S.P.D. worried unduly about the weakness which a small majority would entail. But German party discipline is a good deal looser than British and more work is done in committees where majorities would have been narrower still. Another possibility would have been for a S.P.D./F.D.P. coalition to have taken office and, as soon as they were defeated in the *Bundestag*, put a vote of confidence and gone to the country under article 68 of the Basic Law. But this course could have been frustrated if the C.D.U., who were afraid of an election in which they seemed at the time likely to lose, had arranged for enough of their members to abstain to ensure that the government was not defeated on the vote of confidence.

politics entered on what was clearly a new phase. The juncture
seems therefore appropriate for breaking off this historical narra-
tive, especially as the historian lacks the ability of the space-scientist
to land his projectile accurately on a moving target. Something,
however, needs to be said about problems facing the Federal
Republic in the present and future.

Chapter 12

Four German Problems

(a) *Education and Research*

THE GERMAN educational system has a deservedly high reputation but, like those of many other countries, it is now facing serious difficulties in the process of adapting to present needs methods devised to meet the requirements of the past. Just as in industry ways have to be found of applying to quantity production the high standards of quality and precision achieved in the laboratory, so in academic affairs institutions designed for a few students have to be adapted to turn out the large numbers of highly educated men and women needed by contemporary society.[1] There have been four main factors holding back expansion. One is that the channels of entry to higher education are too restricted. The second is the excessive wastage at almost all levels. The third is the out-of-date view taken by the universities of their function. The fourth is the lack of qualified teachers.

Entry to higher education is virtually confined to boys and girls who at about the age of ten have satisfied the teachers in their *Volksschulen*[2] (primary schools, virtually uniform since 1919 for the first four years for the entire population) that they are qualified to attend *Gymnasien* (grammar schools, also called *Oberschulen*) teaching scientific and modern subjects as well as arts. Parents dissatisfied with the teacher's verdict can apply for special tests, but the method of selection does not appear to provoke dissatisfaction and the principal complaint seems to be that too few children rather than too many are encouraged to think of grammar-school education. This in spite of the fact that although 'a

[1] In Western Germany this need was to some extent obscured till 1961 by the influx of trained manpower from the D.D.R.; one in four of those receiving higher education there are believed to have emigrated on or before its completion. 'Guest' workers from Southern Europe have not been qualified to make good the drying up of this flow, as they have to some extent done for unskilled jobs.

[2] *Kindergarten*, though a German word, is not a West German institution. There is little or no public schooling for children till they are six.

255

second educational route' to higher education through schools other than *Gymnasien* does exist, the percentage of university students who have arrived by it is at present 6.6 (about the same as in England and Wales).

There were in 1964–5 some 1,720 *Gymnasien* in the Federal Republic with about 890,000 pupils (or around 16 per cent of the age-group) as compared with 2,025 and 968,000 (12.5 per cent) in England and Wales.[1] The percentage of the age-group at *Gymnasien* varies considerably from one part of the country to another and in spite of the fact that education in all public schools is free (and there are relatively few private schools), children of workers, of country dwellers and of Catholics, along with girls of all social origins, are under-represented in proportion to their strength in the age-group as a whole. The chief obstacle to be overcome in remedying this is thought to lie in the parent's attitude : a working man once explained that to the likes of him 'Universities are strange, like Picasso; far away in space'. Much attention has, however, been given to this problem recently and as a result the numbers entering *Gymnasien* are beginning to rise faster than the most optimistic forecasts assumed.

The situation has not been improved by the fact that in 1964 nearly 15 per cent of German children were attending primary schools with only one or two classes (there is even one such Gymnasium). These 'dwarf' schools are almost always due to invocation by the Churches (and particularly the Catholic Church) of clauses in the Basic Law and *Länder* constitutions guaranteeing to parents the right to send children to schools of their own faith wherever there is the bare minimum of them to justify separation. Efforts to combine such schools into larger 'community' schools containing children of different religions are making progress but still encounter resistance; in this respect, German education is now meeting something of the trouble which nonconformacy caused to English education throughout the nineteenth century. Comprehensive schools are relatively unknown, though facilities for the technical education of those who do not go on to *Hochschulen* are extensive and efficient.[2]

Sixty per cent of the pupils entering *Gymnasien* either fail to

---

[1] The figures in this section are principally drawn from the Robbins Report on Higher Education, pp. 41–4 and Appendix V, and the 1960 and 1967 *Empfehlungen des Wissenschaftsrates zum Ausbau der wissenschaftlichen Hochschulen*. The reader is, however, warned that comparative statistics are even more treacherous in education than in most other fields.

[2] *Hochschulen* means *not* our 'High Schools' but all institutions of higher education, including universities and institutes of technology.

complete the course or leave without taking the *Abiturientenprü-fung* (a test broadly corresponding to G.C.E. 'A' level but with a broader spread of subjects at a rather lower standard and conducted primarily by the schools' own staff). This wastage compares broadly with that in England and Wales. The proportion of each age-group to pass the *Abitur* was at the beginning of the 1960s 7 per cent (as compared with 8.5 per cent passing 'A' level in two or more subjects in 1964–5). The total figure has been steadily rising; in 1950 it was 31,000 : in 1959 52,000; in 1967 65,000, and it is now expected to be 127,000 in 1979. Ninety-eight per cent of the boys and 86 per cent of the girls who do pass the *Abitur* go on to higher education in one form or another (including teachers' training colleges), a much higher figure than the average in Western Europe.

By long tradition there is no entrance requirement for the universities other than the *Abitur*. The student who had passed that test had hitherto been free to study where he liked, to attend what courses of instruction he chose, to change from one university to another when it suited him and to postpone his final examination until he considered himself ready for it. This examination, however, is not usually for a university degree but for admission to a profession and is set by the State (or by the staff of *Hochschulen* acting on the State's behalf, much like the examiners for Britain's Civil Service Commission). For 'first degrees' have hitherto been unknown in Germany, the only grades (other than diplomas) given by universities being the doctorate and the *venia legendi* (*Habilitation*) or qualifying test for would-be university teachers. The doctorate is awarded for original research, usually to students who have already taken a State examination. For the majority of subjects, a minimum of four years' study at a *Hochschule* is required by the State as qualification for taking its examination, but the average student has been taking five and some six or more years. The doctorate is likely to require two or three in addition, and the total average length of study rose by three semesters (one and a half years) between 1955 and 1965. As a number of professions (notably law, so important for the Civil Service) require a training period of several years after the *Staatsexamen*, a young German is likely to start on responsible work some five years later than a young Briton, though when he (or she) does start, he is likely to be more highly trained.

This situation is fundamentally due to the German tradition, dating back to Wilhelm von Humboldt, according to which all those destined to occupy posts of high responsibility, whether in teaching, administration or the professions, should be trained as scholars. Higher education has culminated in individual research done in close association with professors whose main task is the advancement of learning. Up to this stage, however, teaching (at any rate in the arts) has been by lectures at which attendance has been optional. The training of students in methods of thought and the imparting of the knowledge needed to do a job have assumed a distinctly more subordinate role than in Britain. If the British have looked on German universities as institutions of scholarship remote from the needs of everyday life, the Germans have despised British universities as mere extensions of secondary school instruction. The British problem is to give sufficient instruction in a three-year course to students coming forward in such numbers as to make anything in the nature of individual teaching difficult. The German problem is to find room in universities for the numbers expected to present themselves in 1980 if all are to remain there for the five to seven years which the current system requires. A system in which the individual is largely left to find his own way, though it may often in the end produce excellent results, does require time and cannot easily be hurried up. A particular cause of recent student criticism is the lack of facilities for discussion.

Because of this fundamental difference a comparison of the numbers attending *Hochschulen* in the Federal Republic with those at equivalent institutions in Britain is apt to be misleading. Thus in 1954 the figures were 122,540 and 82,000 respectively but, on the assumption that the first contained 5.5 and the second 3.5 annual intakes, the numbers in each were very nearly the same.[1] In 1958–9 only 3 per cent of each age group were actually finishing courses of British degree level (or higher) compared with 5.6 per cent in Britain and 10 per cent in the U.S.[2] This is partly because 40 per cent of those in the German institutions leave without obtaining any qualification as against 14 per cent in the U.K.

In 1965–6 the total numbers of students at *Hochschulen* in Germany were 251,000 and at universities in Britain 167,000. By 1980, on the assumption already mentioned as to the number taking the *Abitur*, they would rise in Germany to 550,000 which is almost exactly the same figure as envisaged by the Robbins

---

[1] The German figure included about 12,000 medical students, some of whom in the U.K. would not have gone to a university at all but direct to a teaching hospital.
[2] Robbins Report, p. 44.

Report for the U.K. Although this would mean a distinctly lower annual intake in Germany, the problems involved in providing the necessary number of student places are regarded as almost insuperable. The obstacles are only in part financial, though costs, five-sixths of which are born by the *Länder*, have been rising steeply from £93 m. in 1960 to £330 m. in 1966.

In some respects German education is cheaper than British. Although students from poor homes have been paid grants on a uniform basis since 1955, only some 20 per cent at present receive them and they are relatively low. (University fees average around £50 a year.) The salaries of German professors have, however, always been good and now rise to about £8,400 a year. Moreover, it was stated in 1967[1] that the cost of providing each new student place amounted to DM 200,000 or £21,000, whereas the Robbins Report envisaged a total capital expenditure of £1,140 m. for a period in which student numbers were to rise by 344,000 or £3,300 per head. Even allowing for wide differences in the bases on which these figures have been calculated, German building standards look as though they were a good deal more lavish than British. Those in charge of German finances cannot be blamed for looking with alarm at the prospect of an annual cost of nearly £450 m., especially when this comes on top of the extra expenditure needed to accommodate an additional two million children in the schools between 1964 and 1970 (partly as a result of raising the school leaving age to fifteen). Expenditure on all education in 1950 was only £183 m. or 2.5 per cent of g.n.p. By 1960 it was £693 m. or 3 per cent, compared with a British figure of £1,018 m. or 4.4 per cent. In 1965 it would seem to have been £1,400 m. or 3.1 per cent compared with £1,613 m. or 5.2 per cent. Education has been something of a Cinderella; the German public are growing alive to the dangers which this involves but the cost of meeting all needs would be heavy.

Even if the money could be found, however, the staff almost certainly could not. The universities were slow to recover from the running down of teachers which they underwent in the Third Reich.[2] Whereas the student population was in 1960 nearly double what it had been in 1928, the number of professors had only grown by 4 per cent. Moreover, the traditional system militated against the development of a staff pattern suited to modern conditions. Aspirants to professorial chairs were expected to support themselves, or be supported by their parents, until their

[1] *Die Zeit,* August 1967.
[2] See above, p. 98.

Habilitation at an age of about thirty. Even then their only regular stipend was the fees which they were entitled to charge as *Privatdozenten* to students attending their lectures. As soon, however, as they obtained a chair, which they might hope to do about thirty-five, their finances and status changed dramatically. As State servants they gained an assured salary (plus fees for any lectures over and above a stipulated minimum) and a pension at three-quarters of their pay on retirement. They were able to decide who should study at their university for a doctorate within their field and who should be advanced to the grade of *Privatdozent*. With their colleagues, they ran their faculty and with the other faculties were exclusively responsible for nominating one of their number to be Rector each year. Appointments to chairs were made by the *Land* Minister of Culture but the university was allowed to put forward three names and there neither was nor is any system of advertising vacancies or inviting applications. The number of *Privatdozenten,* though rising, was for long less than that of professors and they had virtually no say in running the university. Small wonder that the rank of professor was keenly sought and widely admired. Even in 1959 a cross-section of Germans, polled as to the relative prestige which they attached to thirty-eight different occupations, put professors first!

Nowadays, however, young scholars are no longer able to support themselves till their *Habilitation,* while the growing complexity of all subjects has been tending to push back to thirty-five the age at which this occurs and the age of appointment to a chair towards forty-five. Consequently the whole career structure of German university teaching has had to be revised, so as to provide, as in other countries, a variety of posts subordinate to that of professor. In 1960 the creation of 1,200 new chairs and 11,000 other teaching appointments was recommended and in practice the teaching staff went up between then and 1966 by 104 per cent. Fees for lectures having been abolished, everyone depends upon his salary. The aim is to provide a chair for each teacher within six years of his *Habilitation* (i.e. around forty) and in some cases this gap can be much shorter. The teacher-student ratio is said to have dropped to 8.4—lower than in Britain— though in some crucial sectors, such as law and the social sciences, it is still over 20. The amount of responsibility allowed to junior staff remains small.

Attempts are also being made to shorten the time which students spend at a university. The four-year attendance hitherto required for a *Staatsexamen* is moving from being a minimum to a maximum and syllabuses revised accordingly. The Council of Rectors have decided to institute a preliminary examination at the end of two years, though without agreeing on what is to happen to those who fail to pass or even to take it. Experiments have also been made with M.A. degrees. Each student is to be given an adviser who will guide him as to his curriculum; this change may materially help to reduce student unrest[1] which seems in part due to lack of contact between teachers and taught. The suggestion has also been made that some universities should experiment with halls of residence in which students would be expected to spend their first eighteen months. When the increasing importance attached in Britain to post-graduate work is remembered, the wide differences between the two systems would seem to be on the way out.

Even so, grave doubts are felt as to whether German universities are in a position to take the load which will come on them if present forecasts prove correct. A calculation has recently been made of the number of students who could be effectively taught in 1970, on the assumption of (*a*) 142 additional chairs and 1,650 other posts being created and filled, (*b*) teaching loads and size of classes approximating to those in Britain. This would allow the admission of 50,000 students a year, which if all finished in four years, would mean a total of 200,000 (plus those going on to doctorates and *Habilitation*). This is well below the 1966 numbers, let alone those expected in 1970. A more rapid expansion is ruled out as impracticable, for even if all who take doctorates were to be kept on for a few years in university teaching instead of going in many cases, as at present, to other occupations, the number currently coming forward do not suggest that extra posts could be satisfactorily filled, except by abolishing and not merely (as is proposed) relaxing the requirements of the *Habilitation*.

In face of this dilemma, two solutions are being canvassed. One is to restrict the number of students admitted to the universities, at any rate temporarily and in the most popular faculties. This would involve the abandonment of one of Germany's most cherished traditions, even if it would not violate article 12 of the Basic Law which guarantees to all Germans freedom to choose their place of vocational training. A variant of this scheme, though in the longer term, is an attack upon the equally deep-seated convention that all taking the *Abitur* should go on to a *Hochschule* or teachers' training college.

[1] For the political aspects of this unrest, see below, p. 284, 294.

A more radical plan on similar lines has recently been proposed for the *Land* of Baden-Württemberg. This starts from the recognition that those now seeking higher education of some description do not all need to be treated as though they were potential candidates for a doctor's degree. It proposes to group all institutions of higher education—including some like schools of engineering, which do not at present count as such—under one umbrella and to make the *Abitur*—probably in a revised form—the entrance requirement for them all. It then proposes to provide, both in the universities and in the other institutions, a three-year 'short-study' course leading to a first degree or equivalent diploma. Alongside this in the universities there would still remain the 'long-study' course taking not more than five years with a preliminary examination at the end of the second. Those who aspired to a doctorate could stay on longer. Provided that sufficient students opted for the short course, this change might be expected to reduce the number in universities by something between one and two fifths—but it could also be expected to reduce the 40 per cent fall-out rate and this, though a good thing in itself, would counteract the drop in total numbers.

The introduction of a *numerus clausus* (limit on intake) not only breaks with tradition but runs counter to the modern need for providing as many people as possible with a university education. If the excluded surplus are directed to other institutions, there will still remain the problem of providing those institutions with teachers, who should preferably have had a university education. Moreover, teachers in *Gymnasien* are required to have attended a university while teachers in other schools are normally required to have been to a *Gymnasium*. During the Third Reich the number of people taking up teaching of any kind was allowed to drop, so that the age-structure of the profession is out of balance; 44 per cent of those teaching in 1961 were due to retire before 1970. A low birth-rate during the war was followed by a high one during the '50s and the effect of this is beginning to be felt. The claim was made a few years ago that in the next decade the needs of the teaching profession would absorb all the people taking the *Abitur,* leaving none over for anything else. This has proved unduly alarmist, but the fact remains that the whole way up the educational ladder, staff is at present a bottle-neck with the effects at each level creating complications for the others. For a time there will almost inevitably have to be a lowering of the qualifications for teachers (an idea bitterly resisted by the teaching profession) or a lowering in teaching standards (in the shape of shorter hours for pupils, larger classes, etc.). Not surprisingly there are those in Germany who feel that more should have been done to foresee the present emergency (which one writer has gone so far as to call a catastrophe) and get remedial action taken at an earlier stage. A large share of the blame for the failure is with some justification ascribed to the Federal system. Education has always been regarded as the concern of the individual *Länder* and Germany's experience with a national Minister of Education from 1933 to 1945 has been a powerful argument against centralisation. Accordingly in 1949 no Federal Ministry was given any responsibility for the subject; it is not even mentioned in the article (74) of the Basic Law listing the matters on which the Federal government has a right to legislate if the laws passed at *Land* level prove inadequate. The various *Länder* Ministers of Culture have met at regular intervals since 1948 but lacked an adequate staff to present them with the conclusions of research done on a nation-wide basis. In 1957, however, President Heuss secured agreement to the creation of a *Wissenschaftsrat* (Council for Knowledge) bringing together Federal and *Länder* officials with the leaders of the academic world. This Council carries such prestige that its recommendations, based on considerable research both by its secretariat and outside organisations, are not lightly disregarded; many of the reforms mentioned in previous paragraphs stem from its initiatives. Indeed its example proved so valuable that in 1966 a *Bildungsrat* (Council of Education) was set up on a similar basis to deal specifically with primary and secondary education.

In 1962 the Ministry for Nuclear Power was expanded to become the Ministry for the Promotion of Knowledge (*wissenschaftliche Forschung*) and in addition assigned responsibility for all questions arising at Federal level in relation to education. As the Basic Law cannot be amended without the consent of the *Länder* governments as represented in the *Bundesrat,* and as such consent would not be forthcoming for any change materially reducing their powers, there is no prospect of securing by constitutional means any radical alteration in the way responsibilities are allocated. In these circumstances Western Germany seems in process of working out pragmatically a hybrid form of machinery which will remedy the worst defects of particularism without forfeiting the considerable advantages of local autonomy.

The responsibilities of the *Wissenschaftsrat* are not confined to the *Hochschulen* but extend to all research. This is a subject which was specifically mentioned in the Basic Law (in spite of some opposition) as a matter on which the Federal government should be entitled to legislate concurrently with the *Länder*. Research for military purposes is the concern of the Ministry of Defence while a body called the *Deutsche Forschungsgemeinschaft* (German Research Community) distributes funds for specific projects of research in natural science (including agriculture, building and town-planning).

In 1962 expenditure on research of all kinds only amounted to $20.1 per head of the population or 1.3 per cent of g.n.p., as compared with $23.6 (1.5 per cent) in France, $33.5 (2.2 per cent) in Britain and $93.7 (3.1 per cent) in the U.S. Awareness of these figures has combined with awareness of the importance of research in an industrial state to create considerable alarm in Germany. As will be seen in the next section, Germany's chances of prosperity depend upon her developing new technological products and in most of the relevant fields the costs of development are too great for them to be shouldered by industry. The German Research Community recently reported that, while the country held its own in the established fields of research, it was behind some others in the more modern fields. This applied particularly to research on the boundaries between two or more established subjects. In many directions Germany's reputation rested on the achievements of a few individuals rather than on an overall effort.

By 1966 the government had raised the annual outlay on research to 2.4 per cent of g.n.p. and announced its intention of making this 3 per cent by 1970. The 1967 Budget provided for a 21 per cent increase in government expenditure on this head and the Cabinet approved an annual growth rate of 16 per cent down to 1971. Outside the military field, however, the costs are shared between the Federal government, the *Länder* governments and industry, so that the second two parties will have to match the action of the first if the full proposed increase is to be achieved; in 1967 the *Forschungsgemeinschaft* got £2 m. or 6 per cent less than it asked for because last-minute cuts by the *Länder* in their contributions led to consequential cuts in the Federal grants. But though the scale of effort proposed will involve a considerable burden on the resources of all concerned, the amount of publicity now being organised about the subject makes it reasonable to suppose that targets will be met.[1]

---

[1] In 1965 Western Germany paid out over £30m. more than she received in respect of patents and licensing agreements, whereas Britain earned a surplus of £7m. (*Die Zeit*, 21 October 1966; *The Times*, 21 July 1967).

(b) *Economic Affairs*

Owing to war casualties and the raising of the school age, the working population of Germany is unlikely to show any significant increase until after 1970. Thereafter it will grow absolutely but decline as a percentage of the total population. The hours of work are expected to show a small decline. Any growth in the economy can therefore only come from increased efficiency. Some contribution to this may be made by a better distribution of manpower. For instance, 11 per cent of the total labour force was in 1965 occupied in agriculture (as compared with 25 per cent in Italy, 18 per cent in France and 3 per cent in the U.K.) although it is only responsible for 5.3 per cent of the gross national product. But in 1950 the figure was 24 per cent (in Bavaria 28 per cent) and there is every reason to suppose that the shrinking process will continue; the expectation is that by 1970 another 3 per cent will have gone, principally to the service industries. Similar shifts will occur between declining and expanding sectors in the extracting and manufacturing industries. But except for such shifts, an increase in industrial output (and so in ultimate standards of life) can only come as a result of higher output per worker and will therefore be intimately connected with the rate of investment and the installation of new plant.[1]

The pressures on the economy will be considerably relieved by a rapid drop in the volume of house-building now that most of the post-war back-log has been made good. The preceding section of this chapter has, however, shewn that education and research are both going to increase their claims on the national resources and can only be disregarded at the cost of holding up growth. The same is true of transport and communications; though Germany led Europe in the building of motor-roads, this was done to some extent at the expense of secondary roads while the two-lane *Autobahnen* of the 1930s are proving too small for the traffic of the 1960s. Forty-six people a day were killed on German roads in 1965, while the Federal railways ran a deficit of about £300 m. in 1967. This led the Minister of Transport to produce in September 1967 a drastic plan for curtailing railways and improving roads but diverting heavy traffic from road to rail. Pensions will cost more money as the proportion of the elderly in the population grows and as the rates go up in line with rising prices. All in all, the expectation is that public expenditure will increase over the

[1] The forecasts in this and the two succeeding paragraphs are taken from the Medium-Term Economic Programme of the European Economic Community 1966.

years 1965–70 by 3.2 per cent per annum (as compared with 6.4 per cent in 1960–5) and public investment by 8.2 per cent per annum (as compared with 11 per cent).

For German industry as a whole, an average annual increase in productivity of 4.8 per cent is anticipated over the period with investment growing at 4.4 per cent (the first figure being slightly higher than those for 1955–65 and the second distinctly lower). Such an increase may not be altogether easy to reach. For Western Germany is beginning to run into the problem of obsolescent industries with which Britain is painfully familiar. The most obvious case is coal. Rising labour costs and the exhaustion of the easier seams have made a number of German pits unable to compete with imports, particularly from the United States. A good deal has been done to improve the efficiency of German mining. The proportion of coal cut mechanically has been raised from 17 per cent to 82 per cent in the last ten years, the labour force has been brought down by 50 per cent and ninety-two pits have been closed. But the increasing use of oil and nuclear power is reducing the demand for even the cheapest coal. By the end of 1966 20 million tons of unwanted coal had accumulated at the pitheads. Output had dropped by 1967 from 145 to 100 million tons.

Such a situation called for a bigger change in traditional attitudes than either mineowners, workers or governments were at first prepared to make. The fall in demand was for some time treated as a temporary phenomenon and several new opportunities of bringing new industries (notably an automobile assembly plant) to the Ruhr were missed. A limit was set on coal imports and various incentives were devised at public cost to keep up the use of coal in steel mills and power stations. But if a dramatic signal was needed to bring home the gravity of the crisis, it came in March 1967 with the announcement that Krupps, so long the big name of the coal and steel industry, were so much in debt that they could get no further credit and (to the dismay of the Socialist left wing) would be given government help to stave off collapse. Drastic action was clearly needed; one leading industrialist declared that nationalisation was the only remedy. When in the autumn the closure of the two leading pits was announced, demonstrations and red flags sprouted all along the Ruhr valley; the miners' leaders demanded a limit on oil imports, a ban on nuclear power stations and a six-year hold-up on pit closures. To his credit, Dr Schiller refused to listen but presented to the *Bundestag* a plan which he had proposed six months earlier for drastic rationalisation of all pits under a single holding company.

Considerable sums of public money are to be given to the industry but only to smooth and soften the process of contraction. Eighty thousand more miners, or over a quarter of those still employed, are expected to leave the industry while capacity is to fall by nearly as much by the end of 1970.

Another step taken in 1967 was the approval by the Coal and Steel Community, despite doubts on the part of the French (who have to do most of the paying), for a scheme permitting governments to subsidise coke and coking coal. For the troubles of Krupps and the rest of the Ruhr are not confined to the mines. Excessive installation of steel-making plant all over the world, particularly outside Europe and North America, led to a temporary surplus of capacity over demand. Since the plant is capital-intensive, failure to use it fully involves heavy loss and producers everywhere have preferred to cut prices rather than output. In these circumstances the use of the more expensive German coking coal aggravated the steel-makers' losses, yet if the cheaper American supplies were used instead, demand for German coal would drop even further. As Krupps illustrated, the close connections between the coal and steel industries which have for so long been prominent in Germany and which have excited so much left-wing criticism are now beginning to prove an embarrassment rather than an advantage.

The subsidy for coking coal, which was to last in the first instance until the end of 1968, was intended to provide a breathing space rather than a final solution. Some parts of the German steel industry should remain viable especially as demand expands. But since most of the raw materials now have to be imported, modern plants on the sea-coast are bound to have an advantage. Some of the older and less efficient German plants will have to be closed, notably that built by the Third Reich to use low-grade ore at Salzgitter in Lower Saxony which is still publicly owned and each year increases its losses. Prejudices against cartellisation have been overcome to the extent of allowing thirty-one firms to form themselves into four sales organisations but even more drastic concentration seems inevitable. The process will be expensive and, for the time being at any rate, there will be an end to the steady growth which the industry enjoyed ever since it was freed from Allied controls. For the next few years profits will be small or non-existent.

The position is not markedly more satisfactory in other industries, such as textiles, shipbuilding and shipping, exposed to competition from low-cost producers overseas or to dislocation due to new techniques such as the use of containers. It would not be surprising if the automobile industry found further expansion up-hill work : Volkswagen, the largest firm, had to go on to short time in 1967 for the first occasion in its history and its great dependence on a single model puts it increasingly at risk until an equally popular successor is established. Forty per cent of the industry is in any event American-owned. Resources have clearly got to be shifted into the growth industries of the future. Yet, with the exception of chemicals, pharmaceuticals and to some extent electronics, Germany is backward in all of these. For aviation, space-exploration, nuclear power and electronics are all closely connected with defence. Until 1955 Germany was prohibited from engaging in them and even after rearmament began, it was quicker and simpler to buy ready-made equipment from abroad (and particularly America) or produce foreign types under licence than to embark on the expenditure and research needed to make domestic production possible. As has been seen, German official expenditure on research was for some time relatively small and industry did not make up the deficiency.

The result is that Germany's aviation industry was in 1967 only employing some 40,000 men, as compared with 250,000 in Great Britain. Most of them are occupied in building foreign designs under licence and no German models have been produced in quantity for either airlines or air forces. Much effort has been concentrated on the development of vertical take-off planes; a good deal will depend in future on the extent to which orders for these can be obtained and prospects are distinctly dubious. Nuclear power has been held back in the interests of coal and the first full-scale generating station only came into operation in 1966, five years behind Bradwell and Berkeley. The firms in a position to accept orders build American designs under licence and though German prices compare favourably with American, Germany is neither in a position—nor likely to get quickly into a position— where it can supply the enriched fuel which these types need. A good deal of attention is being paid to fast breeder-reactors but in these Britain has a long start. In computers the story is even worse. Seven out of every ten machines installed in Germany are supplied by the German subsidiary of I.B.M. and the chief German manu-facturer, Siemens, works under an American licence, whereas Britain has two native companies whose designs are mostly their own. Seventy-five per cent of the German oil market is in the hands of foreign (and mostly American) concerns.

The question-mark hanging over Germany's future is how far

the pacemakers in recent industrial growth, such as engineering, vehicles, chemicals, electrical equipment and optical and precision equipment can improve their sales performance at home, in the Common Market and in world exports, and how far, if they do not, other even newer industries can be developed to support them. One thing which seems clear is that, like other West European countries, West Germany has not herself got the resources to make headway in all fields against American competition, and that development can only be effective if it is on a supranational basis. This is likely to make West Germany anxious for technological cooperation with Britain. Most German activity in connection with space research is already being conducted under the auspices of the European Space Research Organisation, while something of the same kind applies with Euratom in the nuclear field. But even on this plane Germany will only make up lost ground and hold her own if a formidable amount of new investment is undertaken and since it will not be of a character to offer quick or assured profits, much of the money will have to come from the government. For this outlay, the resources will have to be found by saving.

In face of these needs for public expenditure on 'infra-structure' and investment in productive capacity, the German economic equation is only going to balance if private expenditure can be kept firmly in check. This in spite of the fact that in recent years investment has been taking 27 per cent of the g.n.p., government current expenditure 16 per cent and private consumption only 57 per cent, as against 18 per cent, 17 per cent and 65 per cent in Britain (for whom the need to sacrifice the present to the future is at least as urgent). Forecasts anticipate a drop in the growth rate of consumption over the period to 1970 from 5.4 per cent to 3.5 per cent, or, on a *per capita* basis, from 4.1 per cent to 2.9 per cent. The days of the Economic Miracle are indeed over, and the question which therefore arises is whether the government will itself have enough resolve and exercise enough authority over the public to curb and keep curbed the public's desire for better living. A number of rash commitments entered into during the past ten years are beginning to make themselves felt. Projections of the budgetary position in the spring of 1967 suggested that, if nothing were done, the short-fall of income behind expenditure would have risen from 8 per cent in 1967 to 13.3 per cent in 1970. There are politicians both in the S.P.D. and in the left wing of the C.D.U., who maintain that the social services should be the last place in which to look for economies. Moreover, pressure groups have become well organised in recent years. A flagrant example of their behaviour occurred when Herr Rehwinkel, the leader of the Farmers' union, threatened that if there was any interference with the payments made to his members, he would advise them to vote for the National Democratic Party. Such an open display of political blackmail probably did his cause more harm than good, especially as German industrialists and economists have for some time been highly critical of the generosity shewn to agriculture and of the high costs with which exporters have in consequence been burdened. But clearly the Great Coalition, even with its overwhelming majority, has a stiff task ahead.

Its initial performance, however, was not unimpressive. Wage increases were kept within bounds. The Federal Bank was persuaded to reduce the interest rates. The Stabilisation Bill introduced by Erhard in the autumn of 1966 was redrafted and rechristened the Law for Stabilisation and Growth. As passed in June 1967, it required the Federal and the *Länder* governments to draw up forecasts of revenue and expenditure for five years ahead and gave them power to put the main taxes up or down by 10 per cent for twelve months in the light of economic expectations, as assessed by an advisory council. (The number of Councils which the Republic has acquired has given rise to the saying that it has become a *Räterepublik*—i.e. what the left wing wanted to establish in 1918.) Other powers to suspend investment allowances or remit taxation and to freeze or release balances held by the banks and other sources of finance give the governments at all levels a variety of tools with which to steer the economy and keep it on an even course. The main doubts must be whether the trend of the economy can be foreseen accurately and early enough for remedial measures to be taken in time for them to be effective, and whether the readiness of the political leaders to unloose the purse-strings will be matched by an equal determination to tighten them if that should seem to be what is called for.

In the spring of 1967, soon after taking office, the Cabinet was able to agree on measures for balancing the 1967 Budget and in the following July also agreed on a financial scheme for the next five years including the 1968 Budget. Such an attempt to assess priorities and to plan ahead was of course a new departure and for it to have had flaws was only natural. A real growth rate of 4 per cent and a nominal one of $5-5\frac{1}{2}$ per cent were assumed, which may well prove optimistic. Resistance to cuts was so strong that the chief result achieved was to put limits on the increases which would otherwise occur in certain sectors and even so most of the extra expenditure contemplated will go to consumption rather than investment.

Moreover, the only acceptable way in which the figures could be made to balance out was by savings on defence. As this solution was pressed by Strauss, the Finance Minister, on a reluctant Defence Minister, it looks as though a repetition of the 1956 operation was involved.[1] The *Bundeswehr* has never been raised quite to the 500,000 level promised in 1961 and the new cuts would bring it back to something like 430,000. Their military effect would presumably be offset by the provision of more powerful (i.e. less conventional) weapons. Any such change is bound to increase nervousness in Eastern Europe and so run counter to the government's professed objective of relaxing tension. The policy had to be decided on without there being time to consult the other members of N.A.T.O. (for the Cabinet seems to have been within sight of break-up) and was obviously unwelcome in Washington. But even if it is not carried through, pressure may be expected for Germany to develop even more of her own military equipment instead of buying it (or its designs) abroad. Industrial opinion has become acutely conscious of the extent to which American superiority in the production and sale of the most sophisticated products is due to research contracts given for defence, and is keen for the Bonn government to follow suit. Support for collaboration in joint European projects is likely to be accompanied by insistence that Western Germany gets her full share of work and is no longer hampered by restrictions on the kind of arms which her troops are allowed to possess. Certainly British and American requests for higher German contributions to support costs are unlikely in the present context to get a sympathetic hearing.

Those in charge of the German economy need, however, to walk a narrow tight-rope between inflation and deflation. The crisis of confidence which developed at the end of 1966, with rapid falls in fresh orders, and a sharp rise in unemployment, showed how easily the country could think itself into a depression. A cutting-back of expenditure was essential if the economy was to be kept under control and runaway increases in prices and wages avoided. But higher taxation discourages fresh enterprise while cuts endanger jobs. As Brüning found in 1930, austerity at the wrong time and in the wrong direction can make things worse instead of

[1] See above, p. 234.

better. Even if it were economically desirable, such a course has become politically impracticable now that everyone knows it can be avoided by government action. Professor Schiller, as Minister of Economics, tried therefore to put into practice a recipe of 'controlled growth', by adding to the normal Budget special programmes by which money obtained through short-term borrowing is used for capital expenditure designed to increase the productive resources of the country. Funds were made available for such things as railway electrification, road construction, telecommunications, computer development and the building of halls of residence for *Hochschulen*. The first programme in the spring of 1967 failed to achieve the desired restoration of confidence because, while the Federal government was embarking on it, the *Länder* and communal authorities were cutting their capital expenditure back. A second instalment in the summer of 1967 was more carefully coordinated and showed signs of being more successful. An obvious danger, which has not been wholly avoided, is that the investment funds will be used not to speed progress but to bolster up uneconomic concerns and areas on the ground of their social (and political) importance. West German economic policy gives every appearance, however, of being on the right lines; the question is whether it can be pushed through and here there is no doubt that Schiller and Strauss are a formidable combination. At the very least they seem to have succeeded in reassuring the German investor : stock exchange prices rose in the course of 1967 by 40 per cent.

By contrast with the two preceding years, West Germany in 1967 earned an export surplus of approximately DM 17,000 m., thereby causing considerable embarrassment not merely to her neighbours but even to her own government. This clearly cannot continue. But it has been largely due to the effect of falling domestic demand in reducing imports and setting goods free for export. A revival of activity in the home market might be expected to cancel much of it out and Germany may also find herself exposed to more British competition as a result of devaluation. German exports have done so well in the last fifteen years that the world has come to take them for granted. But they depend on Germany continuing to turn out the goods which the world wants at competitive prices. From what has already been said in this section, neither can be regarded as absolutely assured. And, as already mentioned[1] Germany needs an annual surplus of some DM 7,000 (£730 m.) on visible trade in order to meet her

[1] See p. 249.

growing invisible deficit, in the absence of any appreciable income from foreign investments. For whereas at the end of 1965 German gold and dollar reserves at DM 30,000 m. were large enough to pay for six months' imports (as against British reserves of only half the size which would only have paid for about eleven weeks' imports), German foreign investments were little more than a quarter the size of her reserves, as compared with British ones which at £11,000 m. were ten times as big as the reserves. On the other hand Germany had little or no overseas debt, whereas Britain's debts, taken altogether, amounted to almost as much as her assets and, as far as the official sector is concerned, are nearly three times the size of the assets.

Thus although Western Germany does not have the commitment of running a reserve currency, she is in the position of a self-made man whose chief assets are his skill and a well-equipped modern factory, but who lacks any accumulated savings to see him through difficult times (though, as he has succeeded in writing off the debts incurred before two previous bankruptcies, he is also unencumbered by any serious liabilities). If his skill or equipment were to get out of date, or if his customers ran short of money, or if he were to start spending too much on himself, his earning power would quickly be at risk. Consequently Germany would be as vulnerable as Britain, though for different reasons, to a depression in world trade or to any other development which caused her exports to fall. To some extent, the Common Market should serve as a safeguard since its six members taken together are more nearly self-sufficient than any one of them in isolation. But this connection can cut both ways, as was shewn in 1965 when recession in France and Italy was largely responsible for Germany running a deficit on her current balance of payments which was larger than the worst ever incurred by Britain. Moreover, the E.E.C. agricultural policy is a handicap to exports. Of course an alternative to a steady and considerable export surplus would be a steady influx of foreign money for investment. But America, the only obvious large-scale source of this, is trying to eliminate her deficit, while there is already concern among Germans over the size of America's stake in their industry.

Considering her apparent condition in 1947, West Germany is a country of remarkable wealth and resources. But she largely owes this wealth and these resources to a combination of exceptionally favourable factors, many of which have lost or are losing their validity. She cannot hope to go on growing—in real terms—at the rate achieved in the '50s and indeed has already ceased to do so. Unless her people are prepared to rein themselves in and accept a significantly lower growth (though not a halt) in consumption, she could easily find herself in economic difficulties. Her future largely depends on how far and how widely this situation is understood. Democracy owes a large measure of its acceptance during the last fifteen years to its having brought prosperity. But this creates a danger that Germany's democratic governments may in the future be judged by their ability to match the standards of growth set under Adenauer (especially if, as seems likely, they have to compete with a high rate of growth in the D.D.R.). If so, they will all be judged incapable and run the risk of being superseded in favour of any alternative able to persuade the electorate of its ability to do better. On the other hand excessive alarmism about the economic future, besides being unjustified, might easily shake confidence and so help to make its forecast come true. The years ahead are therefore likely to put to the test not merely the skill and authority of the Federal Republic's politicians and the adequacy of its political system but also the maturity of its voters.

(c) *Internal Politics*

The British observer of German politics cannot help being struck by the relative lack of authority over its followers possessed by the Bonn government—though the impression on an American observer might be the opposite! It is hard to believe that even Dr Adenauer could have imposed his views on the *Bundestag* in the way in which the House of Commons has been made to accept Cabinet decisions on such secondary matters as summer time and decimal currency.

There are a number of possible reasons for this. Something may still be due to the fact that German parties began in the Second Reich as pressure groups trying to exert influence on a government which was not of their own making. Moreover, the Federal form of state means that there are legal limits to the authority of the central government, whereas the rights of British local authorities can always be overridden by Parliament. The possibilities of amending the German Basic Law are limited by the need to get a two-thirds majority not only in the *Bundestag* but also from the nominees of the *Länder* governments who form the *Bundesrat*. Not surprisingly the *Länder* governments have shewn themselves very sensitive over any development which might reduce their powers and their relations with the Federal government more often take the form of contest than of cooperation. The existence of these governments also implies the existence of strong party organisations at *Land* level, whose importance has been enhanced by the provision, deliberately inserted to reduce the power of the centre, that they should be the bodies to draw up lists of Deputies for election by proportional representation. The need to depend on the centre for party finance is reduced by the system by which the parties are allowed £9 m. of public money, distributed according to fixed rules, for the expenses of each election. (It is symptomatic of the German preoccupation with legal forms that party organisations should be regulated by a Federal law!)

A further explanation of the government's relative weakness is the small extent of the patronage available to the Chancellor. The Cabinet is approximately the same size as in Britain but there were until 1967 no Junior Ministers at all and even then the number created was only seven. They cannot therefore be compared with the fifty British M.P.s (and more if Parliamentary Private Secretaries are included) whose jobs depend on their voting as the Whips wish. A number of influential party figures, such as Dufhues and Barzel, who could have posts in the German Cabinet, prefer to remain outside it. They thus avoid becoming committed to its measures and do not hesitate on occasion to criticise them. Indeed there is nothing in Germany comparable to the doctrine of collective Cabinet responsibility so that Ministers are free to propound in public views which are not necessarily endorsed by their colleagues. This outlook spreads to the rank-and-file who not merely have their own ideas about legislation but on occasion vote, particularly in *Bundestag* committees, in a sense unwelcome to Ministers. Official proposals for legislation can even get stuck in such committees, though not to the extent to which this happens in the United States.

A balance between anarchy and servility is never easy to achieve and the domination of the British executive over the legislature may well have gone too far. In a country accustomed, like Germany, to strong government, there is much to be said for a degree of independence. But if safeguards are written into a constitution to limit a government's powers, only the good sense of the Deputies will enable that government to act with vigour when vigour becomes necessary. German Chancellors have had difficulty in pleasing their public; Adenauer was criticised for being too autocratic, Erhard and to a lesser extent Kiesinger for being too pliable.

The limits to the central government's power might have been expected to diminish with the formation of the Great Coalition having a majority of 398. But the causes of German party indiscipline are too deep-rooted to be removed by a big majority, which may indeed make Deputies less rather than more compliant. Though the new government has had a fair measure of success in getting its way, most of its proposals have proved unwelcome to one group or another of its supporters. The Coalition was itself in part a reaction to the defects which the present political system revealed when led by a weak man and its very formation has been represented as an abnegation of party government. For a democratic party system rests on the belief that the best way to resolve the conflicts which are inevitable in any society is to provide a mechanism for bringing such conflicts into the open, along with generally-accepted rules as to how decisions about them are to be reached. Any change which impedes this process is of questionable wisdom (unless the predominant conflict is not inside the particular society but between it and others when a 'national effort' to conduct the conflict is appropriate). This point is misunderstood by Germans who complain that a party should not be an umbrella organisation representing a collection of miscellaneous interests but a compact group united by adherence to a common creed and who accordingly view with misgiving the trend towards a two-party instead of a multi-party system. If, however, those two parties coalesce, policy tends to be evolved by bargaining behind the scenes rather than by debating in public.

The Great Coalition would have been unlikely to come into existence if it had not been for the economic recession. But such a recession is bound to create dissatisfaction with the people in charge of the country no matter who those people may be. If there is no adequate parliamentary opposition to act as the focus for such dissatisfaction, it is bound to find alternative foci. The inadequacy of the F.D.P. as a parliamentary opposition has been so obvious that the rise of other movements outside Parliament both to right and left should cause no surprise. The important question is how far those movements are to be regarded as permanent rather than temporary.

Reference has already been made[1] to the probability that at the end of the war there were still some 4 million convinced Nazis in Germany, along with another 8 million people who had been involved less whole-heartedly in the apparatus of the Third Reich. Many of these will by now have died; some, such as Drs Kiesinger

[1] See p. 156, 167.

and Schröder, may be given the credit for having suffered a genuine and permanent change of heart; many more have suffered a change of head and decided to cast in their lot with the new order for the sake of their careers. Certainly living conditions since 1948 have not been such as to encourage radical policies. But traditions die hard and for reasons explained in the first part of this book, traditions of an authoritarian kind are deeply ingrained in Germany. Moreover, there are in any society, no matter how prosperous, misfits and people who for one reason or another have a chip on their shoulder. Such people tend to find satisfaction by involvement in divergent heterodox movements, whether political, religious or social. Many adherents of authoritarian parties hold strong views on such matters as capital punishment, modern art, the emancipation of women, diet and the influence of the stars! In a society where government by discussion and toleration of minority opinion is deeply rooted, such people can be held in check and have relatively little influence—though Britain has its Empire Loyalists and America its John Birch Society. Where, as in Germany, the tradition has been repressive rather than permissive, such lunatics can be expected to be more than a fringe.

A major reservoir for such extremists is of course to be found in the twelve million people living in West Germany who were born (or whose parents were born) east of the Iron Curtain. The surprising success which has been achieved, thanks to economic prosperity, in providing these people with jobs and homes has fostered the hope that they were ceasing to be a menace. Many have undoubtedly made good in the West and have not the least desire to return whence they came. Many more, equally well-off, like to foregather with former neighbours in order to gratify that desire for reminiscence which is one of human nature's more innocent foibles! Unfortunately this is not the whole story. To begin with, the refugees, though employed and housed, have not as a body gone as far as the average West German in recovering their pre-1945 status. The number receiving national assistance was in 1964 still nearly three times as high as in the rest of the population, the number owning their houses half as many. People who used to be their own masters, even if only in a small way, now have to work for others and resent the degradation. Few refugees as yet possess any appreciable capital. Though many of the second generation accept the new situation with equanimity, children in other cases inherit the resentment of their parents; the problem will not necessarily die out in proportion as those born in the East come to the end of their natural lives. Moreover, the refugees have formed themselves into associations, led by paid officials. As with all interest groups, the leaders feel an obligation to prove that they are doing their job.

Outside observers sometimes say that the majority of Germans are not genuinely interested in reunification or the recovery of the lost provinces, and will never run risks in an attempt to reverse what has happened. It is true that at the end of 1966 a public opinion poll found that only 26 per cent considered partition 'intolerable' as compared with 38 per cent two years previously. But as against this the refugee leaders have made it their business to prevent hopes and aspirations from fading. The main parties have been, and still are, afraid that if they disregard the refugees, they may lose the marginal votes making all the difference between victory and defeat. Moreover, the refugees come largely from those frontier areas where awareness of other nations and therefore national feeling has been strongest. The kind of sentiments which they have voiced are the traditional ones of German nationalism and very few German political leaders have been ready to risk incurring the stigma of disloyalty by speaking out against them.

Much is made of the so-called 'Right of the Homeland' (*Heimatrecht*). The failure of international law to recognise any such thing is countered by the argument that international law is notoriously incomplete. And refugee spokesmen do not weary of pointing out that, if former colonial peoples all over the world are being allowed to decide the form of government they wish to have, the right to such self-determination should know no frontiers and be equally valid in Eastern Europe.[1] Moreover, Western spokesmen are apt to find their own objections to Nazi methods turned against them by the argument that the new order in the East should be based on agreement and justice rather than force. Herr Rehs, the East Prussian who had just been chosen as leader of the Socialist Refugees Association, said in an interview in February 1967 :

> We certainly ought not to ignore those who advise the Germans to bury their illusions and accept the eastern frontiers as final. But a nation should not allow itself to be irritated by the

[1] This argument, if strictly applied, tells against the Germans, for the colonial peoples being allowed self-determination are the actual inhabitants of the territory at the moment, not the former dominant groups who have been expelled! A closer equivalent to the Germans is afforded by the white populations of South Africa and Rhodesia.

views of its neighbours. What is involved here is a precedent for the whole of Europe, and the way it is dealt with will make clear whether a future Peace settlement is going to come into existence based on moral and legal principles or on the facts of power politics. Concern for Germany's eastern lands is not the product of national aspirations for territorial expansion but is a test case for the integrity of the European conscience.[1]

Like any skilful advocate, Herr Rehs takes it for granted that all the right is on the German side. He does not explain what happens when ideas about right differ nor how settlements are to be based on 'moral and legal principles' when the various parties have different ideas as to how such principles are to be applied (though it is significant that the refugees' objections to basing principles on force disappear when, as in the case of the attempts of the *Sudetendeutsch* refugees to uphold the validity of the 1938 Munich Treaty, the result seems to tell in their favour).

The truth is, of course, that the right of an individual or a group to self-determination cannot be absolute. It must bow to the interests of the community at large, which have to be judged in the light of history and geography. The Germans, by their behaviour in Eastern Europe, have set narrow limits to the readiness of third parties to attach weight to their claims. It is easy to say that two wrongs do not make a right but it is equally true that penalties for wrong-doing have often to be paid by people other than the wrong-doers. A settlement in the East will never be achieved by the relentless exchange of legalistic claims and counter-claims but only by the establishment of a new spirit which aims at the achievement of mutual understanding and good-will rather than a self-interpreted justice. But when the German Evangelical Churches, in a remarkable report published in October 1965, tried to advance this argument, the scrupulous care with which the case of the refugees was reproduced and weighed did not protect the authors from a storm of abuse and misrepresentation. The sad fact is that the refugee movement is in the hands of men who, perhaps as a result of failure to make good in their new surroundings, are guided by emotion rather than reason, sufficiently educated to expound their case in conceptual terms yet incapable of admitting its limitations and inconsistencies.

Such is the background against which it is necessary to assess the rise of the National Democratic Party, a body formed in November 1964 from the remnants of the German Party, the

[1] *Die Zeit*, 17 November 1967.

Socialist Reich Party and other unsuccessful right-wing groups.[1]
By the Federal elections of September 1965 it had about 12,500
members and secured 640,000 votes but no seats. A year later when
it attracted world attention in the Hesse and Bavarian elections[2]
membership was said to have risen to 20,000; a year later still
(autumn 1967) it was 33,500. To judge by a 1965 opinion survey
its strength lies in Schleswig-Holstein, Lower Saxony (where in
1951 the Socialist Reich Party polled 400,000 votes), Bavaria,
Hamburg, Bremen and Baden-Württemberg; its membership is
disproportionately low in North Rhine-Westphalia and Berlin.
It is a man's party rather than a woman's and appeals particularly
to those in the age-groups from thirty to fifty-nine, to Protestants
rather than Catholics (in Bavaria it is partly a protest vote against
the Catholic C.S.U.), to the middle classes, officials and independent
tradesmen, and to those with secondary (rather than merely
elementary) education.[3] On the whole it is disproportionately strong
in large and middle-sized towns and villages, so that it cannot be
dismissed as a 'grass-roots' agitation. In short, with the important
exception of youth, its strength lies precisely among those who
throughout the last century have been the main upholders of the
German national tradition.

After any disaster such as Germany experienced in 1945, those
who had associated themselves with the people responsible for it
naturally find themselves out of favour and lie low. A good number
went abroad to places like Egypt and South America; there is
evidence of funds being sent back to help those remaining behind.
In due course when the precautions taken by the victors have
largely lapsed, the moment arrives for a come-back; that it has
taken over twenty years to arrive in West Germany may be due
in varying proportions to the magnitude of the disaster, the success
of the new régime and the various steps taken to put Nazis under

---

[1] See above, pp. 187, 226, 240.
[2] See above, p. 252.
[3] There seem to be interesting differences between the age-structure of
the party and that of the N.S.D.A.P. in 1930.

Age-group	N.S.D.A.P.	N.D.P.
16–29	37%	23%
31–44	40%	30%
45–59	18.5%	31%
60+	4.5%	16%

Schoenbaum, *Hitler's Social Revolution*, p. 30, *Die Zeit*, 20 January 1967.
The N.D.P. have more recently claimed to have found a 'ready response'
in the younger generation but the extent of this should be viewed with
some scepticism in the absence of objective confirmation.

a handicap (such as the action taken by the British security authorities in 1953 against the groups forming round Werner Neumann, formerly State Secretary to Goebbels in the Propaganda Ministry). But a revival at some stage was almost inevitable and the autumn of 1966 when everything seemed to be going wrong for the government was the natural time for it to occur. The party's continued progress, after a temporary relapse (due to internal dissension) in the spring of 1967, is certainly disquieting. But there is only limited cause for alarm as long as the C.D.U. and S.P.D. can get, as they did in June 1967, 85 per cent of the votes in Lower Saxony, a *Land* in which reactionary opinion has been steadily conspicuous since 1945. The real danger may well be that, once the main parties do start losing votes, they (or at any rate the C.D.U.) will themselves move to the right out of self-protection.

To reach a balanced judgement on the outlook, account must be taken of the considerable evidence of the opposition that any reversion to nationalism would encounter. As has been shewn, the Basic Law contains a number of provisions designed to remedy the most obvious faults in the Weimar constitution, such as splinter parties, weak governments, Presidential interference and freedom to rule by decree. It also stipulates that the democratic character of the State cannot be made a matter of constitutional amendment, and provides for banning parties which seek to alter or abolish that character—policed as these clauses are by the Constitutional Court. Certainly no paper document can prevent a country from taking a course on which a sufficient number of resolute men are determined. But it is very doubtful whether, under the new conditions, an authoritarian ruler could achieve power as Hitler did without openly violating the constitution, especially as a greater reluctance on the part of democratic parties to help him towards a two-thirds majority may not unreasonably be expected. The fact that the *Länder* have greater power under the Basic Law than under the Weimar constitution is a further safeguard. Moreover, the Federal membership of the Common Market puts a certain brake on the ability of the government to pursue a policy of autarchy; this could, of course, be reversed but not legally (since the Treaty of Rome makes no provision for its denunciation) and not without material loss.

Behind these more formal defences stands evidence that plenty of Germans have made a real effort to think over their country's history and to change its character. One of the most interesting developments has been the new series of Nazi trials conducted by the Germans themselves since 1958. Trials conducted by the

Allies in the years after the war had evoked a wave of hostility culminating in 1953 in a campaign by the F.D.P. leader Mende to secure the release of all those who had been sentenced on the ground that the acts for which they had been condemned were not genuine crimes. A number of prosecutions before German courts resulted in acquittals. People were ready to say and apparently to believe that most of the stories about concentration camps had been invented by the Allies; a favourite assertion was that the only gas chamber had been one used for sanitary purposes. Things began to change after the Allies handed over their intelligence files to the Germans and as new evidence was unearthed. A series of prosecutions for crimes against humanity, starting with a deputy-commandant of Dachau, must have left all except the incorrigibles in very little doubt as to what really happened (and with the incorrigibles it is less a question of knowing the facts than of facing up to the implications of the facts!). In this process the publication and dramatisation in 1957 of the Diary of Anne Frank played a significant part, translating the horrors into personal terms which touched the emotions. When in 1965 the existing law would have ruled out trials for offences committed more than twenty years previously, public opinion forced its amendment and the resignation of the Minister of Justice who opposed the change. It is possible, however, that this process has now yielded all the dividends which can be expected of it and is beginning to provoke a reaction. Horrible as the crimes were, and important as it is that justice should be done, there is a danger that advocates of punishment will alienate sympathy by appearing too relentless. A public opinion poll in 1966 suggested that 73 per cent of Germans would favour ending the trials and a demand for such an end has been a prominent feature in N.D.P. propaganda.

Serious steps have also been taken to revise the accepted picture of German history. In contrast to the period immediately after the war, many text-books are now available both for schools and universities which give a version not differing markedly from that current in England and America. Professor Franz Fischer of Hamburg caused a great sensation in 1961 by his book *Germany's Aims in the First World War*. Though passionate answers have been made and though Fischer has been denied a passport to prevent him lecturing in America, it is safe to say that the account given by German historians of the 1914–18 war and its origins will never be the same again and that the crude interpretation of it as a war forced on Germany by a jealous world is now finally discredited. Such a result is important not just in itself but because it logically necessitates a fresh approach to the Versailles Treaty and its War Guilt clause.[1] This is a field where argument is continuing and by no means all the books published have shaken themselves free from the outlooks propagated between 1918 and 1945—but it would have been remarkable if they had.

Moreover, it would be quite wrong to suppose that nationalist activities since 1945 have met anything like the public tolerance which they encountered after 1918. In 1953 the students of Göttingen forced by means of a strike the resignation from the post of Lower Saxon Education Minister of a right-wing publisher whose speciality was the memoirs and apologia of former Nazis and their widows. In the same year a proposal by Adenauer to centralise official facilities for giving news to the Press in a Ministry of Information caused such a storm that it had to be dropped. In 1957–61 a similar storm backed by a decision of the Constitutional Court forced the abandonment of a proposal for a second television service on a Federal basis. (Thanks originally to American and British policy after the war, radio and TV are organised under independent regional authorities who would have to be taken over by a series of operations since there is no single centre of command.) In 1959 the desecration of a synagogue in Cologne called forth vigorous student demonstrations. In addition to the compensation which the State has paid to Israel[2], numbers of young Germans have served in work camps in that state as a gesture of personal compensation. The successes of the N.D.P. in 1966 led quickly to counter-demonstrations by both students and trade unionists; for a long time the party was unable to find a city which would allow them the use of a hall for their party conference. The vigilance of *Der Spiegel* on behalf of democracy, particularly in relation to Franz-Josef Strauss, has already been mentioned. German television has been active in the same cause though at the cost of some collision with authority and much public controversy; after the formation of the Great Coalition, it was widely considered to have provided the real opposition. The supporters of democracy are by no means unaware of the lesson of 1933 that resistance must not be left until it is too late.

In the summer of 1967 the government stirred up a hornet's nest of controversy by trying to solve the problem of emergency legislation. In the 1955 settlement[3] the Western occupying Powers reserved the right to reassume authority if any emergency

[1] See p. 79.
[2] See p. 220.
[3] See p. 211.

threatened to undermine the security of the country before the Federal government had passed legislation enabling it to deal with such a contingency. Although there has ever since been a natural desire to expunge the last relic of an inferior status, political agreement has not been forthcoming on the nature of the extraordinary powers to be allowed to the government and the circumstances under which they could be assumed. A nuclear war might obviously make the due processes of law impossible but there has been considerable nervousness lest, if the government was authorised to circumvent them, advantage might be taken of the concession to suppress liberty in peacetime on the analogy of 1930–2. The government proposed that the *Bundestag* should elect an emergency committee of twenty-two members, to whom there would be added by the *Bundesrat* one representative from each *Land*. This body would have the right to decide by a two-thirds majority that the *Bundestag* was incapable of acting and if it did could then proclaim an emergency and bring into operation some forty previously prepared (and debated) emergency laws. The task of enabling the government to act effectively without thereby enabling it to act arbitrarily is complicated by the national concern for precise legal definitions. The difficulty found in reaching a compromise well illustrates the healthy suspicion with which many Germans regard their rulers.

A similar suspicion of authority has recently become manifest among university students, chiefly, though by no means exclusively, in Berlin, and has led to many charges of high-handed action by the police. The climax came during the Shah of Persia's visit to the city in June 1967 when in the course of a demonstration against him, a student called Bruno Ohnesorg was shot. The students got little sympathy from the Press and particularly from the large part of it owned by Herr Axel Springer; in retaliation they demanded an end to the situation in which 80 per cent of the eleven daily papers with national circulation (three-quarters of which is contributed by the tabloid illustrated *Bild*) and 90 per cent of the Sunday Press can be in the hands of one man.

This student unrest is part of a wave sweeping the world and it is probably heightened in Germany by the fact that the generation now at universities is the product of the chaotic years 1943–8. There is widespread disenchantment with some of the less lovely manifestations of the affluent society and with it is combined a refusal to take at face-value the official condemnation of communism and the D.D.R. What is disturbing about the movement is not its lack of respect for the existing order : German middle-class youth has for so long vacillated between submissiveness and a fondness for right-wing radicalism that a change to the other extreme would be important and even encouraging. But there is as yet no clear evidence of any positive ideals at all; what seems instead to be involved is a rejection of existing society *in toto*, a non-political attempt to contract out. Such an attitude is too unrealistic to last and the possibility of a new form of right-wing radicalism taking its place—at any rate in some cases—cannot be excluded. If on the other hand the development is leftwards—and the reaction of respectable opinion to the disturbances has been so unsympathetic as to encourage this—then a left-wing movement of some strength may develop in the near future. For this there would be a number of potential recruits, though the ability of the leadership is more open to question. The tradition of dissident left-wing socialism is far from dead and many members of the S.P.D. have been alienated by the Godesberg Programme and the alliance with the C.D.U. In the last election before they were suppressed, the Communists polled 600,000 votes. Not all the miners who want revenge for the S.P.D.'s refusal to safeguard their jobs will be willing to vote N.D.P. An independent left party has already been brought into existence to fight the Baden-Württemberg *Land* elections in 1968 and the example may prove contagious.

This development on the left, taken in conjunction with the growth of the N.D.P., leads back to the crucial question of future Federal politics. When the Great Coalition was formed it was regarded as a transient and emergency phenomenon which would not last beyond the elections of 1969. But if the C.D.U./C.S.U. and S.P.D. are to fight in that year as opponents, they can hardly be expected to govern as a harmonious team right up to the eve of the campaign; their manoeuvrings would have a devastating effect on solidarity long before the present programme of legislation has been brought anywhere near completion. All the evidence, particularly in the *Länder* elections, suggests that most of the credit for anything which the Kiesinger government has achieved has gone to the C.D.U./C.S.U. who are no longer in the bad odour of late 1966. The Socialists, by contrast, have lost ground and may have missed their chance of emerging from an election as the strongest party; the compromises inevitable in a coalition have made their rank-and-file restive. Yet they would be unlikely to do themselves much good among the vital marginal voters by quitting the government. Until the elections, neither party can well get on without the other; they are reminiscent of a cat and dog whose tails have been tied together.

Moreover, any appreciable success in the elections by radical parties to right and left (which on present showing is highly probable) may mean that no party will emerge in 1969 with a clear majority and that a coalition government will continue to be inevitable. This result might well be prevented by the abolition of proportional representation and exclusive reliance on majority voting in single-member constituencies on the British pattern. Such a system would probably reduce the right- and left-wing radicals, and in addition the F.D.P., to insignificance. But the S.P.D. are afraid that, in current conditions, it would strengthen the C.D.U./C.S.U. at their expense. They have therefore been reluctant to depart from the bargain made when the Great Coalition was formed, by which the electoral law was to be changed in time for the 1973 elections, but not (or only to a minor extent) for the 1969 ones. But parties which have worked together for six or more years are unlikely ever to be quite the same again. Both the C.D.U./C.S.U. and S.P.D. embody a considerable spread of opinions and many Deputies have more in common with moderate opinion in the other party than with their own extremists.

These facts suggest that the German political system may be in process of transformation away from a left-right confrontation towards the kind of pattern familiar in the Weimar Republic and in Austria until 1966, in which the democratic system is maintained by a coalition of moderates, based essentially on Christian and working-class opinion, with extreme parties of doubtful allegiance to left and right. For the development needed to arrest the trend, namely a break-up of the Great Coalition, appears unlikely. If the trend becomes established, the fundamental reason for it will be that there are not in Western Germany—at any rate in the opinion of the Social Democrats—enough potential voters left of centre to give a party of the democratic left adequate prospect of achieving office either on its own or as the major partner in a stable coalition.

There is, however, no reason why a return to the Weimar pattern should mean a repetition of the Weimar experience. The vital question both for Germany and the world is how far those who think in terms of a German culture, distinct from East and West and dominating Central Europe, authoritarian, irrational and emotional, are the last survivors of an outdated point of view or people with a message which will appeal to coming generations. Much has altered in Germany since 1945 and many of the social changes made between 1933 and 1945, though ostensibly the work of the Nazis, represented a response to general economic trends and are therefore irreversible. Even more influential than the impact of defeat has been the impact of full employment and of middle-class living conditions on the mass of the population along with the impact of the outer world (particularly the U.S.A.) thanks to mass media and air travel. Established ideas are coming under scrutiny and in some cases being thrown overboard. The Germans are probably better informed about the outside world than ever before.

On the other hand Germans are now more inclined than at any time in the past twenty years to look critically at Western values. Britain's inability to solve her economic problems is contrasted with German prosperity; America's preoccupation with Asia and colour troubles at home are casting doubt on her commitment to Europe. The failure of the Cold War policies has created a feeling that West Germany, having done what was asked of her by the West, has been cheated of the reward which she was encouraged to expect, and would be well advised to take a line of her own in future. Just as her economic and military integration with the West cannot be said (in spite of optimistic affirmations to the contrary) to have passed the point of no return, so her political and cultural integration is still in doubt. Changes in the character and structure of the Federal Republic are only to be expected; there neither is nor can be any finality in human affairs. But they need not necessarily involve a regression to a more authoritarian and aggressive society. For though this may still prove to be their character, the result of the continuing struggle in Germany between these influences and their antitheses is by no means a foregone conclusion.

In any case Hitler and his ideas are too inseparably connected with disaster for a crude revival to have much prospect of success. The term 'neo-Nazis' is calculated to focus attention in the wrong direction. The real dangers in a situation are seldom those for which one is on the alert; what people were expecting when they got Hitler was a revival of the monarchy! A fresh nationalist movement will have to devise a new formula and even then it will only stand a chance of becoming more than a 'brown back-lash' and gaining control over German policy if appreciable numbers of voters start to lose confidence in and patience with the two parties which at present dominate the scene. The chances of this happening depend on the ability of those parties, either on their own or in coalition, to satisfy the chief desires of the German people. These are for prosperity, international status and reunification. We have seen that the prospects for continued prosperity are reasonably good though by no means assured (and indeed excessive prosperity might lead to over-confidence). A great deal therefore depends on the prospects for reunification and the acceptability of the sacrifices needed to get it.

(d) *Foreign Policy*

Shortly before Erhard resigned office, the State Secretary of the Foreign Office is reported to have told him and his senior colleagues that Germany's foreign policy had run into a dead end. The strategy of reunification by intimidation had broken down, owing to the proven impossibility of building up a strength which was overwhelming and to the consequent refusal of the Americans, whose support was essential, to accept the risk of nuclear war which the offensive prosecution of the policy involved. The various German ancillaries to the policy, such as the claim to exclusive representation, non-recognition of the D.D.R. and the Hallstein Doctrine, could by themselves at best prevent the situation from getting worse but not make it any better. A new initiative was needed and with Kiesinger's appointment of Willy Brandt to the Foreign Office, the occasion for it was believed to have come. A public opinion poll suggested that he would have the support of 59 per cent of the population (as compared with 48 per cent a year earlier).

The spirit in which Brandt approached his task was that outlined by Herr Bahr,[1] whom he brought in as his policy adviser. The old concept of 'relaxation of tension through reunification' was to be exchanged for one of 'reunification through relaxation of tension'. The hope was, by establishing working arrangements on minor matters with Communist states, and particularly the D.D.R., to win their confidence sufficiently for negotiations on wider issues to become possible. At the very least, some amelioration might thus be secured in the living conditions of the East German population. The difficulty about this policy of 'small steps' is that, for it to be successful, two players are required. As long as the West German attitude was uncompromising, East Germany made effective propaganda by appearing eager for negotiations. But as soon as Bonn began to show a readiness for minor concessions, this appearance was abandoned.

Already in the summer of 1966 the S.E.D. had proposed to the S.P.D. that debates should be held between representatives of the two parties on both sides of the frontier. The West, after swallowing hard, accepted the proposal, whereupon the East found excuses

[1] See above, p. 244.

for not proceeding with it. In April 1967 Brandt and Wehner persuaded Kiesinger to let the S.P.D. send a letter to the S.E.D. with
practical suggestions for improving communications between the
two Germanies. Rather over a month later a reply arrived in the
shape of a letter from Willi Stoph, the chairman of the D.D.R.
Council of Ministers, to Kiesinger. This indicated that the best
way to get such improvement going would be a meeting between
the two of them but indicated that no such meeting could take
place until the Federal government abandoned its claim to be the
sole legal representative of the German people. In spite of
opposition from the C.D.U. 'hardliners', who thought that any
answer addressed to Stoph might impute to his government a legal
right of existence, Kiesinger continued the correspondence, address-
ing Stoph as 'Dear Chairman' without saying of what. He indicated
his view that conversations would best be left to subordinates but
added that, if recognition were to be insisted on as a precondition
of talks, he would be obliged in return to demand a secret plebiscite
of all Germans about their future. The exchange of letters went
on for several more months until just before Christmas the D.D.R.
made it clear that recognition of their legal existence was an
indispensable precondition of any negotiations at any level. An
attempt by the new Lord Mayor of West Berlin to initiate talks
with his opposite number in the Eastern sector of the city not
merely met a similar fate but evoked a reaffirmation of the East
German claim that the city as a whole rightly belongs to the
D.D.R. of which it is the capital.

Who gained most out of these exchanges is a matter of opinion,
but the reasons for East Germany's up-stage behaviour are not
hard to guess; they are indicated by the description of the 'small
steps' policy as 'aggression in carpet slippers'. Although the immediate object of the West is said to be the easing of life for the
D.D.R.'s citizens, and although Dr Kiesinger has stated openly
that for the time being the German problem is incapable of solution, there can be no denying that the ultimate object of all these
moves is reunification. Indeed they would not be acceptable in
West Germany on any other terms. A wide variety of schemes for
gradual reunification has been proposed with greater or less
authority during the last few years. All have envisaged that a
point should ultimately come at which the inhabitants of the
D.D.R. are allowed an opportunity of changing their form of
government. It is therefore hardly surprising if the D.D.R. régime
shows reluctance to join in working out schemes intended to bring
about its demise. That demise may be desirable and Herr Brandt's

policy stands a better chance of achieving it than those previously followed. But the real question to be faced is whether it can be achieved at all in the foreseeable future.

Some well-qualified observers believe that, if a free vote were allowed in the D.D.R., the people thereby brought to power would not rush into the arms of the Federal Republic but would at least make conditions, some of which would be far from welcome. It is certainly true that the situation has changed considerably since 1953. The standard of life has improved greatly during the last ten years and can be expected to go on doing so. The growth in the national product has probably not led to as great a growth in consumer expenditure as it would have done in a liberal democracy because it is in the nature of centrally-controlled economies to siphon off a larger share for communal purposes (such as research and education!) and productive investment. Consequently, the average inhabitant of the D.D.R. does not benefit from living in the world's ninth largest industrial country as much as might be expected. But the enforced saving must to some extent protect the economy from the pressure of excess demand, such as are complicating the future of the Federal Republic, and if the present is being sacrificed to the future, things may be counted on to improve as the future arrives.

The new generation of technician-managers who are coming to the top in the D.D.R. (as in all Communist countries) are both more acclimatised to the conditions in which they have to live and more resigned to them. All those under forty have never known anything but autocratic rule. There are a great number of aspects of life in the West which they have been taught to despise and the Federal Republic's economic problems have recently made a sense of superiority easier to adopt. They take some pride in a society which, in spite of all difficulties and depredations, has been made to work. Any attempt at revolution, given the risks disclosed in 1953 and 1956, seems highly unlikely. The question, however, is whether the loyalty of these cadres to the régime is such, and is believed by the régime to be such, as to last if they were given freedom, either to decide on their future or merely to cross the frontier.

In Yugoslavia, Romania and some other Communist countries, relaxation has taken the form of polycentrism, the development of a distinctive brand of communism which makes a claim to loyalty not simply on grounds of doctrinal truth but also on those of national sentiment. But in the D.D.R. an appeal to national sentiment is for the present hardly thinkable. In time an East

German loyalty may very well develop, like an Austrian German or a Swiss German loyalty. But for the present the 'nation' for East Germans still means the Germany of Bismarck and the Kaiser, so that putting national before doctrinal objectives would mean giving priority to reunification. Paradoxically polycentrism, by reducing the amount of support which the Soviet Union can expect from the other Communist countries, has made East Germany more important to it and has thus increased the D.D.R.'s ability to extort its aid.

Undoubtedly the differences of outlook which have grown up between East and West would mean grave headaches for any reunited German state, however loose its constitutional form. But it is hard to believe that these would at present be foreseen clearly enough to counteract all the traditional pulls of loyalty. It would be surprising if the East Germans really felt themselves at home in the Slav camp. The lack of free discussion, of freedom to travel to the West, of access to Western literature, are all resented. Closer contact with Western technology is regarded as vital to rapid progress. Accordingly, the chance of a free vote working out in their favour is not one which the leaders of the D.D.R. can be expected to take. Communists are trained to think in terms of power and do not easily let power out of their hands.

Ulbricht, however, is an old and by all accounts a tired man of seventy-four who cannot last much longer. Western commentators at times hold out the hope that he will be succeeded by someone less doctrinaire, less dependent on the Russians and more flexible. The prospect might certainly offer a chance of progress if the East Germans were on their own but if that were the case, many other things would be altered. The Russians have twenty divisions in the country and show no disposition to withdraw them. Moscow can be expected to see that the power remains in the hands of people it can depend on. And indeed, a split in the East German ranks or an attempt by the leadership to defy the Russians would present the West with an almost intolerable dilemma between standing aloof and risking a full-scale war by intervention.

There are, however, those in Bonn and elsewhere who maintain that pressure can be brought to bear on the Soviet Union and the D.D.R. by the policy of 'being nice to the Gomulkas' or, in other words, exploiting polycentrism. The aim proposed is to improve relations with all other Communist states so as to sow dissension between them and the D.D.R. which accordingly would find itself in growing isolation and difficulty. This policy seemed to have scored an encouraging success in January 1967 when the

Romanians agreed to establish diplomatic relations with the Federal
Republic and even accepted a statement that this implied no
relaxation of that Republic's attitude to the D.D.R. But the Romanians, who were engaged in nailing their colours to the fence, had
special reasons for wanting Western contacts to play off against
their Eastern ones and it remains to be seen whether West Germany, by accepting with such alacrity the outstretched hand of
the trouble-maker in the Communist camp, improved her prospects
of reaching agreement with that camp's other members. Certainly
the immediate result was a flurry of activity by the Poles and
East Germans which compelled the Bulgarians, Hungarians and
Czechs to reaffirm their links and loyalties, while even the
Romanians have been careful to treat West Germans on exactly
the same footing as Eastern ones. If developments suggest that
Romania has on balance clearly gained by resuming diplomatic
relations the other Balkan countries may one by one follow suit.
This process may be accelerated by the agreement with Yugoslavia, especially as such a step clearly implies the abandonment of
the Hallstein Doctrine. But the length of time taken over reaching
such an agreement suggests that the price of any further ones
would be the eating of more humble pie than the Bonn government
can make palatable to its right-wing supporters, while even then
it will not necessarily have done much to achieve its somewhat
transparent object of sowing discord in the enemy ranks.

It is not the Communist satellites which decide who holds power
in East Germany but the men in Moscow and to a lesser extent
in Warsaw. To say that there are no circumstances in which the
Kremlin would let go its hold on the D.D.R. may be unrealistic.
Indeed some observers argue that the Russians are even more over-
extended than the Americans, that the Presidium must realise the
impossibility of maintaining indefinitely the division of Germany
and that its members must therefore be anxious to find their way
out of a commitment which could so easily involve them in full-
scale war. Moreover, they are supposed to be anxious for an early
settlement in Europe, before China's strength has reached a stage
where it must absorb most of their attention. But such a picture
involves wishful thinking. The division of Germany has now lasted
twenty years and, thanks in particular to de Gaulle, the present
situation must in many ways look less alarming to the Russians
than that of ten years ago. They are anyhow likely to be so trained
in Marxist ways of thought as genuinely to expect the capitalist
states to grow weaker with the passage of time and the Communist
ones stronger. Though they would no doubt be glad to liquidate

their stake in Germany, they have no intention of doing so at any cost and probably believe that the longer they wait, the better the terms they are likely to get.

The kind of terms for which they are holding out are by now fairly clear. Their main objective is assurance that a reunited Germany would either remain a friendly and satisfied Power or else be unable to recover its 1937 frontiers by violence. They are too realistic to trust to verbal promises. Therefore they want to ask terms which any pro-Western German is going to find difficulty in accepting so as to ensure that the concessions are made by a régime well-disposed to themselves. The main items would be:

1. The complete abandonment of the Hallstein Doctrine and of the Bonn claim to be the only government entitled to represent Germans.

2. The recognition of the D.D.R. as a fully-fledged state with its capital in Berlin.

3. A neutral status for West Berlin, possibly under U.N. guarantee. This would presumably involve the cessation of Bonn's financial support, and therefore a rapid economic decline.

4. The recognition of the Oder-Neisse line and of the other frontiers established in 1945.

5. A reaffirmation of the West German promise not to manufacture nuclear weapons, accompanied by a promise not to acquire or control them. This would have to be accompanied by arrangements for inspection, on the lines agreed in the proposed non-proliferation agreement. Non-possession would apply to means of delivery as well as to warheads.

6. The reunited Germany to leave N.A.T.O. and pledge itself to neutrality (probably with a limit on the size of its armed forces and a guarantee by America, Britain and France to respect and maintain such neutrality).

7. Freedom of activity for the Communist/Socialist Unity Party in West Germany.

8. Judging by the attitude which they have taken to Austria's wish to join the Common Market, the Russians might well argue that full membership of the European Economic Community was incompatible with neutrality. They might, however, be prepared to yield on this or at least to allow the reunited Germany to sign a Trade Treaty with the Five, giving it most of the economic advantages of membership but precluding any surrender of sovereignty. (Such an arrangement would chime in with de Gaulle's views as to the future form of the Community.)

Obviously no West German government would consider such terms until it had explored all other possibilities first, and there is always a hope of some fresh factor inducing the Russians to settle for less. But enough has been said to suggest that the balance of probabilities is against this in the foreseeable future. What then will the likely reaction in West Germany be as the cost of reunification slowly becomes clear to the public?

There are, as has already been said, signs of restiveness among the younger generation (personified by the novelist Günther Grass and the Berlin student leader Rudi Dutschke). Such people are refusing to take their elders' views about communism on trust and argue that all these elders are being asked to do is to accept the world as it is and as they have made it rather than as they would like it to be. To the young, the legal theories about Germany's continuing unity are nothing more than a hollow sham. In the summer of 1967 40 per cent of German students favoured the recognition of the Oder-Neisse line, as compared with 34 per cent of the general population, while 60 per cent did not believe in the possibility of early reunification, as compared with 44 per cent. Later evidence suggests that the movement for recognition is growing. The view that the D.D.R. offers better facilities than the Federal Republic for sport is widespread, while there is an almost equal division of opinion about the relative superiority of its educational and cultural arrangements. But while those on the newly emerging democratic left who think in these terms may have the future on their side, in the present they are nothing like strong enough to decide the policy of the country, and the coalition government has made it clear that abandonment of the claim to sole representation (and with it the recognition of the D.D.R. as a legally constituted state) is not and cannot be a matter of negotiation. The furthest that West German Ministers can go without splitting the coalition was indicated in August 1967 when **Brandt** on a visit to Bucharest spoke of 'two political régimes which coexist on German soil'.

The only conceivable source from which a majority could be found for a policy of conciliation with the East is German nationalism. Nationalists tend to be violently anti-Communist and anti-Slav : they see in the U.S.S.R. the main source of their humiliation. The Soviet government in return regards a revival of German nationalism as the most dangerous threat to its security in Europe. A deal between the two seems hardly on the cards. Yet as many earlier pages of this book have shewn, the heart of German nationalism belongs to Central rather than to Western

Europe. It shares with the East an inclination towards authoritarian rule. German-Russian cooperation has a long, if intermittent, history. Nationalist foreign policy is by tradition realist and if the interests of the nation are once again to be given priority over everything else, realism would seem to indicate that a reunification which cannot be obtained by alliance with the West should instead be sought by a bargain with the East.

Yet at the most only a section of nationalist opinion could be expected to swallow such a line, while the opposition to it would be formidable. The reversal of attitude which it would involve would be too much for most refugees. It would be abhorrent to liberal opinion and to all those who have been schooled to see in communism the arch enemy to Western and Christian values. It would be powerfully contested by the Springer Press. The country would be split from top to bottom and the considerable degree of political integration achieved since 1945 would be reversed. The chances of any government obtaining a majority for such a policy in this or any prospective *Bundestag* seem as remote as the chances of the Russians proving amenable to negotiations. If by any chance the deal were carried through, its conclusion would not end the controversy and, to maintain their position, those responsible would be drawn into increasingly close cooperation with the East, which in turn would provoke increasing resistance. A civil war would not be unthinkable.

In such a situation the other countries of the West could hardly afford to look on with impartiality. For the Germans and the resources at their command are too numerous for their passage from one camp into another to be a matter of indifference. It may be that the Russians would be prepared to leave a reunited Germany in a genuinely neutral position; 70 million German Communists might cause them just as much trouble as 70 million German nationalists. The Kremlin must have learnt a great deal in recent years about the difficulties and disadvantages of trying to control alien peoples. Internally and externally they have so many problems on their hands that they may well lack any desire to acquire more. Russia may in short be a satisfied Power like America and Britain. Equally, lasting collaboration between Teuton and Slav may be impossible; the precedent of 1939 was hardly auspicious. Yet none of these hypotheses is firm enough to justify the West in allowing its policies of Atlantic defence and European integration to be scrapped on the strength of them.

Yet coming back to Germany the question remains of what other routes to reunification in the full sense of the word are available if acceptance of Russia's probable terms for it is ruled out. A return to the policy of intimidation is not a rational alternative. There has been no fundamental change in the factors which caused it to fail in the 1950s. Both the United States and Britain are now less rather than more inclined to support it than they were. The appeal to arms means the risk of annihilation and is therefore only justifiable to prevent annihilation. We are not in a position to coerce the Communists and we are unlikely ever to become so.

Great hopes were at one time pinned in Germany on the possibility of mediation by General de Gaulle, or on his cooperation in building up a European nuclear force which would allow the policy of intimidation to be resumed without the need for extra-European support. But the extent of the General's influence in Eastern Europe was always open to doubt as was his readiness to re-establish German strength. The Federal Republic was an essential tool which he used with some skill in his attempts to build up a Western Europe independent of the United States. But when it comes to the point of helping Germany to reassume her status as a Great Power, and particularly of putting nuclear weapons into her hands, France is always likely to remember that, as Clemenceau said, there are twenty million Germans too many. Franco-German relations in the 1960s have had something of the character of a poker-game played in the atmosphere of a veterans' reunion. The German zest for taking part has certainly been impaired by a growing awareness that France under de Gaulle has been exploiting the atmosphere in order to win the game. But in spite of growing disillusion, the German leaders are reluctant to break off play, for fear of thereby provoking the other party into kicking over the table, or even burning down the club! In other words, they fear that, by standing up to France, they might well jeopardise both the future of the European Economic Community and also the work of Franco-German reconciliation, the two big positive achievements of German policy since 1949, the two supranational ends to which Adenauer sacrificed the chance of early national reunification. Such a clear admission that Adenauer's priorities had been wrong could only play into the hands of the nationalists. A reluctance based on motives like these is as much to be respected as the shortsightedness of French policy is to be deplored.

The suggestion is often made that the problem of reunification can only be solved in the context of European unity. Though this may well be true, it is hardly encouraging. The process of integrating the Common Market has proved laborious and is now in danger of stopping half-way. Yet its members were roughly compatible in economic development and shared broadly the same political and social institutions. Much the same can be said of Britain and other E.F.T.A. countries, yet grave doubts have been expressed—and not only by de Gaulle—as to whether the fabric of the Six could survive their entry. To absorb the countries of Eastern Europe would obviously be a much tougher proposition altogether. Yet only if the Communist satellites could be detached from Russia and merged in a Europe-wide Federation would a solution to German disunity be in sight within such a Federation. The day for this is clearly far ahead.

The upshot of the discussion would therefore seem to be that there is in present circumstances *no* policy which offers an early prospect of territorial reunification or even of a significant relaxation of living conditions in the D.D.R. The best course for the world as a whole, and probably for Germany as well, is that at present being followed by Kiesinger and Brandt, by waiting in patience yet taking every opportunity which offers of proposing relaxations. This policy well deserves the full support which Britain has given it. And the time may come when, as part of a world-wide Russo-American agreement, a security framework can be established within which relaxation would be possible for both sides. Even if this heart-warming dream should never ripen, the time may all the same come when East Germany can be given its freedom with every confidence that it will not quit the Eastern camp.

Such a development would happen all the faster if West Germany could convince the Russians that it is not trying to lure the D.D.R. away. That is to say, it must make credible the assertion, now not unfrequently heard, that the aim is simply and solely to ease the lot of the 'other Germans'. But such a gesture, which is precisely what the other Eastern nations are asking for in their demands for renunciation of past claims, seems too much for West Germany as yet to make. For it would in fact mean acquiescing in part of Germany remaining Communist for the foreseeable future and one cannot help doubting whether many West Germans have really yet reconciled themselves to such a scaling down of their objectives. All that can be said is that at present East and West Germany, like East and West Europe, seem to be moving internally towards greater similarity rather than towards greater divergence. The Kiesinger government has indeed said that its aim is to bridge the gulfs rather than widen them.

Yet the Brandt policy is not one which can hope for quick

results. It involves patience and perseverance in face of rebuffs, in the hope that, as time goes on, the German public will gradually be educated as to the realities of the situation and abandon excessive hopes. Such an attitude of renunciation requires, like policy in the economic field, a high level of restraint and intelligence on the part of the public. It is hardly a policy with which to win elections. The danger is that, before it can show dividends, some unforeseeable turn of home or foreign politics will put its exponents at a disadvantage compared to those who argue that action and vigour are the way to get results, that liberal policies are lost on Communists. If, as has been said, lack of progress towards reunification were to coincide with a serious interruption in economic growth, such activists, whether inside or outside the established parties, might well get enough support to gain office.

The question may fairly be asked as to what, in the light of previous pages, a fresh nationalist régime in West Germany could do. The Federation at present only possesses twelve (incomplete) divisions and lacks its own nuclear arms. The only solution which the Kiesinger government could find in July 1967 to its budgetary headaches was to cut defence expenditure.[1] Admittedly Germany will soon have available from civilian reactors plutonium which could be used to make bombs. But the processing involved is intricate and extremely costly. It is not therefore merely international undertakings which stand in the way of West Germany 'going it alone' in atomic weapons and the means of delivering them. She would have drastically to alter her present distribution of income before she could afford such things and even then her striking power would not begin to compare with Russia's. If the whole of N.A.T.O. could not intimidate the East, West Germany on her own has not got the resources to do so.

There is, however, a policy which a government of the kind envisaged could pursue, perhaps accompanied by a limited amount of rearmament. It is one of calculated provocation, the deliberate taking of risks and provocation of incidents in the belief that, if the East could be needled into action, the Western Powers could not allow it to succeed nor to advance further into Western Europe but, no matter how much they disliked Western Germany, would feel compelled in their own interests to prevent that country from being defeated by Communists. The hope would presumably be that, in the ensuing mix-up, Western armies would advance to the 1937 frontiers of Germany which would then remain in

1 See p. 271.

their hands. The enterprise would not be prohibited by the possibility that what might get to those and other frontiers would be nuclear-headed missiles rather than men nor by the thought that it might be largely Germany which would be devastated. The menace of superior American arms would be reckoned on to deter the Soviets from having recourse to nuclear weapons. Once again German policy-makers would be gambling on a quick and relatively cheap victory.

In the past such German aspirations have been met by an East-West alliance. But that alliance has been effective in winning wars, not in preventing them. In the circumstances envisaged the need would be not to stop a German victory but to stop the war from 'escalating'. The fear of mutual self-destruction has caused Soviet-American cooperation to grow far faster than was dreamt of in the 1950s. But the arrival to power in West Germany of a radical nationalist government would present it with its stiffest test yet.

The time has come to answer the question on p. 131 : has the gold been returned to the Rhine? Is the German nation (and more particularly its Western section) prepared to be content with its position and boundaries, or is desire for a radical improvement in that position likely to bring destruction again upon the world? Is a divided Germany going to prove just as dangerous as a united one did?

But the question is one to which an answer cannot yet be given because, for most at any rate of the inhabitants of the Federal Republic, the moment of truth has not yet arrived. Successive governments have led them to believe that, by one means or another, reunification, in one sense or another, could be achieved without war and without abandoning any other of their basic principles, such as Western integration, democracy and anti-communism. The testing time will come if and when it grows evident to even the most optimistic that these hopes are incapable of anything like their full realisation. Should this happen, will the voice of reason prevail and the ring be returned whence it came? Or will those whose patriotism takes the form of seeking a Valhalla reject reason and sober calculation in favour of tradition and emotion?

There are good grounds for expecting the advocates of the first course to prevail and it may even be regarded as unfriendly so much as to question their ability to do so. And since it is among the older generation that the advocates of the second course are mostly to be found, they may be expected to grow progressively weaker the longer that the crisis can be postponed. The Atlantic spectator must have difficulty in remaining impartial. For the risks now involved in establishing a Valhalla are even greater than in the days of the Nibelungs and the victory of those who prefer the siren voice of a Lorelei to the caution of the Rhinemaidens might result in a *Götterdämmerung* indeed. Spectators, however, are not being asked, as are the Germans, to surrender values which they have been brought up to cherish; they merely stand to benefit immensely by that surrender. They would therefore do well to show appreciation of what has been achieved in West Germany since 1945 and sympathy for the choice which faces that state—even if they can leave it in no doubt as to the course which, in its interest as well as their own, they confidently hope to see it pursue.

List of Statistical Tables

I

THE GREAT COALITION GOVERNMENT

Department	Minister	Parliamentary State Secretary
Chancellor	Dr Kurt Georg Kiesinger (C.D.U.)	Baron von und zu Guttenberg (C.D.U.)
Vice-Chancellor and Foreign Affairs	Willy Brandt (S.P.D.)	G. Jahn (S.P.D.)
All-German Affairs	Herbert Wehner (S.P.D.)	—
Interior	Paul Lücke (C.D.U.)	E. Benda (C.D.U.)
Justice	Dr Gustav Heinemann (S.P.D.)	—
Finance	Franz-Josef Strauss (C.S.U.)	A. Leicht (C.S.U.)
Economics	Prof Karl Schiller (S.P.D.)	K. Dieter (S.P.D.)
Budget	Kurt Schmücker (C.D.U.)	—
Defence	Dr Gerhard Schröder (C.D.U.)	E. Adorno (C.D.U.)
Agriculture	Hermann Höcherl (C.S.U.)	—
Labour	Hans Katzer (C.D.U.)	—
Transport	Georg Leber (S.P.D.)	H. Boerner (S.P.D.)
Posts	Dr Werner Dollinger (C.S.U.)	—
Housing	Dr Lauritz Lauritzen (S.P.D.)	—
Refugees	Kai-Uwe von Hassel (C.D.U.)	—
Bundesrat	Carlo Schmid (S.P.D.)	—
Families & Youth	Dr Bruno Heck (C.D.U.)	—
Promotion of Knowledge	Dr Gerhard Stoltenberg (C.D.U.)	—
Economic Assistance	Hans-Jürgen Wischnewski (S.P.D.)	—
Health	Frau Käte Strobel (S.P.D.)	—

The Cabinet thus consists of 8 C.D.U., 3 C.S.U. and 9 S.P.D. As at
1 January 1968.

II
PARTY STRENGTHS IN BUNDESTAG

Election in *Party*	1949	1953	1957	1961	1965
C.D.U./C.S.U.	139 (5)	243 (6)	270 (8)	242 (9)	245 (6)
S.P.D.	131 (9)	151 (11)	169 (12)	190 (13)	202 (15)
F.D.P.	52 (5)	48 (5)	41 (2)	67	49 (1)
Refugees	—	27	—	—	
German	17	15	17	—	
Centre	10	3	—	—	
Others	53	—	—	—	
Total	402	487	497	499	496

NOTE: Figures for West Berlin are given in brackets and, since W. Berlin Deputies do not vote, are excluded from the larger figures for the rest of the Federal Republic.

III
PARTY STRENGTHS IN LÅNDER
Votes cast in Election of 1965

Land	C.D.U./C.S.U.	S.P.D.	F.D.P.	Others
Schleswig-Holstein	682,600	549,900	132,800	51,500
Hamburg	446,100	572,900	112,000	56,000
Lower Saxony	1,855,100	1,614,500	440,900	142,900
Bremen	150,900	215,500	51,900	25,900
North Rhine-Westphalia	4,595,300	4,149,900	740,000	268,100
Hesse	1,130,900	1,366,000	359,000	132,200
Rhineland-Palatinate	1,013,600	754,200	209,000	79,000
Baden-Württemberg	2,219,800	1,470,000	582,900	179,500
Bavaria	3,136,500	1,869,500	413,700	221,800
Saar	295,300	250,800	54,100	30,400
	15,526,100	12,813,200	3,096,300	1,187,300

IV

THE LÄNDER

Name of Land	Area in sq. km.	Population end 1965	% of total population	Pop. per sq. km.	Religious adherence m. Ev : R.C. (1960)	Capital	Name of Minister President Autumn 1967	Composition of Government
Schleswig-Holstein	15,658	2,438,800	4·1	148	2·0:0·1	Kiel	H. Lemke	C.D.U./F.D.P.
Hamburg	747	1,854,400	3·1	2452	1·4:0·1	Hamburg	H. Weichmann	S.P.D.
Lower Saxony	47,393	6,921,000	11·7	140	5·1:0·1	Hanover	G. Diederichs	S.P.D./C.D.U.
Bremen	404	742,500	1·3	1,749	0·6:0·1	Bremen	H. Koschnick	S.P.D./F.D.P.
North Rhine–Westphalia	34,045	16,735,700	28·2	467	6·9:8·3	Düsseldorf	H. Kühn	S.P.D./F.D.P.
Hesse	21,109	5,170,400	8·7	228	3·0:1·5	Wiesbaden	G. A. Zinn	S.P.D.
Rhineland Palatinate	19,831	3,582,000	6·0	172	1·4:1·9	Koblenz	P. Altmeier	C.D.U./F.D.P.
Baden–Württemberg	35,750	8,426,200	14·2	217	3·8:3·6	Stuttgart	H. Filbinger	C.D.U./S.P.D.
Bavaria	70,550	10,100,900	17·0	135	2·5:6·8	Munich	A. Goppel	C.S.U.
Saar	2,568	1,127,400	1·9	413	0·3:0·8	Saarbrücken	F. J. Röder	C.D.U./Saar Democrats
West Berlin	479	2,197,300	3·7	4,588	1·6:0·25	Berlin	K. Schütz	S.P.D./F.D.P.
Totals	248,534	59,296,600		237 average	28·6:23·55			
By comparison: U.K.	240,779	54,500,000			51·3%:44·1%			
Oregon	251,000	199,780						

Sources: *Statistisches Jahrbuch* 1967, *Statesman's Year Book* 1967–8.

FEDERAL AND LAND FINANCES
Figures for 1965. DM million

Income

Income and Corporation Tax	39,706
Capital Gains Tax	1,351
Total	41,057
of which 16,012 (39%) goes to *Bund*; 25,045 (61%) to *Länder*	
Federal Taxes	44,888
among which:	
Turnover Tax	21,568
Turnover Tax Adjustment	2,651
Mineral Oil Tax	7,428
Tobacco Tax	4,697
Customs Duties	2,898
Spirits Monopoly	1,508
Coffee Tax	954
Land Taxes	7,322
of which	
Property tax	1,880
Vehicle tax	2,624
Beer tax	979
Communal taxes	13,063
of which	
Trade tax	9,350
Ground tax	2,110
Other income of *Länder and Communes* (Rent, Interest, Debt repayment, dues, profits, fines, etc.)	38,261

Expenditure

Heading	Federation	*Länder* and Communes	Total
Social Security	17,389	10,240	27,629
Defence	18,230	—	18,230
Education, Research and Culture	953	16,590	17,543*
Transport	3,769	7,704	11,473
Commercial undertakings, and trade development	5,359	5,644	11,003
Building	224	7,697	7,921
Food and Agriculture	1,798	5,086	6,884
Communal institutions and organisations	—	6,154	6,154
Health, etc.	41	5,615	5,656
Public Security	360	4,628	4,988
Administration, debt repayment, war compensation, etc.	8,261	22,376	30,637
	56,384	91,734	148,118

* 16,023 for Education and Research, of which 903 was provided by Federation.

VI

GROWTH OF POPULATION IN SEVEN COUNTRIES
1871–1966
(millions)

Country	1871	1891	1913	1936	1946	1956	1966
Germany	41	49.4	66·8	68·8[1]	65·2[2]	69·2	76·1
W. Germany					46·7[3]	51·6[4]	59·3
France[5]	36·1	38·2	39·7	41·9	40·5	43·4	49·15
Italy	n.a.	30·2	34·7 (1911)	42·4	45·6	49·2	53·0
Sweden	4·2	4·8	5·6	6·2	6·8	7·2	7·8
U.K.	27·4	34·2	45·6	47·1[6]	46·8	51·2	54·7
U.S.A.	38·5	63	97[7]	128	143·7	168	197·6
Russia/U.S.S.R.	76·5	118	175	193 (1939)	n.a.	202 (1955)	227·3

SOURCES: *Statesman's Year Book, Whitaker's Almanack, British Economy Key Statistics.*

NOTES:
1. Within 1936 frontiers
2. Excluding areas under Russian & Polish administration
3. Including W. Berlin
4. Including the Saar (1m.)
5. Metropolitan France
6. Excluding Eire
7. Continental U.S.

VII

COMPARATIVE BURDENS OF TAXATION

1. % Tax paid on extra £1 or equivalent earned by married man with two children 1965.

Income Level £	W. Germany	France	Sweden	U.K.	U.S.
500	13	6	28	Nil	4
1,000	13	11	28	23	19
2,500	25	18	45	32	20
5,000	40	25	57	37	28
10,000	45	32	66	74	48
50,000	53	47	71	91	69

Tax paid includes both social security payments and income tax. Purchasing power exchange rates used to convert other currencies into £: Germany DM 10.42; France NF 13.05; Sweden Kr 15.35; U.S. $3.72.

SOURCE: *Economist* 26 June 1966.

2. Total taxes as % of gross national product 1965.

W. Germany	France	Italy	Sweden	U.K.	U.S.
39·6	45·5	33·4	44·2	34·2	30

Figures include local taxation and social security contributions.

SOURCE: *The Times* 19 June 1967 based on O.E.C.D. National Account Statistics.

3. Direct taxes as % of total tax revenues. Average 1963–5.

W. Germany	France	Sweden	U.K.	U.S.
32·1	16·1	49·8	37·9	50·1

SOURCE: As for § 2.

VIII

GROSS DOMESTIC PRODUCT AT FACTOR COST PER HEAD
Constant Prices in U.S. dollars 1955

	1899	1913	1929	1937	1950	1957 (a)	1957 (b)	1961	1965
Germany	525	560	625	687	—	1,070	849	—	—
W. Germany	—	—	—	775	665	1,070	849	1,140	1,292
France	360	400	605	540	775	1,015	1,054	1,188	1,380
Italy	185	225	275	260	360	520	439	540	617
Sweden	360	475	720	705	1,020	1,225	1,148	1,325	1,557
U.K.	830	920	915	1,055	1,245	1,280	932	1,015	1,115
U.S.	790	1,000	1,380	1,330	1,940	2,185	2,163	2,229	2,600

SOURCES: 1899–1957(a). A. Maizels: *Industrial Growth and World Trade*, p.533. 1957(b)–1965. O.E.C.D. National Account Statistics combined with U.N. figures for population and index numbers of per capita g.d.p.

IX

ANNUAL GROWTH IN REAL GROSS NATIONAL PRODUCT

	Average 1955–60	Average 1960–65	Average 1965–70
	Actual		*Forecast*
Canada	3·3	5·5	5·1
United States	2·2	4·5	4·2
Japan	9·7	9·6	7·4
France	4·6	5·1	4·7
West Germany[1]	6·3	4·8	3·2
Italy	5·5	5·1	5·2
U.K.	2·3	2·8	
Smaller Industrial Countries	3·7	4·8	3·8

NOTE: 1. Including the Saar and West Berlin, except for 1955–60 period. U.K. Figures from *The Economist*.

SOURCE: *N.I.E.S.R. Review* February 1967, Table 5, Page 15 (based on O.E.C.D. Economic Growth 1960–70 and N.I.E.S.R. Estimates).

X

NATIONAL EXPENDITURES ON CONSUMPTION AND INVESTMENT

A. Proportion of Gross Domestic Product devoted to Private Consumption.

Country	1938	1948	1952	1957–9 average	1962–4 average	1965
West Germany	60[1]	65[3]	56	59	57	57
France	n.a.	72	67	66	65	64
Italy	62	70	69	64	61	62
Sweden	71[2]	69	63	61	58	n.a.
U.K.	77	72	68	66	65	65
U.S.	75	68	62	63·5	63	63

B. Proportion of G.D.P. devoted to Public Consumption.

W. Germany	20[1]	18[3]	17	13	15	15·5
France	n.a.	12	18	14	13	13
Italy	20	12	12	14	16	15
Sweden	11[2]	13	16	18	18·5	n.a.
U.K.	14	15	19	16	17	17
U.S.	12	11	20	18	19	18

C. Proportion of G.D.P. devoted to Domestic Capital Formation.

W. Germany	19[1]	20[3]	25	24	27	27
France	n.a.	19	16	21	22	22
Italy	19	21	22	21·5	23	19
Sweden	19[2]	19	21	21·5	24	n.a.
U.K.	10	13	12	16	17·5	18
U.S.	11	18	18	18	17·5	17

SOURCE: O.E.E.C. Statistics of National Production and Expenditure 1938, 1947–52. O.E.C.D. National Accounts Statistics 1955–64.

NOTES: 1. 1936. 2. 1938–9. 3. Second half 1948.

XI

*PERCENTAGE OF G.N.P. DERIVED FROM DIFFERENT SEC-
TORS WITH, IN BRACKETS, PERCENTAGE OF EMPLOYED
WORKERS IN EACH SECTOR.*

Year 1965

	Agriculture	*Industry*	*Services*
Germany	5·3 (11)	50·8 (49)	43·9 (39)
France	8·8 (18)	40·5 (39)	50·7 (42)
Italy	13·4 (25)	39·5 (39)	47·1 (32)
Netherlands	8·3 (10)	41·2 (42)	50·5 (47)
Belgium	6·3 (6)	42 (45)	51·7 (47)
E.E.C. average	8·2 (17)	44·9 (47)	46·9 (39)
U.K.	3·4 (3)	47·5 (47)	49·1 (49)
U.S.	3·6 (6)	39·0 (31)	57·4 (58)

SOURCE: E.E.C.

XII

WEEKLY WORKING HOURS

Country	*1929*	*1938*	*1950*	*1955*	*1960*	*1966*
Germany	46	48·5	—	—	—	—
W. Germany	—	—	48·2	48·8	45·6	43·7
France	48	38·7	45	45·4	45·9	46·2
Italy	47·5	41·3	41·8	42·6	42·4	41·4
Sweden	47·7	46·3	46·3	45·5	43·5	n.a.
U.K.	46·9	46·5	45·9	46·9	46·1	46
U.S.	44·2	35·6	40·5	40·7	39·7	41·6

SOURCE: A. Maddison: *Economic Growth in the West*, Table G.I.,
p. 228.

1966 figures from International Labour Office Year Book,
Table 13A.

Italian figures multiplied by 5·25 to bring them from a daily to
a weekly basis.

XIII

TIME LOST IN STRIKES

(Minutes per year per member of economically active population)

	1953	*1959*	*1964*
West Germany	88·7	3·6	0·9
France	730	142·4	179·4
Italy	n.a.	621·3	942·9
Sweden	270	10·6	14·7
U.K.	134·8	316·2	130·1
U.S.A.	679	1,380	424·6

SOURCES: *Statistisches Jahrbuch* 1954, 1960, 1965. I.L.O. *Yearbook*
1960, 1966.

XIV
OUTPUT PER MAN HOUR
1913 = 100

Country	*1929*	*1938*	*1950*	*1955*	*1960*	*1966*
Germany	113	137	—	—	—	—
W. Germany	—	—	140	188	250	330
France	155	178·5	180	221	264	354
Italy	144	191	200	244	298	398
Sweden	116	151	205	241	290	n.a.
U.K.	140	168	190	206	231	280
U.S.	155·5	209	241	276	305	377

SOURCE: A. Maddison: *Economic Growth in the West*, p. 232 for 1929–60.

Figures for 1966 approximated from series in *N.I.E.S.R. Review*, August 1967, p. 60.

XV
EARNINGS IN MANUFACTURING
Pence per hour

	1948	*1953*	*1958*	*1963*	*1965*
West Germany	29·3	42·2	53·5	74·8	83·7
France	21·3	24·1	33·8	48·5	49·6
Sweden	56·3	70·2	81·4	99·1	98·4
U.K.	48·5	49·9	57·0	66·9	73·1
U.S.A.	103·2	123·9	132·3	149·7	154·2

Calculated at constant prices and converted at purchasing power exchange rates in 1965. Based on U.N. figures for wages, consumer and retail prices. The table is subject to a considerable margin of error and should only be regarded as a rough indication of relative earnings.

XVI
CONSUMER PRICE INDEX NUMBERS
1958 = 100.   All items.

Country	*1948*	*1953*	*1958*	*1963*	*1965*
West Germany	92	92	100	111	118
France	57	82	100	105[1]	111[1]
Italy	78	88	100	117	129
Sweden	65	84	100	115	125
U.K.	64	84	100	112	121
U.S.	83	93	100	106	109

SOURCE: U.N. *Yearbook*, 1966. Figure for U.K. in 1948 from London and Cambridge Key Statistics.

NOTE: 1. French figures for 1963 and 1965 based on 1962 = 100. Prior to 1963, figures refer to Paris alone.

XVII. *BALANCE OF PAYMENT*

	1950	1951	1952	1953	1954	1955	195
A. *Balance of Transactions* in Goods, Services, Transfer Payments and Capital.							
I. *Current Items*							
1. *Goods and Services*							
(a) Goods. Exports f.o.b.	8,356	14,577	16,894	18,477	21,938	25,580	30,712
Imports f.o.b.	10,670	13,084	14,732	14,848	18,046	22,339	25,079
Merchanting trade (net)				+23	+28	−4	+87
Net transactions in goods	−2,314	+1,493	+2,162	+3,652	+3,920	+3,237	+5,720
(b) Services Receipts	930	1,716	2,879	3,690	4,656	5,935	7,388
Expenditures	1,088	2,397	2,673	3,098	4,493	6,133	7,408
Net	−158	−681	+206	+592	+163	−198	−20
Net transactions in goods and services	−2,472	+812	+2,368	+4,244	+4,083	−3,039	+5,70
2. *Net Transfer Payments*	+2,065	+1,529	+160	−451	−474	−834	−1,223
Net Balance of Current Items	−407	+2,341	+2,528	+3,793	+3,609	+2,205	+4,477
II. *Capital transactions.* Outflow − Inflow +							
1. *Long-term Capital*							
(a) German capital investment abroad (net)	−51	+50	−403	−1,229	−162	−258	−584
(b) Foreigners' capital investments in Germany (Net)	+509	−199	−183	−416	−356	−123	+29
Net long-term Capital Transactions.	+458	−149	−586	−1,645	−518	−381	−555
2. *Short-term Capital*							
(a) Private Capital Movements (net)	−251	+236	+477	+395	+305	+119	+894
(b) Official Capital Movements	—	—	+86	+1,300	−162	−188	−287
Net short-term capital transactions	+207	+87	−23	+50	−375	−450	+52
Net Balance of Total transactions	−200	+2,428	+2,505	+3,843	+3,234	+1,755	+4,529
B. *Overall Increase* (−) or *Decrease* (+) in German Gold and Foreign Exchange Holdings.	+564	−2,038	−2,761	−3,614	−2,782	−1,851	−5,014
[=balance of payments surplus(−) or deficit (+)]							
C. *Net Errors and Omissions*	−364	−390	+256	−229	−452	+96	+485

Monthly report of *D. Bundesbank*, June 1967, pp. 26–7.

XVIII (a)

WEST GERMAN EXPORTS BY COMMODITIES
in total value (DM milliards) and per cent of total

	1952		1959		1966	
	DM mld	per cent	DM mld	per cent	DM mld	per cent
Commodity						
Food and agriculture	0·4	2·2	1·0	2·5	2·0	2·5
Raw materials	1·3	7·4	2·0	4·8	2·9	3·6
Semi-finished products	2·5	15	4·3	10·5	7·1	9
Components	3·5	21	8·0	19·4	14·8	18·3
Finished articles	9·3	54·4	25·9	62·8	53·9	66·6
The last two categories include						
Machines	3·7	22	7·7	18·7	17·3	21·4
Vehicles (excl. ships)	1·4	5·7	5·6	13·5	11·8	14·7
Chemicals	1·5	8·9	5·3	12·8	10·3	12·8
Iron and steel goods	2·6	15·9	5·8	14·1	9·2	11·4
Electrical goods	1·0	5·9	3·7	9·0	7·2	8·9
Textiles and clothing	0·9	5·6	2·1	5·0	4·7	5·8

SOURCE: *Statistisches Jahrbuch.*

1950–1966	*DM million*								
1957	*1958*	*1959*	*1960*	*1961*	*1962*	*1963*	*1964*	*1965*	*1966*
35,831	36,849	41,031	47,855	50,876	52,884	58,288	64,788	71,408	80,388
28,509	29,443	33,242	39,698	41,368	46,694	49,148	55,032	66,522	68,855
+99	+57	−161	+275	+77	−19	−20	−212	+152	+200
+7,421	+7,463	+7,628	+8,432	+9,585	+6,171	+9,120	+9,544	+5,110	+11,733
9,247	10,228	10,856	12,077	11,992	13,307	13,947	15,337	16,743	18,878
8,925	9,725	10,989	12,402	14,219	16,396	17,068	19,412	21,899	23,919
+322	+503	−133	−325	−2,227	−3,089	−3,121	−4,675	−5,156	−5,041
+7,743	+7,966	+7,495	+8,107	+7,358	+3,082	+5,999	+5,469	−46	+6,692
−1,879	−2,018	−3,300	−3,453	−4,471	−5,224	−5,086	−5,243	−6,381	−6,264
+5,864	+5,948	+4,195	+4,654	+2,887	−2,142	+913	+226	−6,427	+428
−992	−1,690	−5,125	−2,319	−3,042	−2,624	−2,565	−3,180	−3,168	−5,580
+397	+133	−542	+2,220	−1,194	+2,350	+4,347	+2,309	+4,108	+3,129
−595	−1,557	−5,667	−99	−4,236	−274	+1,782	−871	+940	−2,451
−55	−761	−1,163	+2,844	+281	+358	+743	+276	+611	+1,320
−1,810	−87	+398	−957	−1,272	+425	−346	−1,427	+870	+1,065
−2,460	−2,405	−6,432	+1,788	−5,227	+509	+2,179	−2,022	+2,421	−66
+3,404	+3,543	−2,237	+6,442	−2,340	−1,633	+3,092	−1,796	−4,006	+362
−5,122	−3,188	+2,204	−8,007	+1,928	+552	−2,572	−12	+1,506	−1,030
+1,718	−355	+33	+1,565	+412	+1,081	−520	+1,808	+2,500	+668

XVIII (*b*)

WEST GERMAN EXPORTS BY DESTINATION
in total value (DM million) and per cent of total

	1952		*1959*		*1966*	
	DM	per cent	DM	per cent	DM	per cent
E.E.C.	4,872	28	11,562	28·0	29,470	36·5
E.F.T.A.	5,443	32	11,717	28·4	21,422	26·6
E. bloc	522	3·15	1,737	4·25	3,539	4·4
US-Canada	1,138	6·7	4,331	10·5	8,097	10·0
Rest of America	1,744	10·3	3,154	7·6	3,859	4·8
Africa	677	4·6	2,050	5·0	3,075	3·8
Asia	1,191	7·0	4,412	10·7	6,475	8·0
Australasia	186	1·1	534	1·3	817	1·0
Other (mainly Europe)	1,225	7·15	1,636	4·0	3,885	4·9
Total	16,998		41,184		80,639	

SOURCE: *Statistisches Jahrbuch.*

XVIII(c)

WESTERN GERMAN EXPORTS TO THE EASTERN BLOC
DM million

Country	1952		1959		1964		1966	
	Value	Per cent of total exports	Value	Per cent	Value	Per cent	Value	Per cent
U.S.S.R.	0·6	—	382·5	0·93	774·3	1·19	541·3	0·67
Poland	65	0·38	294·3	0·71	313·9	0·48	375·5	0·47
Czechoslovakia	34	0·2	251·6	0·64	331·9	0·51	503·1	0·62
Hungary	65	0·38	151·1	0·37	296·2	0·46	371·3	0·46
Yugoslavia	310	1·9	417·2	1·01	532·7	0·82	756·6	0·94
Romania	41	0·24	69	0·17	330·8	0·51	558·1	0·69
Bulgaria	6·2	0·04	171·0	0·42	155·8	0·24	433·0	0·54
Totals	521·8	3·14	1736·7	3·25	2735·6	4·21	3538·9	4·39
D.D.R.	145		1078·5		1151		1625	

SOURCE: *Statistisches Jahrbuch.*

XIX

% SHARES OF WORLD TRADE IN MANUFACTURES

Year	Germany[1]	France	U.K.	U.S.	Japan	Others[2]
1899	22·4	14·4	33·2	11·7	1·5	13·4
1913	26·6	12·1	30·2	13	2·3	13·4
1929	20·5	10·9	22·4	20·4	3·9	18·6
1937	16·5	5·8	20·9	19·2	6·9	23·5
1950	7·3	9·9	25·5	27·3	3·4	26·6
1955	15·5	9·3	19·8	24·5	5·1	25·8
1958	18·5	8·6	18·1	23·3	6·0	25·5
1963	20·3	9·2	15·4	19·7	7·7	27·7
1966	19·7	8·9	13·1	19·5	9·5	29·2

SOURCES: 1899–1937. Maizels: *Industrial Growth and World Trade,* p. 189.

1950–66 *N.I.E.S.R. Review* November 1959, T. 19: May 1967, T. 23.

NOTES:

1. First 2 figures for 1871 frontiers; third for 1919 ones; thereafter (including 1937) for *Bundesrepublik* only.

2. Belgium-Luxembourg, Canada, Italy, Switzerland and (after 1913) Netherlands.

XX

BURDEN OF DEFENCE
% of gross national product devoted to defence

	West Germany	France	Italy	U.K.	U.S.A.
1958	2·7	5·6	4·3	6·6	10·1
1960	3·3	5·3	n.a.	6·2	9·3
1962	5·9	7·2	4·4	6·7	11·3
1963	6·1	6·4	4·2	7·2	9·8
1964	5·5	6·7	4·1	7·0	9·0
1966	3·6	4·4	3·3	6·4	9·2

SOURCES: 1958, 1960: O.E.C.D. *Statistics of National Accounts.*
1962–6: Institute of Strategic Studies, *The Strategic Balance.*

XXI

COMPARATIVE LIVING STANDARDS

	W. Germany	France	Italy	Sweden	U.K.	U.S.	U.S.S.R.	Year to which figures apply
Calories per head per day	2,920	3,070	2,800	2,950	3,300	3,100	—	1964/5
Total energy consumption per head per year (t.e.c.)	4,422	3,320	2,043	6,100	5,400	9,200	3,800	1965
Total steel used per head per year (kg.)	579	356	221	623	438	615	355	1964
Average no. of persons per room	0·9	1·0	1·1	0·8	0·7	0·7	1·5	1960/62
% of dwellings with bathroom per 1000 population	51·9	28·0	10·7 (1951)	61·0	78·3	88·1	—	1960/62
Passenger cars per 1000 population	159	183	106	232	167	385	4	1966
Radio receivers per 1000 population	301	312	207	381	294	1244	320	1966
TV receivers per 1000 population	192	130	117	268	247	408	68	1966
Circulation of daily papers per 1000 population	326	245 (1964)	113	505	479	310	264	1965
Doctors per 1000 population	144	112	171	104	118	149	204	1964/5
Cost of class daily paper	10d.	10d.	9½d.	9½d.	5·6d.	10d.	3½d.	Autumn
Cost of 20 ordinary cigarettes	2/1d.	2/4d.	2/11d.	7/1½d.	4/7d.	3/2½d.	1/10d.	1967
Cost of internal letter	7½d.	6d.	9½d.	8½d.	4d.	6d.	4½d.	1967
Cost of one (imperial) gallon petrol	6/0½d.	7/6d.	6/6½d.	6/5½d.	5/7½d.	3/-d.	4/8d.	1967

SOURCE: E.E.C. *Basic Statistics of the Community* (except for last 4 items). Cost of last four items converted at exchange rates obtaining on 21 November 1967.

XXII

WEST GERMANY'S BIGGEST FIRMS

The following list includes all those which had a turnover exceeding DM 1,000,000,000 in 1966.
(See note at end.)

a Rank	b Name	c Place in European List	d Nature of Business	e Turnover 1966 DM millions	f Capital DM millions	g Return on Capital	h Number of Employees
1	Volkswagen	5	Motors	9,998	5,781	12·9	124,581
2	Siemens	6	Electric	7,831	4,933	3·3	257,000
3	Thyssen	8	Steel	6,780	4,332	1·6	91,800
4	Bayer	11	Chemicals	5,912	3,840	7.0	83,600
5	Daimler-Benz	34	Motors	5,900 (est)	1,574	9·9	101,000
6	Vereinigte Elektrizitaets und Bergwerks Aktiengesellschaft		Electricity and Coal	5,831	—	—	80,212
7	Hoechst	9	Chemicals	5,827	3,991	7·1	79,416
8	Krupp	25	Steel	5,000	2,386	1·05	102,415
9	AEG-Telefunken	19	Electric and Communications	4,861	2,701	3·45	138,153
10	Badische Aniline Soda Fabrik	10	Chemicals	4,707	3,884	6·5	65,400
11	Rhein-Westfaelische Elektrizitaet	12	Electric Power	4,684	3,703	6·85	17,215
12	Guete-Hoffnungs Huette	—	Steel	4,312	—	—	73,969
13	Rheinstahl	22	Steel	4,303	2,528	1·9	79,800
14	Mannesman	18	Steel	4,265	2,719	2·6	73,116
15	Esso	—	Oil	4,237	—	—	5,271
16	Opel (General Motors)	—	Motors	4,006	—	—	55,465
17	Hoesch	16	Steel	3,791	2,857	1·2	69,238
18	Reemtsma	—	Tobacco	3,705	—	—	7,237
19	Salzgitter	—	Steel	3,571	—	—	81,592
20	Metalgesellschaft	68	Chemicals	3,519	727	4·9	30,531
21	Deutsche Shell	—	Oil	3,465	—	—	6,478
22	Aral	—	Oil	3,400	—	—	3,044
23	Edeka-Zentrale	—	Department Stores	3,329	—	—	1,715
24	Kloeckner	—	Mining	3,320	—	—	9,500
25	Deutsche Unilever	—	Food, Soap, Detergents	3,271	—	—	37,640
26	Karstadt	60	Department Stores	3,255	803	10.9	50,399
27	Ford	21	Motors	3,169	2,539	6·6	38,517
28	Bosch	51	Electric	3,000	1,008	1·3	85,720
29	Kaufhof	67	Department Stores	2,980	732	11·0	48,977
30	Gelsenberg	27	Coal, Oil	2,721	2,301	0·45	49,970
31	Quelle	—	Mail Order	2,464	—	—	24,000
32	B.P.	—	Oil	2,352	—	—	5,501
33	G.E.G.	—	Trade	2,189	—	—	11,257
34	Otto-Wolf Gruppe	—	Steel Trading	2,100	—	—	1,947
35	Deutsche Erdoel	41	Oil	2,050	1,309	0·005	20,800
36	British American Tobacco	—	Tobacco	2,000	—	—	4,000
37	Baywa	—	Trade	1,995	—	—	11,567
38	Kloeckner Werke	45	Steel	1,851	1,163	1·7	43,100
39	Feldmuehle-Nobel	—	Paper	1,726	—	—	28,440
40	Horten	—	Department Stores	1,650	—	—	25,000
41	Buderus	—	Machinery	1,600	—	—	32,500
42	Deutsche Gold und Silber-schmiede Anstalt	91	Chemicals	1,520	507	6·5	12,764
43	Glanzstoff	70	Synthetic Fibres	1,452	709	10	27,480
44	Deutsche I.B.M.	—	Business Machines	1,436	—	—	15,000
45	Brinkmann	—	Tobacco	1,435	—	—	4,968
46	Neckermann	—	Mail Order	1,400	—	—	15,402
47	Brown Boveri	—	Electric	1,352	—	—	35,600
48	Kloeckner Humboldt	66	Commercial Vehicles	1,340	727	1·65	30,500
49	Norddeutsche Affinerie	—	Alloys	1,330	—	—	2,780
50	Henkel	—	Detergents	1,300	—	—	23,000
51	Wintershell	85	Alkalis, Oil	1,279	560	5.3	9,700
52	Continental Gummi	76	Tyres	1,268	669	5·9	28,481
53	R.E.W.E.-Zentrale	—	Retail Trade	1,260	—	—	5,587
54	Grundig	—	Electrical	1,250	—	—	30,000
55	Deutsche Philips	—	Electrical	1,200	—	—	25,300
56	V.I.A.G.	—	Holding	1,181	—	—	21,000
57	Lufthansa	55	Aviation	1,166	857	5·1	16,483
58	Standard Electric Lorenz	—	Electric	1,080	—	—	32,058
59	Preussag	61	Alkali, coal, Oil	1,008	780	2·0	18,053
60	Huettenwerke Oberhausen	52	Coal, Steel	1,006	998	1·1	24,299

NOTES: Columns *a*, *b*, *d*, *e* and *h* are taken from a table of leading German firms in *Die Zeit* (1 September 1947). Columns *c* and *f* are taken, and column *g* is calculated, from figures given in a table of leading European firms in *The Times* on the same day. *The Times*, however, ranks firms according to amount of capital, *Die Zeit* according to turnover. Consequently a firm can appear on this list above a firm whose position on the European list (Column *c*) is higher. *The Times*'s list also excludes publicly-owned companies and subsidiaries of foreign firms.

XXIII

THE WEST GERMAN PRESS

At the end of 1966, there were 496 daily papers in the Federal Republic, selling 21 million copies. The most important of these, in order of circulation, are:

Name	Circulation	Head Office	Remarks
Bild	4,879,000 S	Hamburg	Illustrated.
Hamburger Morgenpost	405,900	Hamburg	Favours S.P.D.
Ruhrnachrichten	370,900	Dortmund	
Mittag	354,500 S	Düsseldorf	Early evening.
Berliner Ztg. (BZ)	341,000 S	Berlin	
Hamburger Abendblatt	333,000 + S	Hamburg	Evening
Rheinische Post	314,000	Düsseldorf	Committed to support of C.D.U.
Abendztg.	291,300 +	Munich	Evening
Frankfurter Allgemeine Ztg.	287,200 +	Frankfurt	
Die Welt	287,200 + S	Hamburg	
Neue Ruhr Ztg.	246,800	Essen	Favours S.P.D.
Nürnberger Nachrichten	246,300 +	Nuremberg	
Süddeutsche Ztg.	235,900 +	Munich	
Westfälische Rundschau	233,200	Dortmund	Favours S.P.D.
Express	225,800	Cologne	
Berliner Morgenpost	214,100 + S	Berlin	
Kölner Stadt Anzeiger	207,500 +	Cologne	
Hannoversche Allgemeine Ztg.	205,800	Hanover	
Augsburger Allgemeine Ztg.	201,600	Augsburg	

(4 papers with a circulation of between 200,000 and 160,000)

Stuttgarter Ztg.	156,700	Stuttgart

(19 papers with a circulation of between 155,000 and 100,000)

Tagesspiegel	99,400 +	Berlin	
Telegraf	80,000 +	Berlin	Favours S.P.D.

+ = higher circulation at week-ends.
S = Owned by Axel Springer.

There were also 55 weeklies selling 1·2 m. copies and 745 Trade and Technical papers selling 64·4m. copies. Among the most notable of these were:

Die Zeit	259,700	Hamburg	Cross between U.K. *Observer* and *Spectator*.

Name	Circulation	Head Office	Remarks
Der Spiegel	833,000	Hamburg	See p. 244.
Christ und Welt	175,600	Stuttgart	Current affairs from religious angle.
Sonntagsblatt	139,800	Hamburg	
Handelsblatt	40,500	Düsseldorf	The two chief economic papers Published 5 & 3 times weekly
Industriekurier	31,500	Düsseldorf	
Bayernkurier	102,500	Munich	Organ of C.S.U.
Deutsche National-Ztg. und Soldaten-Ztg.	102,500	Munich	Nationalist
Heimatwacht	146,700	Hanover	Biggest refugee paper
Hör Zu	4,077,400	Hamburg	Radio & TV programmes. Owned by Axel Springer.
Neue Revue	2,143,300	Hamburg	Biggest of illustrated weeklies. 4 others with circulation of over 1m.
Für Sie	1,144,500	Hamburg	Biggest of women's weeklies.

Notes on the Illustrations

2. This statue in Bamberg Cathedral may possibly be of the Emperor Frederick II (1194–1250). It was much in vogue at the beginning of the present century among advocates of a return to German traditions, such as the poet Stefan Georg, on the ground that it symbolised their ideal of the aristocratic ruler. It lent its name to a crack cavalry regiment, to which belonged Count Klaus von Stauffenberg, the author of the attempt on Hitler's life on 20 July 1944.

3(*a*) Cologne Cathedral, one of the outstanding examples of German Gothic, was begun in 1248 to the designs of Gerhart. But only the choir, containing the supposed shrine of the Three Wise Men, was finished in the Middle Ages. After a long interlude since the sixteenth century, building started again in the nineteenth and the structure was finally finished, to the original design, in 1880. Much damaged by bombing during the war, it has since been restored and was in April 1967 the scene of the Requiem Mass for Konrad Adenauer.

(*b*) Marienburg was formerly in East Prussia on a branch of the Vistula thirty miles south-east of Danzig. It is now under Polish rule and has been renamed Malbork.

4. This drawing was clearly intended as an allegory of the Christian journeying through the dangers of the world. Nietzsche said that it should be regarded 'as a symbol of our existence'. Following his line of thought, nationalist writers have interpreted it, with little or no historical justification, as symbolising the situation of the German *Volk*. The heroic German, dedicated to restoring the greatness of his people, must ride on undisturbed and full of hope through present dangers to the vision of the future. A book called *Ritter, Tod und Teufel: der heldische Gedanke*, which was published in 1924,

321

established its author Hans F. K. Günther as a leading theorist of National Socialism.

5. This picture, now in the Unterlinden Museum at Colmar, Alsace, is one of nine panels in an altar painted for a monastic hospital at Isenheim, fifteen miles away. The painter, about whom little is known, was a friend of Dürer; his life and paintings inspired Hindemith's opera *Mathis der Maler*. In this picture he has given physical shape to all the lusts and terrors which assault men's minds. Although it belongs essentially to German art, for 267 out of the 453 years since its creation, the place the picture has been in has belonged to France.

6. The baroque architect Schlüter built much of the Royal Palace in Berlin for the first King of Prussia, Frederick I, who spent on it and similar projects a good deal of the money which his father, the Great Elector, had amassed. Schlüter had never seen the Great Elector who died eight years before the statue was begun. It stood at the end of the Long Bridge leading to the Palace and so had a first-hand view of the revolutions of 1848 and 1919. When in 1884–5 Germany gained the bulk of her colonies, the Emperor William I said that at last he could look his ancestor in the face when he rode home. The palace (in East Berlin) has been pulled down and the statue has been re-erected in front of the Charlottenburg Palace in West Berlin.

8. This statue came from the abbey of Salem near the Lake of Constance, later owned by Prince Max of Baden, Germany's first democratic Chancellor, and used as a school under Kurt Hahn, the founder of Gordonstoun.

9(a) One of the achievements of the Romantic Movement in Germany was to revive interest in and embellish the national past. In this picture, Caspar David Friedrich, Germany's greatest romantic painter, invented a tomb for Hermann or Arminius, the almost legendary chieftain who defeated the Roman general Varus in A.D. 9.

(b) Frederick the Great was a patron of musicians, including C. P. E. Bach, and used to play the flute with them. In the time of national reunification a century later, Menzel's paintings of such scenes brought him great success, somewhat to his detriment as an artist. On one occasion the Emperor William II, to compliment Menzel, invited him to come to dinner dressed as a figure from this picture and on his arrival led him into a room where the other guests had been staged to reproduce the scene as a whole.

Books for Further Reading

There are so many books about Germany that it has seemed best to confine the following list (which is far from exhaustive) to secondary works in English. Many of the books listed contain fuller bibliographies. No book is mentioned more than once.

CHAPTER 1 & GENERAL

G. Barraclough: *Factors in Modern German History*. Oxford, 1946

E. K. Bramstead: *Aristocracy and the Middle Classes in Germany*. Revised edn., Chicago, 1964

E. M. Butler: *The Tyranny of Greece over Germany*. London, 1935

F. L. Carsten: *The Origins of Prussia*. Oxford, 1954

Sir John Clapham: *The Economic Development of France and Germany*. 2nd edn., London, 1936

G. A. Craig: *The Politics of the Prussian Army 1660–1945*. Oxford 1955

W. H. Dawson: *The Evolution of Modern Germany*. London, 1908

L. Dehio: *Germany and World Politics in the Twentieth Century*. Eng. trs., London, 1959

Sir John Dunlop: *A Short History of Germany*. 3rd edn., London, 1965

K. Epstein: *The Genesis of German Conservatism*. Princeton, 1966

R. Flenley: *Modern German History*. London, 1964

W. Goerlitz: *History of the German General Staff*. London, 1953

T. Hamerow: *Restoration, Revolution, Reaction: Economics and Politics in Germany, 1851–71*. Princeton, 1958

W. O. Henderson: *The Zollverein*. 2nd edn., London, 1959

H. Kohn: *German History, Some New Views*. London, 1954

L. Krieger: *The German Ideal of Freedom*. Boston, 1957

G. Mann: *The History of Germany Since 1789*. Eng. trans., London, 1968

F. Meinecke: *The German Catastrophe*. Eng. trs., Harvard, 1950

R. P. Morgan: *The German Social Democrats 1864–72*. Cambridge, 1965

E. J. Passant: *A Short History of Germany 1815–1945*. Cambridge, 1959
K. Pinson: *Modern Germany*. New York, 1962
N. Pounds: *The Economic Pattern of Modern Germany*. London, 1963
A. Ramm: *Germany 1789–1919, a Political History*. London, 1967
D. G. Rohr: *The Origins of Social Liberalism in Germany*. Chicago, 1963
W. M. Simon: *Germany, a Brief History*. New York, 1966
A. J. P. Taylor: *The Course of German History*. London, 1945
V. Valentin: *1848, Chapters in German History*. Eng. trs., London, 1940

CHAPTER 2

L. Albertini: *The Origins of the War* (3 vols.). Eng. trs., Oxford, 1952–7
M. Balfour: *The Kaiser and His Times*. London, 1964
G. A. Craig: *From Bismarck to Adenauer*. Baltimore, 1958
K. Demeter: *The German Officer Corps*. Eng. trs., London, 1965
E. Eyck: *Bismarck and the German Empire*. London, 1950
F. Fischer: *Germany's Aims in the First World War*. Eng. trs., London, 1967
H. Gatzke: *Germany's Drive to the West*. Baltimore, 1960
I. Geiss (ed.): *July 1914, the Outbreak of the First World War, Selected Documents*. Eng. trs., London, 1967
D. J. Goodspeed: *Ludendorff*. London, 1966
H. Hartmann: *Authority and Organization in German Management*. Princeton, 1959
W. O. Henderson: *Studies in German Colonial History*. London, 1962
Journal of Contemporary History, Vol. I, No. 2. (on 1914). London, 1966
H. Jacob: *German Administration Since Bismarck*. New Haven, 1963
M. Knight: *The German Executive 1890–1933*. Stanford, 1952
H. Kohn: *The Mind of Germany*. New York, 1960
W. Laqueur: *Young Germany*. London, 1962
V. L. Lidtke: *The Outlawed Party, Social Democrats in Germany 1878–90*. Princeton, 1966
J. P. Mayer: *Max Weber and German Politics*. 2nd edn., London, 1956
W. N. Medlicott: *Bismarck and Modern Germany*. London, 1965
G. Mosse: *The Crisis of German Ideology*. New York, 1964
G. A. von Müller (ed. Goerlitz): *The Kaiser and His Court*. Eng. trs., London, 1961
J. A. Nichols: *Germany After Bismarck*. Harvard, 1958
O. Pflanze: *Bismarck and the Development of Germany, 1815–71*. Princeton, 1963
P. J. Pulzer: *The Rise of Anti-Semitism in Germany and Austria*. New York, 1964

N. Rich and M. Fisher: *The Holstein Papers* (4 vols.). London, 1955–63
——*Life of Holstein* (2 vols.). London, 1965
W. Richter: *Bismarck*, Eng. trs., London, 1964
G. Ritter: *The Schlieffen Plan.* Eng. trans., London, 1958
J. Röhl: *Germany Without Bismarck, the Crisis of Government in the Second Reich, 1890–1900.* London, 1967
A. Rosenberg: *Imperial Germany, the Birth of the German Republic.* Eng. trs., London, 1931
G. Roth: *Social Democracy in Imperial Germany.* Totowa, 1963
R. H. Samuel and R. H. Thomas: *Education and Society in Modern Germany.* London, 1949
C. Schorske: *German Social Democracy, 1905–17.* Harvard, 1955
J. Steinberg: *Yesterday's Deterrent.* London, 1964
F. Stern: *The Politics of Cultural Despair.* Berkeley, 1961
G. Stolper (and others): *The German Economy, 1870 to the Present.* Eng. trs., 2nd edn., New York, 1967
A. J. P. Taylor: *Bismarck.* London, 1955
T. Veblen: *Imperial Germany and the Industrial Revolution.* New York, 1915
Sir John Wheeler-Bennett: *Hindenburg, the Wooden Titan.* London, 1936

CHAPTER 3

W. T. Angress: *Stillborn Revolution.* London, 1963
E. H. Carr: *German-Soviet Relations 1919–39.* Baltimore, 1951
F. Carsten: *The Reichswehr and Politics, 1919–33.* Oxford, 1966
R. T. Clark: *The Fall of the German Republic.* London, 1935
A. Dorpalen: *Hindenburg and the Weimar Republic.* Princeton, 1957
H. L. Dyck: *Weimar Germany and Soviet Russia, 1926–33.* London, 1966
K. Epstein: *Matthias Erzberger and the Dilemma of German Democracy.* Princeton, 1959
E. Eyck: *History of the German Republic* (2 vols.). Eng. trs., Oxford, 1962
H. Gatzke: *Stresemann and the Rearmament of Germany.* Baltimore, 1954
H. Gordon: *The Reichswehr and the German Republic, 1919–26.* Princeton, 1957
R. Grunberger: *Germany 1918–45.* London, 1964
S. W. Halperin: *Germany Tried Democracy 1919–33.* London, 1963
R. N. Hunt: *German Social Democracy 1918–33.* London, 1964
L. Kochan: *The Struggle for Germany 1914–45.* Edinburgh, 1963

I. F. D. Morrow: *The Peace Settlement in the German-Polish Borderlands.* Oxford, 1936

J. P. Nettl: *Rosa Luxemburg* (2 vols.). London, 1966

A. Nicholls: *Weimar and the Rise of Hitler.* London, 1968

A. Rosenberg: *The History of the German Republic.* Eng. trs., London, 1936

A. J. Ryder: *The German Revolution of 1919.* Cambridge, 1967

H. A. Turner: *Stresemann and the Politics of the German Republic.* Princeton, 1963

Sir John Wheeler-Bennett: *The Nemesis of Power, the German Army in Politics 1918–45.* London, 1953

CHAPTER 4

W. S. Allen: *The Nazi Seizure of Power.* Chicago, 1965

E. K. Bramsted: *Goebbels and National Socialist Propaganda.* London, 1965

A. Bullock: *Hitler, a Study in Tyranny.* London, 1952

C. W. Guillebaud: *The Economic Recovery of Germany 1933–9.* London, 1939

K. Heiden: *Hitler.* Eng. trs., London, 1936

T. L. Jarman: *The Rise and Fall of Nazi Germany.* London, 1955

K. von Klemperer: *Germany's New Conservatism, Its History and Dilemma in the Twentieth Century.* Princeton, 1957

E. Kogon: *The Theory and Practice of Hell.* Eng. trs., London, 1950

D. Lerner: *The Nazi Elite.* Stanford, 1951

G. Lewy: *The Catholic Church and Nazi Germany.* London, 1964

R. Manvell and H. Fraenkel: *Doctor Goebbels.* London, 1960

——*Hermann Goering.* London, 1962

——*The July Plot.* London, 1964

——*Heinrich Himmler.* London, 1965

H. Mau and H. Krausnick: *German History 1933–45, an assessment by German Historians.* Eng. trs., London, 1959

P. de Mendelssohn: *The Nuremberg Documents.* London, 1946

A. Milward: *The German Economy At War.* New York, 1964

T. Prittie: *Germans Against Hitler.* London, 1964

H. Rauschning: *Germany's Revolution of Destruction.* Eng. trs., London, 1939

——*Hitler Speaks:* Eng. trs., London, 1939

G. Reitlinger: *The Final Solution.* London, 1953

——*The SS, Alibi of a Nation.* London, 1956

G. Ritter: *The German Resistance.* Eng. trs., London, 1958

E. M. Robertson: *Hitler's Pre-war Policy and Military Plans.* London, 1963

S. H. Roberts: *The House That Hitler Built*. London, 1937

H. Rothfels. *The German Opposition to Hitler, an Assessment*. London, 1961

D. Schoenbaum: *Hitler's Social Revolution*. London, 1967

A. Schweitzer: *Big Business in the Third Reich*. London, 1964

W. Shirer: *Berlin Diary 1934–41*. New York, 1941

——*The Rise and Fall of the Third Reich*. New York, 1960

G. H. Stein: *The Waffen SS, Hitler's Elite Guard at War 1939–45*. London, 1966

R. H. Stevens (trs.): *The Testament of Adolf Hitler*. London, 1961

H. Trevor-Roper: *The Last Days of Hitler*. London, 1947

——(ed.): *Hitler's Table Talk*. London, 1953

——(ed.): *Hitler's War Directives 1939–45*. London, 1964

UNESCO: *The Third Reich*. London, 1955

Sir John Wheeler-Bennett: *Munich, Prologue to Tragedy*. London, 1948

E. Wiskemann: *Czechs and Germans*. London, 1938

——*The Rome-Berlin Axis*. 2nd edn., London, 1966

——*Undeclared War*. 2nd edn., London, 1967

Z. A. B. Zeman: *Nazi Propaganda*. London, 1964

CHAPTERS 5 & 6

N. Balabkins: *Germany Under Direct Controls*. New Brunswick, 1964

M. Balfour: *Four-Power Control in Germany 1945–6* (in series *Survey of International Affairs 1939–46* ed. A. J. Toynbee). London, 1956

L. D. Clay: *Decision in Germany*. New York, 1950

H. Feis: *Churchill, Roosevelt, Stalin*. Princeton, 1957

——*Between War and Peace, the Potsdam Conference*. Princeton, 1960

A. Grosser: *West Germany From Defeat to Rearmament*. London, 1956

W. Heidelmeyer and G. Hindrichs: *Documents on Berlin 1943–63*. Eng. trs., Munich, 1963

W. Leonhard: *Child of the Revolution*. Eng. trs., London, 1957

Drew Middleton: *The Struggle for Germany*. New York, 1950

J. P. Nettl: *The Eastern Zone and Soviet Policy in Germany*. London, 1951

B. Ruhm von Oppen (ed.): *Documents on Germany 1945–55*. London, 1955

J. L. Snell: *The Origins of the East-West Dilemma Over Germany*. New Orleans, 1959

E. Wiskemann: *Germany's Eastern Neighbours*. London, 1956

H. Zink: *The United States in Germany*. Princeton, 1957

CHAPTER 7

W. P. Davison: *The Berlin Blockade*. London, 1958

P. M. Boarman: *Germany's Economic Dilemma—Inflation and the Balance of Payments*. New Haven and Geneva, 1964

R. G. Opie: 'Western Germany's Economic Miracle' (*Three Banks Review*, March, 1962)
J. E. Smith: *The Defense of Berlin*. London, 1963
H. C. Wallich: *Mainsprings of the German Revival*. New Haven, 1955
Supplement to *The Economist*, 15 October 1966

CHAPTERS 8 to 11

K. Adenauer: *Memoirs*. Vols. I and II. Eng. trs., London. 1966–8
R. Augstein: *Konrad Adenauer*. Eng. trs., London, 1964
K. Bölling: *Republic in Suspense*. Eng. trs., London, 1964
G. Braunthal: *The Federation of German Industry in Politics*. Ithaca, 1965
√R. Chaput de Saintonge: *Public Administration in Germany*. London, 1961
D. Childs: *From Schumacher to Brandt*. London, 1966
K. W. Deutsch and L. Edinger. *Germany Rejoins the Powers*. London, 1959
L. Edinger: *Kurt Schumacher*. Oxford, 1965
F. Erler: *Democracy in Germany*. Harvard, 1965
F. Golay: *The Founding of the Federal Republic of Germany*. Chicago, 1958
W. F. Hanrieder: *West German Foreign Policy 1949–63*. Stanford, 1967
A. Hartley: *Germany East/West*. London, 1968
F. H. Hartmann: *Germany Between East and West*. Englewood Cliffs, 1966
A. Heidenheimer: *Adenauer and the CDU*. The Hague, 1960
——*The Governments of Germany*. London, 1966
R. Hiscocks: *Democracy in Western Germany*. London, 1957
——*Germany Revived*. London, 1966
U. Kitzinger: *German Electoral Politics*. Oxford, 1960
G. Loewenberg: *Parliament in the German Political System*. Ithaca, 1966
G. Mann: 'Bismarck and Adenauer' (*Encounter*, April 1964)
P. H. Merkl: *The Origin of the West German Republic*. New York, 1963
——*Germany, Yesterday and Tomorrow*. New York, 1965
E. Plischke: *The West German Federal Government*. London, 1964
T. Prittie: *Divided Germany*. London, 1961
J. Richardson: *Germany and the Atlantic Alliance*. London, 1966
H. Speier: (ed.): *German Rearmament and Atomic War*. Evanston, 1957
——(ed.): *West German Leadership and Foreign Policy*. Evanston, 1957
W. Stahl (ed.): *The Politics of Post-war Germany*. New York, 1963
F. J. Strauss: *The Grand Design*. London, 1965
Survey (No. 61), October 1966 ('Germany: Today and Tomorrow')
P. Weymar: *Konrad Adenauer*. Eng. trs., London, 1957

Index

Bosch, Hieronymus, 19
Boulogne, 117
Bourgeoisie, 18, 24, 27, 33, 34, 41,
43, 44, 56, 75, 89, 90, 93, 124,
200–1, 280, 284
Brandenburg, 23
Brandt, Willy, 226, 243; Leader of
Socialists, 250; Vice-Chancellor and
Foreign Minister, 253, 288, 289,
297, 304; visit to Bucharest, 294
Brauer, Max, 226
Bremen, *Land*, 159, 195, 226, 280,
305–6
Brentano, Heinrich von, 228, 243
Brest-Litovsk, Treaty of, 71
Brüning, Heinrich, 90–93, 95, 271
Brussels, 154, 197, 246
Bucharest, 294
Bückeburg, 172
Bulganin, Nikolai, 218
Bulgarians, 292
Bundesbank, see Banks
Bundesrat (Federal Council): in 1871
constitution, 38–9, 76; in 1949
constitution, 191, 195–6, 198–9, 274,
284; Ministry for B. Affairs, 201;
Presidency, 201
Bundestag (Federal Assembly), 211,
247, 253 n, 274, 284, 295; powers of,
194, 199; Committees of, 195, 198,
233, 275; events in, 227, 235, 244,
245, 246, 251, 266; composition of,
224, 301, 305; Berlin representation
in, 192
Bundeswehr (Federal Defence Forces),
233–5, 239, 244, 271
Byrnes, James, 160, 161

C

Cabinet: *Bundesrat* intended as, 38;
in Republic, 72, 80, 82, 83, 86, 93,
97; Absence of under Hitler, 105; in
Federal Republic, 196–7; under
Adenauer, 203, 224, 245; under
Erhard, 250, 251; under Kiesinger,
252, 270, 271, 304; authority of,
196, 274, 275
Calais, 117
Calvinists, 23
Canossa, 17
Cars, 52, 152, 268, 317, 318
Cartels, 56, 147, 181, 267; *see also*
Decartellisation
Casablanca, 124
Casualties: 1914–18, 73; 1939–45, 122,
130, 265
Categorical imperative, 26
Catholics, 20, 21, 27, 31–2; in Second
Reich, 41–2, 44, 54, 60; in Third

Catholics—*continued*
Reich, 100–2; in Federal Republic,
157, 183, 185, 188, 242, 280;
attitude to education, 256; present
strength, 306
Caucasus, 124
Celts, 15
Centre Party: in Second Reich, 41–2,
59–60, 70; in Weimar Republic, 77,
79, 93, 94, 96, 97, 101, 157; since
1945, 189, 225, 226, 306
Chamberlain, Joseph, 55
Chamberlain, Neville, 112, 113, 115,
203 n
Chancellor: in Second Reich, 39–41,
60, 71; in 1918, 72; in Weimar
Republic, 76, 91, 94, 101, 185;
Hitler as, 94, 96, 103; in Federal
Republic, 186, 196–7, 201, 241, 245,
247, 250–52, 275; *see also* Bismarck,
Bethmann Hollweg, Stresemann,
Marx, Brüning, Papen, Schleicher,
Adenauer, Erhard, Kiesinger
Charlemagne, 16
Charles V, Emperor, 18
Chemicals, 52, 147, 152, 268–9, 318
Cherusci, 16
China, 61, 247, 292
Christian Democratic Union (C.D.U.):
foundation, 143, 157, 183–7;
composition, 186, 224, 226, 247,
304–6; views on Basic Law, 189–91,
196; form government 1949, 200–2,
225; policies of, 186, 224, 243–4,
246, 269, 289; relations with S.P.D.,
226, 228, 252–3, 285, 286; in
elections, 200, 224, 226, 241, 250,
281, 301–2; in North Rhine-
Westphalia, 225, 251
Christian Socialist Union (C.S.U.):
foundation of, 159; views on Basic
Law, 189–91; composition of,
304–6; in elections, 200, 224, 226,
241, 250, 280, 301; policies of, 233,
246; relations to Adenauer, 201,
202, 234; to Strauss, 233, 245, 252,
253; to S.P.D., 228, 252–3, 285–6
Churches, *see* Calvinists, Catholics,
Confessional Church, Evangelical
Church, Free Churches, Lutherans,
Protestants, Papacy,
Reformation
Churchill, Winston: threat to continue
war overseas, 119; meeting with
Roosevelt at Casablanca, 124–5;
Yalta and zone boundaries, 136–8;
reparations, 139, 143; Potsdam, 145;
refusal to join E.D.C., 211
Cimbrians, 15

Printed in Great Britain by The Garden City Press Limited, Letchworth, Herts.